Philosophy Made Simple

Second Edition, Revised

**Richard H. Popkin, Ph.D., and
Avrum Stroll, Ph.D.**

A MADE SIMPLE BOOK

BROADWAY BOOKS

NEW YORK

A MADE SIMPLE BOOK
Published by Doubleday, a division of
Bantam Doubleday Dell Publishing Group, Inc.
1540 Broadway, New York, New York 10036

MADE SIMPLE and DOUBLEDAY are trademarks of Doubleday,
a division of Bantam Doubleday Dell Publishing Group, Inc.

Library of Congress Cataloging-in-Publication Data
 Popkin, Richard Henry, 1923–
    Philosophy made simple / Richard H. Popkin and Avrum Stroll. —
 2nd rev. ed.
      p.   cm.
    "A Made simple book."
    1. Philosophy—Introductions. I. Stroll, Avrum, 1921–
 II. Title.
 BD21.P6   1993
 100—dc20   92-34537
                                                              CIP

ISBN 0-385-42533-3

 20 19 18 17 16 15 14 13

CONTENTS

Chapter 6:   **Logic**   237

Preface

Some years ago the *New Yorker* magazine ran a typically witty cartoon. The scene was a bookstore and four books were prominently displayed for sale on a table. Their titles could easily be read: the first was "Philosophy Made Simple" and the next "Philosophy Made Simpler." The third said "Philosophy Made Still Simpler," and the fourth was "Philosophy Made Simplest." Since the first title was that of our own *Philosophy Made Simple,* the book you are reading now, it occurred to us to ask whether the new edition of this work, the first since 1985, should, following the cartoon, perhaps be entitled "Philosophy Made Simpler," or even "Philosophy Made Simplest." But when we read over the first edition of the work, we realized that we had made philosophy about as simple as it could be made without distorting the subject drastically, and so in this new edition we'll leave the title intact.

Apparently, several hundred thousands of readers have agreed with us that the book is simple enough. *Philosophy Made Simple* has been translated into foreign languages, is sold in nearly every country of the Western world, and in Nigeria, Hong Kong, Singapore, Israel, and Australia. We had expected that this book would be used by ordinary readers, most of whom would have no special training or background in philosophy but would like to know something about this supposedly "abstract" subject. And many of our readers fall into exactly that category. But the book has also been used as a text in dozens of universities throughout the world. We have received many letters from undergraduate the graduate students, as well as instructors, indicating that it is one of the best and *simplest* introductions to philosophy to be found anywhere.

Nevertheless, there have been important developments in philosophy during the past three decades. We therefore felt that a new, reworked, and updated edition would be desirable at this time. This new edition thus has extensive changes throughout—too numerous to be mentioned here. Of course, we should stress that our main focus continues to be on fundamental philosophical problems. These may take new and sophisticated forms, but the great philosophers of the past who addressed these issues are not really dated. Questions about the nature and purpose of human life, about the ideal form that a political association should have, whether one can obtain absolutely certain knowledge about the world—these questions go to the heart of the philosophical enterprise and will endure as long as human beings are able to use their rational faculties to examine their lives and the environment they inhabit. *Philosophy Made Simple* is devoted to these important issues. Our update continues this focus but goes on to describe often innovative forms these matters take as we move toward the end of the twentieth century.

Richard H. Popkin
University of California, Los Angeles

Avrum Stroll
University of California, San Diego

What is philosophy?

Philosophy is generally regarded as perhaps the most abstruse and abstract of all subjects, far removed from the affairs of ordinary life. But although many people think of it as being remote from normal interests and beyond comprehension, nearly all of us have some philosophical views, whether we are aware of them or not. It is curious that although most people are vague about what philosophy is, the term appears frequently in their conversation.

Popular usages

The word "philosophy" is derived from the Greek term meaning "love of wisdom"; but in current popular usage many different ideas are involved in the ways we employ the term. Sometimes we mean by "philosophy" an attitude toward certain activities, as when one says "I disapprove of your philosophy of doing business" or "I am voting for him because I favor his philosophy of government." Again, we talk about being "philosophical" when we mean taking a long-range, detached view of certain immediate problems. When one is disappointed, we suggest to him/her that he/she ought to be more "philosophical," as when one misses a plane. Here we mean to say that the person should not be overconcerned with the events of the moment but should try instead to place these in perspective. In still another sense, we think of philosophy as an evaluation or interpretation of what is important or meaningful in life. This usage may be indicated by the story of two men who were drinking beer together. One of them held his glass to the light, scrutinized it thoughtfully, and then observed, "Life is like a glass of beer."

His companion looked up at the glass, turned to his friend, and asked, "Why is life like a glass of beer?"

"How should I know," the other answered, "I'm not a philosopher."

Popular conceptions

By and large, in spite of the many different ways we may use the words "philosophy" and "philosophical" in ordinary speech, we tend to think of philosophy as some extremely complex intellectual activity. We often imagine the philosopher (as in Rodin's statue of *The Thinker*) as one who sits pondering questions of the ultimate significance of human life while the rest of us have only the time or the energy to live it. Occasionally, when our newspapers or magazines publish a story about the important philosophers of the past, such as Bertrand Russell or Aristotle, the impression is given that they devoted themselves to contemplation of the problems of the world in a most abstract manner and arrived at views or theories that may sound splendid but can hardly be of much practical value.

While this picture has been created of the philosopher and what he/she is trying to do, there is also another image. This is that the philosopher is one who is ultimately responsible for the general outlook and the ideals of certain societies and cultures. Thinkers such as Karl Marx and Friedrich Engels, we are told, were the ones who created the point of view of the Communist party; while others, such as Thomas Jefferson, John Locke, and John Stuart Mill, developed the theories that prevail in democratic societies.

The Philosophical Enterprise

Regardless of these various conceptions of the role of the philosopher, and regardless of how remote we may think his/her activities are from our immediate concerns, the philosopher has been engaged in considering problems that are of importance to all of us, either directly or indirectly. Through careful critical examination, he/she has tried to evaluate the information and beliefs we have about the universe at large and the world of human affairs. From this investigation, the philosopher has attempted to work out some general, systematic, coherent, and consistent picture of all that we know and think. As we gain more information about the world through the sciences,

new interpretations of accepted pictures need to be considered.

This sort of understanding has provided an outlook or framework in which the ordinary person can place his/her own— possibly more limited—conception of the world and human affairs. It has provided as well a focus through which we can see our own roles and activities, and determine if they have any significance. Through such an examination and evaluation, we may all be better able to assess our ideals and aspirations, as well as understand better why we accept these, and possibly whether we ought to.

From the very beginnings of philosophy in ancient Greece, over two and a half millennia ago, it has been the conviction of the serious thinkers who have engaged in this pursuit that it is necessary to scrutinize the views that we accept about our world and ourselves to see if they are rationally defensible. We have all acquired much information and many opinions about the natural and human universe. But few of us have ever considered whether these are reliable or important. We are usually willing to accept without question reported scientific discoveries, certain traditional beliefs, and various views based upon our personal experiences. The philosopher, however, insists upon subjecting all this to intensive critical examination in order to discover if these views and beliefs are based upon adequate evidence and if a reasonable person may be justified in adhering to them.

The Socratic Contention

Socrates, at his trial in 399 B.C., maintained that the reason he philosophized was that "the unexamined life was not worth living." He found that nearly all of his contemporaries spent their lives pursuing various goals, such as fame, riches, pleasure, without ever asking themselves whether these were important. Unless they raised such a question, and seriously sought the answer, they would never be able to know if they were doing the right thing. Their entire lives might be wasted pursuing useless or even dangerous goals.

All of us have some general outlook about the kind of world we think we live in, the sort of things that are worthwhile in such a world, and so on. Most of us, like Socrates' contemporaries, have never bothered to examine our views to discover their foundations, whether we have adequate or acceptable reasons for believing what we do, or whether the totality of our views has any general consistency or coherence. Hence most of us, in one sense, have some kind of a "philosophy," but we have not done any philosophizing to see if it is justified.

The philosopher, following Socrates' contention, insists upon bringing to light what our implicit beliefs are, what assumptions we make about our world, ourselves, our values. He/she insists that these can only be accepted by reasonable and intelligent people if they can meet certain tests set up by the logical mind. Rather than merely possessing an unorganized mass of opinions, the philosopher feels that these must be inspected, scrutinized, and organized into a meaningful and coherent system of views.

What does a philosopher do?

One may be tempted to observe at this point that these initial comments give some slight idea, perhaps, of what philosophy deals with, but that they are too vague to make clear what it is all about. Why can't one just give a straightforward definition of the subject, and then proceed, so that one can see clearly at the outset what a philosopher is trying to do?

The difficulty is that philosophy can be better explained by doing it than by trying to describe it. It is in part a way of dealing with questions, as well as an attempt to resolve certain problems that have been the traditional interest of the persons who have called themselves, or have been called, "philosophers." As we shall see throughout this book, one of the subjects that philosophers have never been able to agree upon is what philosophy consists in.

Varieties of philosophy

The people who have engaged seriously in philosophizing have had varying aims. Some have been religious leaders, like St. Augustine, and have tried to explain and justify certain religious points of view. Some have been scientists, like René Descartes, and have attempted to interpret the meaning and importance of various scientific discoveries and theories. Others, like John Locke and Karl Marx, have philosophized in order to effect certain changes in the political organization of society. Many have been interested in justifying or promulgating some set of ideas which they thought might aid mankind. Others have had no such grandiose purpose, but merely wished to understand certain features of the world in which they lived and certain beliefs that people held.

Who Are Philosophers?

The occupations of philosophers have been as varied as their aims. Some have been teachers, often university professors giving courses in philosophy, as in the instance of St. Thomas Aquinas in the Middle Ages, teaching at the University of Paris; or John Dewey in the twentieth century, lecturing at Columbia University; or Martin Heidegger at the University of Freiburg; or Ludwig Wittgenstein at Cambridge University. Others have been leaders of religious movements, often taking an active part in the affairs of their organizations, like St. Augustine, who was Bishop of Hippo during the decline of the Roman Empire; or George Berkeley, who was the Bishop of Cloyne in Ireland in the eighteenth century. Many philosophers have had ordinary occupations, like Baruch Spinoza, who was a lens-grinder by profession. John Locke was a medical doctor; John Stuart Mill was a writer for magazines, and briefly a member of Parliament. A good many of the most prominent philosophers have been scientists or mathematicians. Some have had careers which kept them far removed from the excitement and crises of everyday life; others were continually occupied in the most active pursuits.

Regardless of their aims or their occupations, philosophers have, by and large, shared a common conviction that thoughtful examination and analysis of our views, and our evidence for them, are important and worthwhile. A philosopher thinks about certain matters in certain ways. He/she wants to find out what various fundamental ideas or concepts that we have mean, what we base our knowledge on, what standards should be employed in arriving at sound judgments, what beliefs we ought to adhere to, and the like. By reflecting upon such questions, the philosopher feels that one can achieve more significant comprehension of the universe, natural and human.

Some years ago, one of the authors of this book began his lectures in a course entitled "Introduction to Philosophy." He tried to give the class some idea of what sort of material they would be considering throughout the course by raising a question that Plato had asked over twenty-three hundred years ago: "What is justice?" To suggest what this question might mean, he raised related problems, among them: "How do we distinguish just acts from unjust ones?" "How do we tell what we ought to do, or what is right?" "Is justice based only on legal conventions, or are there other, more basic standards?" After the lecture, a student remarked to the professor that many questions had now been asked and he wondered if the answers would be forthcoming in the near future. The teacher told him that they would consider some *possible* answers in the course, but he could not guarantee that they would be the *right* answers. The student answered, "That's all right, so long as we get answers—just so that we don't have to think."

The philosopher does not want *any* answers, and he/she is unwilling to accept them merely because they purport to be answers. The student might be willing enough to live "the unexamined life," but the philosopher wants to find the right answers, those that a rational man can feel are warranted after most thoughtful consideration. The fact that some answers have been offered, or even that some have been accepted by almost everybody in a given society, does not suffice for the philosopher. Even the fact that one might feel certain answers to be the right ones is not an adequate basis for relying upon them. Rather, the philosopher insists, it must be completely certain that these answers are the true ones before a rational person can adopt them as his/her own. Otherwise, the best that we may be able to accomplish by philosophical examination is only to realize the inadequacy of all answers that have thus far been presented.

That particular student, like so many people in all ages, was willing to sell his "birthright" rather than undertake the effort required to philosophize. He was abdicating his proper function as a rational human being in order not to have to be bothered with the problem of finding some justification for what he believed, with discovering some consistent and coherent system for his views. But the philosopher claims that fundamentally the questions to be considered are too important to be answered in any quick and lazy fashion. It would be far better to have no answers than unexamined answers or, worse, answers that might be wrong.

Two examples

In order to make clearer what the philosopher is seeking and what he/she does, let us consider briefly two examples from the earliest history of philosophy that indicate the sort of situations that have given rise to intellectual consideration of various fundamental beliefs. The first instance is that of the first Greek philosophers, who lived in the sixth century B.C., in one of the Greek colonies in Asia Minor, the part that is now Turkey.

The Greek Philosophers

From the little we know of this era, apparently the vast majority of the populace was willing to accept a mythological explanation of events, an explanation like those we find in the works of Homer. Natural occurrences were accounted for in terms of the activities of gods or spirits who inhabited the natural world. The wars, jealousies, and rivalries among the gods, and their relations with men and women, were taken to account for the events of the visible world.

The thinkers who began the philosophical quest were those who found that when they scrutinized these accepted beliefs, they were seen to be inadequate. Different societies had different legends and mythologies. Most of these conflicted either with the others or with themselves. The explanations were always based upon insufficient evidence and could never adequately account for all the information people had acquired about the world. The philosophers, to the dismay of their contemporaries, challenged the believers in mythology to prove their views or to find a better theory, one that would satisfy reasonable people. Out of this rejection of traditionally accepted beliefs, and the search for more plausible or more defensible theories, came the attempts of thoughtful people to explain the natural world in some consistent and rational fashion.

The Book of Job

Similarly, in the Bible, in the Book of Job, we are given a picture of the beginning of the philosophical quest. Job is portrayed as living in a world in which people accept the view that the universe is governed by a just and good God who rewards the just and punishes the wicked, and that this system of divine retribution works out immediately in everyone's lifetime. Job, we are told, "was perfect and upright, and one that feared God, and eschewed evil," and yet he was punished.

Job and his "comforters" discuss this apparent conflict between the accepted belief in God's goodness and justice and what is happening before their very eyes, i.e., the torments of Job. The "comforters" refuse to examine their view with critical eyes and, instead, deny the facts. They attempt to convince Job that he must have been a wicked man; otherwise, he could not be in his predicament. Job, on the other hand, sees that the accepted system of belief cannot be adequate to account for what we do in fact know about the world, namely, that the wicked flourish and the just suffer in this supposedly divinely governed cosmos.

The Book of Job reveals the defects of the traditionally held view about the nature of the world. Because of these, a different, more rationally defensible theory has to be sought. Several possible ones are examined in the course of the book, and finally the only remaining solution is that man is unable by means of reason to discover any satisfactory answer.

Rather than rest content with inconsistent theories, or unjustifiable ones, the philosophical writer of the Book of Job could only pose a question. The people who lived "the unexamined life" tried their best to avoid facing the problem. But the philosopher, because of his need for intellectually satisfactory beliefs, had to examine it. Even if he could not find a better theory than the traditional one, at least he would not accept a view that he knew was inadequate.

In these examples—both instances from the beginnings of philosophical activities in ancient times—we can discern some of the drive that sets the philosophical quest in motion. There are always people who are ready to accept almost any view. But there are others who are troubled by what appear to be inconsistencies in these views, or are troubled because they do not see why these views ought to be accepted or why they are true. These philosophers begin to raise questions and seek solutions. How they do this, and what they have accomplished, are the subject matter of philosophy.

Conclusion

If one asks what is the point of all this searching for some consistent and coherent system of beliefs, of demanding rationally satisfactory explanations, possibly a kind of answer is contained in a story about a relatively recent catastrophe. According to the newspaper accounts, a Georgia bootlegger ran out of liquor with which to supply his clients. There was a great demand, and to satisfy this, he concocted a brew out of some antifreeze and other ingredients. The results were disastrous—some thirty people died from drinking the beverage. When the bootlegger was arrested, he was asked if he had anything to say about what had happened as a result of his nefarious activities. "Well," he commented, "it makes a man think."

Philosophy, in a less dangerous way, also makes a person think—think about the basic foundations of his/her outlook, his/her knowledge, his/her beliefs. It makes one inquire into the reasons for what one accepts and does, and into the importance of one's ideas and ideals, in the hope that one's final convictions, whether they remain the same or whether they change as a result of this examination, will at least be rationally held ones.

Whether this desired consequence is actually superior to declining to examine one's life is a philosophical question, and one that can better be decided after reading this book. One may well decide, after seeing what philosophy is and what philosophers have done, that it is all a waste of time. On the other hand, one may find that the consideration of problems in the various branches of philosophy—logic, ethics, theory of knowledge, metaphysics, and so on—provides solutions to the most urgent questions. Any conclusion that the reader comes to, we hope, will be based upon a thoughtful consideration of the material that is to follow, and hence will be the result of the reader's philosophizing.

We repeat: The best way to discover what philosophy is, is by studying it, and by philosophizing.

CHAPTER ONE

Ethics

The definition of "ethics"

As with so many words in common use, the term "ethics" has a number of different meanings. In one of its most frequent uses, it refers to **a code or set of principles by which people live.** Thus, we speak of "medical ethics" and mean by this phrase the code that regulates and guides the behavior of doctors in their dealings with each other and with their patients. Or again, when we speak of "Christian ethics," we are referring to the principles that prescribe the behavior of those who are Christians, such as the rules for conduct that are found in the Ten Commandments.

Philosophers, however, do not only employ the word in this sense when they speak of "ethics." They also mean by it a **theoretical study,** very much as the physicist means by "physics" a theoretical study. But whereas the physicist studies certain natural phenomena, such as moving bodies and their laws, the objects that are studied in ethics are theories. These theories, sometimes called "ethical theories," deal with such questions as "How ought men to behave?" "What is the good life for man?" and so on. An example of an ethical theory studied in the branch of philosophy called "ethics" is **hedonism.** This is an ancient theory that contends that the good life is ultimately one of pleasure.

Philosophers study such theories as hedonism not merely because these doctrines have important consequences for living and for understanding human nature, but also because many ethical doctrines that appear plausible at a first glance, such as hedonism, are found upon careful examination to suffer from certain defects. For example, does it not make sense to speak of "bad pleasures," i.e., of the things that may give us momentary pleasure, such as drinking alcohol, but that may result in a life of subsequent pain and travail? If this is so, then how can the good life be identical with a life of pleasure, since there are pleasures that are bad? But if it is not pleasure that constitutes the good life, then what does? Part of the motivation for studying ethics lies in the attempts by philosophers to construct satisfactory answers to questions like those we have mentioned above. In what follows, we will consider some of the famous classical and modern ethical theories to see how they answer such questions. We will examine their advantages and their defects, and by so doing, we will engage in the philosophical study we have designated as "ethics."

Ethics originates in everyday life

It would be a mistake to regard ethics as a purely "academic" study, having no intimate connections with the daily lives of men. Every person who is reflective and who is troubled by certain situations in his or her daily life is a philosopher of ethics to that extent. Suppose a person believes that no one should take a human life, and also believes that one has an obligation to defend one's country against foreign enemies. What should that person do when his/her country is at war? If one refuses to fight for his/her country, then one reneges on the belief that one has an obligation to do so. On the other hand, if one does fight for it, in the course of doing so one may take human life. What should be done in the circumstances? How can one decide? Reflections of this sort, which engage the attention of ordinary people, are the raw material of which ethical theories are made. The difference between the reflections of the ordinary person and the reflections of the philosopher is that the latter are frequently more systematic, although not always so, and are usually more general. The ordinary individual may merely be trying to solve a particular problem and may try to do this by deciding on a particular course of action in the relevant circumstances. The philosopher tries to **generalize.** The question is not "What is the right course of action for this individual in these circumstances?" but rather, "What is the good life for all? What is the goal for which all should

strive? Is it the accumulation of pleasure? Is it happiness? Is it identical with doing one's duty?" Like the ordinary person, the philosopher begins a consideration of ethics by reflecting about common situations, but then goes beyond these to discussions of a more general sort. It is this sort of abstract speculation that constitutes "ethical theory" as we shall employ the term.

Classification of ethical theories

There are many ways of classifying ethical theories. All of these different classifications are important not only because they help to organize the various types of doctrines into groupings that make them simpler to understand, but also because they help direct our attention to certain features that make the theories distinctive. The simplest and most obvious classification is a historical one. We can divide theories into those that are "classical" and those that are "modern." Roughly speaking, a theory will be classical if it does one of two things, or both: if it attempts to answer the question "What is the good life for people?"; and if it attempts to answer the question "How should people act?" We shall discuss the characteristics of modern theories later in this chapter.

Classical theories

Most classical theories do not carefully distinguish between these two questions. **It is generally assumed in such theories that if we know what the good life is, we**

will naturally act in such a way as to try to achieve it. This is the basis of the first famous classical theory we will consider.

Platonism

Although the philosopher Plato did not put forth philosophical views under his own name (his writings are mainly in the form of conversations, called "dialogues," between Socrates and other Greek philosophers of the fifth century B.C.), nevertheless, certain views are often attributed to Plato as being his own. Although there is some controversy about whether Plato or Socrates held the position that if a person knows what the good life is, he/she will not act immorally, in what follows we shall speak as if this is Plato's own view. According to this position, **evil is due to lack of knowledge.** If people can discover what is right, Plato believes, they will never act wickedly. But the problem is to discover what is right, or as Plato calls it, **"the good."** How can this be done when people differ so greatly in their opinions about the good life?

Plato's answer is that **finding the nature of the good life is an intellectual task very similar to the discovery of mathematical truths.** Just as the latter cannot be discovered by untrained people, so the former cannot be either. In order to discover what the good life is, people must first acquire certain kinds of knowledge. Such knowledge can be arrived at only if they are carefully schooled in various disciplines, such as mathematics, philosophy, and so on. Only when they have been through the long period of intellectual training that Plato suggests will they have

the capacity to know the nature of the good life.

It is important for an understanding of Plato to make a distinction at this point. Plato does not maintain that one must have knowledge in order to lead the good life. He maintains only the weaker doctrine that *if one does have* knowledge, that person will lead the good life. Even without the possession of knowledge it is possible for some individuals to lead the good life, but they will do so haphazardly or blindly. It is only if we have knowledge that we can be assured of leading such an existence. And this is why, in his suggested program for training people to lead good lives, Plato believes that they must be instructed in two different ways. On the one hand, they must develop **virtuous habits of behavior;** and on the other, they must develop their **mental powers** through the study of such disciplines as mathematics and philosophy.

Both of these types of instruction are necessary. To begin with, some people may not have the intellectual capacity to acquire knowledge; they will not be able to understand what the "good life" is, just as others do not have the intellectual power to apprehend higher mathematics. But if they **imitate and are guided** by those people who have knowledge of the good and who accordingly act virtuously, they, too, will act virtuously even though they do not understand the essential nature of the good life. On the basis of this sort of reasoning, Plato goes on to advocate the necessity of censorship in what he calls an "ideal society"—the society that is portrayed in his most famous book, the *Republic*. Plato feels that it is necessary to prevent young people from being exposed to certain sorts of experiences if they are to develop virtuous habits and thus lead a good life. Secondly, it is necessary for some especially gifted people to develop their mental powers and consequently to undergo rigorous intellectual training that will do more for them than to develop virtuous habits. This is so because they must finally be the rulers of the ideal society.

Plato so long ago envisaged a ruling class of both men and women. In such a society, the rulers, having developed their intellectual capacities, would also have acquired knowledge; and having acquired knowledge, they would understand the nature of the good life. This would guarantee their acting rightly, or morally, and hence would ensure their being good rulers. For, as we have seen, it was Plato's belief that if a person could acquire knowledge, in particular knowledge of what was good, then such a person would never act evilly.

A second basic element in Plato's philosophy is what contemporary scholars term his **"absolutism."** According to Plato, there is fundamentally **one and only one** good life for all to lead. This is because goodness is something that is not dependent upon humans' inclinations, desires, wishes, or upon their opinions. Goodness in this respect resembles the mathematical truth that two plus two equals four. This is a truth that is absolute; it exists whether anyone likes such a fact or not, or even whether one knows mathematics or not. It is not dependent upon mankind's opinions about the nature of mathematics or the world. Likewise, **goodness exists independently of mankind and remains to be discovered if people can be properly trained.**

This can be put another way. Plato is arguing for the **objectivity** of moral principles as opposed to all philosophies that contend that morality is merely a "matter of opinion" or "preference." Plato's view can be roughly summarized as saying that a certain course of action is right or wrong **absolutely** and **independently of anyone's opinion,** just as the statement "This is a typewriter" is either right or wrong independently of anybody's opinion. Thus the Nazis who murdered 6,000,000 Jews in gas chambers were *absolutely* wrong in their behavior; it was not that we, with differing ethical standards, merely *thought* them to be wrong—but more than that, we were *right* in so thinking, for they were *wrong*. It is an absolutely objective moral law that "Thou shalt not commit murder," and the Nazis violated this law.

Platonism has had a tremendous impact upon religious philosophy, for most theologians have assumed that moral laws such as "Thou shalt not steal" and "Thou shalt not commit murder" are **absolute and objective** in the Platonic sense. The development of Plato's philosophy that is known as Neoplatonism was the nearest that Greek philosophy itself came to becoming a religion, and it had a direct influence on the development of Christian and Islamic theology. But it should be pointed out that although Platonism and most theologies agree in contending that moral standards are objective, there is a fundamental difference between them that should not be overlooked. Plato himself believed that **moral standards were superior even to God;** goodness is anterior to God, and God is good if and only if he acts in accordance with a standard. This is quite distinct from the traditional Judeo-Christian or Islamic view, for example, that God creates goodness. This point will be examined more fully in Chapter 4.

Criticism of Platonism

As we have seen, Platonism as a moral philosophy rests upon two basic assumptions. One is the assumption that if a person has knowledge of the good life, he/she will never act immorally. The other is that there is one and only one good life for all, just as there is no moral alternative, in certain circumstances, to the command "Thou shalt not steal." Let us now examine criticisms of these basic assumptions, beginning with the belief that those who have knowledge of the good will never act immorally.

Most philosophers who criticize Plato have interpreted this thesis as expressing a **psychological judgment about how people will act under certain conditions.** The conditions are that if they have a certain kind of knowledge, they will behave in a certain way. Let us see if Plato's view is true. Suppose I intend to embezzle money from the bank where I work. Suppose it is pointed out to me that stealing is wrong. Now I may not agree with this assertion. I may think, and even argue, that stealing is right. If so, ordinary people would consider me deficient in moral knowledge, since stealing is in fact wrong. It is much as if I had argued that two plus two equals five. In holding such a view, I am simply mistaken. If I proceed to steal money from the bank, it is plausible to say that I have acted immorally because of a deficiency

in knowledge. And this is indeed what Plato would say about me—that I simply do not understand what is meant by the "right way of life." Insofar as Platonism can be applied to this case, it seems in accord with commonsense views of morality. On the other hand, interpreted as a psychological account of how people behave *in every case*, the theory seems to have grave defects. For some people may well understand that stealing is wrong, but they may still persist in stealing. Plato would say of them that they really do not understand what is meant by "stealing," since no people willingly will do what they know to be wrong. But if we talk to such people and if they give the usual signs of understanding what it means to steal, and further, if they admit it to be morally wrong but still persist in doing it, it appears as if Plato's account must be rejected, since it seems that some people will act evilly while knowing what the right course of action is. This is the view of human nature taken by Aristotle.

But Plato's account is much more subtle than the above discussion would indicate. What makes it attractive is that it attempts to supply a general solution to a common type of difficulty that arises in daily life. People often find themselves in situations where they do not know how to behave because they do not know what the right course of action would be in those circumstances. Is it right to defend my country if this means killing someone, or is it right never to kill anyone? What Plato suggests is that if we had more information, if we had been more carefully trained, we could discover the answer. We would know what the right course of action would be in those circumstances, and thus our perplexity would be relieved. The situation seems analogous to many problems that doctors face. Should they operate now or wait until tomorrow? Should they administer this drug or not? These are problems that would be hopelessly bewildering to the average person, since he/she does not have the training and hence the knowledge to solve them. But to a trained person, the difficulty disappears. Plato's point is that moral difficulties in many cases are theoretically solvable by the acquisition of further knowledge— and this is a point of view that cannot be lightly dismissed.

The major objection to it, however, is this. Moral conundrums do not, in the final analysis, seem to be analogous to scientific questions. When all the relevant facts have been gathered in a scientific issue, we can in principle always decide the issue or decide what is the most suitable answer. But this is not so in a moral situation. We may know all the relevant facts in a given situation. We may know, for instance, that the effect of dropping a nuclear bomb on a certain area will be to kill a million people, to make that area uninhabitable for one century; and, on the other hand, we may also know that if we drop the bomb, a currently disastrous war will be shortened by years. But our perplexity still exists. Should we or should we not drop the bomb? It must be conceded that sometimes the acquisition of further information about a situation will solve difficulties we have about acting in that situation, but it must also be recognized that this is not always so, and if not, Platonism cannot be accepted without considerable qualification. Moral knowledge is not analogous to scientific or mathematical knowledge, and Plato's mistake was to think that it is.

A further criticism that arises from this is that since Plato regards morality as being a matter of knowledge, a prerequisite of moral behavior is the intellectual ability necessary to apprehend the abstract truths of morality, so that he seems to exclude the possibility of fully moral behavior for all but a few intellectually gifted individuals. It is not sufficient to say that those of us who lack this ability can live good lives by allowing ourselves to be ruled or advised by those who have, since to behave morally presupposes that one has responsibility for one's actions. An action is not truly moral—or immoral, for that matter—unless it is the result of the free choice of the individual performing it. To make this choice, the individual needs the kind of moral understanding that Plato says is possible only for a few. Again, we shall find Aristotle showing a clearer awareness of this basic feature of moral behavior than Plato.

The second basic assumption of Platonism is that there is one and only one right course of action for all: we have called this Plato's "absolutism." Since we shall discuss this problem in more detail when we come to modern ethics, we shall not consider it directly here. However, even in ancient times this view was tellingly criticized, again by Plato's greatest pupil, the philosopher Aristotle. Let us turn, then, to Aristotle's moral philosophy in order to see how it differs from Plato's and, in particular, how it rejects the Platonic tenets that there is one and only one right course of action in a given moral situation, that good behavior is possible without moral understanding, and that a knowledge of the good will necessarily lead to virtuous behavior.

Aristotle: The Doctrine of the Mean

It was characteristic of Greek philosophy to be highly speculative. This trait is exhibited most strikingly in **metaphysics, where many Greek philosophers attempted to discover the true nature of the world by the use of reason alone.** It is found less commonly in the ethical writings of the Greeks, but even here it is a noticeable feature of their philosophizing. Such philosophers as Heraclitus, Plato, and the Stoics **derived their ethical views in part from certain metaphysical positions they held.** The Stoics, for example, believed that **all behavior is rigidly determined by natural laws.** This led them into puzzles about whether one can behave **freely, for if not, no one can be held morally responsible for what one does.** In general, such speculation is of a nonscientific sort: it does not patiently try to collect facts and then derive conclusions from them; rather, it tries to *deduce* facts about the nature of the world and the nature of man by the use of reason alone. Aristotle is, of course, one of the great metaphysicians in this sense. But curiously enough, in his ethical writings he departed from this tradition and adopted a **scientific or empirical approach to ethical problems.** Instead of trying to discover the nature of the good life for all by reflection alone, he examined the behavior and talk of various people in everyday life. He noticed that plain men regard some people as leading what they call "good lives" and others as leading what they call "bad lives."

He noticed further that the various lives that people of common sense consider to be "good" all contain one common characteristic: **happiness.** And similarly, the lives that ordinary people regard as being bad lives all have in common the characteristic of being unhappy. Therefore, in answer to the question "What is the good life for man?" Aristotle's answer can be stated in one sentence: **"It is a life of happiness."**

But this answer is in a way too simple. We still would like to know, beyond this, what the common man means when he says the good life is a "happy" one. Does he suggest that it is a life of pleasure, of success, of fame, or what? Exactly what does the word "happiness" mean? Unfortunately, the ordinary person is unable to help us if we ask what is meant by "happiness." Either one is inarticulate, or one gives different and contradictory answers. Aristotle's work in ethics is a philosophical attempt to supply the answer: he tries to explain more clearly than the ordinary person can what moral words like "happiness" mean. The *Nicomachean Ethics*, which is the title of Aristotle's chief work on ethics, can thus be regarded as one of the earliest essays in what is now called "analytical philosophy." Aristotle in this work was trying to analyze or explain the use of certain moral terms that occur in everyday speech in a clearer way than the average person could do, even though the ordinary person could use these words quite properly in everyday speech.

In the *Nicomachean Ethics*, Aristotle gives a definition of the word "happiness" that has since become famous. "Happiness," he says, "is an activity of the soul in accord with perfect virtue." Unfortunately, this definition may not be much clearer to the reader than the original question "What is happiness?" since it is couched in obscure terminology. In fact, it has been a source of puzzlement to philosophers for centuries, and various interpretations of it have been offered. A plausible interpretation, although not the only one, is this: Aristotle is stressing the fact that happiness is not something static, but that it is an **activity.** What does he mean by saying it is not "static"? People tend to think that happiness is something we arrive at—a certain fixed goal that awaits us if we behave in certain ways. Those who hold this view tend to think of happiness as an object of a certain sort, just as London is an object one can reach at the end of a trip. Once we finish our tour through life's daily activities, so to speak, then we will have arrived at this goal called "happiness."

But this is precisely what Aristotle is *denying.* Happiness is *not* a goal in this sense. Rather, it is something that *accompanies* certain activities, instead of being the *goal* of these activities. Happiness, as a characteristic of men's lives, is something like persistence. A person who engages in a course of conduct persistently does not arrive at a goal called "persistence." Instead, it is **a way of doing things;** for instance, of refusing to be defeated by circumstances. Happiness is like this: it is **a way of engaging in the various activities of life,** such as eating, making love, working, and so on. If one engages in these activities in a certain way, then we can declare that person to be happy. For instance, if a person enjoys eating, intellectual pursuits, friendship, and so on, and is not frequently downcast, depressed, anxious—then he/she is happy. This roughly is what Aristotle means by saying that happiness is an activity—but it should be stressed that these brief remarks are to be regarded as a preliminary aid to the reader rather than an exhaustive account of the doctrine.

As we have mentioned already, classical ethical theories attempt to answer two questions: "What is the good life for people?" and "How ought people to behave?" Aristotle is a classical moralist in both senses. In answer to the first question, his reply is: **"The good life for people is a life of happiness."** The answer to the second question is equally direct: **"People ought to behave so as to achieve happiness."** But again, this answer seems vague. If we ask, "More specifically, how should we behave in order to achieve happiness?" Aristotle's answer is to be found in the well-known formula called the **"doctrine of the mean,"** sometimes popularly referred to as the **"golden mean."** We shall now turn to a discussion of the doctrine of the mean, and in this way we will show how Aristotle's moral philosophy differs from that of Plato.

Being happy, according to Aristotle, is like being well fed. How much food should a person eat in order to be well fed? Aristotle's contention is that there is no general answer to this question in the sense of fixing a specific amount like one kilo of meat per day. It depends on the size of the person, what sort of work he/she does, whether he/she is ill or well, and so on. A person who works at digging ditches will need more food, in general, than one who sits at a desk; and a large person will need more food, in general, than a small one. Now the proper amount for anyone to eat can be ascertained only by trial and error: if we eat a certain amount of food and still feel hungry, we should eat more; if we eat the same amount and feel uncomfortable, then we should eat less. The correct amount is a "mean" between eating too much and too little. It is important here not to interpret the word "mean" as being synonymous with "average." Suppose that one kilo of food per day is too little and that two kilos is too much. Does this suggest that the average amount (i.e., one and one-half kilos) is the correct amount? Aristotle's answer is that it may or may not be—but in general, one cannot say that the correct amount is exactly one and one-half kilos; all one can say is that it is an amount *somewhere* between one and two kilos, and this is what he intends by the word "mean." We should eat an amount of food that is more than one kilo and less than two; but the exact amount can be ascertained only after we eat various portions and see how we feel.

The important consequences of this doctrine for ethics are that **there are various correct ways of living for different people. What is good for one person may not be good for another. And, further, one cannot tell prior to actual experimentation, by the use of reason alone, which is the correct way of living for someone. This can be ascertained only by experimentation and by trial and error.** We can summarize these two points by saying that Aristotle is both a **relativist** and an **empiricist** in ethics.

So with happiness. **The proper way for one to behave in the moral sphere is in accordance with the mean.** For example, in order to be happy, one must be courageous, liberal, proud, witty, modest, and

so on. But all of these "virtues," as Aristotle designates them, are virtues of **moderation:** courage is the mean between cowardice and rashness; liberality, between prodigality and frugality; pride, between vanity and humility; and so forth. Aristotle's philosophy of the **"golden mean"** can be condensed as follows: **In order to achieve happiness, people must act moderately, they must act so as to be striving for the mean between two extremes.** If they do this, then they will be happy. But the mean will vary from person to person: some can be more courageous than others, and some less; and each will be proper for that person. Plato, it will be remembered, contended that "goodness" is an absolute characteristic. Either a person is "good" or not—there is one and only one proper way for him/her to behave in a given set of circumstances. But this is precisely what Aristotle is disputing: there are *many* "good" lives—in fact, there may be as many as there are differences between people. All of these have in common the fact that if people behave in accordance with the mean, they will achieve happiness; but there may be many ways of so behaving, thus many ways of being happy.

Aristotle shows a similar disagreement with Plato over the question of whether people are really acting morally if they are without a full understanding of the situation. He makes an important distinction between actions done "willingly" and those done "not unwillingly," pointing out that we do not praise or blame someone if we believe that he/she did not understand what he/she was doing. Moral behavior in the full sense requires moral understanding, and all people can hope to achieve this, since what is involved is not a purely intellectual appreciation of absolute moral truths but the kind of practical wisdom and awareness of the need for moderation that we have just described.

Furthermore, Aristotle does not agree with Plato that a knowledge of the good will necessarily lead to virtuous behavior. He shows a more realistic view of human nature by introducing into his discussion of ethics the notion of moral weakness or lack of self-control. He tells us, much as St. Paul was to tell us later, that the evil that we would not, that we do, and the good we would, we do not. A knowledge of what we ought to do is not sufficient without the kind of self-discipline necessary to ensure that we do it. For we can be too easily led astray by the pleasures of other forms of behavior. We must, therefore, receive a sound training in good habits when we are young, so that when we come to understand what the golden mean is for us, we will also have the self-control to follow it.

Aristotle is one of the first great philosophers of common sense in dealing with ethical matters. Unlike Plato, who lays down rigid requirements for everyone to follow, regardless of his/her inclinations, desires, temperament, station in life, and so on, Aristotle is much less narrow. And this can be seen in his **doctrine of pleasure.** Aristotle rejects the view that pleasure is entirely bad. His view is that no one can be happy without a certain amount of pleasure in life; this is expressed in his famous epigram **"No man can be happy on the rack."**

In spite of its commonsense outlook, however, the Aristotelian view of ethics is not without its difficulties, and we will consider some of these now.

Criticism of Aristotle

Although at first glance it seems plausible to hold that everyone always ought to follow the middle course between certain kinds of activities, there seem to be situations in which this advice will not do. For example, there is no middle course between keeping a promise and not keeping one. We tend to feel that any person is moral insofar as he/she keeps a promise, and immoral insofar as he/she breaks it (unless there are certain other overriding factors). But the main point is that in such a case there is no middle ground between the two: either one keeps a promise or one does not. The same applies to telling the truth—either one does or does not tell the truth—and once again the doctrine of the mean cannot be applied to such cases. Such virtues as keeping promises and telling the truth seem to be better analyzable by the Platonic view: they seem to be *absolute* virtues, and are *not relative* to various people and situations as are virtues like courage (which is the mean between rashness and cowardice).

A second and perhaps more important criticism of the Aristotelian doctrine is this: **Aristotle is primarily proposing a philosophy of moderation.** His view is that happiness will result from moderate behavior. This is true in some cases, of course, but there are hosts of cases where only "immoderate" behavior is *proper* behavior. A person who is temperamentally passionate and romantic may find that "moderate" behavior does not suit him/her. One cannot be happy if forced to control oneself in all situations of life. For people of this temperament, the Aristotelian ethic is not an appealing one; and the rise of Romanticism in philosophy can be regarded in this way as criticism of the Aristotelian way of life.

Hedonism: The Philosophy of Epicurus

As we have indicated, Plato maintained that the good life is in no way connected with pleasure. Aristotle moderated this doctrine. Although denying that the good life was *identical* with a life of pleasure, he admitted that **"pleasure must be in some way an ingredient of happiness."** Epicurus was the exponent of a type of philosophy that has persisted down to the present time. He held a view that is sometimes called **"hedonism," the doctrine that pleasure is the sole good.** The influence of his philosophy can be judged from the fact that the English language still contains the word "epicure," which is based upon the view of Epicurus. As with so many words, however, the connotations of the word "epicure" as it is now employed do not represent accurately the sort of philosophy that was held by Epicurus himself. An "epicurean" is now depicted as a *gourmet*, as a person whose main delight consists in the enjoyment of exotic or fastidiously prepared food and rare wines. As a matter of fact, Epicurus himself suffered for years from stomach trouble and was never an "epicure" in the modern sense. He ate frugally, allegedly drank only water, and, in general, lived in a highly abstemious fashion.

(His letters contained such sentences as the following: "I am thrilled with pleasure in the body when I live on bread and water, and I spit on luxurious pleasures, not for their own sake, but because of the inconveniences that follow them.")

The ethical philosophy of Epicurus consists mainly of advice for living moderately but pleasurably. He considered pleasure to be *the* good, but he also realized that **if a person pursues pleasure too arduously, pain will follow.** If a person drinks too much, he/she will suffer headaches and stomach pains the next day. The proper way to proceed in life is to **live pleasantly without suffering from any of the undesirable effects of such living.**

In fact, Epicurus' philosophy may be regarded as containing instructions that are designed not only to enable one to acquire pleasure but also to enable one to avoid pain. If one engages in a life of pleasure that leads to pain, then such a life would be regarded as a bad one by Epicurus. Since some pleasures are obviously accompanied by pain, Epicurus distinguished between those pleasures that are accompanied by pain and those that are not, and regarded only the latter as good. He called the former **"dynamic"** pleasures and the latter **"passive"** pleasures. Sexual love, for example, is bad because it is accompanied by fatigue, remorse, and depression. Other "dynamic" pleasures are gluttony; the fame that one achieves through a life of public service; drinking; and marriage. All of these are bad because they are accompanied by pain: gluttony will lead to indigestion, fame may be accompanied by all sorts of distress, drinking will lead to headaches, disease, and so forth. The result is that Epicurus advocated (and himself led) a life that we would now consider highly ascetic. This is because he seemed to believe that **it is bet-**

ter to avoid pain than to seek pleasure if it will produce pain. Friendship, on the other hand, is a passive pleasure. It is not accompanied by pain and hence is permitted and, indeed, encouraged by him.

Hedonism, as a philosophical doctrine, has two forms. We can call the first form **"psychological hedonism"** and the second type **"ethical hedonism." Psychological hedonism is the doctrine that in fact people pursue pleasure, and only pleasure, in their lives. All activities, according to this theory, are directed toward the acquisition of pleasure and the avoidance of pain.** Eudoxus, who was a famous Greek mathematician and an earlier contemporary of Aristotle, is supposed to have held such a view. Aristotle says of him:

> Now Eudoxus thought pleasure to be the chief good because he saw all, rational and irrational alike, aiming at it: and he argued that, since in all what was the object of choice must be good and what most so the best, the fact of all being drawn to the same thing proved this thing to be the best for all: "For each," he said, "finds what is good for itself just as it does its proper nourishment, and so that which is good for all, and the object of the aim of all, is their chief good."

Epicurus is generally interpreted as being a psychological hedonist in this sense. He apparently believed that all were motivated in their daily lives to attempt to acquire pleasure: did not people strive for riches, for fame, for sensual delights because the attainment of these produced pleasure?

Epicurus is also an ethical hedonist (with certain important qualifications). **Ethical hedonism is the view not only that people in fact seek pleasure but, further, that they ought to do so, since pleasure alone is good.** It is obvious that psychological hedonism does not entail ethical hedonism. One might hold either doctrine without necessarily holding the other. For example, one might believe that people are motivated to seek pleasure, and one might also believe that they ought *not* to do so. In fact, this is roughly what Epicurus held, as we have seen. His view was that even if people are motivated to acquire pleasure, certain pleasures are bad and ought to be avoided. On the other hand, he held that some pleasures, such as friendship, conversation about philosophy, and so on, are such as ought to be cultivated; and the good life consists in acquiring pleasures of this sort. He can consequently be interpreted as holding a modified form of ethical hedonism, as well as adhering to the psychological version of the theory.

Criticism of Hedonism

Hedonism is a complex moral philosophy consisting of at least two parts, one of them a psychological theory, the other an ethical theory. The psychological account is supposedly a true description of how people are motivated to action in conducting their daily lives. According to this account, every conscious action is motivated by the search for pleasure. Whether one is a hermit or whether one seeks fame, in either case—if we are to accept psychological hedonism—one is motivated to act as one does because one is striving for pleasure. Ethical hedonism, on the other hand, goes beyond the psychological account: it contends that people *ought* to seek pleasure, for ultimately this is the only thing worth having for itself.

Both aspects of hedonism seem plausible not only to the unsophisticated reader but even to professional thinkers. Let us show in somewhat more detail why this is so, considering **psychological hedonism** first. What the theory attempts to do is **to provide a single explanation for every possible type of conscious or voluntary action human beings engage in**. It is a source of satisfaction to all thinkers to find the most general explanation for a group phenomenon, especially if this explanation turns out to be a very simple one. And psychological hedonism tries to provide an explanation of this sort. Consider any kind of conscious behavior—why do people do it? The answer is always the same—they are seeking pleasure. At this point, we can mention a famous philosophical distinction that can be used to support psychological hedonism. The distinction has various names, one of the most common of which is the **"means-ends" distinction**. The point of the distinction is this: **Some things may not be worth having in themselves, but are worth having because they enable us to achieve certain goals**. On the other hand, other things may be worth having in themselves. They are, as philosophers say, **"intrinsically valuable."** We value them not because they enable us to achieve something else, but for their own sakes. Exercise, for instance, may not be worth doing in its own right, but it has value in that by doing it, we will become healthy, which *is* valuable in itself. In terms of the above distinction, exercise is valuable as a "means," while health is valuable as an "end." Now the position of the psychological hedonist is that the ultimate end toward which all activity is directed is

pleasure; such things as fame, riches, success are all means to this end. Thus, all conscious human behavior can be explained by saying that individuals are motivated *ultimately* or *basically* by pleasure—it is the end for which all strive. Put this way, psychological hedonism has been a theory that has attracted philosophers and ordinary people, and it has accordingly had a great influence throughout the history of Western thought.

However, insofar as this part of hedonism is interpreted as a purely scientific account of conscious behavior, it does not withstand present-day scientific scrutiny. Psychologists agree that people are *sometimes* motivated by the search for pleasure, but they go on to point out that such is not always the case. For although some individuals may begin by trying to acquire riches as a means to pleasure, after a time they may come to regard wealth as an end in itself. In psychological language, they become "fixated" upon the acquisition of wealth and disregard the use to which it may be put for acquiring pleasure. (Such people are commonly called "misers.") Psychologists point out that these people may be so strongly motivated by the attempt to acquire money that they may disregard or even reject the pursuit of pleasure as being of any value to them if it interferes with the acquisition of money. We are all familiar with newspaper accounts of men and women who are found living in squalid conditions even though they may possess a fortune hidden in the mattress. The acquisition of money, not pleasure, becomes an end for them—and for this reason, psychologists tell us that psychological hedonism cannot be accepted as an accurate picture of *all* conscious human motivation. And this is merely one instance of such exceptions.

Unfortunately, psychological hedonism is not simply a scientific theory, and it cannot be refuted merely by an appeal to the latest scientific findings. This can be seen when we consider the sort of reply the psychological hedonists will make to the objection we have just considered. They will claim that the miser *actually* gains pleasure by hoarding money. The miser is merely giving up the usual means for acquiring pleasure, such as living in a decent home, eating well, and so on. All he/she has done, the hedonists argue, is to limit the means for acquiring pleasure to the collecting of money. Money has not become an end in itself—rather, it has become the sole means for achieving pleasure; but pleasure is still the end for which he/she strives.

At this stage, the theory has been removed from the area where any scientific finding can possibly confirm or refute it. It has now become a philosophical rather than a scientific problem, for no collection of facts can be gathered that would resolve the problem. But when psychological hedonism is interpreted in this way, it can still be attacked on philosophical grounds. **For when any theory cannot be refuted by facts, then it loses its explanatory force**. It becomes true **"by definition" but no longer refers to the world in the way in which genuine scientific theories do,** since its truth or falsity no longer depends upon the *facts*. When this happens, the theory may be rejected on the ground that it has lost its power to provide us with a satisfactory explanation of the facts it started out to explain. It has now

defined "pleasure" as what people "desire," so that in asserting that all people are motivated by a desire for pleasure, it is asserting no more than the tautology that all people are motivated by a desire for what they desire. It has become irrefutable by becoming trivial, i.e., it is not worth refuting.

Ethical hedonism, as contrasted with psychological hedonism, can be divided into two parts, which may be regarded as answers to the questions "What is the good life for people?" and "How *ought* one to behave?" The answers, according to the ethical hedonist, are that the good life consists of a life of pleasure and that one *ought* to act so as to acquire pleasure. Let us now examine objections to these replies.

We have already pointed out that even Epicurus, the founder of hedonism, recognized that some pleasures may be accompanied by pain or that they may produce pain. For example, smoking cocaine may give us pleasure, but it will produce physical and mental deterioration if persisted in. It thus appears that some pleasures are bad; and if so, we cannot contend simply that the good life is *identical* with a life of pleasure. Epicurus attempted to avoid this difficulty by finding pleasures that do not produce painful consequences, and argued that such pleasures constitute the good life. But this approach will not do, since even friendship, which he regards as a passive pleasure, may sometimes be accompanied by tribulation. For example, if a friend dies, one may suffer intensely from sadness at the death.

A second way of defending the view that pleasure is good is to hold that pleasure itself is never bad—even the pleasure one gets from smoking cocaine. It is only the painful consequences themselves that are bad. For example, if a drug could be devised that would eliminate the painful consequences of smoking cocaine—who would deny that the pleasure one got from it was good?

This defense is logically unassailable, but it has practical difficulties that make it dubious that ethical hedonism can offer acceptable guidance for one's conduct in daily life. For we cannot, as a matter of fact, always separate the painful consequences of a course of action from the pleasurable ones. If we use cocaine, we may be given pleasure, to be sure, but we will also suffer pain as a result of doing so. To advise one, as ethical hedonists do, to seek pleasure is in effect frequently equivalent to advising one to seek pain as well, since the two sometimes cannot be dissociated. Ethical hedonism, consequently, must sometimes advise one not to pursue pleasures when those pleasures are followed by pain, and thus its practical effect seems incompatible with the theory.

Finally, let us consider the doctrine that people ought to behave so as to acquire pleasure. This view likewise seems plausible at first glance, but further reflection shows that it violates our commonsense beliefs about how we ought to behave. Consider the following case: A soldier is put on guard duty at an important post. He is forced to walk back and forth, and this is monotonous for him. It is a hot night. It would be more pleasant not to remain at his post but to leave for a bar where he can have a cool drink. Most people would say that if he deserted his post for this reason, then he would be acting wrongly. If he says that he acted as he ought to have done because he was seeking pleasure, this defense would be laughed out of court. The ordinary person feels that sometimes one ought to act so as to acquire pleasure, but not always. Sometimes one has certain obligations that one must fulfill, and in these cases one ought to behave so as to fulfill them even if in doing so one does not acquire pleasure. If ethical hedonism is interpreted as a systematic theory about how people ought to behave in society, the objection we have just cited shows that it cannot be regarded as an adequate account of such behavior.

Hedonism, even though theoretically attractive, can thus be seen to violate our ordinary feelings about what constitutes moral behavior. Do we object on moral grounds to the "playboy"? The objection is not merely that he seeks superficial pleasures, such as those of the table, the grape, and so on; but more fundamentally, that pleasure is not the sole object that people should strive for. The ordinary person is, with regard to pleasure, more an Aristotelian than an Epicurean. He/she feels that sometimes pleasure is a worthwhile object, and in fact that no life can be happy without some pleasure in it; but finds the doctrine that pleasure is the *only* worthwhile goal, objectionable—and rejects it as containing advice that cannot in fact be followed.

Cynicism

We have spoken of Platonism, Aristotelianism, and Epicureanism as if they were ethical philosophies that were devised by their authors in isolation from the social conditions of the time. For many purposes, this sort of abstraction is useful; but at the same time, it should be stressed that moral philosophies to a great extent *are* products of their times. If one does not recognize this fact, it may be impossible for one to account for the widespread appeal that such theories have had for so many people. Great philosophies, especially moral philosophies, may be regarded as saying more clearly and usually more strikingly what many common people only vaguely realize. This is especially true of **Cynicism** and **Stoicism**, whose attraction for so many cannot be fully appreciated apart from some knowledge of the social conditions from which they developed. To some extent, this is even true of hedonism. **When people suffer great catastrophes, they may grasp at pleasure as providing some comfort and security in a collapsing world. Hedonism is a philosophy that justifies their behavior,** and under such conditions they will be attracted to it. In this regard, **hedonism may be considered a philosophy that arises out of despair.**

Cynicism and Stoicism resemble hedonism in being, generally speaking, philosophies of consolation. But instead of suggesting that the acquisition of pleasure is the proper goal of life, they offer different advice. Let us turn to these doctrines now in order to see why they arose when they did and what sorts of answers they give to such persistent questions as "What is the good life for people?" and "How should people act?"

There are various ways that people can deal with adversity. They can succumb to it, fight it, escape from it, accept it, and so on. For each of these types of behavior there is a corresponding ethical theory that justifies it. **Quietism**, for example, is an Oriental ethical philosophy that advises one to accept and succumb to adversity; hedonism can be looked at as a way of escaping from it; and **utilitarianism,** as a way of combating it. **All ethical theories arise because people are dissatisfied either with their personal lives or with the world in which they live.** If a person is content with his/her lot and with the situation in which the world finds itself, he/she will not in general seek to change it. What would be the point of trying to do so? But when one is dissatisfied, one will attempt to alter the circumstances in which one finds him/herself—as we have said, one may fight these circumstances or try to escape from them. Likewise, philosophers do not develop theories about how one *ought* to behave unless they are discontent with the way people do in fact behave: they offer these theories as advice for altering the situation as they see it.

This is particularly true of Cynicism. It can be regarded as having prescribed behavior for those whose lives became intolerable due to the collapse of the world about them or for reasons of personal despair. This collapse in part began with the decline of the Greek city-state (note the frequent wars between Sparta and Athens, or Sparta and Corinth, with the incredible loss of life and destruction that they entailed) and was considerably accelerated by the turmoil that was attendant upon the collapse of the Alexandrian Empire. When social institutions of this magnitude break down, people are naturally led to consider how they may achieve *personal* salvation, and Cynicism offers one answer to this question. **It holds** that all the fruits of civilization are worthless—government, private property, marriage, religion, slavery (in the ancient Greeks' social order), luxury, and all artificial pleasures of the senses. If salvation is to be found, it is to be found in a rejection of society and in a return to the simple life—to a life of ascetic living.

The early Cynics, such as Diogenes, practiced frugal and even miserable lives to such an extent that they were likened to animals in their mode of life. In fact, the word "cynic" comes from the Greek word *kunos*, which means "doglike" (we find a cognate of it in the English word "canine"). Diogenes, for example, is supposed to have lived in a large tub and rejected all refinements—of dress, food, personal cleanliness, and so on. There is a famous story told about him and Alexander the Great, then the strongest potentate in the world. Alexander came to visit Diogenes and asked him if there was anything he could do for him to relieve him of the miserable conditions in which he existed. Diogenes is supposed to have replied: "Yes, you can stand out of my light and let me see the sun."

The Cynics believed that the world was fundamentally evil; in order to live properly, people must withdraw from participation in it. But at the same time, even if one lives a private life, such a life may be devoted to acquiring the usual goods of the world—such as money, a house, fine clothes, and so on. And all of these things are precarious, too—for **if we trust our happiness to the possession of them, we may find ourselves again betrayed.** Consequently, all externals, whether private or public, must be dispensed with. **If a person is to find salvation in the world, he/she must find it within him/herself—this is what virtue consists in.** The Cynics thus advocated a rejection of the goods of the world, and in this way tried to show people that by ignoring such externals they would be emancipated from fear. (We will indicate later that a much more sophisticated version of this theory is to be found in the philosophy of Spinoza, and considerable elements of it occur in Stoicism.)

It is interesting to speculate upon how the word "cynical" acquired its modern meaning. The rejection of external goods included the rejection of other people, so that a complete indifference and lack of feeling for others resulted. Furthermore, although the early Cynics such as Diogenes and Antisthenes lived moral and upright lives of extreme frugality in accordance with the precepts we have mentioned above, later followers used the doctrine for personal advantage. They borrowed money and food from friends, and then applied the doctrine of "indifference" when it came time to repay these debts. People gradually came to feel that the doctrine was being applied insincerely and callously—and out of such feelings the word "cynic" developed its modern meaning.

It can be seen that Cynicism is primarily a doctrine that is **antisocial**. It does not attempt to describe how people can be happy as social beings, but instead, it tries to propose ways for achieving individual salvation. In this way, **it contributed considerably to the philosophical undermining of social standards, arguing that only individual virtue was of fundamental importance.** This outlook considerably abetted the moral chaos into which the ancient world fell after the collapse of the Alexandrian Empire.

Not only is Cynicism antisocial, but it is also one of the forerunners of **asceticism**. By rejecting the claim that worldly possessions are of value, it was one of the precursors of the sort of asceticism that we find so brilliantly pictured in Anatole France's novel *Thaïs*, where men are depicted as living solitary, miserable lives in the Egyptian desert—lying on hard ground at night, fasting for days at a time, and in general subjecting themselves to physical and mental torture.

Not only has Cynicism as a philosophy had great influence upon plain men, but it was a considerable factor in the development of early Christian philosophy. The monk, in a way, can be pictured as a man who follows the advice of the Cynic: he lives a simple, frugal, cloistered life, shunning the world's goods—such as marriage, the accumulation of private property, and fame—and all this so that he may develop his character as an individual and cast aside the world for the unencumbered devotion to God. The general effect of Cynicism is thus otherworldliness, and this is why it has played so great a role in influencing the way of life advocated by **pietistic** religions such as Christianity.

Stoicism

It is fair to describe **Stoicism as the most influential ethical doctrine of the ancient Western world before Christianity.** It swept over Greece after the death of Alexander and dominated Roman thought until it was superseded by Christianity. But unlike hedonism and Cynicism, which remained more or less unchanged from the time of their inception, Stoicism was a doctrine that went through a number of radical developments in its long history. It began as a development of Cynicism and ended as a form of Platonic idealism. Most of the changes that took place, however, were in the metaphysical views of the Stoics and in their logic. Their ethical views remained relatively stable, and consequently in this section, since we are concerned with ethics, we can ignore the minor variations that took place in Stoic moral theory and treat the doctrine as if it had persisted unaltered.

The founder of Stoicism was named Zeno (not to be confused with Zeno of Elea, the originator of the famous logical paradoxes). Zeno is supposed to have lectured in the third century B.C. from a porch, and Stoicism gets its name from this fact, since *stoa* is the Greek word meaning "porch."

Like the Cynics, the Stoics were tremendously depressed by the collapse of the Greek city-states and the Alexandrian Empire. They felt that no hope for social reconstruction was possible. Consequently, **their philosophy consists of advice to individuals for attaining personal salvation in a crumbling world.** Although Stoicism, as we shall see, is a fairly complex moral theory, its basic tenet for achieving personal salvation is very like that of the Cynics and can be stated in one sentence: **Learn to be indifferent to external influences!**

Epictetus, who began life as a Roman slave and who rose to be an official in the Roman government, was one of the most famous and influential of the Stoics. In his famous discourse on "Progress or Improvement," he tells us why one must learn to cultivate a philosophy of indifference:

> Where then is progress? If any of you, withdrawing himself from the externals, turns to his own will to exercise it and to improve it by labor, so as to make it conformable to nature, elevated, free, unrestrained, unimpeded, faithful, modest; and if he has learned that he who desires or avoids the things which are not in his power can neither be faithful nor free, but of necessity he must change with them and be tossed about with them as in a tempest, and of necessity must subject himself to others who have the power to procure or prevent what he desires or would avoid; finally, when he rises in the morning, if he observes and keeps these rules, bathes as a man of fidelity, eats as a modest man; in like manner, if in every matter that occurs he works out his chief principles as the runner does with reference to running, and the trainer of the voice with reference to the voice—this is the man who truly makes progress, and this is the man who has not traveled in vain. But if he has strained his efforts to the practice of reading books, and labors only at this, and has traveled for this, I tell him to return home immediately, and not to neglect his affairs there, for this for which he has traveled is nothing. But the other thing is something, to study how a man can rid his life of lamentation and groaning, and saying, Woe to me.

As can be inferred from the above quotation, the Stoics believed that **good or evil depends upon oneself.** Others have power over external matters that affect you— they can put you in prison and torture you, or they can make a slave of you; but nonetheless, **if a person can be indifferent to these events, others will not in a significant sense have power over him/her.** Epictetus expressed this by saying that **virtue resides in the will—that only the will is good or bad.** If one has a good will (and

one can have one by remaining indifferent to external happenings), one's essential character cannot be destroyed by the external events in one's life. When a person is indifferent to such happenings, **he/she is a free person.** He/she is no longer bound by adherence to events outside of him/herself. **By practicing indifference one becomes independent of the world**—and thus, even though the world may be in chaos, this will not prevent one from achieving personal salvation.

The ethical view of the Stoics cannot be fully understood apart from their metaphysics. They believed in **predestination, i.e., that all happenings in the world are fixed by God according to some preconceived plan.** Nothing happens fortuitously. Virtue consists in a will that is in agreement with the happenings of nature. In less complicated terminology, **one is virtuous if one can learn to accept what happens and if one can understand that all this is part of a divine arrangement, which one is powerless to alter.** Consequently, one can avoid frustration, heartbreak, and despair in trying to alter the course of events if one understands that prior to making any such attempt, these events have been *ordained* to take place. A person becomes *free* when he/she understands this; it is only the person who struggles to change things who is *not* free. By practicing an indifference to events one puts oneself in a frame of mind such that the events cannot affect one's fundamental character—and when one does so, one is being virtuous. In particular, the **Stoics felt it was important to free oneself from desires and passions.**

Stoicism differs from Cynicism in a fundamental respect. The Cynics felt that they were powerless to prevent the collapse of the world in which they lived and hence they renounced it. They lived like "dogs." But the Stoics argued that this sort of renunciation was unnecessary. One does not have to renounce the material things of the world; one can live a life of pleasure or of material success, **provided that one does not become trapped by these things. One must remain indifferent to them,** so that if one should lose material possessions, one's feeling toward them will not change. It is only insofar as one is affected by these things that one is not free; but if one can remain unaffected in the sense indicated, there is no reason why one should not continue to enjoy them.

The main effect of Stoicism is to place the responsibility for becoming good or bad directly upon the individual rather than upon society. If an individual can cultivate a frame of mind that makes him/her indifferent to the usual goods of the world, then he/she will be virtuous; and nothing that happens can alter his/her essential character.

Criticism of Stoicism

There are three major difficulties in Stoicism: (1) a logical difficulty involving the notions of **freedom** and **predestination;** (2) the difficulty that the doctrine of **indifference** has consequences that seem paradoxical to common sense; and (3) the difficulty that Stoicism appeals only in **unusual circumstances** and hence cannot be accepted as a *universal* ethic. We will consider each of these, turning to the logical difficulty first.

The Stoics held that *every* event that occurs, whether it is the falling of a meteor or whether it is one's thinking about having dinner tonight, is predestined to occur according to a divine plan. If this doctrine is accepted, then it becomes impossible to alter any of the circumstances in which we find ourselves. If these events were *destined* to occur, then there is nothing we can do about it. In a very significant sense, we are powerless to alter our lives. This can be put by saying that we are not "free" but, instead, are chained to our destinies in accordance with the divine plan. **But this outlook is inconsistent with the Stoic view that a person can alter his/her character.** According to the latter, a person can learn to change his/her frame of mind in such a way that he/she will become indifferent to things that were formerly prized. In holding this position, the Stoics were implying that people are free to alter their character; that they can change some of the natural events in the world, namely, those that go into making up their will. It thus appears there is a fundamental inconsistency at the basis of Stoic theory: man is *both* free and not free. It can be seen that if we accept the latter of these alternatives (i.e., that man is not free), it is pointless to tell one to change one's character. If a character is rigidly determined by natural laws, then how can it be changed? On the other hand, if a man is free to alter his character, then the thesis that all events are predetermined by some master plan must be false.

This dilemma, which is sometimes called **"the problem of freedom of the will,"** is one of the most persistent and troublesome of philosophical problems. Not only has it appeared in Stoic philosophy, but it also occurs in religious philosophy, as well as in modern psychology. For example, to take up the last case, modern psychologists have sometimes contended that our environment and past experience cause us to be the sort of people we are. Thus, if I murder somebody, the view is that I have done so because of events in my past life. Given these events, plus a certain physical and mental constitution, it was impossible for me not to have murdered the person I did murder. In short, my behavior was completely determined by factors over which I had no control; hence I was not free. But if I was not free, then how can I be punished by the law? For the law assumes that I have control over my actions. There is no point in punishing a meteorite that kills somebody, since we believe the meteorite had no control over its path. But we do believe that some criminals *do* have control over their actions, and when we punish them, it is because we hold them responsible for what they do. Thus, it seems as if the findings of modern psychology are inconsistent with the existence of criminal law. As we have tried to indicate, this difficulty occurs at the basis of Stoic philosophy, and the Stoics were never able to solve it.

Modern philosophical techniques have enabled us to see that this perplexity is in part "linguistic," that a solution to it involves clarifying the notions of "freedom," "compulsion," and "casual determinism."

Another major difficulty in Stoicism stems from the doctrine of indifference. People of common sense do not believe it is right to cultivate indifference to the exclusion of all other "virtues." If a friend dies, it would appear callous to most of us to suggest that indifference is the proper way to react to such an event. Moreover, it seems to follow from Stoic theory that acts that would normally be regarded as immoral are right if performed indifferently. Murder committed from a sense of indifference would seem to be proper if we follow out the implications of Stoic theory—and such a moral outlook is obviously inconsistent with our usual ethical beliefs.

Finally, Stoicism gives plausible advice for living only when one is living under very special circumstances. If one knows beforehand that he/she may be tortured for military secrets by the enemy in time of war, it makes sense to try to develop an attitude that will enable him/her to withstand the torture. The philosophy of indifference may be helpful in such a situation; by trying not to think about the pain that is being inflicted upon him/her, he/she may be able to avoid giving in to it. Or again, it is frequently the case that men brood over events that are not really important in their lives. Suppose a man's car is accidentally scratched and the paint is ruined—this may cause him extreme mental distress. Stoic philosophy may be helpful here in contributing to his equanimity. Stoicism suggests that it is stultifying to be easily upset by events that are not basic to the conduct of one's life; by practicing a certain indifference to the minor distractions that occur in everyday life, one may avoid considerable unhappiness. But apart from these sorts of circumstances, it would seem to most that to practice consistently a doctrine of indifference would be to rob life of many of the things that make it most enjoyable: love, friendship, achievement, and so on. For this reason, Stoicism loses its appeal when the external circumstances in which people live greatly improve. If all's well with the world, people feel it is pointless to be indifferent toward it; instead, they feel they should enjoy it. Stoicism arose when the world of the Greeks was in a state of collapse, and it offered useful advice for withstanding the rigors of life at that period. But once people came to feel that circumstances could be changed, Stoicism could not provide them with a positive program for building a better world, and for this reason it was replaced by a more dynamic moral philosophy—Christianity. Like Stoicism, Christianity is a philosophy of consolation that offers guidance in time of trouble; but unlike Stoicism, it also suggests constructive measures that people can take to overcome these difficulties.

Christian Ethics

When one studies the history of Christianity, one is quickly impressed by the variety of doctrines that have been subsumed under that name. It soon becomes evident that there is no *homogenous* philosophy that can simply be labeled as "Christian ethics" without considerably distorting the facts, or at least without considerable qualification. For this reason, it would be an almost impossible task to trace the many and often subtle differences among these doctrines. A discussion of heresies alone would fill a tome, not to mention any attempt to follow the variations within orthodoxy itself. But even conceding that such a multiplicity exists, it seems possible, without undue violence to the subject matter, to distinguish three

main streams of ethical thought that can be labeled as "Christian," and we will turn to a discussion of these now.

Let us call the first type of Christian ethical thought **"pastoral Christian ethics."** This name refers to the moral views of certain early Christian sects—views that developed out of **Judaism** and **Persian mystical religions.** They emphasize the **Decalogue** (i.e., Ten Commandments), **ritualistic** practices (e.g., baptism), and the **moral teachings of Christ.** Christ is considered to be a holy prophet, giving divinely inspired guidance for living (e.g., "Whatsoever a man soweth, that shall he also reap"). We call this sort of outlook "pastoral" because it has little connection with abstruse philosophical speculation. The subtle controversies that we find in the later writings of the Church Fathers are almost entirely unrepresented in early Christianity. Instead, the emphasis is upon **morally correct behavior.** Metaphysics, when it occurs, is mainly restricted to the beliefs in a supernatural order, a personal God, and immortality. But in all these cases, systematic speculation about the beliefs themselves is lacking—or at least is negligible when compared with later developments.

The second type of Christian ethics is much more analytic than the "pastoral" standpoint we have just considered. It appears only after the Catholic Church has developed as a social and political, as well as a religious, institution. We may call the ethics of this period **"church ethics."** But even church ethics, it should be mentioned, has undergone profound changes in its long history. These changes are due to a number of factors. For example, the influence of Plato and Aristotle upon the

Christian Fathers altered the entire Christian concept of "otherworldliness," bringing to it a metaphysical interpretation that was lacking in pastoral Christianity. Again, the concept of the soul changes from the time of Origen, who regards it as being the same in all human beings, to the time of St. Thomas Aquinas, who considers every soul to be unique. This had important consequences for the **doctrine of immortality.** Other causes of the change in church ethics are the following: (*a*) The rise of religious institutions such as the monastery and nunnery led the church officially to favor **asceticism,** and this view greatly affected its doctrines concerning sexual morality. (*b*) The growth of the church as a factor in political and social life caused its ethical doctrine to vary depending upon the state of the continuing conflict between church and state over the direction of people's lives. (*c*) Difficulties about the interpretation of Scripture of the sort that finally resulted in Luther's withdrawal from the church (the Protestant Reformation) also caused some alteration in the official doctrine.

As a result of these influences, the ethical views of St. Augustine, which could be regarded as expressing official church philosophy in the fourth century, were considerably revised by St. Thomas in the thirteenth century, and differed so radically in certain respects as to constitute almost a new ethical outlook. A major difference, for example, was the shift from a moral philosophy based upon **Neoplatonism** (in St. Augustine) to a philosophy based upon Aristotle (in St. Thomas).

Finally, the third great change in Christian ethics came about with the Reformation and the development of Protestantism. Protestants rejected the ethical views of Catholicism (as represented by St. Thomas) in many respects (whether the clergy could marry, for example), but even within Protestantism no consistent ethical system has prevailed. It is perhaps not an exaggeration to say that there are nearly as many variations in ethical doctrine among Protestants as there are Protestant sects.

In spite of this considerable diversity, however, all these moral doctrines possess certain features in common that serve to distinguish them from other religious codes such as Judaism, Buddhism, and Islam. Because of the existence of these pervasive traits, we are justified in speaking of "Christian ethics" as a single and distinct doctrine. But in doing so, we wish to emphasize that our description will be a highly general one, which does not serve to distinguish the various ethical strains within Christianity from each other; instead, its main function is to bring to light certain basic features that form a common doctrine to which all adhere.

All such ethical views as can be called "Christian" assume the existence of a divine being, and they further assume that this being is in some manner identified with Christ. Because of the latter assumption, Christianity can be sharply distinguished from Judaism, for example. Christian sects vary in the powers they ascribe to the divine being, and they also disagree about the exact relation the divine being has to Christ. In some it is the relation of simple identity; in others this is not so (e.g., the conflicts that arose between the Monophysites, the Nestorians, and orthodox Christians). Similar differences exist with respect to an interpretation of the nature of Christ (to what extent He is human, to what extent divine).

However, even those early Christian sects that denied that Christ was identical with God agreed at least that God made His will known by means of Christ; hence the preachings of Christ about the proper way to live are assumed by all Christian moral theories to be the expressions of the divine will.

The preachings of Christ, together with certain other ethical prescriptions such as the Decalogue and certain of the writings in the New Testament, such as the Sermon on the Mount, are regarded as forming a moral "code." A person is considered by all Christian doctrines to be behaving rightly insofar as he/she behaves in accordance with the code, and immorally insofar as he/she violates any of its provisions, such as "Thou shalt not steal."

Christian ethics may thus be summarized as the view that there is a divine being who has laid down certain rules for moral behavior, and that incorrect conduct consists in violating them.

In actual practice, however, Christian sects are not in agreement about which rules make up Christian conduct. For example, the practice of artificial birth control is regarded as immoral by proclamations of the Catholic Church but is not so regarded by most Protestant sects. In order to understand why Christian religions can differ in practice, even though they all agree to the above theoretical picture, we must refer to a distinction between what has been called "ethical theory" and what has been called **"casuistry."** Roughly speaking, casuistry is applied ethics. Once one decides what is good or bad in general (and this is the function of ethical the-

ory—hedonists, for instance, decide that pleasure is the sole good), then one can go further and compile a list of things that are conducive to the production of goodness and things that are conducive to the production of badness. **Casuistry is the practice of compiling such lists.** Now the difference between the various Christian moral codes concerning practical conduct can be regarded not so much as a difference in theory as it is a casuistical difference; they all agree that God has ordained a system of rules that must be followed; but they disagree as to which rules belong to the system, and this latter disagreement may be regarded as **one of casuistry, not of theory.** Of course, not all disagreements between various forms of Christianity should be regarded as differences about which rules belong to the system; quite frequently they may agree that a certain rule belongs, but still interpret it differently. This kind of difficulty often arises when one tries to apply teachings of the past to those problems of the present (such as the problem of birth control) that were not envisaged when the original statements of the doctrine were made.

We cannot, of course, here follow out the casuistical differences between the forms of Christianity, but in order to indicate the nature of casuistry, as opposed to ethical theory, we shall examine some of the pronouncements of St. Thomas concerning sexual morality. These pronouncements still form the orthodox outlook of the Catholic Church upon such matters. According to St. Thomas, there are certain general ways in which people should behave—for instance, they should love God and their neighbors. There are also certain specific ways in which they should not behave. For example, the moral code disapproves of adultery. It also forbids sexual relations between husband and wife save for the purpose of procreation—that is why artificial birth control is prohibited. Divorce is not allowed, because the father is essential in the education of the children.

Turning from these injunctions to more theoretical matters, the general view of Christian ethics (regardless of sect) is that the good life consists in the love of God, and that one can attain this good life by behaving in accordance with God's precepts (i.e., by behaving in accordance with the rules ordained by God, as interpreted by the clergy).

In speaking of Christian ethics, we have not stressed what is perhaps its most important element from a standpoint of theoretical ethics: its **authoritarianism.** The church regards the moral code as an **objective and infallible** guide to correct behavior, which cannot therefore be questioned. This is because **the code is regarded as an expression of God's will.** Anyone who deviates from its precepts is by definition behaving immorally.

In practice, Christian sects have divided over how one is to discover God's will. Fundamentalist sects stress the written word, as found in the Bible, as literally revealing God's will. Catholics hold that the church is the "vicar" of God and that His will is expressed through the edicts of the church. Protestants who refuse to accept this doctrine maintain that the relation between people and God is a *personal* one, requiring no intermediary; and that, finally, in deciding what God wishes, one must consult his/her own conscience. The theoretical exposition of a "conscience

theory" is to be found most clearly stated in the writings of Bishop Butler.

Criticism of Christian Ethics

The success of Christian ethics can be measured both by its perdurance through immense social and political changes over a period of almost 2,000 years, and by the fact that it has been widely accepted all over the world. In the latter respect, Christianity is strikingly more successful than Judaism, which is similar in its ability to persist through difficult times. But many philosophers have had serious reservations about Christianity, for reasons which we shall consider now.

The major difficulty with Christian ethics stems from its assumption that the moral code expresses God's will. A violation of the code is thus equivalent to disobedience toward accepted authority. Immorality in this view is equated with disobedience. Some philosophers have pointed out that this is an acceptable moral position only if it can be shown that God is good. Why obey the prescriptions of a divine being who may be evil? And why is disobedience in itself bad if one is disobedient toward a malevolent authority? At this point, Christian ethics is faced with a dilemma. Either it must be *proved* instead of being *assumed* that God is good, or one must attempt to justify God's precepts on purely ethical grounds rather than on theological ones. Both tasks offer major difficulties. For example, the existence of evils such as plague, cruelty, and premature death seems a powerful argument against the unqualified goodness of God; if one adopts the other alternative and attempts to justify Christian ethics on nontheological grounds, then one seems to be sacrificing what is distinctive in the theory.

However, there is another argument that is put forward by many people to stress the need for a nontheological justification of Christian ethics. We have seen the importance Aristotle placed on understanding, as well as his insistence that an action is moral only if done from free choice and in full knowledge of the situation. Many people feel that this is an essential prerequisite of any moral action. This view of the nature of morality precludes actions done out of obedience—even to the will of God—from being regarded as truly moral. To act morally, we must do something **because it is right** and not merely because God says we must. Hence some nontheological justification of Christian ethics seems necessary.

This becomes apparent when we consider the effects of arguments that deny or at least question the existence of God. If God does not exist, then it is impossible to justify the moral code as expressing His will. Philosophers who were atheists or agnostics, such as the British **utilitarians,** could not accept this sort of justification. They frequently agreed with many of the particular moral laws of Christianity (e.g., "Thou shalt not steal"), but felt they had to be justified ultimately on nonreligious grounds.

A third difficulty arises, even within Christianity, over how we can decide what God ordains. If we accept the writings in the Bible as evidence of God's will, then God's will can be shown to be inconsistent. To avoid these inconsistencies, some interpretation of the Bible is required—and this is in any case necessary if we are to show how the teachings of the Bible relate to present-day problems—but then it is open to a critic to challenge the authority of the interpretation. If we take the Catholic position that the church knows God's will, we fall into similar difficulties and if we finally abide by the authority of conscience, then when people's consciences differ, we have as many authorities as we have differing intuitions. Who is to decide whose conscience really expresses God's will?

Puzzled by such questions, some philosophers have felt that it was necessary to think about ethical problems independently of any official doctrine. This led, in some cases, to systems that were incompatible with Christianity. We turn to one such now—the philosophy of Baruch Spinoza.

The Philosophy of Spinoza

The estimation of Spinoza as a philosopher has varied considerably since his death in 1677. Some critics unhesitatingly label him as the greatest of all ethicists. Others who read the intricate body of discourse in which most of his ethical opinions are found, *Ethics,* consider it to be a collection of muddles. They hold that it is confused in two ways: first, because it uses the geometrical method of Euclid to attempt to arrive at ethical conclusions, which, these critics contend, is a method not fitting to moral subjects. Second, they argue that the system is poorly constructed. The definitions of crucial terms are often not clear, and certain proofs of the theorems do not go through. But both of these opinions are now regarded by the majority of philosophers as extreme. The consensus seems to be that, even granting the defects of this methodology, Spinoza must be reckoned one of the towering figures in the history of ethics. Those who adhere to this appraisal say it is no over-estimation to rank him as **one of the two or three greatest writers on morals to appear in the European tradition since the time of the Greeks.**

Spinoza was born on November 24, 1632, in Amsterdam, where his family had settled as Jewish refugees from the Inquisition in Spain and Portugal.

Spinoza studied in the school run by the Spanish and Portuguese synagogue, which taught Jewish religious subjects as well as some of the general courses then being followed in Spain. Spinoza became familiar with the works of certain medieval Jewish thinkers, such as Abraham Ibn Ezra and Moses Maimonides. He also seems to have imbibed some of the early ideas of the biblical critics, and possibly some of the new scientific ideas of the time. Apparently, he rebelled against the religious teachings of the Jewish community, and he was excommunicated in the summer of 1656.

The excommunicating document reads, in part, as follows:

> The heads of the Ecclesiastical Council hereby make known that already well assured of the evil opinions and doings of Baruch de Espinoza, they have endeavored in sundry ways and by various promises to turn him from his evil courses. But as they have been unable to bring him to any better way of thinking: on the contrary, as they are every day better certified of the horrible heresies entertained and avowed by him, and of the insolence with which these heresies are promulgated and spread abroad, and many persons worthy of credit having borne witness to these in the presence of the said Espinoza, he has been held fully convicted of the same. Review having therefore been made of the whole matter before the Chiefs of the Ecclesiastical Council, it has been resolved, the Councillors assenting thereto, to anathematize the said Espinoza and to cut him off from the people of Israel, and from the present hour to place him in Anathema with the following malediction . . .
>
> Let him be cursed by the mouths of the Seven Angels who preside over the seven days of the week, and by the mouths of the angels who follow them and fight under their banners. Let him be cursed by the Four Angels who preside over the four seasons of the year, and by the mouths of all the angels who follow them and fight under their banners . . . Let God never forgive him for his sins. Let the wrath and indignation of the Lord surround him and smoke forever on his head. Let all the curses contained in the book of the Law fall upon him . . . And we warn you, that none may speak with him by word of mouth nor by writing, nor show any favor to him, nor be under one roof with him, nor come within four cubits of him, nor read any paper composed by him.

Driven out by the Jews, Spinoza at first lived with some unaffiliated Christians, the Collegeants, and then spent the remainder of his short life living quietly without any riches or luxuries. He ground lenses for a living (in fact, is supposed to have died of a lung infection contracted from glass dust) and wrote philosophy in his spare time. In his personal life, Spinoza of all the great philosophers comes closest to being a saint: on the day of his death he was calm and unafraid; in his life, in spite of vicious attacks made upon him, he rarely became angry, rarely lost his reasonableness. When Jan de Witt, the leader of the Dutch Republic, was murdered, Spinoza is supposed to have become very angry, and denounced the populace who cheered the deed.

In order to understand the attraction that Spinoza's philosophy has had for subsequent thinkers, we shall here quote at length from the opening of his unfinished treatise entitled *On the Improvement of the Understanding*, which is one of the most brilliant pieces of philosophical writing in existence. The undogmatic, honest attempt to discover the good life comes through to the reader with a tremendous impact. Spinoza writes:

After experience had taught me that all the usual surroundings of social life are vain and futile; seeing that none of the objects of my fears contained in themselves anything either good or bad, except insofar as the mind is affected by them, I finally resolved to inquire whether there might be some real good having power to communicate itself, which would affect the mind singly, to the exclusion of all else: whether, in fact, there might be anything of which the discovery and attainment would enable me to enjoy continuous, supreme, and unending happiness. I say "I *finally* resolved," for at first sight it seemed unwise willingly to lose hold on what was sure for the sake of something then uncertain. I could see the benefits which are acquired through fame and riches, and that I should be obliged to abandon the quest of such objects, if I seriously devoted myself to the search for something different and new. I perceived that if true happiness chanced to be placed in the former I should necessarily miss it; while, if, on the other hand, it were not so placed and I gave them my whole attention, I should equally fail.

I therefore debated whether it would not be possible to arrive at the new principle, or at any rate at a certainty concerning its existence, without changing the conduct and usual plan of my life; with this end in view I made many efforts but in vain. For the ordinary surroundings of life which are esteemed by men (as their actions testify) to be the highest good, may be classed under the three heads—riches, fame and the pleasures of sense: with these three the mind is so absorbed that it has little power to reflect on any different good. By sensual pleasure the mind is enthralled to the extent of quiescence, as if the supreme good were actually attained, so that it is quite incapable of thinking of any other object; when such pleasure has been gratified it is followed by extreme melancholy, whereby the mind, though not enthralled, is disturbed and dulled.

The pursuit of honors and riches is likewise very absorbing, especially if such objects be sought simply for their own sake, inasmuch as they are then supposed to constitute the highest good. In the case of fame the mind is still more absorbed, for fame is conceived as always good for its own sake, and as the ultimate end to which all actions are directed. Further, the attainment of riches and fame is not followed as in the case of sensual pleasures by repentance, but, the more we acquire, the greater is our delight, and consequently, the more we are incited to increase both the one and the other; on the other hand, if our hopes happen to be frustrated we are plunged into the deepest sadness. Fame has the further drawback that it compels its votaries to order their lives according to the opinions of their fellowmen, shunning what they usually shun, and seeking what they usually seek.

When I saw that all these ordinary objects of desire would be obstacles in the way of a search for something different and new—nay, that they were so opposed thereto that either they or it would have to be abandoned, I was forced to inquire which would prove the most useful to me: for, as I say, I seemed to be willingly losing hold on a sure good for the sake of something uncertain. However, after I had reflected on the matter, I came in the first place to the conclusion that by abandoning the ordinary objects of pursuit, and betaking myself to a new quest, I should be leaving a good, uncertain by reasons of its own nature, as may be gathered from what has been said, for the sake of a good not uncertain in its nature (for I sought for a fixed good), but only in the possibility of its attainment.

Further reflection convinced me that if I

could really get to the root of the matter, I should be leaving certain evils for a certain good. I thus perceived that I was in a state of great peril, and I compelled myself to seek with all my strength for a remedy, however uncertain it might be—as a sick man struggling with a deadly disease, when he sees that death will surely be upon him unless a remedy be found, is compelled to seek such a remedy with all his strength, inasmuch as his whole hope lies therein. All the objects pursued by the multitude not only bring no remedy that tends to preserve our being, but even act as hindrances, causing the death not seldom of those who possess them, and always of those who are possessed by them. There are many examples of men who have suffered persecution even to death for the sake of their riches, and of men who in pursuit of wealth have exposed themselves to so many dangers that they have paid away their life as a penalty for their folly. Examples are no less numerous of men, who have endured the utmost wretchedness for the sake of gaining or preserving their reputation. Lastly, there are innumerable cases of men who have hastened their death through overindulgence in sensual pleasure. All these evils seem to have arisen from the fact that happiness or unhappiness is made wholly to depend on the quality of the object which we love. When a thing is not loved, no quarrels will arise concerning it—no sadness will be felt if it perishes—no envy if it is possessed by another—no fear, no hatred, in short no disturbances of the mind. All these arise from the love of what is perishable, such as the objects already mentioned. But love toward a thing eternal and infinite feeds the mind wholly with joy, and is itself unmingled with any sadness, wherefore it is greatly to be desired and sought for all our strength. Yet it was not at random that I used the words, "If I could go to the root of the matter," for, though what I have urged was perfectly clear to my mind, I could not forthwith lay aside all love of riches, sensual enjoyment, and fame. One thing was evident, namely that while my mind was employed with these thoughts it turned away from its former objects of desire, and seriously considered the search for a new prin-

ciple; this state of things was a great comfort to me, for I perceived that the evils were not such as to resist all remedies. Although these intervals were at first rare, and of very short duration, yet afterward, as the true good became more and more discernible to me, they became more frequent and more lasting; especially after I had recognized that the acquisition of wealth, sensual pleasure or fame, is only a hindrance, so long as they are sought as ends, not as means; if they be sought as means, they will be under restraint, and, far from being hindrances, will further not a little the end for which they are sought, as I will show in due time.

I will here only briefly state what I mean by true good, and also what is the nature of the highest good. In order that this may be rightly understood, we must bear in mind that the terms good and evil are only applied relatively, so that the same thing may be called both good and bad, according to the relations in view, in the same way as it may be called perfect or imperfect. Nothing regarded in its own nature can be called perfect or imperfect; especially when we are aware that all things which come to pass, come to pass according to the eternal order and fixed laws of nature. However, human weakness cannot attain to this order in its own thoughts, but meanwhile man conceives a human character much more stable than his own, and sees that there is no reason why he should not himself acquire such a character. Thus he is led to seek for means which will bring him to this pitch of perfection, and calls everything which will serve as such means a true good. The chief good is that he should arrive, together with other individuals if possible, at the possession of the aforesaid character. What that character is we shall show in due time, namely, that it is the knowledge of the union existing between the mind and the whole of nature. This, then, is the end for which I strive: to attain such a character myself, and to endeavor that many should attain to it with me.

The essence of Spinoza's moral philosophy is contained in the above quotation, but in a highly condensed form. Let us try in what follows to expand and perhaps to clarify it.

To begin with, Spinoza is a rigid determinist. As he says, "All things which come to pass, come to pass according to the eternal order and fixed laws of nature." In holding this view, **Spinoza was in the metaphysical tradition of the Stoics and of Descartes.** No one is free to act capriciously or by chance; all actions are determined by past experience, by physical and mental constitution, and by the state of the laws of nature at that moment. **Secondly, Spinoza is a relativist. He holds that nothing is good or bad in itself, but is only so in relation to someone.** Thus it makes no sense, he avers, to say that castor oil is inherently good; it is good relative to a given person in particular circumstances. If one is ill and castor oil helps one to recover, then in those circumstances it can be declared to be good for that individual. But if one is suffering from an inflamed appendix and takes castor oil, and in doing so should be killed, then under those conditions it would not be good for one. Since the same thing (e.g, castor oil) may at different times affect the same person differently, the goodness or badness of such a thing cannot be considered as an *inherent* property of it, like its density, but only as a property that comes into existence depending upon what relation it has to a human being. This view of goodness or badness is important, because it leads Spinoza to the position that riches, fame, and sensual pleasure are not *inherently* worthwhile. They are not worth acquiring for their own sakes, **but only as means to make human life more happy.** When these things affect people in desirable ways, they are good; but when they affect them in undesirable ways, they are bad. As Spinoza says, "There are many examples of men who have suffered persecution even to death for the sake of their riches, and of men who in pursuit of wealth have exposed themselves to so many dangers that they have paid away their life as a penalty for their folly."

Given, therefore, the two facts that all events are determined by natural laws, so that people are not free, and also that things are not good or bad in themselves, then what does the good life consist in? According to Spinoza, such a life consists in the possession of a certain attitude toward the world. This attitude is in part emotional and in part rational. **The rational part of it consists in the recognition of the truth that all events are determined; the emotional part in an acceptance of this fact.** It is, as he says, "the knowledge of the union existing between the mind and the whole of nature."

Otherwise put, **Spinoza is arguing that a person will be happy when he/she comes to understand that there are limits to human power; by understanding that everything that happens must happen necessarily, one will no longer dissipate one's energy in struggling against these events.** If a friend dies, it is pointless to give vent to emotion; it is part of the natural pattern. By looking at every event as part of a large system ("in the context of eternity," to use his phrase), one will no longer be upset and frightened by the events that occur in life. In this way, one can live a happy life.

Spinoza's philosophy can thus be interpreted as offering guidance that, if followed, will enable people to avoid fear, anxiety, and unhappiness. These arise only when we become slaves to our emotions—the person who does not take the broad view is "in human bondage." But one can liberate oneself by understanding that the course of nature is predestined and also by understanding that "nothing is good or bad in itself," but that it only becomes good or bad depending upon how it affects us. By adjusting our outlook, we can finally develop an attitude toward the world that will liberate us from our emotional slavery to it—and when this happens we will be living the good life.

As we have already pointed out, Spinoza's masterpiece is *Ethics*. This great work is regarded by many philosophers as one of the most difficult philosophical texts to understand; hence any interpretation of Spinozistic philosophy, such as the one we have given above (which is in part based on *Ethics*), must be considered by the reader as a brief introduction rather than as a definitive passage, which briefly summarizes the book. Spinoza writes:

> I have finished everything I wished to explain concerning the power of the mind over the emotions and concerning its freedom. From what has been said we see what is the strength of the wise man and how much he surpasses the ignorant who is driven forward by lust alone. For the ignorant man is not only agitated by external causes in many ways and never enjoys true peace of soul, but lives also ignorant, as it were, both of God, and of things, and as soon as he ceases to suffer ceases also to be. On the other hand, the wise man insofar as he is considered as such, is scarcely ever moved in his mind, but, being conscious by a certain external necessity of himself, of God, and of things, never ceases to be and always enjoys true peace of soul. If the way

which, as I have shown, leads hither seems very difficult, it can nevertheless be found. It must indeed be difficult, since it is so seldom discovered, for if salvation lay ready to hand and could be discovered without great labor, how could it be possible that it should be neglected almost by everybody? But all noble things are as difficult as they are rare.

Criticism of Spinoza

Spinoza's ethics has difficulties similar to those we find in Stoicism. To begin with, **Spinoza did not effectively resolve the conflict that exists between determinism and freedom.** He believed that if an individual could come to understand that what comes to pass *must* come to pass, he/she could learn to accept this fact and in this way could achieve "peace of mind." But if all events in nature are determined, then one is essentially powerless to alter his/her attitudes. Either one will be determined to have the sort of attitude Spinoza suggests, or one will be determined not to have it. But if the latter, there is nothing one can do about acquiring it.

A second difficulty concerns the Spinozistic doctrine of taking the broad view of human life, or the view *"sub specie aeternitatis,"* as he puts it—"in the context of eternity." At times this is useful advice to follow; men do become enslaved by their emotions in trivial causes. But at other times this is not so. Most people believe there are occasions when one should feel deeply about the things that happen to him/her; to suggest that one should never feel this way would be *to eliminate some of the most profound of human experiences.* If followed, such an ethic might, for example, make artistic creation impossible. Moreover, in a significant sense, it would seem to violate human nature, since some persons are temperamentally so constructed that it is psychologically impossible for them to adopt the Spinozistic outlook. For these reasons, such an ethic could not be expected to have a widespread and permanent appeal—and this has indeed been the fate of Spinoza's system.

Utilitarianism: Jeremy Bentham and John Stuart Mill

Utilitarianism has had a long and vigorous existence as a moral theory. It is still accepted by many American and British philosophers, although the original form of the theory has been somewhat modified in current versions. One of the earliest exponents of utilitarianism was Francis Hutcheson, who is known to have advocated it in 1725; David Hume's moral theory has also been interpreted as being a form of utilitarianism. The most famous exponents of it, however, are Jeremy Bentham (1748–1832) and John Stuart Mill (1808–73).

Both Bentham and Mill had very interesting lives. Bentham was an extremely shy and sensitive person, who always felt insecure in the company of strangers. He wrote voluminously but published practically nothing of his own volition; friends would literally force him to publish material, and when he refused, they would surreptitiously publish it for him. Yet this man became one of the most controversial figures of the nineteenth century in England. In spite of his reclusive tendencies, he became the head of a group of reformers called **"the philosophical radicals,"** who were to a great extent responsible for social and political changes in England; the British criminal code, for instance, was considerably improved because of the efforts of Bentham and his group.

Bentham opposed both monarchy and hereditary aristocracy, advocated complete democracy, including women's suffrage, and opposed British imperialism in India and the other colonies. In matters of religion he was an atheist.

John Stuart Mill is perhaps the most incredible prodigy in the history of philosophy. His father, who was a disciple and friend of Bentham's, was greatly influenced by the Benthamite doctrine that a man's character and even his intellect can be completely determined by his education. As a result, John Stuart Mill was not allowed to go to public school but was very carefully educated from infancy under the tutelage of his father. His achievements were amazing: at the age of eight he had mastered several languages, and by the time he was twelve, had worked carefully through many of the great literary and philosophical classics. Mill's *Autobiography*, which is mainly concerned with relating the story of his education, is a fascinating document, revealing the psychological effects of this kind of training upon a young man.

The utilitarians conceived of their philosophical work as **an attempt to lay down an objective principle for determining when a given action was right or wrong.** They called this maxim the **"principle of utility." The principle states: An action is right insofar as it tends to produce the greatest happiness for the greatest number.** Both Bentham and Mill interpreted this principle as a form of hedonism by identifying happiness with pleasure. Interpreted in this way, the principle states that an action is right if it produces the greatest amount of pleasure for the greatest number; otherwise, it is wrong. However, it is not necessary to interpret utilitarianism in this way, and as we shall show later, many modern philosophers who are utilitarians are not hedonists. **The essence of utilitarianism as a philosophy is that it lays stress upon the effects that an action has. If an action produces an excess of beneficial effects over harmful ones, then it is right; otherwise, it is not.** The fundamental point is this: The *consequences* of a given action determine its rightness or wrongness, not the *motive* from which it is done. We all know of cases where men act from the best intentions yet do something that has horrible consequences. Even in his crazy way, Hitler may have believed that he was acting from a desire to improve Germany, yet his acts led to torture, pain, genocide, and to the ultimate collapse of Germany itself. The utilitarians would thus condemn his behavior on the grounds that the effects of his actions produced a balance of pain over pleasure, and hence were wrong for that reason.

They regarded this principle as being completely objective. In terms of it, anybody can measure whether an action was right or wrong. For example, if we accept hedonism, it becomes a purely scientific matter to determine whether a given action caused an excess of pleasure over pain for the greatest number. We merely calculate the amount of pleasure the act caused, and the amount of pain, and we have our answer as to whether it was right or wrong. Bentham even went so far as to develop in detail a method of making such calculations, which he called the **"hedonic calculus."** This calculus has seven ingredients that allow one to measure the amount of pleasure or pain an act causes—ingredients such as the *intensity* of the pleasure, its *duration,* and so on.

The main result of utilitarianism as a moral theory is to separate the rightness or wrongness of an action from the goodness or badness of the agent who performs the action. A person may be morally good in the sense that one may always act from good intentions (e.g., one may always act from a sense of honesty or from the desire to tell the truth). But the worth of the *action* is to be distinguished from the worth of the *agent;* for as we have indicated, a person may be morally good and yet do something that has undesirable effects. If so, utilitarians would pronounce the action wrong in spite of its being done from good motives.

Utilitarianism has often been regarded as a **political philosophy that entails democratic government as a political institution.** Whether this is so or not is a difficult question to answer briefly, but it is easy to see how the belief arose. To begin with, the great utilitarians were democratically minded. They fought for civil liberties and for women's suffrage, for the conduct of government by law, and so on. This served to identify their philosophical doctrines with democratic causes. Secondly, in regarding each individual as of equal importance in calculating the amount of pleasure and pain an action evoked, their views came to be identified with the democratic tenet that each counts equally before the law. And finally, the rightness or wrongness of an act is to be determined by how it affects the majority—and this seemed to point to rule by the majority, another provision of democracy.

Criticism of Utilitarianism

Let us turn now to some of the objections that have been made to utilitarianism:

There are both theoretical and practical difficulties about how to determine how much happiness (i.e., pleasure) an action causes. For example, it is assumed by Bentham that in computing the amount of happiness or unhappiness an action creates, each will count equally for one unit of happiness. Thus, we add up the number of people who are made happy by the act, add up the number of those made unhappy, and presumably we can then determine whether the act produces an excess of happiness over unhappiness. Some philosophers, such as Friedrich Nietzsche, objected violently to this assumption. Nietzsche believed that **some people were inherently more important than others;** their happiness or unhappiness counted for more than the happiness or unhappiness of the average person. He described John Stuart Mill as a "blockhead" for this presupposition. Nietzsche wrote about Mill as follows:

> I abhor the man's vulgarity when he says "What is right for one man is right for another." Such principles would fain establish the whole of human traffic *upon mutual services,* so that every action would appear to be a cash payment for something done to us. The hypothesis here is ignoble to the last degree; it is taken for granted that there is some sort of *equivalence in value between my actions and thine.*

A second and perhaps more serious difficulty is this: it is assumed in utilitarianism that it is the *total* number of effects that must be taken into account before an action can be determined to be right or wrong. If we merely count the immediate amount of pleasure and pain, we may be mistaken, since the long-range effects may give different results. Thus the explosion in 1945 of the A-bomb over Japan may have had beneficent effects in ending what could have been a longer war, yet the long-range effects of such weapons may be highly undesirable. But this leads to a theoretical difficulty, for if we can never assess the rightness or wrongness of an act until we know *all* of its effects, we shall have to wait infinitely long before declaring an act to be right or wrong, since there may be an infinite number of effects. The principle of utility was developed as a practical test for deciding whether an action is right or wrong, but if we cannot apply the principle until *all* the effects are known, **then its practical value is useless,** particularly as what we require of a moral principle is that it should help us to decide **in advance** what the right course of action is.

The objection we have just mentioned is usually countered by utilitarians who say the rightness or wrongness of an action can be determined with a high degree of **probability** without waiting for the total consequences to happen. Thus, one should do the act that **seems most likely, according to probability theory, to have desirable consequences in the long run.** But when we interpret the theory in this way, we introduce another difficulty that the theory was expressly created to avoid. The rightness or wrongness of an action now apparently depends upon *subjective* considerations. It seems to depend upon one's belief that the act in question is *likely* to have desirable consequences. One may believe this, act in accordance with the best scientific information about the probable consequences of his/her action, and yet the act may not have the effects one believed it would have. One may be mistaken, as future events will show. Are we then to say one acted wrongly in acting upon the best probabilities, or are we to say one acted rightly? Either answer has difficulties for the theory. If we maintain one acted rightly—but was mistaken—then we have given up the view that a right action is one that *in fact* has the most desirable consequences in the long run; on the other hand, if we adopt the position that one acted wrongly in acting from subjective considerations, we seem to be saddled with a criterion that cannot be used for practical purposes.

Another objection to utilitarianism is that it violates the beliefs of plain men who frequently think our actions cannot be properly evaluated apart from some concern about the *motives* from which they are done. We hesitate to say that an act is right when it is done from an evil motive (such as the intention to cheat someone) just because it has desirable effects. One consequence of utilitarianism is that a world in which everybody acted from evil motives and yet had all their acts turn out to be desirable would be a good world, but the thought of actually living in such a world would be highly repugnant to people of common sense. Thus, the theory if pushed to the extreme seems to have implications that many people would not accept.

Some philosophers have accordingly rejected utilitarianism on the ground that consideration in assessing the moral worth of an action must be given to the motive from which it came. Let us turn to one such view now—the moral theory of Immanuel Kant.

Kantian Ethics

Although Kant is famous mainly for his work in the theory of knowledge and in metaphysics, he believed that ethics was the most important subject in philosophy. He even used ethical arguments to establish the existence of God after showing that all proofs derived from so-called "pure reason" are invalid. **His argument is that the moral law requires that people be rewarded proportionately to their virtue.** Since in everyday life people who are not virtuous may often be happier and more successful than those who are, such rewards evidently are not assured in this life. He therefore infers that there must be another existence where they are so rewarded, and this leads him to the conclusion that there are a God and an eternal life.

Like his work in metaphysics and epistemology (the theory of knowledge), Kant's contribution to ethical theory is of a very high order; but as one who has glanced at Kant's writings in those areas might expect, his writings in ethics are difficult to understand and even more difficult to summarize. This is in part due to the compactness of his style, to the use of many technical terms, and in part to the awkwardness of his mode of expression; but it is also due in part to the subtle cast of his ideas and to the fine distinctions he draws. Nevertheless, let us try here to state the main points of his theory as simply as possible, illustrating these points with relevant quotations.

The main question that Kant's moral theory was designed to answer is **"What is the nature of morality?"** This question can also be put in different ways: **"What** is a moral action as contrasted with a nonmoral one?" or, again, "What is the difference between a person who acts morally and one who does not?" Kant believed that this question, or set of questions, could be answered and that the key to it lay in distinguishing between **acts done from "inclination" and acts done from a "sense of duty."** What, then, is meant by these terms?

People often indulge in a certain course of action because they are forced to. For instance, if I am waylaid by a thief, I will be forced to turn my money over to him if I have any, or if I refuse, I am forced to suffer the consequences. In such a case, we would not ordinarily describe my actions as being "voluntary actions," or "actions done because I wanted to." Nor would we say that I was "doing my duty." In this instance, I am not a free agent; I am properly described as not acting either from "inclination" or "from duty" but, rather, as "being compelled to do so." Hence it is a requisite of any act being done from "inclination" or from "duty" **that it be the act of a free agent.** Now, obviously, individuals are often free in the above sense—nobody is forcing them to behave in a certain way or is otherwise constraining their behavior. For instance, I am free tonight either to go to a movie or to stay at home and read a book, or even to continue to type this chapter. In a significant sense, it is up to me which of these I will do. But which of these *ought* I to do? If I have promised my publisher to finish this chapter tonight, then I am under an "obligation" to continue to work on it. On the other hand, if the matter is not pressing, if there exists no "demand" on me, we could say that it is a matter of "taste" or "inclination" which I should do. I should do that which I want to do, or which it pleases me to do, provided, of course, that no obligation exists which it is my duty to fulfill. Now, as can be seen from this example, **"inclination" is to be distinguished from "obligation." An obligation is that which one ought to do despite one's inclination to do otherwise.** Once under an obligation, one ought to attempt to fulfill it. If no obligation exists, then it becomes a matter of inclination or of taste what one should do.

Now some philosophers have held that in matters of morality one should act upon one's inclinations. He/she should do that act which pleases him/her or which he/she wants to do in those circumstances; but Kant strongly rejects such an account of morality. He feels that **a person is acting morally only when he suppresses his/her feelings and inclinations and does that which he/she is obliged to do.** Thus, "doing one's duty" is doing something that one is not inclined or willing to do, but that he/she does because he/she recognizes that he/she ought to do it; an obligation exists and he/she must fulfill it. Thus a person who does something merely because he/she is afraid *not* to do it (such as the fear of being imprisoned for not repaying a debt) is not a moral person; nor is a person moral who repays a debt merely because he/she wants to, or inclines toward doing that rather than something else. It is only when a person recognizes that he/she *ought* to repay a debt because he/she has incurred an obligation that he/she is genuinely a moral person. **Thus morality, as Kant sees it, is closely bound up with one's duties and obligations.**

One further point must be made before we can proceed to other elements of Kant's moral theory. It is important to distinguish actions that are "in accord with duty" from those done "from duty," as Kant puts it. The former are not moral acts, but the latter are. For instance, most parents are inclined to take care of their children; they may be so inclined because they are fond of them or because they fear police action if they neglect them. But anyone who takes care of one's children for these reasons is not acting morally. One is acting "in accord with duty" but not "from duty." One would be acting from duty only if one recognized that one has a special obligation to one's children because they are one's children. A person who understands the nature of this obligation and acts upon it is moral; otherwise, one is not. Kant explains this brilliantly in the following passage from his *Theory of Ethics:*

> I omit here all actions which are already recognized as inconsistent with duty, although they may be useful for this or that purpose, for with these the question whether they are done *from duty* cannot arise at all, since they even conflict with it. I also set aside those actions which really conform to duty, but to which men have no direct inclination, performing them because they are impelled thereto by some other inclination. For in this case we can readily distinguish whether the action which agrees with duty is done *from duty* or from a selfish view. It is much harder to make this distinction when the action accords with duty, and the subject has besides a *direct* inclination to it. For example, it is always a matter of duty that a dealer should not overcharge an inexperienced purchaser; and wherever there is much commerce the prudent tradesman does not overcharge, but keeps a fixed price for everyone, so that a child buys of him as well as any other.

> Men are thus *honestly* served; but this is not enough to make us believe that the tradesman has so acted from duty and from principles of honesty; his own advantage required it; it is out of the question in this case to suppose that he might besides have a direct inclination in favor of the buyers so that, as it were, from love he should give no advantage to one over another. Accordingly, the action was done neither from duty nor from direct inclination, but merely with a selfish view.

> On the other hand, it is a duty to maintain one's life; and in addition, everyone has also a direct inclination to do so. But on this account the often anxious care which most men take for it has no intrinsic worth, and their maxim no moral import. They preserve their life *as duty requires*, no doubt, but not *because duty requires*. On the other hand, if adversity and hopeless sorrow have completely taken away the relish for life; if the unfortunate one, strong in mind, indignant at his fate, rather than desponding or dejected wishes for death, and yet preserves his life without loving it—not from inclination or fear but from duty—then his maxim has a moral worth.

As can be seen from the above quotation, Kant differs sharply from the utilitarians in stressing that **the essence of morality is to be found in the motive from which an act is done.** All such motives reduced to one—that **a person is moral when he/she acts from a sense of duty.** A person who keeps promises by accident, or who repays debts to avoid punishment, or who feels that it is to his/her advantage in the long run to do so, is not moral. He/she is moral if and only if he/she understands that he/she must keep promises and repay debts because it is his/her duty to do so—regardless of the consequences that doing so or not doing so will bring. Thus, a good person is a person of "good will," i.e., a person who acts from a sense of duty. As Kant puts it in a famous phrase, **"Nothing can possibly be conceived in the world, or even out of it, which can be called good without qualification, except a good will."**

In criticizing utilitarianism for confusing the results of people's actions with the motives for committing such actions, Kant develops a distinction between **"prudential action"** and **"moral action."** A person who repays debts because he/she fears the legal consequences acts from a sense of prudence; he/she is not a moral person. He/she would be moral only if he/she acted from the sense that he/she has incurred a monetary obligation and thus is "duty bound" to repay it. Kant's criticism of utilitarianism is contained in the following passage:

> A good will is good not because of what it performs or effects, not by its aptness for the attainment of some proposed end, but simply by virtue of the volition, that is, it is good in itself, and considered by itself is to be esteemed much higher than all that can be brought about by it in favor of any inclination, nay, even of the sum total of all inclinations. Even if it should happen that, owing to special disfavor of fortune, or the niggardly provision of a stepmotherly nature, this will should wholly lack the power to accomplish its purpose, if with its greatest efforts it should yet achieve nothing, and there should remain only the good will (not, to be sure, a mere wish, but the summoning of all means in our power), then, like a jewel, it would still shine by its own light, as a thing which has its whole value in itself. Its usefulness or fruitlessness can neither add to nor take away anything from this value . . . Let the question be, for example: May I when in distress make a promise with the intention not to keep it? I readily distinguish here between the two significations which the question may have: Whether it is prudent or, whether it is right, to make a false promise? The former may undoubtedly often be the case. I see clearly

that it is not enough to extricate myself from the present difficulty by means of this subterfuge, but it must be well considered whether there may not hereafter spring from this lie much greater inconvenience than that from which I now free myself, and, as with all my supposed cunning, the consequences cannot be so easily foreseen but the credit once lost may be much more injurious to me than any mischief which I seek to avoid at present, it should be considered whether it would not be more *prudent* to act herein according to a universal maxim, and to make it a habit to promise nothing except with the intention of keeping it. But it is soon clear to me that such a maxim will still be based on the fear of consequences. Now it is a wholly different thing to be truthful from duty, and to be so from apprehension of injurious consequences.

In short, we may summarize Kant's answer to the question "What is a moral action as contrasted with a nonmoral one?" as follows: **A moral action is one done from a respect for duty,** and correspondingly, a moral person is a person who acts **from duty,** not from **inclination** or even in **accord with** duty.

With the above distinctions, Kant has outlined the sphere of morality for us. He had indicated the difference between behaving morally and not behaving morally; but this outline does not complete his system of morals. A person may still not *know* what his/her duty will be in a given situation. Is there any test for determining what one's duty will be in a particular set of circumstances? Kant answers that there is. Since human beings are rational creatures, they ought to behave in a rational way, and for Kant this means that one ought always to behave as if one's course of conduct were to become a universal law. That is, **every action must** be judged in the light of how it would appear if it were to be a universal code of behavior. This is why lying, even if it is expedient, cannot be accepted as moral under *any* circumstances; for if we were to regard lying as a universal law to which people ought to conform, we could see that morality would be impossible. On this point, Kant writes as follows:

> The shortest way, however, and an unerring one, to discover the answer to the question whether a lying promise is consistent with duty, is to ask myself, should I be content that my maxim (to extricate myself from difficulty by a false promise) should hold good as a universal law, for myself as well as for others? and should I be able to say to myself, "Everyone may make a deceitful promise when he finds himself in a difficulty from which he cannot otherwise extricate himself?" Then I presently become aware that while I can will the lie, I can by no means will that lying should be a universal law. For with such a law there would be no promises at all, since it would be in vain to allege my intention in regard to my future actions to those who would not believe this allegation, or if they overhastily did so, would pay me back in my own coin. Hence my maxim, as soon as it should be made a universal law, would necessarily destroy itself. I do not, therefore, need any far-reaching penetration to discern what I have to do in order that my will may be morally good. Inexperienced in the course of the world, incapable of being prepared for all its contingencies, I only ask myself: Canst thou also will that thy maxim should be a universal law? If not, then it must be rejected, and that not because of a disadvantage accruing from it to myself or even to others, but because it cannot enter as a principle into a possible universal legislation, and reason extorts from me immediate respect for such legislation.

The Categorical Imperative

Kant invented a phrase, **"the categorical imperative,"** that makes the above point

in a different way. He distinguishes **"the categorical imperative"** from so-called **"hypothetical imperatives."** A hypothetical imperative is a directive to the effect that if you wish to achieve such and such an end, you must act in such and such a way. Hypothetical imperatives are thus concerned with **prudential action.** For example, if you wish to drive from point A to point B by the shortest route, directions for doing so can be given to you by means of a hypothetical imperative: "If you wish to drive to point B by the shortest route, take roads X, Y, and Z." On the other hand, the categorical imperative enjoins action without any ifs or without regard to the effect such an action may have. It enjoins you to do such and such *without qualification.* It thus lays down **a rule that, if followed, will ensure that the person behaving in accordance with it is behaving morally.**

Kant formulates the categorical imperative in several different ways, the first of which is this:

"There is therefore but one categorical imperative, namely this: **act only on that maxim whereby thou canst at the same time will that it should become a universal law."**

As we have pointed out, Kant means by this statement that a person should always act as if every action were to become a universal law. Thus no person should steal, because if he/she were to steal and if everyone were to steal (if stealing should become a general rule), then moral relations based upon the possession of private property would become impossible. Similarly with regard to telling lies. One should never lie, since if lying were to become a universal law, all human relations based upon trust and the keeping of promises would become impossible. In short, the view is that all acts should be entered into as if they were to become general laws—this is what the categorical imperative tells us. If an act that one commits can pass the test of thus being universalized, it will be a moral act.

Another, and equally famous, formulation of the categorical imperative is the following:

"So act as to treat humanity, whether in thine own person or in that of any other, in every case as an end withal, never as a means only."

This formulation of the categorical imperative has a long tradition in the history of ethics. It is another way of stating such maxims as "Do unto others as you would have them do unto you." It is an injunction to us to respect other people because they are rational human beings like ourselves. We should treat others as ends in themselves because that is how we regard ourselves. To treat another person **only** as a means of achieving what we want is to disregard his/her humanity, to treat a person as a **thing** and to fail to show due respect for his/her status as a rational human being. Consequently, this doctrine has had important consequences for democracy. It supports the democratic views that "all people are created equal," where this is interpreted to mean that no person should be discriminated against before the law. Certain criticisms directed against this formulation of the categorical imperative have been based upon misunderstanding. If this version of the categorical imperative is interpreted literally, it might be thought to mean that no one's interests and desires should be sup-

pressed. But with such an interpretation, the view has the consequence that when conflicts between people arise, it would be impossible for the courts (say) to decide between them; for by deciding against one of the people, they would be acting against his/her interests. Such an interpretation of Kant's view would lead to a form of anarchy, thus making moral life inconsistent with life in society. However, as we have pointed out, such an interpretation of Kant is mistaken. In saying that each person should be treated as an end in him/herself, Kant is not implying that each person's interests should be granted or acceded to. He is merely saying that in any sort of conflict between people, each person must be counted as being of *equal value* in the conflict. Regardless of a person's history, his/her present social status, or his/her present economic worth, he/she is not to be discriminated against. All must be treated equally with others in the eyes of the law.

Criticism of Kant

Kant's moral view may be regarded as an attempt to save what is valid in such conflicting accounts of the nature of morality as **Platonism** and **hedonism.** The Platonist stresses the *objectivity* of moral standards, a thesis that Kant accepts **(the categorical imperative represents an action as objectively necessary).** At the same time, some account of **human motives** must be taken into consideration in assessing the moral worth of an action. **The mistake of the Platonist, on the one hand, is to divorce goodness and badness from human motives in his/her desire to seek objectivity; the mistake of the hedonist is to identify**

moral motivation with the search for pleasure. The Kantian theory is an interesting and plausible one because it attempts to do justice to both of these factors: (*a*) **that morality to some extent depends upon human motivation** and (*b*) **that morality is not merely a matter of inclination or of taste, or preference, but is something objective.**

Common sense recognizes that morality involves both of these elements. If, as the utilitarian would have it, objectivity is identified with the kind of effects a person's actions have, then, according to Kant, common sense would not identify morality with such objectivity. It makes a difference what intentions a person has when he/she acts. If he/she acts from "the best will in the world" but makes a mistake, we do, ordinarily, tend to excuse him/her. The surgeon who operates upon a patient and kills her through a mistake is not *morally* blamed. He is, as Kant says, regarded as inefficient, as a bungler; but we do not consider him an immoral person merely because he has failed. This shows that some consideration of human motives is necessary in assessing an act as right or wrong. At the same time, Kant points out that morality is not entirely a matter of human motivation if human motivation is regarded as stemming from desire, caprice, or inclination. Some motives are wrong motives (e.g., the search for pleasure). It is only when one acts out of respect for duty that we regard him/her as a moral being—and in such cases, he/she is acting *against* his/her inclinations.

A further argument in favor of the Kantian view is the commonsense outlook that **to behave morally one must behave consistently, i.e., "universalize his behavior."**

It is a legitimate objection to a draft dodger to tell him, "What if everybody behaved as you do?" We do feel that one ought to behave in a consistent way—it is not morally right at one time to evade paying your taxes and morally right at other times to do so. We feel that one should always pay taxes if obliged to do so—one should behave in accordance with a universal rule or maxim.

These considerations show that the Kantian ethic is a highly plausible one. What criticisms can be directed against it? There are three main criticisms that have been made of Kant's view. The first holds that although Kant tried to prove that the moral worth of an action depends only upon the motive from which it is done, in fact he surreptitiously introduces considerations of the *consequences* that an act has into a determination of its rightness or wrongness. For, according to this objection, he is tacitly showing that the *effect* of not behaving in accordance with the categorical imperative would be to make human life as we know it impossible. For instance, he says, "Then I presently become aware that while I can will the lie, I can by no means will that lying should be a universal law. For with such a law there would be no promises at all, since it would be in vain to allege my intention in regard to my future actions to those who would not believe this allegation, or if they overhastily did so, would pay me back in my own coin." In citing such an example, Kant is referring to the *consequences* of lying (e.g., "being paid back in my own coin"), so that his theory seems inconsistent insofar as he has not held to his original claim that he is concerned solely with *motive*.

The second major criticism that has been made of Kantian ethics is that it does not handle cases where we have **a conflict of duties**—and these seem to be some of the most pressing and serious types of moral perplexity. Suppose I promise to keep a secret, and then someone else asks me about it. I cannot both tell the truth and keep my promise—yet according to the Kantian position, I should do both. In such a situation, I cannot, logically, universalize my behavior; if I tell the truth, I will break my promise to keep the secret. If I keep my promise, I will not tell the truth.

A third difficulty, analogous to the above, is that Kant is urging too strong a claim when he insists that we should never tell lies or never break promises. According to more moderate versions of objectivism, no claim as strong as this need be made. Moral rules are to be interpreted, this objection urges, as *generalizations* rather than as *categorical* propositions without exception. In general, we should tell the truth, but there may occur circumstances where we would feel morally obliged to lie. For example, if a maniac, armed with a revolver, comes looking for a relative in order to kill her, we would consider it highly immoral to inform the maniac of the whereabouts of the relative merely because one ought to tell the truth. Telling the truth, keeping promises, repaying debts are obligations that one should keep, provided that no other overriding factors are present. W. D. Ross has called such obligations **"prima facie duties."** One is obliged to perform such obligations, provided that no other overriding factors are present, or provided that all other conditions are equal.

Such a criticism still allows room for an objective morality, without adhering to what runs contrary to common sense, i.e., that one must *always* tell the truth, *always* keep one's promises, *no matter what* circumstances or conditions obtain. Would we not morally disapprove of the captured soldier who gave away military secrets on the ground that he was following the categorical imperative?

With this brief discussion of Kant, we come to the end of the classical view we shall deal with here. The above disquisition should not be regarded as containing a complete discussion of all classical philosophers, but only as a set of introductory remarks to some of the more famous moralists. Such writers as Butler, Spencer, Nietzsche, Schopenhauer, Hume, Locke, Hobbes, Rousseau, and Lucretius have not been treated, mainly because they hold views that are variants of those we have considered, or because they are not now regarded as of first importance.

We turn now to a consideration of modern ethics.

Modern ethics

Definition of "Modern Ethics"

As we pointed out in an earlier discussion, so-called "classical" ethical theories are characterized by their efforts to answer two questions: "What is the good life for people?" and "How ought they to behave?" If we examine these questions from a slightly different perspective, we might interpret them as requests for advice by people who are puzzled by certain aspects of daily living. And the various answers that the classical theories give can be regarded as statements of advice to the individual. Thus hedonism can be regarded as telling us that the good life consists of a life of pleasure and, further, that we *ought* to act so as to acquire pleasure.

It is assumed in asking such questions and in giving such answers that the meaning of the questions and the meaning of the answers are clear. But in recent years, philosophers have come to realize that many of these questions and answers are not clear at all; that before we can give an answer to them, we must find out *precisely* what they mean. To discover what they mean requires that the questions be clarified. The process of clarifying the meaning of questions and answers is called *"philosophical analysis."* The use of this process persistently in modern ethics causes it to differ enormously from ethics pursued in the classical tradition. **The main difference is that one can engage in philosophical analysis without necessarily being committed to giving any sort of advice for living**—for instance, one may analyze a theory like utilitarianism without necessarily advocating that doctrine. Of course, it is assumed that the process of analysis is not an end in itself; once one becomes clear about the meaning of the crucial terms and statements that occur in moral theories, it is assumed that one will be in a better position to decide which of them one ought to adhere to. Thus, modern ethics is not regarded as an alternative to propounding ethics in the classical tradition so much as it is regarded as a preparation for the further study of such theories.

We might therefore define "modern ethics" as that branch of philosophy that applies analysis to moral theory. In order to state somewhat more clearly what this definition implies, let us give both an ethical and a nonethical example of philosophical analysis. Consider, to begin with, a simple word like "brother." What does it mean when it occurs in a sentence like "John is the brother of Joan." (It will have a different meaning, of course, in a sentence like "All men are brothers.") In order to answer this query, an analysis of the term "brother" is required. In order to analyze the meaning of the term, we must find a set of characteristics that belong to all those people who are brothers and only to those. Thus the property of "having blond hair," while attributable to some brothers, is not a quality that every brother must have in order to be a brother (many things, such as women and dolls, may possess this trait without being brothers). On the other hand, every brother must be male. But being male, it should be noticed, is not sufficient to determine whether someone is a brother or not, since a given person may be male and yet be the only child in the family. If so, he would not be a brother. To be a brother requires not only that he be male but also that he be a sibling, i.e., stand in the relation to some other person having a common parent. The complete analysis of "brother" reveals that it means the same as "being a male sibling." In more technical language, "being a male" and "being a sibling" provide the correct meaning of the term "brother" because they give us the **necessary and sufficient conditions** that a person must satisfy in order to be such. To say that "being a male" is a necessary condition means that no one who is not a male can be a brother. This condition plus the other necessary condition of "being a sibling" *together* are sufficient conditions for being a brother—anyone who has both characteristics will be a brother. **Philosophical analysis is frequently considered to be the search for the necessary and sufficient conditions that determine the meaning of a term, although this is not its only job.**

Sometimes the phrase "philosophical analysis" is used to refer to any process that attempts to clarify the meaning of a term, whether or not this process results in the sort of definition we have just considered (i.e., in a definition that leads to the discovery of necessary and sufficient conditions). **The function of analysis is to make the question precise so that we will know how to reply to it.**

Upon examination, classical moral theories like hedonism, utilitarianism, Stoicism, Christianity, and so forth, turn out to be highly complex doctrines. Before we can assess the merits of the advice they give, we require first of all to understand the advice—and this can be achieved only if we first analyze the meaning of the terms they use, such as "good," "bad," "right," "wrong," "ought," and so on. Modern ethics, as contrasted with classical ethics, stresses this task—the task we have called "analysis." Many modern philosophers believe that this process of analysis shows that the methods of the classical moral philosophers have been mistaken, that the questions they asked were not clearly formulated, and that, as a result, their answers do not have the validity they have claimed for them. In other words, many philosophers now feel that in attempting to give us positive moral guidance, the classical theorists were attempting the impossible and that

the most any moral philosopher can do is to attempt to clarify for us the implications of the language we use when we are expressing moral judgments. This is the most important way in which what has been called the "twentieth-century revolution in philosophy" has affected moral theory.

If any one philosopher is responsible for this revolution in the approach to moral philosophy, it is G. E. Moore, who claimed in his *Principia Ethica*, published in 1903, that the classical theories were attempts to deduce moral precepts from theological, metaphysical, or scientific premises and that such arguments are fallacious, since one cannot argue from premises of one logical type (i.e., from factual or descriptive judgments) to premises of another logical type (i.e., to prescriptions). This is a point that David Hume had made much earlier, but Moore developed it to show that what was involved was an attempt to define moral words like "good," "bad," and so on, in nonmoral terms, in terms of descriptive statements about God or about human nature, i.e., to make "good" synonymous with "approved by God," "conducive to the greatest happiness of the greatest number," and so on. To do this, he claimed, was to leave out of consideration the essential moral or prescriptive element in the meaning of such words. This is what he means when he tells us that "good," like all moral words, is indefinable and that goodness is a simple, unanalyzable property. To attempt to define it is to commit what he called the **"naturalistic fallacy,"** since any attempted definition of moral words will be in terms only of their descriptive meaning, and the moral element, with which we are primarily concerned, will be lost.

Many philosophers have taken this as an indication that a new approach to the problems of moral philosophy is needed, an approach based on an analysis of the language of morals rather than an examination of factual statements about God, about "goodness," or about human nature, and they have come to see that moral statements are not analogous to theological, metaphysical, or scientific statements but have a peculiar logic of their own.

Let us turn to a discussion of some modern theories and their classifications.

Classification of Modern Theories

Modern theories are now commonly classified in three different ways. They may be classified (*a*) as either **subjectivistic** or **objectivistic,** (*b*) as **naturalistic, nonnaturalistic,** or **emotivist consequence,** or (*c*) as **motivist,** or **deontological theories.** In this section we shall briefly define each of these terms and then show why the classifications are important for an understanding of modern ethical theory.

Subjectivism and Objectivism (Moral Realism)

In beginning a discussion of this classification, it is important to reiterate that **modern ethical theories are primarily concerned with the analysis of the language of morals.** Therefore, a theory will be classified as either subjectivistic or objectivistic (but not both, of course) depending upon how it analyzes ethical language. **We can define the term "objectivistic" by saying that any theory that is nonsubjectivistic is objectivistic.** This raises the question of defining "subjectivism."

There are two characteristics that determine a theory to be subjectivistic:

1. If the theory holds that what are ordinarily called "ethical" judgments (such as "Stealing is wrong") are **neither true nor false,** it is subjectivistic.

2. If the theory holds that ethical judgments are true or false but **that they are always about the psychology of the person who utters them** and only that person, then again it is subjectivistic. Thomas Hobbes's moral theory is usually interpreted as being subjectivistic because he held that such judgments as "This is good" can be analyzed into "I desire this." Moral language, in his view, merely uses another form of words to speak about one's desires, inclinations, feelings, and so forth. The moral theory of Immanuel Kant is also subjectivistic, according to some interpretations, because it analyzes ethical judgments into commands, and commands are neither true nor false (e.g., it makes no sense to say that "Right face!" is either true or false).

Both Platonism and utilitarianism are objectivistic doctrines according to the above definition. Plato held that moral judgments *are* true or false in exactly the same sense as judgments like "Two plus two equals four." Likewise, he held that such statements as "This is good" are not about anyone's psychology, if true, but are about a certain feature of the world called "goodness." Plato holds that there are moral facts in the world, and that goodness is such a fact. This is why such views are today often labeled as "moral realism." Utilitarianism resembles Platonism in both of these respects. Judgments such as "This is right" mean "This will produce an excess of pleasure over pain," and in this translation are simply, ordinary *scientific* judgments; likewise, although these judgments are about psychological entities, such as pleasure and pain, they are not about the speaker's psychology *alone*—but about the psychology of a number of people. For this reason, such judgments go beyond the speaker alone and refer to a group of individuals. In this sense, moral language is not subjective but objective. It is important to note, however, that such theories are based on a view of moral statements as analogous to scientific statements.

This classification is extremely important because it draws attention to the status of moral standards. If moral standards are merely subjective (like tastes), then there seems to be no way of settling disputes about whether behavior is immoral or not. If something tastes sour to me and sweet to you, we cannot say I am wrong or that you are wrong—this is just the way things are. Likewise, if in saying "Stealing is wrong," I am merely asserting "I dislike stealing," and if in saying "Stealing is right," you are merely asserting that you like stealing, there seems to be no way of showing that one of us is wrong, the other right. You feel about it one way, I the other, and that is all there is to it.

The question whether moral judgments are merely subjectivistic pronouncements or not is thus an important one—and in the next section we shall consider arguments for and against both subjectivism and objectivism.

Naturalism, Nonnaturalism, and Emotivism

The classification of theories into those that are naturalistic, nonnaturalistic, or emotivist raises issues that are more academic but still important. Let us define these terms now, and then show why the issues they raise are of significance.

A theory will be regarded as **naturalistic** if it holds **both that moral judgments are true or false, and also that such judgments are reducible entirely to the concepts of some natural science (usually psychology).**

A theory will be defined as **nonnaturalistic** if it holds **that moral judgments are true or false, but that they are not reducible to any natural science.**

A theory will be called **"emotivist"** if it contends that **moral judgments are neither true nor false but are merely expressive of the feelings** of those who utter them and evocative of the feelings of those who hear them. Since all the judgments of science are *either* true or false, it follows that if the emotivist analysis is correct, moral judgments cannot be reduced to scientific ones.

The importance of the issue that is raised by these classifications is this: Is ethics a unique discipline, with laws of its own, or is ethics merely a branch of some science like psychology? If the latter, in order to make valid ethical judgments, one would be advised to study science; if not, there is an autonomous body of human knowledge that must be studied in its own right.

Utilitarianism and the Hobbesian moral doctrine can be seen to be naturalistic theories; both contend that **moral**

judgments are really disguised ways of making psychological assertions (they merely differ over the question of whether the judgments are subjectivistic or not).

Platonism and Christian ethical theories are nonnaturalistic doctrines. Plato believed that the world contained **moral entities** (goodness, rightness, etc.) in the same way as it contains *natural* entities, like chairs and tables. Moral judgments, when true, are about these entities and not about the entities found in nature; hence ethics, which is the discipline that concerns itself with moral entities, cannot be reduced to one of the known sciences. The same considerations hold for Christian ethics, which regard moral judgments as being expressions for the divine will; these expressions are true or false, but they cannot be confirmed or refuted by scientific experimentation—hence Christian ethics again is nonnaturalistic. However, in both Platonism and Christian ethics, moral statements, although not being in themselves empirical scientific statements, are nevertheless analogous to statements of this kind, since they are assertions about something, i.e., they are **descriptions** of something.

The **emotive theory**, which has been supported by a number of twentieth-century philosophers—A. J. Ayer, C. L. Stevenson, Rudolf Carnap, to mention a few—avers that *both* naturalism and nonnaturalism are mistaken. This theory takes up Moore's point and asserts that moral statements are not analogous to scientific statements in that the moral element in them is not an assertion or a description of anything. It agrees with nonnaturalism that **moral judgments cannot be verified or falsified by scientific proce-** dures, and it also agrees with naturalistic forms of subjectivism (like Hobbes's position) in holding that **moral judgments are about one's feelings**—but the sense in which they are "about" these feelings is not that which traditional naturalistic theories have claimed. For moral statements are not descriptions at all. They are not even descriptions of one's feelings. Rather, they are expressions of feelings, much as a grunt of pleasure after eating is an expression of satisfaction. Since one would not say that grunts are true or false, **it is a mistake to say that moral judgments, which express feelings, are true or false.**

We shall consider arguments for and against these views in the next section.

Motivist, Consequence, and Deontological Theories

The classification of theories into motivist, consequence, and deontological doctrines also raises issues of importance. After defining these terms, we shall proceed to a discussion of the issues in question.

A theory will be called a **"motivist ethical theory"** if it holds that the **rightness or wrongness of an action depends upon the motive from which the act was done.** Kant's ethics is an example of such a theory.

A theory will be called a **"consequence theory"** if it holds that the **rightness or wrongness of an action depends entirely upon the effects that the action has.** Utilitarianism is a classic example of a consequence theory. It is worth mentioning that consequence theories usually fall into two groups: **hedonistic consequence theories** and **agathistic consequence the-**

ories. The former hold that the rightness or wrongness of an action depends upon whether it produces consequences that are painful or pleasant; the latter hold that goodness is not to be identified with pleasure, or badness with pain, but is something unique, just as redness is unique and cannot be reduced to anything else. Such a theory was held by G. E. Moore, who himself maintained that the rightness or wrongness of an act depends upon the amount of goodness or badness the act produces. It is thus a consequence doctrine, but of a nonhedonistic sort.

Deontological theories (held by W. D. Ross, A. C. Ewing, and H. A. Prichard, among others) reject both motivist and consequence theories. They claim that the **rightness or wrongness of an act depends neither upon the motive from which the act was done nor upon the consequences of the act—but solely upon what kind of an act it was.** Thus it is right to keep one's promises, because in making a promise one has performed an act that by its very nature obligates one to carry it out, regardless of one's inclinations or the effects that carrying it out will have. Because they stress the notions of **obligation and duty,** deontological theories are often described as **"duty ethics."**

The disagreements among these doctrines have important practical consequences. Consider, for instance, the question of punishment. How can we justify punishing criminals? According to motivist theories, we can justify punishing people if their intentions were evil. If a person kills someone accidentally, we do not punish him/her; but if his/her *intentions* were to kill someone whom he/she hated,

we punish him/her because he/she acted from bad motives. Consequence theories deny this. They argue that the only justification for punishment is to prevent further crime. If we leave a killing unpunished, then everyone will feel free to kill those whom they hate. We punish people because the *effect,* or *consequence,* of punishing them will be to deter further crime. Deontologists disagree with both positions. Their view, put roughly, is that we punish people for crimes because the acts they performed were wrong. It is inherently wrong to commit a crime, and by punishing people for their crimes, we are acting justly. A person who does a good deed deserves to be rewarded; a person who commits a crime deserves to be punished, and this is the reason for imposing sanctions upon him/her.

With these definitions explained, let us now consider some of these issues in greater detail. Let us consider, as a specimen case, the arguments for and against subjectivism and objectivism.

Analysis of Subjectivism and Objectivism

Subjectivism

ARGUMENTS FOR

The main argument for subjectivism is the argument based on an analysis of the language that we use to make moral judgments. As we have already seen, such judgments are more than statements or **descriptions** of something. They are also **prescriptions.** They are imperatives—commands to someone; and they are evaluations—expressions of one's own personal values. It is the latter that are the

truly moral elements in such judgments, and since these elements are not descriptions, it does not make sense to ask whether they are true or false. Consider what I am saying when I tell a child, "Stealing is wrong." I may be telling him that stealing is forbidden by the law of the society we both live in, but this is far from all that the sentence contains. For I am also saying to him **in the same words,** "Do not steal!" and, in addition, I am expressing my own disapproval of stealing. It does not make sense to ask whether the sentence "Do not steal!" is true or false, since it is not an assertion but a command, and equally it is not sensible to ask whether my feelings are true or false. Hence it would appear that all moral judgments must be subjective.

The second argument that supports subjectivism may be called the **"argument from sentience."** Imagine a world in which there were no creatures that had feelings, desires, appetites, attitudes, knowledge—in short, a world in which there were no sentient beings. All the objects that made up such a world would be inanimate. Would it really make sense to say that anything good or bad could happen to the things in such a world? Would it be "bad" for water to erode away a rock or for a landslide to fill a valley with boulders? The subjectivistic answer is that it would not make sense to ascribe such predicates as "good" or "bad" to these occurrences. Only if some sentient being were affected by these events, or could be affected by them, would it make sense to say that they were "good" or "bad." Goodness and badness thus seem to depend upon the feelings, attitudes, and desires of sentient beings. If we continue to reflect upon the problem, the subjectivist goes on to say, we can see that ultimately what is good or bad depends upon the individual psychology of the person who has certain attitudes toward events, such as liking or disliking them. From considerations such as these, it is argued that some form of subjectivism must be true.

A third argument in favor of subjectivism is the **egoistic argument.** This is used to reject objectivistic theories such as utilitarianism. What is the point of working for the greatest happiness of the greatest number if *you personally* become unhappy by so doing? In the final analysis, who can be more important than *you*? If a course of action leads to the well-being of others, but not to *yours*, can it really be for the good? The subjectivistic answer is a firm "No!" We can justify working for the good of the many only if we at the same time, or at least in the long run, increase our own good; otherwise, doing the action is wrong.

ARGUMENTS AGAINST

The first argument against subjectivism is that if we accept such a theory, we can never settle any moral dispute. How can we say "Hitler was wicked in killing six million Jews" if we accept subjectivism? All this would mean would be: "I disapprove of Hitler's killing six million Jews." But if Hitler objects to this and claims he did right in murdering these people, then he will mean by such a judgment: "I approve of killing six million." We thus have no real conflict, for he is saying "I approve of this action," and we are saying "I disapprove of it." It turns out that we are both merely talking about how we feel; we are not talking about the act of killing these people. Both of us are expressing our feelings: I disapprove and he approves—but if so, there is no real conflict between us. Ordinary people think that such a consequence makes subjectivism as a moral theory paradoxical. In ordinary life, we seem to be talking not only about our feelings when we say "Hitler was wrong," but about Hitler and about the acts he committed. But to say that such a theory is paradoxical is not to say that it is untenable or that ordinary people are not mistaken in what they think they are asserting in such contexts.

A second difficulty in subjectivism is this. Ordinary people believe that words like "good," "bad," "right," "wrong," and so on, have more or less the same meaning for everybody who knows how to use the English language. If they did not, it would be impossible to communicate with other people. Since we obviously can communicate with them, these words must have some interpersonal meaning. But it seems to be a consequence of subjectivism that two different people will never mean the same thing when they utter these words. For if I say "That's good," I mean the same as "I like it," whereas if you say "That's good," you mean that you like it. The word "good" in the first use refers to a different person from the one referred to in the second use of the word "good." If this is indeed a consequence of subjectivistic theories, then ordinary people would reject such views on the ground that these words do have common meanings in the ordinary employment of daily English. It is not, however, a necessary consequence. For the subjectivist will not want to deny that the complexities of words like "good"

are such that they can carry both of these meanings at the same time. When I say that something is good, I am not only expressing my approval of it; often I am also drawing attention to the fact that most people approve of it too.

The third difficulty with subjectivism is that such theories cannot give a justification of the concept of "doing one's duty." This is obviously an important notion in morals. One may often, in everyday life, be faced with issues that involve one's duty. The person who has pacifist inclinations and also believes it is his/her duty to defend his/her country may suffer moral agony in trying to decide which of these courses he/she should follow. The notion of "doing one's duty" seems to involve acting against one's inclinations at least some of the time. One may desire to drink alcohol, but it may be his/her duty (if he/she is a doctor "on duty," let us say) to remain sober. In short, the ordinary person feels that at least sometimes it is right for an individual to do that which he/she does not want to do or like to do— and if so, it is difficult to see how subjectivistic theories can explain such a concept if they reduce all moral behavior to liking and disliking.

Objectivism

ARGUMENTS FOR

The main argument in favor of objectivism is that it provides a **theory that corresponds more closely to the views of people of common sense about moral matters** than does subjectivism. Consider the question of moral disagreement. Subjectivists hold that what *seem* to be moral disputes, if we judge merely from the sentences that each party uses (A saying "That's good," and B saying "That's bad"), turn out upon analysis not to be such (A means "I like it," and B means "I dislike it"—and each can be right). Now **objectivists contend that there is no essential difference between a dispute about moral matters and a dispute about factual ones.** In both cases, there can be genuine disagreement in which one faction is right and the other is wrong. Thus, if I say "There is extraterrestrial life" and you deny this, one of us is right and one wrong. Similarly, the objectivists say, if I assert "Stealing is wrong" and you deny this, one of us is right and one wrong. We are not simply talking about ourselves and how we feel about stealing, but we are talking about stealing and whether that is right or wrong. In short, **our sentences have an objective reference** in exactly the same way as sentences about extraterrestrial life do. Philosophers who defend this point of view are often called moral realists.

Now the ordinary person believes this too. He/she believes that it is not just a question of individual preference as to whether Hitler was right or not, but that in some objective sense, anybody who tortures and murders people is committing deeds that are wicked. Hitler may have defended his behavior on the ground that he was acting properly, but all this shows is that either he did not understand the right way to behave, in which case he lacked moral knowledge; or if he did and acted against it, he was simply an immoral person. Objectivistic theories allow us to account for the strong feeling we

have that there are *genuine* disputes about moral matters.

Secondly, such theories allow us **to explicate the nature of "duty."** Ordinary people feel that there are certain duties in their lives that must be performed regardless of whether one wants to or not. These duties are objective facts that exist whether one chooses to ignore them or not. Thus, if I am a doctor and see a man injured in an accident, it is my duty to treat that man, even if it should prove highly inconvenient to do so. I may have another course of action in mind (I may be going to a party, say) that is much more pleasant; yet if I ignore the injured individual and proceed to the party, I am behaving wrongly. Sometimes there are things we *have* to do even though we do not *wish* to—and in stressing this fact, objectivism seems more in accord with common sense than with subjectivistic theories. It must be pointed out, however, that the subjectivist is not committed to a denial of the fact that we have feelings of duty and obligation; it is merely that he cannot accept that such feelings have any objective status.

ARGUMENTS AGAINST

The main difficulties with objectivism, or moral realism, center about **how we establish or prove** that a certain action is right or wrong. The objectivists claim that there is no real difference between the method of establishing a scientific hypothesis and a moral one; but critics of objectivism deny this. What seems essential in proving a scientific claim is (*a*) the acceptance by both sides of a common method, sometimes called the experimental method, and (*b*) the willingness of both sides to accept the judgments of disinterested observers after they have examined the evidence. Both of these characteristics seem lacking in the case of moral disputes. For example, it is difficult for the disinterested observer of a moral conflict to know what counts as evidence for or against either side. Suppose one side holds that euthanasia is right, the other that it is wrong. Both sides may completely agree about the facts of the case. They both agree, for instance, that the patient was dying of a disease with no known or foreseeable cure; the patient was in great pain; he/she insisted that he/she be killed to relieve him/her of his/her agony. It is further agreed that the killer was acting from the highest motives (i.e., to relieve pain). But nonetheless one side holds that the killer did wrong in killing someone, the other side that the killer acted rightly. What further facts could be relevant to deciding this dispute? If the evidence in scientific matters is not decisive, no one has any more reason to believe any scientific hypothesis than its denial; the proper course of action is the suspension of judgment—but if we are members of a jury trying the killer, can we actually take this course? It seems we must decide, but how? The subjectivistic answer at this point is that we finally examine our feelings and preferences and we decide in terms of them—this is the only possible answer. The objectivist claims that this will not do, but he/she is hard put to it to tell us what evidence would show one side to be right, the other wrong. This is the kind of difficulty that leads the subjectivist to believe that moral statements are not like scientific

statements and cannot, therefore, have the same objectivity.

Applied Ethics

As the case of euthanasia we have just discussed indicates, theoretical issues in ethics and practical dilemmas that people face are intimately intertwined. Practical problems give rise to theoretical questions, and theoretical solutions must be tested against the all too human issues that ordinary people face every day. The philosopher, as we have seen, attempts to formulate systematic and coherent sets of principles that not only will deepen one's understanding of the issues at stake but will allow for the justification or rationale of certain sorts of actions. Practical problems of a moral kind arise in nearly all of the domains of human life: Should a society prohibit divorce? Should abortion be legalized? Should homosexuals and lesbians be allowed to become policemen/women or soldiers? Should physicians be given the right to decide when a critically ill patient should no longer receive life-support systems? The list is endless, and with respect to nearly all such issues—the above set is a good example—society has often been split, with some persons vigorously supporting positive answers to the above questions, and with some supporting negative answers.

Let us take the issue of gay rights as an example of a moral dilemma of an applied kind. What is the issue, and can philosophers assist in arriving at a reasonable solution to it? Here, to show how a philosopher could argue an unpopular position, let us—for purposes of the exercise—defend the gay rights position.

The issue can be described in a variety of ways, but let us make it explicit. Should gays and lesbians be allowed to become members of the San Francisco police department, for example? Why should this even be a question? Those who oppose such a recommendation would argue that gays and lesbians are not normal people. From a psychoanalytic standpoint, they have not reached the kind of personal maturity—normally measured by the development of heterosexual relationships leading to marriage, a family, social integration in the community, and so forth. From this perspective, it can be argued that homosexuals and lesbians are not merely psychologically immature but also "sick," and that this sickness results in perverted sexual practices, the inability to form normal relationships, and especially the inability to work as a full-fledged member of the "outside" community. Even worse, it is charged that many homosexuals and lesbians are potential child molesters and thus cannot be trusted with normal police duties.

A philosopher weighing these various charges might begin by asking what evidence there is for the claim that all homosexuals and lesbians are psychologically immature. It can be pointed out that some of the evidence depends on the truth of specific psychoanalytical theories, such as Freud's, whose scientific validity has itself been challenged. It can also be pointed out that the range of human behavior exhibited by gays and lesbians is as vast as is found in the "straight" population. Finally, it can be pointed out that under the Constitution of the United States, and especially under the Fourteenth Amendment, it would be of dubi-

ous legality to restrict the employment of any group of persons because of their particular sexual orientation. A philosopher who argues this way might end by urging that gays and lesbians be given a chance to see how they would perform in the police department. Such a course of action could begin on an experimental basis, and if it were found that their performances were acceptable, the practice of employing them could be expanded. In making such a recommendation, the philosopher would, in the end, have to justify his/her proposal by showing that it derived from a set of rational and consistent principles. In this case, the principles might be those of fairness and justice, supported by particular provisions in the United States Bill of Rights. The practical consequence of this theoretical appeal thus would issue in a practical decision that could affect the lives of many persons in society.

Another example of applied ethics can be seen in the current discussion about whether it is right to assist people to commit suicide if their lives are medically hopeless, and full of pain, and they rationally come to the conclusion that they have nothing to live for. Society has regarded suicide not only as terribly immoral—as contrary to the religious teachings of Judaism and Christianity—but also as illegal. It consists in taking a life; it is murder, at least self-murder. Therefore, the law is quite clear that assisting anyone to commit suicide amounts to being an accessory to murder. The person attempting suicide, if stopped or if unsuccessful, can be charged with a crime; but he/she is usually regarded as mentally unbalanced and is sent to a mental institution for treatment. It is contended that the person, when properly treated, will realize that it is wrong to try to end one's life.

On the other hand, it is argued that whether one should continue living is a personal matter, to be decided according to the individual's particular circumstances. So, if one considers the medical situation and is fully cognizant of the prognosis for one's ailments, he/she should be allowed to decide whether it is worthwhile to continue a life full of pain, with no known possible cure.

If it is objected that the decision is not just a personal one, but one affecting family and friends, then the person in question can take this into account when deciding what to do.

In spite of the legal sanctions, the Hemlock Society, which distributes information about how one can end one's life, has come into being in recent years. A book entitled *Final Exit* (a bestseller in the United States but banned in the United Kingdom) has described various painless ways of committing suicide. A doctor in Michigan has devised a "death machine" and has assisted some people in ending their lives; he has come under investigation for possible criminal activity. He and the would-be suicide hold lengthy discussions about the use of his machine, during which the doctor ascertains that the person fully understands what he/she is about to do and has thought through the objections. Then it is the person who makes the death machine operate.

The question of whether suicide and assisted suicide are morally defensible has now become a serious issue. Some people no longer feel restrained by religious teaching, and they also feel that the law is obsolete in that it does not take into con-

sideration the rational decision to commit suicide. The ethical heart of the matter is whether anyone is allowed to take a life, including his/her own, under any circumstances. Is living, under any conditions, a positive value that supersedes any other values?

Another major current problem with some similar aspects is that concerning abortion of unwanted fetuses. Those who favor preserving the legal right to have an abortion emphasize that the woman carrying the fetus has the right to choose what to do with her own body, that it is a private, personal decision in which the state should have no interest. Opposed to this is the view that the fetus has the right to live and that the state should have the duty to protect the fetus. Central in arguments pro and con is the question whether the fetus is a living person entitled to be treated just as any other person. For decades scientists and medical doctors and theologians have argued about (*a*) when life begins and (*b*) when the fetus is considered a viable person. Even if the factual questions could be answered to everybody's satisfaction, there would still remain basic ethical issues concerning the rights of the woman carrying the fetus. Many opposed to legalized abortion are willing to grant that in some circumstances an abortion may be justified. Such circumstances may involve saving the life of the mother, preventing the birth of a severely deformed child, and preventing the birth of a child who resulted from the rape of the mother. These considerations of the physical well-being of the mother or the child, or the circumstances causing the pregnancy, can lead to further considerations: the mental health of the potential mother, the economic and social viability of the offspring, and many other matters.

The ethicist would first have to determine when life begins and when an unborn child is a person. If preserving life is taken as the principal value, then one has to consider the competing life claims of the mother and the potential child. If the quality of the life being preserved is taken into consideration, then all sorts of medical, psychological, economic, and social factors have to be evaluated. And the Supreme Court of the United States can spell out only what the present members think is lawful under the Constitution, rather than what is right or good. Hence the ethical debate is sure to go on as different aspects of the abortion question are decided in courts, and different laws are passed by Congress and the states, dealing not only with the right to abortion itself but also with whether doctors, nurses, social workers, etc., can advise people if they should have an abortion or not.

A related but rather different ethical issue is involved in discussions about curbing violence on TV and about limiting the possession of firearms. Those in favor of some limitations stress that they are trying to save lives. The projecting of violence as an ordinary part of life, they contend, leads to viewers' acting out violent scenarios they have watched. The fact that in America guns are so easily obtained makes such acting out possible, often with tragic results—the killing of other people.

However, some may argue that their right to freedom of expression covers their right to produce violent TV programs. The viewers' freedom should also cover the right to watch what they wish. And, regarding a question similar to one raised as part of the debate about pornography, is there compelling evidence that people become violent from watching violent TV, or can it have a beneficial effect, of letting people express their violent feelings by just watching? Within this argument there is another: whether there are some degrees of violence that should be suppressed, such as actual murder scenes of live people, rapes, etc.

How can one tell where to draw the line? It is partly a factual question of which experiences influence people to commit bad acts. It is also partly a value judgment about what people ought to see. Even if it could be proved that viewing had *no* bad influences, would we want people to see others tortured to death, drawn and quartered, etc.? And if it could be shown that people could be influenced to behave better by what they have experienced, would we want TV programs to consist of nothing but uplifting experiences?

The issue of gun control involves both whether it contributes to bad, violent behavior and whether there are other rights involved that may be more important. Some people insist that the use of guns for hunting, sport shooting, and other recreational activities is beneficial—and desirable within the context of a good life. Further, they would say that the ability to protect themselves and their loved ones from bad people is also good—and important in society as it presently exists. They would insist that theirs is an inherent right to self-defense. In the United States, they would point out, the Founding Fathers saw the importance of gun possession when they made it part of the Bill of Rights—that the right of citizens to bear arms shall not be abridged, thus allowing them to protect themselves from threats by other people and by tyrannical governments.

On the other hand, those advocating gun control would stress how dangerous gun possession is in the present world. The number of people injured or killed by guns in private hands in the United States is enormous compared with the number in those countries that control gun possession. Even in benign situations, accidental firings of guns occur and cause death or injury. In recognition of this, slight attempts to control the situation have been offered and adopted in an effort to keep guns out of the hands of criminals and crazy people. But these efforts do not work without stringent actions that threaten everyone's freedom of action. In the current situation in the United States, there could be more adequate control of gun sales and purchases, as there are of sales and purchases of prescription drugs. With present-day computers, one could quickly ascertain if a prospective purchaser had a criminal record. One probably could not determine his/her mental status beyond obvious behavioral symptoms. If one had a time period to check on would-be purchasers, more of the potentially violent ones could be weeded out. But the problem would probably not be seriously alleviated, since the availability of guns from other sources, legal or illegal, is so great.

So, treating the matter as an applied ethical problem, one would first have to determine which was more important— the freedom to bear arms and to protect oneself thereby, or the protection of the society through limiting access to guns. If one decided in favor of the latter, then one would have to determine how much people's freedom should be curtailed to bring about a gun-free environment. Should authorities be able to search every home? Should authorities be allowed to seize people's property?

The issue of freedom versus control has had a long history, with both practical implications and theoretical stumbling blocks, from the time of Plato to the present, and one of its most penetrating instances arises in the case of pornography. As we have seen, in the cases of television, films, and literature, language and behavior have become less and less inhibited. It is common today for theatrical plays and films to contain language that would have been ruled illegal in the United States and in most Western countries not many decades ago. A film such as *Deep Throat* exhibits overt sexual behavior, such as oral intercourse; and even on TV, simulations of such behavior are now commonplace. There is no doubt that such permissiveness takes cyclical forms in human history. In the plays of Aristophanes and in Restoration drama, we find explicit sexual comments and the depiction of various forms of intercourse; and of course, in the works of the Marquis de Sade, extremes of such activity. Each society faces these changes either with equanimity or with more definite degrees of approval or disapproval. There are arguments on all sides of the question, ranging from those demanding that such activities be outlawed to those suggesting that they be fully tolerated.

The main theoretical issue that arises

here is that of censorship, and it arises in an acute form for democratic societies. In nondemocratic societies, free speech is not in general tolerated, so what is permissible is determined by autocratic authorities. Those authorities usually argue that they, or some subset of those in authority, such as the church, say, believe that certain types of behavior are immoral or injurious to society or to subgroups within society, such as children, and therefore can justifiably be excluded by fiat. But in a democratic society, the argument is that no sort of free discussion should be constrained *a priori*, so that citizens can make unfettered and free choices about the kinds of lives they wish to lead. The classic defense of this point of view is found in John Stuart Mill's *On Liberty* (1859), especially in the second and third chapters. A powerful argument in favor of this point of view, used by defenders of democracies against autocratic forms of governance, is that *no* society has ever instituted or justified *total* censorship. Even those societies dominated by religious conviction have allowed some persons—say, certain priests—to read and discuss everything in order to decide what among those items should be allowed dissemination. That this is so presupposes that in order to have a good society, at least those governing society should be immune from censorship. They must be exposed to all the facts, as well as to a free and unfettered discussion of them, in order to make the best judgments about what is desirable for that society. But in a democratic society, since it is the people who govern, then the argument is that they should not censor themselves. They must also have all the facts at their disposal if they are to make judicious decisions about matters of public policy.

This is a powerful argument, but even proponents of democracy, such as Walter Lippmann and Alexander Meiklejohn, have held that freedom of information applies only to matters of public policy, and that prohibitions on extreme sexual behavior and talk, and violence on TV and the stage and in film, can therefore be censored without inhibiting free discussion of political issues. But this objection faces the difficulty of setting up a group of censors who can decide, independently of the people, what does or does not affect matters of public policy, so it has its own liabilities. From the time of the Greeks to today, these have been the central issues, and they are still debated by philosophers and members of the public along the preceding lines.

Suggested further reading

History of Ethics

Broad, C. D. *Five Types of Ethical Theory.* 1930. Excellent account of the moral views of Spinoza, Butler, Hume, Kant, and Sidgwick.

MacIntyre, A. *A Short History of Ethics.* 1967. Very clear and interesting treatment of the history of ethics.

Olafson, F. A. *Ethics and Twentieth Century Thought.* 1973. Beautifully written; broad-ranging to include not only philosophy but related disciplines such as anthropology and sociology.

Sidgwick, H. *Outlines of the History of Ethics for English Readers.* A classic work first published at the end of the nineteenth century. Read the 1962 edition.

Classical Works in Ethics

Aristotle. *Nicomachean Ethics.* Aristotle's greatest work on ethics, dedicated to his son Nicomachus.

Butler, J. *Fifteen Sermons upon Human Nature.*

Kant, I. *Critique of Practical Reason.* A motivist theory of ethics.

Moore, G. E. *Principia Ethica*. The "naturalistic fallacy": an intuitionist theory of ethics.

Nietzsche, F. *Beyond Good and Evil*. Emphasis on the emotions; a type of romantic philosophy.

Paley, W. *The Principles of Moral and Political Philosophy*. A discussion of utilitarianism.

Plato. *Lesser Hippias, Crito, Protagoras, Gorgias, Republic, Philebus, Laws*. These works range from brief dialogues such as the *Crito*, to long works such as the *Republic* and the *Laws*.

Price, R. A. *A Review of the Principal Questions in Morals*. An early account of nonmaterialism.

St. Augustine. *The Basic Works of St. Augustine*.

Schopenhauer, A. *The World as Will and Idea*. The philosophy of pessimism.

Spinoza, B. *Ethics*. One of the greatest classics in the field, but difficult reading.

Modern Works in Ethics

Bok, S. *Secrets*. 1983.

Carritt, E. F. *The Theory of Morals*. Oxford University Press, 1928. Defense of nonnaturalism.

Donagan, A. *A Theory of Morality*. 1977.

Gibbard, A. *Wise Choices, Apt Feelings*. Cambridge, Mass.: Harvard University Press, 1990.

Hare, R. *The Language of Morals*. Oxford University Press, 1952. A modern approach to ethical problems.

MacIntyre, A. *After Virtue*. 1981.

Nagel, T. *The View from Nowhere*. Oxford University Press, 1986.

Nowell-Smith, P. H. *Ethics*. Oxford: Blackwell, 1957. Paperback edition published by Penguin Books. Another modern approach to ethical problems.

Rawls, J. *A Theory of Justice*. 1971.

Ross, W. D. *The Right and the Good*. Oxford University Press, 1930. Deontological ethics.

Stevenson, C. L. *Ethics and Language*. New Haven: Yale University Press, 1944. Emotive theory.

Veatch, R. *A Theory of Medical Ethics*. 1981. An excellent discussion of problems in applied ethics.

Williams, B. *Ethics and the Limits of Philosophy*. Cambridge, Mass.: Harvard University Press, 1985.

Wolff, R. P. *About Philosophy*. 1976.

CHAPTER TWO

Political philosophy

Definition of "political philosophy"

It is difficult to formulate a precise definition of "political philosophy" because political philosophy seems to have no special subject matter of its own. Its main tasks are in part to describe past and existing social organizations, in which respect it seems to duplicate the findings of economics, political science, anthropology, biology, and sociology; and in part to evaluate these organizations, in which respect it is like ethics. For example, it describes the essential features of various types of governments (democracy, monarchy, fascism, etc.) and at the same time asks such questions about them as **"What is the ultimate justification for the existence of any form of government?"** The answer to such a question seems most naturally to emerge from ethical theory (e.g., a utilitarian might answer, "To provide the greatest amount of happiness for the greatest number"), and for this reason, political philosophy has sometimes been charged with being merely "applied ethics."

But even though political philosophy has intimate connections with the social sciences and with ethics, it would be a mistake to conclude that it does not have distinctive problems of its own. It deals, for example, with such issues as **"What are (or ought to be) the proper limits of government power over the members of society?" "Is it possible to have rigid control over the economic affairs of people without curtailing their political freedom?" "Should elected representatives to a legislature be allowed to vote as they see fit, or should they merely reflect the majority opinion of their constituencies?"** and so forth. No doubt, these issues in part involve moral considerations, but it should also be remembered that they pose special difficulties of their own as well.

We can further characterize political philosophy by dividing it, like ethics, into **classical** and **modern** theories. **Classical political theories may be defined, roughly, as those that offer advice for achieving an ideal society. Modern theories, on the other hand, are primarily devoted to what we have called "philosophical analysis,"** i.e., to the purpose of clarifying the meaning of this advice and of the terms we use in political discussions. Modern theories deal with such questions as "What is meant by the phrase 'universal human rights' as this appears in the Charter of the United Nations?" "What is the correct analysis of the word 'state'?" and so forth.

These issues raise questions that are often extremely subtle, but the attempts by philosophers to deal with them should not be regarded as mere quibbling. Rather, they should be looked upon as initial moves toward the clarification of problems of political philosophy, so that the merits of the advice given in classical theories can more adequately be assessed and so that we can achieve greater clarity in our discussions of present social and political problems. To illustrate this, we shall briefly indicate the practical importance of providing a correct and rigorous analysis of such a term as "the state."

Some philosophers, notably Hegel, have been greatly impressed by the fact that the state is something different from any individual who belongs to it. For one thing, he noticed that we can describe a state as "populous" but that it would be nonsense to ascribe this property to any individual citizen. From the fact that some characteristics belong to states that do not belong to individuals, **Hegel inferred that the state was a separate, distinct entity that (so to speak) had an existence of its own. He also inferred that the state was more important than any individual citizen,** since it not only united all its citizens into a particular culture but also because its persistence guaranteed the continuance of the culture even though its individual members perished. From this, it was a natural step to the glorification of the state. This glorification resulted in a political philosophy whose practical effects come down to us in such maxims as "Deutschland über alles." Philosophers who reject the doctrine that the state is more important than the individual often do so on the ground that the above analysis of the state is incorrect. They point out that what is called the state is a fictitious entity—it is merely a convenient way of talking about a group of individuals who are related in certain ways (living in a common area, having the same government, abiding by certain laws, and so forth). There is thus no separate existing thing called "the state," apart from certain individuals and the relations they have to each other. Hence to glorify the state at the expense of its citizens is simply wrongheaded philosophy. This attack is closely connected, of course, with the **democratic view that the individual is more important than the state**—and in this respect, philosophical analysis may be regarded as having the important function of showing us that certain kinds of advice ("Die for the fatherland") may be mistaken, i.e., philosophically and logically untenable. In analyzing such terms as "the state" or "inalienable rights," political philosophy reveals itself to be a special discipline that cannot be reduced entirely to the social sciences and to ethics. But for a fuller comprehension of its nature and functions, let us turn to some famous political theories and consider them in greater detail.

Plato's political philosophy

One of the most difficult and perplexing questions in political philosophy is "Who should rule?" Almost all the classical theories have dealt with it, and almost all of them can be classified according to how they attempt to answer it. If one holds that "the people should rule themselves," he is advocating democracy (John Locke);

if he holds that one man should, he may be a monarchist (Thomas Hobbes); and so forth. For Plato, this is the crucial question that every society must face, and his entire political philosophy can be understood as an attempt to answer it. Roughly, the Platonic answer is that a specially trained group of intellectuals should rule. Plato himself called his view "aristocratic." This was because he believed that the intellectuals were best fitted to rule; indeed the Greek words *ariston* and *kratos* together mean "the rule by the best." But it is perhaps a clearer characterization of Plato's political theory to designate it as **"authoritarian," i.e., as defending the granting of absolute authority to a special group for the purpose of ruling the society.**

In order to see why the question "Who should rule?" was of fundamental importance for Plato, it would be fruitful to refer to the social conditions that prevailed in Greece at that time. Greece was composed of a number of small city-states, which had autonomous governments. These states engaged in constant warfare with each other, an even with such large, powerful nations as Persia. Most of them also suffered from a great deal of internal strife. Life for the average citizen was precarious. Dissatisfied with this state of affairs, Plato attempted to outline a society that would be free from such defects, in which people could live peacefully with each other and in which everyone could develop to the fullest capacity. This led Plato to ask what an ideal society would be like if it could be brought into existence. The answer, he believed, depended to a great extent upon who ruled such a society.

In trying to describe the perfect society, Plato was greatly influenced by psychological and biological theories of the time. He assumed, accordingly, that there was an analogy between an individual person and the society in which he/she lived. The only real difference was one of size—a society was nothing but "the individual writ large." If so, the question of what an ideal society would be like could be reinterpreted as the question "What makes an ideal or perfect man?" And Plato's answers to this query came in part from the then current theories of psychology and biology.

The psychology of the day held that everyone is composed of two different ingredients: body and soul. Thus, what makes an ideal person is a matter both of physical and of psychological perfection. By "perfection" Plato here meant the same as "health." To describe such a person, therefore, is to describe someone who is physically and psychologically healthy. A person is physically healthy if he/she is not suffering from disease; but to determine when he/she is psychologically healthy is somewhat more complicated. Plato's reply was that the human soul is divided into three parts—what he called **"the rational element," "the spirited element,"** and **"the appetitive element."** The rational element is that part of a soul that enables one to reason, to argue, and to deliberate. The spirited element is what makes one courageous or cowardly and gives one strength of will. And the appetitive element consists of his/her desires and passions, such as the desire for food, drink, and sex. In terms of this threefold division of the soul, Plato argued that a person will be psychologically healthy **if**

the three parts of one's soul function harmoniously. Reason should be in command of the appetites, and the spirited element should with its strength support the dictates of reason to ensure that the appetites are kept under control. The appetites should not be repressed completely but should be satisfied only when reason says that it is appropriate. If a person is too exclusively controlled by reason, his/her emotional life will be impoverished. (James Mill, if we can trust the reports of his son, John Stuart Mill, seems to have been a man whose rational life dominated his emotional life to the detriment of the latter.) On the other hand, men are frequently dominated by their appetites: in order to satisfy their desires, they engage in conduct that is detrimental to themselves and to others. They are controlled by their passions, their feelings, and in this sense could be described as "unbalanced." In commonsense terms, a person is regarded as being "sound in mind" when he/she is not unbalanced, i.e., if all the parts of his/her soul function harmoniously, each of them playing its role without dominating the other or without being so dominated. Thus the Platonic answer to the question "What makes a healthy or ideal individual?" is "An individual is healthy if all of the elements of his/her soul function harmoniously with each other."

Since the state was nothing but the individual "writ large," the same analysis could be applied to it. An ideal state would be composed of three classes: the rulers to administer it; warriors to defend it; and all other citizens to provide the essentials of life, such as food and shelter. Each of these classes would correspond to a division of the individual soul: the ruling class as the rational element; the soldiers as the spirited element; and the other citizens as the appetitive element. Like the ideal individual, the ideal society would be one in which all these elements functioned harmoniously, with the warriors assisting the rulers to keep the rest of the citizenry under a benign but firm control. It would have no conflicts within it, and each class, by doing what it was best fitted to do, would be happy and contented.

But the fundamental problem that the establishment of such a society raises is "Who shall rule it?" since it is the rulers who ultimately will decide which individuals belong to which class; and it is they who must formulate the laws by which the society functions. Poor leadership will lead to poor laws; a wrong decision in placing someone in a given class will lead to unhappiness, or worse, to rebellion. It is thus essential that proper rulers be chosen if the society is to be ideal.

Plato gave careful directions for choosing rulers and for making sure that, once chosen, they would not work for their own advantage. All children, male and female, would be raised communally, i.e., by the state, until they were about eighteen. At that time, they would be subject to three types of tests in order to determine prospective rulers from those who were to become warriors and artisans. These tests were to take two years. They would be in part physical (since ruling imposes a severe physical strain and also because Plato believed that physical health was a prerequisite of mental health), in part intellectual, and in part moral. If a person could not withstand moral temptation, then he/she might sacrifice the interests of the society in order to satisfy his/her own interests. The individuals who passed these tests would be carefully isolated for further training—most of it intellectual. They would be schooled in the abstract sciences. They would study arithmetic, geometry, solid geometry, astronomy, and harmonics to prepare them for the abstract thinking necessary for their subsequent study of philosophy. The study of philosophy—or "dialectic," as Plato called it—would be the culmination of their theoretical preparation for the task of ruling, since it would lead them finally to a complete knowledge of the good. As we saw in discussing Plato's moral theory in the previous chapter (see page 4), once they had this knowledge, their actions would of necessity be good and they would always, therefore, make decisions which were in the best interests of the state. They would in fact be "philosopher-kings." The second part of their schooling would be practical: they would be appointed to administrative posts of a lesser order and constantly observed in the performance of their duties. Anyone who failed to achieve competence in any of the above subjects would be dismissed as a potential ruler. After all the tests had been passed, the rulers would take part in the active administration of the society. But in order to avoid any chance of their placing their private interests over the public welfare, they would not be allowed to have private families or to possess private property or wealth. Plato felt that family interests and the desire for riches were the two great obstacles to unbiased and impartial leadership. With the elimination of these motivations, which work

against the public good, the guardians were to be given absolute authority in running the society. No one from the "lower" classes would be allowed to intervene in the administration of the government; for the members of the lower groups were not experts, as the rulers were. Plato justified giving the rulers absolute powers on the ground that ruling is a skill, just as medicine is a skill. In order to rule properly, one has to be trained for it; just as in order to practice medicine properly, one requires special instruction. Thus, to allow an untrained person a voice in the direction of the government was as foolish, in Plato's eyes, as to allow an untrained person to give advice for the proper conduct of a surgical operation.

Plato's philosophy leads, by natural steps, to an antidemocratic, authoritarian philosophy. It is government for the people, but not by the people. It is assumed that the rulers will know better than the people themselves what laws and policies will be in their best interest, just as a doctor can decide better than the lay person can whether or not one needs a certain course of treatment.

Criticism of Plato

Plato's argument, when generalized, is perhaps the most powerful argument ever directed against democratic government. Let us first state it carefully and then see what can be said for and against it. The argument goes as follows:

Premise 1: Ruling is a skill.
Premise 2: People differ innately in their capabilities or abilities to acquire and to exercise various skills.

Premise 3: Those who exhibit the greatest capacity for ruling should be trained in this skill, and when trained, they ought to be made rulers of the society.

Premise 4: Because they have the greatest skill in ruling, they ought to be given absolute authority so that their laws will be put into effect.

It can be seen that the basis of the argument is that ruling is a skill. Plato proves this by appealing to common sense; do not ordinary people often decide that the ruler made a mistake in passing such and such a law? But to say that one can make mistakes is equivalent to asserting that ruling does involve knowledge, i.e., is a skill that can be learned. If one possesses knowledge, one will not commit blunders; just as the doctor who is properly trained will not make an incorrect diagnosis. If we grant this premise, then it seems that the rest of Plato's argument follows. For once we admit that some people have a greater capacity for ruling than others, is it not they who should be trained to rule? Moreover, once so trained, will they not have the greatest skill in ruling; and if so, ought they not to be given absolute authority to institute the laws they pass? Plato's point can be put very simply and can be summed up in the questions "Do you want those who are not either fitted or properly trained for ruling to rule?" and "Will they not make mistakes and thus produce the tribulations that we find in existing societies because the rulers lack the knowledge to govern?" One who opposes the Platonic theory at this point seems pinned on the horns of a dilemma. Either the trained must rule or the untrained must rule. But if the untrained rule, one will have improper government. If the trained rule, one will have authoritarian and nondemocratic government. Hence one seems committed either to nondemocratic government or to improper government. Is there any way out of this impasse?

There are several ways of rebutting the argument, some of them stronger than others. The first is to deny that ruling is a skill in the way in which medicine is. Ruling is not simply reducible to a science in the way medicine is. One who prescribes for subjects is doing something different from one who prescribes for patients. The difference might be put as follows. The physician *directs* the conduct of the patient when prescribing for him/her; the physician does not directly take account of the wishes and desires of the patient, prescribing instead a course of action that the patient must follow in order to regain his/her health. But the ruler of a society ought to have a function different from the physician's. Instead of *directing* the interests and activities of the citizenry, the ruler's function (it has been argued) is to reflect these interests and to make their achievement possible. This is a view that has been sponsored by democratic theorists. Substantially, it states that people's interests differ; there is a wide diversity in their aptitudes, abilities, desires, attitudes, and so forth. What will be good for one person may not be good for another. A good society is one that allows for the full expression of all such interests. The function of the ruler is not to direct the citizens' interests or behavior along particular lines, and thus to impose the ruler's standards upon the members of society, but only to make it possible for them to live together as far as possible in accord with their own standards. We must remember, however, a central point about Plato's moral theory, mentioned in the previous chapter. For Plato, there are absolute standards of goodness and, as we have just seen, the philosopher-king knows what these are. In ruling according to them, therefore, he is not imposing his own personal standards on the other members of society but directing their behavior in those ways he *knows* to be right. An adequate refutation of Plato's argument requires a denial that such knowledge is attainable by anyone, so that we can really show that ruling is not a science based on knowledge in the way that medicine is.

A second and more powerful objection to the Platonic argument attempts to show that the conclusion to the argument does not follow from its premises. Thus, for instance, even if it is admitted that ruling is a skill, that individuals differ innately in their abilities to exercise such a skill, and even if it is agreed that such individuals ought to be selected as rulers, it still does not follow that these rulers ought to be given absolute authority. They should always be responsible to the people for their actions, and hence authority is to be vested in the people, not in the rulers. This objection stems from the long experience of tyranny that people have suffered at the hands of absolute rulers. As Lord Acton is reported to have remarked, "Power corrupts, but absolute power corrupts absolutely." In spite of the safeguards that Plato envisaged, experience teaches us that people who are intelligent can always find ways of circumventing such safeguards and of misusing their

authority. The best way, it seems, of preventing rulers from misusing their power is to invest them with as little of it as possible. Again, we are rejecting Plato's basic beliefs that knowledge of the good is possible and that it will necessarily lead to virtuous behavior.

A third objection to Platonism is that a society run by a few will stultify the development of most of the people who live in it. This objection is closely connected with the objection that we have already referred to. The Platonic view is that rulers can be trained in such a way as to become infallible judges of what is best for the people. Modern democratic theories hold that no one is infallible; and if no one is infallible, it is pointless to have someone else making mistakes for you. There is a good reason why one should be allowed to make one's own errors. By doing so, one learns from experience; and by learning, one will become a more mature person and hence a better citizen. The Platonic conception of the relation between the ruler and the citizen is that of a parent-child relation. The ruler is essentially a parent who directs the life of the child-citizen. But if one's life is always directed by some other person, one will never grow up; one will always remain a child. The result will be a society composed of immature people who will never realize their capacities because they will never be given the responsibility to act on their own initiative. As we saw in Plato's moral theory (see page 4), in such a society most of the citizens will never be able to make their own choices and decisions; they will never achieve the kind of moral autonomy that we believe is an essential feature of mature, responsible adulthood. In short, this objection contends that self-government is essential to the development of a mature citizenry ("self-government" here meaning, of course, that the ultimate responsibility *ought* to rest with the people).

The political philosophy of Thomas Hobbes

Not all philosophers have believed that the imposition of authority is the worst possible social evil. **Thomas Hobbes is an example of a philosopher who preferred the evils of absolute power to the evils of life in a society that did not contain such an authority.** It is easy to account for the Hobbesian dread of living in a country without a powerful sovereign. Born in 1588 (prematurely, it is said, when his mother was frightened by the report of the Spanish Armada), Hobbes lived through some of the most unsettled years in English history. He witnessed the rebellion against King Charles in 1642, resulting in civil war, and finally was forced to flee to the Continent, where he remained in exile for eleven years. But he was not safe there either. In danger of assassination by his political enemies, he returned to England only to see his writings condemned as subversive. In 1662, on the threat of imprisonment, he was ordered to refrain from further publication about social and political problems. Against this background of turmoil, **it is understandable that what Hobbes feared most of all was a chaotic society.** In such a society no one's life or property or family could be safe. The only way to assure domestic tranquillity lay in *compelling* people to obey the laws of the society, and in *punishing* them if they did not. But laws are only as effective as the enforcing agency makes them. A sovereign without absolute power to enforce laws is no sovereign at all in the last analysis, according to Hobbes; for he/she cannot settle disputes which may arise among the citizenry unless he/she has such authority. In order to have a peaceful society, it is therefore required that the ruler have absolute control over it. Whatever abuses arise from his/her possession of such power, the society will nevertheless remain a peaceful one—and hence the abuses of such power are to be preferred to living in chaos.

It might be asked in questioning Hobbes's outlook, "Why should a society without an absolute authority necessarily be chaotic?" **Hobbes's answer depends almost entirely upon a psychological theory about the nature of people. According to this view, a person is by nature selfish and egoistic.** He/she is motivated by selfish desires that require satisfaction if he/she is to be happy. For example, all of his/her actions can be explained in terms of the attempt to gratify some desire, such as the desire for sex, for food, for shelter, for fame, for riches, and so forth. If people lived alone, or in small groups, this fact would not have important implications; but when they band together into larger and larger groups, it becomes of paramount significance in explaining their conduct toward each other. For two or more men may have desires that they want to satisfy, yet cannot because the desires are incompatible. Two men may desire the same woman, and therefore (assuming monogamy) both cannot be satisfied. As a result, when men herd together in large organizations, conflicts will break out among them in the effort to satisfy their desires at the expense of others. Life becomes a battle in which the strong will win—but only temporarily; for even the strong will finally succumb in the conflict (a defeated person may organize a group against the victor, for instance). This is the picture of the life of "natural man," or (as Hobbes calls it) the picture of "life in the state of nature." In a famous sentence, Hobbes sums up the horrors of such an existence, telling us that the life of man in the state of nature **"is solitary, poor, nasty, brutish, and short."**

Such a state of affairs cannot continue indefinitely if people are to survive. The development of what we call "society" is a way of ending "the war of each against all." People finally realize that in order to survive the conflicts of the state of nature, they must abandon all efforts to satisfy their egoistic impulses. **Society is thus a compromise** that people enter into; in order to achieve peace, they must give up the attempt to satisfy their desires. No person wishes to compromise; every person would rather satisfy his/her desires, but the compromise is necessary if he/she is to survive.

Hobbes is one of the most important of the political theorists who used the theory of the "social contract" to explain society and the basis of a person's obligations within society. **The compromise, or "covenant," as Hobbes calls it, consists of an agreement among people to abide by a certain set of rules, or "conventions."** These constitute what we now call the "laws of the society." People agree to abide by these laws in order to avoid being harmed in conflicts that would rage

were there no laws in existence. But, as Hobbes points out, laws are effective if, and only if, they are enforced. And the enforcing agency can do so only if it is granted absolute power. If it does not have such power, then it cannot prevent conflict. On this ground, Hobbes argues that the sovereign authority of any nation must be absolute.

Hobbes also suggests that the sovereignty be in the hands of one person—a king. In this respect, he is a monarchist. His reasons for advocating monarchy over other forms of government, such as oligarchy or aristocracy, are these: If the sovereign consisted of a group, then this group might have conflicts within itself. Thus the power of enforcement would be divided, and instead of a peaceful society, conflict would again break out. On the other hand, a monarch cannot be divided against himself. Secondly, a single ruler has more secrecy of counsel. Large groups invariably develop "leaks," and important information may filter down to the people, again causing dissension among them. Finally, a monarch's decisions are "only as inconstant as human nature, but a group has that plus the inconstancy of number." For instance, the absence or presence of a few people can alter the decision that a government will take in framing laws. This can never happen with a monarch. Furthermore, there is no reason to believe that the monarch will work for his own good at the expense of the public welfare. As Hobbes puts it, "The king is only as rich as his country."

Although the power of the monarch is to be absolute, Hobbes also wishes to grant (perhaps this is an inconsistency) the subject certain "liberties." These liberties he defines as "those things the subject may justly refuse to do even though commanded by the sovereign."

Since **sovereignty is created by a covenant, or contract, the subject retains all those natural rights that cannot be transferred by covenant.** To put it differently, since the subject has entered into the contract to preserve and protect his life, he is entitled to refuse to obey the sovereign when to do so would place his life in danger. For instance, the monarch's command to the subject to kill, wound, or maim himself, or not to resist those who assault him, can be justly disregarded by the subject. Further, he is not bound to testify against himself in a criminal action (it was around this time, incidentally, that the historical precedent of the Fifth Amendment to the U.S. Constitution was established). A command for dangerous military duty may be refused if the intention of the sovereign in issuing it is not to preserve the peace (but no man can justly object to defending his country when it is attacked by an outside aggressor). Liberty does not include the defense of any man against the sovereign. Thus rebellion is *always* unwarranted, according to Hobbes; and, similarly, protection of a criminal from the officers of the law is likewise unjust (this tenet has also come down to us from Hobbes and is embodied in most legal codes). People always have liberty to defend their lives against the sovereign; but if they are offered a pardon and refuse, then they are unjust. In a controversy with the sovereign, the subject has the right to sue (another provision that is found in American law). The obligation of the subjects to the sovereign lasts only so long as the sovereign is able to protect them: "**The end** [i.e., the purpose] **of obedience is protection.**" Thus, a prisoner captured by the enemy has the liberty to become an enemy subject if the sovereign is unable to protect him/her.

The powers of the sovereign are imposing. According to Hobbes, no subject can make a new covenant or rebel against the monarch (provided that the monarch is capable of protecting him/her). No breach of the covenant is possible by the sovereign, for according to the Hobbesian theory, **he** has not contracted with his subjects. **They** have agreed among themselves to abide by certain laws and have appointed the sovereign the agency for enforcing such laws. Once appointed, he has absolute authority. **It follows from this that a dissenting minority must now acquiesce to the dictates of the sovereign or be destroyed.** Further, no matter how the sovereign behaves, he cannot—by definition—act unjustly toward anyone. **"Just" behavior consists, according to Hobbes, in abiding by the laws of the community; but since the sovereign makes the law, whatever he does will be law;** hence in a significant sense the ruler **is above the law** and cannot violate it. The sovereign has an **absolute right to control all opinions** (for it is his decision whether or not the expression of an opinion will cause chaos in the commonwealth). Further, **he is to make all civil laws and also to adjudicate disagreements involving the law.** He has the power to make peace or war with other nations and to levy taxes in order to conduct such wars.

Criticism of Hobbes

Since the above doctrine is composed of a psychological theory about the nature of humans and also a political theory about who should govern society, each of these parts should be evaluated separately.

Some philosophers have interpreted Hobbes as attempting to give a true description of the *origin* of society. According to this interpretation, Hobbes is asserting that people originally lived in groups without laws regulating their behavior. When it was discovered that life led in this way turned into a war of each against all, people fabricated an agreement among themselves to give up the satisfaction of their egoistic impulses in order to achieve peace. When Hobbes is thus interpreted, the theory may be attacked on the grounds that there is no historical or anthropological evidence to support it. The earliest information we have about primitive humanity comes only after people had reached a fairly high degree of social organization. What life was like before societies were formed, nobody knows; hence there is no reason to accept Hobbes's imaginative portrayal of "life in the state of nature" as being accurate.

But such an interpretation of Hobbes is exceedingly superficial and misses the main significance of the theory. Hobbes is not trying to give an exact historical or anthropological account of the development of societies; instead, he is trying to give **a philosophical justification for the existence of a certain type of government.** In other words, the notion of the social contract is an analogy designed to illustrate the basis of political allegiance, to show us why we should obey the law. Whether or not people in fact behaved in this way at some early historical moment is irrelevant to the significance of his ac-

count. **What is important is his analysis of human nature and the necessity of having an absolute authority in order to curb the excesses of human nature.** In part, therefore, his account may be regarded as psychological, in part as philosophical. Let us treat each of these independently, beginning with the psychological theory.

The Hobbesian view is that people are basically motivated by the drive to satisfy their desires. From this, he infers that people are by nature egoistic. Is the inference justified? Suppose we grant that people are motivated by desire, does it then follow that all their desires are egoistic? The answer depends in part upon what is meant by saying that people are motivated by desire. To begin with, one might mean that it is the nonrational aspects of human beings that motivate them, namely, that emotions, feelings, and attitudes cause people to act as they do, not reason. So one might hold, as both Hume and Hobbes do, that although reason can reveal various alternatives for possible conduct, and also something about the probable consequences of selecting any of the alternative courses of action, reason does not itself initiate action. The choice of a given alternative or of a given course of action is—according to this view—a matter of emotion or feeling. Now if this is what one means by the phrase "people are motivated by desire," it does not follow that all desire is egoistic. People may indeed be motivated only by nonrational factors—but these, such as the feeling of sympathy, may motivate them to act for the good of others. On the other hand, one might mean by the phrase "people are motivated by desire" that people are always motivated to act for their own interests, and theirs only (regardless of whether it is reason or emotion that so motivates them). But if this is what Hobbes intends, it can be seen that from a psychological standpoint Hobbes is incorrect. People may desire to contribute to the happiness of others as well as to their own. Do we not often sacrifice our interests for the interests of our families, wives, husbands, children, country? This can be put by saying that some of our desires are "altruistic" rather than "selfish." We sometimes desire to contribute to the well-being of others, and if so, it is false that all desires are egoistic. What makes Hobbes's psychological account of human nature attractive is his vacillation between these two different accounts of motivation; but if we accept the former, egoism does not follow from it; and if we accept the latter, egoism is clearly false. Suppose, however, that we did accept the latter, i.e., the position that all people are motivated by egoistic desires (i.e., desires that work only for their own advantage), would it follow then that only the creation of an absolute authority would make for peaceful living in a society? The answer here again seems to be no.

Human interests are diversified and they change from time to time. A ruler who is given absolute power will generally not reflect this change in people's interests but will impose his/her own standards upon them. What seems required for satisfactory living in society is not that there should be *no* conflict at all within the society, **but only that the amount of conflict should not be such as to make certain other goals impossible of achievement.** The Hobbesian view would rule out all conflict, but it would also prevent the realization of many fundamental desires. A sovereign power that does not have absolute authority may yet have enough authority to eliminate most conflicts and still allow for the satisfaction of a wide range of interests. For this reason, it does not seem requisite—as Hobbes's account suggests—that absolute authority is necessary in order to achieve a good society. We may thus reject the philosophical part of the theory as well as the psychological part.

Hobbes's political philosophy is essentially an expression of defeatism: it is a "peace at any price" philosophy. On this ground alone, it would be unacceptable to people of a less submissive temper. Compare, for example, the ringing words of Patrick Henry, "Give me liberty or give me death!" or those of Thomas Jefferson, "The tree of liberty must be refreshed from time to time with the blood of patriots and tyrants!" **Hobbes, in attempting to avoid the evil effects of internecine conflict, was willing to submit to the evils of tyranny and to surrender liberty in return for security.** For him, these were the only choices that a citizen faced. But as Locke was to show, these were not the only alternatives; it was possible to have both law and order and the absence of tyranny.

The political philosophy of John Locke

It is accurate to say that **John Locke was the theoretical architect of democracy as it exists in the Western world today.** His ideas, as expressed in his famous *Second Treatise on Civil Government*, were influential in forming the political philosophy of the founders of the American and French republics. A careful study of the Declaration of Independence and the American Constitution reveals both documents to be replete with phrases such as "All men are created equal," "Life, liberty, and the pursuit of happiness," "We hold these truths to be self-evident," and so forth, which are culled almost literally from the *Second Treatise*. In using the word "men" in what follows, we shall follow the usage of Locke and the constitutional forefathers, who were thinking mainly of the male sex. In contemporary political thought, these views are usually taken as applying to men and women equally.

Like Hobbes, Locke lived in a period of great social unrest. Involved in intrigue against the king, he was forced to flee England twice during his life, once in 1675 and again in 1679. But unlike Hobbes, he did not allow such events to sour his outlook on human nature. Both in this respect and in his theory as to the proper function of government, **he is diametrically opposed to Hobbes.** Let us examine this theory in some detail.

Like Hobbes in the *Leviathan*, Locke begins the *Second Treatise* with what seems to be a historical account of the origin of government, using, like Hobbes, the notion of a social contract. The account begins with an important distinction that was undoubtedly directed at Hobbes: the distinction between life in a "state of nature" and life in a "state of war." In the state of nature, men live on the whole peaceably. They own private property, such as land, and also have private possessions, such as cattle and sheep. Men by

nature are not wholly selfish: they sometimes work for the good of others and they cooperate with each other; but sometimes, on the other hand, they do act egoistically. What property they own they may dispose of without asking the permission of anyone. The only law that governs them is what Locke calls "the law of nature." This is the provision that **"no one ought to harm another in his life, health, liberty, or possessions."** Now although life in the state of nature is as a rule peaceful, men occasionally may transgress the law of nature; they may attempt to kill someone or to steal his property. When this occurs, the injured party has the right to punish the transgressor. **There would be no reason for men to leave the state of nature and to form societies except that difficulties arise in applying punishment to those who transgress the law.** These difficulties are three in number: (*a*) Each man in the state of nature is his own judge of what is right or wrong, and this leads him to make biased judgments. One man may claim that he has been injured; another may deny it. Who is to decide the merits of the dispute? (*b*) Even where it is plain that someone has violated the law, we may not have adequate force to punish him. (*c*) Moreover, the degree of punishment will vary for the same crime. A man who steals a loaf of bread may be hanged by one group of individuals; but another man may merely be fined. In order to overcome these impairments in the state of nature, men require (*i*) a judiciary that will administer the law impartially, (*ii*) an executive who can enforce the law when it is broken, and (*iii*) a legislature that can lay down consistent and uniform laws. **Society originates** in the attempt to develop such institutions for the purpose of remedying the defects of life without organized society. Men create a society by a voluntary agreement among themselves to erect these institutions.

Now all this, Locke argues, is entirely different from a state of war. The state of war is like the Hobbesian "state of nature." It is characterized by one person or a group of people seeking absolute domination over others. In such a case, there is want of a "common judge," and there consequently exists a struggle for survival. Men will assault and maim each other, and life hangs by a thread. But it is an error to confuse this picture with that of life in the state of nature. This, according to Locke, was Hobbes's fundamental mistake. The state of nature (and for that matter even civil society) may become a state of war under certain conditions; but it is a fallacy to *identify* them. The conditions are that someone or some group will attempt to gain control *of an absolute sort* over others. When this happens, such a person creates a state of war between himself and those whom he attempts to dominate. **Opposition to him is not only justified but even required;** for if men were to submit to him, they would in effect be giving up the advantages of social life for the difficulties that they previously encountered in the state of nature. On this ground alone, monarchy may be rejected, Locke argues, since the monarch by seeking absolute domination over the citizenry has established a state of war with them.

The above account when expanded can be seen to contain most of the important elements of democratic theory as we now know it. To begin with, it stresses that **law, not force, is the basis of government. A government without law will be tyrannical.** This is characteristic of monarchy. A king can issue a decree stating that so and so is under arrest. There may have been no previous regulation to cover the alleged crime; the person may not have known that he was doing something that would evoke the wrath of the monarch. Yet the ruler can fabricate at will regulations for the purpose of imprisoning someone whom he does not like. **Such a government operates by caprice, and the society that it controls will be correspondingly unstable.** In a properly conducted government (such as a democracy), such a state of affairs will be ruled out. **Democracy is government by laws that are arrived at after long deliberation by properly chosen representatives of the people, and that are promulgated so that all men may become acquainted with them.** All of this is sharply at variance with government by decree.

Secondly, according to Locke, **there are certain areas of human conduct that are immune from governmental interference.** Locke calls these **"rights." This doctrine is the direct ancestor of the famous Bill of Rights in the American Constitution.** The Bill of Rights maintains that the government is powerless to abridge certain types of conduct of the citizenry, such as the freedom to speak, to worship as one pleases, and so forth. The main right that Locke emphasizes, however, is the right to own private property. According to him, no government can justly take away a person's private property. This is because private property is, to a great extent, the fruit of a person's own labor. In a significant sense, part of the person is invested in his property (in fact, Locke often uses the word "property" to refer to a man's life and liberty as well as to his possessions), and to take it from him is tantamount to an assault upon his physical person. Hobbes and Rousseau both strongly disagreed with this doctrine. They held that **property is a creation of society.** Before society exists, to quote Hobbes, there is "no thine or mine." A man owns what he can hold by force; he has no *right* to anything. This view, as we have seen, is strongly rejected by Locke. His outlook has had profound influence not only upon the creation of such a document as the Bill of Rights but also in the creation of the democratic belief "that all men are created equal by nature." **Locke argues that all men are equal in the sense that they have rights that are anterior to those given them by society, and since they are not given to them by society, they cannot be taken away by society either.** In our time, this doctrine has been interpreted as the view that each man, regardless of his station in life, is to be accorded **equal treatment before the law—"due process"** is an application of it.

But the most important democratic element in Locke's theory is his attitude toward government. Society is created in order to eliminate the defects of the state of nature. When men leave the state of nature in order to enter society, they thereby give up the power of punishment to an executive whom they appoint. But the crucial fact that Locke emphasizes here is that the executive is *appointed* by the people and therefore is *responsible to them.* As he says, "The whole purpose of government is to make laws for the regulation and preservation of property, and for the defense of the community against external aggression, all this only for the **public good.**" Locke's theory is that the government is, so to speak, a glorified secretary. We entrust it with powers to do those things that we find it inconvenient or impossible to do ourselves, just as we appoint a secretary to handle our affairs if we are busy. But if the secretary violates our trust (if he embezzles money, say), we can fire him; and if the government violates our trust by attempting to usurp our rightful authority, we can dismiss it. **Ultimately, the source of authority lies with the people who appoint the government. It is merely a means for carrying out their will.** Locke's way of putting the point is to say that the relationship between the people and their government is a fiduciary relationship—the people entrust the government with certain powers. But these are never entirely relinquished; they are merely delegated.

In order to safeguard the people against the concentration of power, **Locke envisaged a government divided into three branches, each of which would function as a check upon the other.** Locke called these divisions the "executive," "legislative," and "federative" branches of government. The executive and legislative branches would have had much the same function as they do in the United States government, but the duties of the federative branch consisted in carrying on negotiations with foreign powers.

Locke greatly feared the possible concentration of authority in the executive. Consequently, his theory sharply restricts its powers. To begin with, **the legislature is to be the supreme authority in the ideal**

commonwealth. It, and only it, has the power to make laws; the executive merely has the function of enforcing them. It cannot punish anyone unless this peson has violated an explicitly promulgated law, and even this punishment is to be reviewed by an impartial judiciary. Further, the executive's right to obedience stems only from the fact that it is the person or body vested with the power of the law. It has no authority of its own and cannot claim obedience except when it is enforcing the law of the society. In this respect, Locke's system resembles British parliamentary government. The executive may be removed immediately from office if the legislature, or the people, feel that he has violated the limits of the power given him.

At the same time, in order to carry out the duties of the office, the executive is to be given certain powers. For one thing, he can dismiss the legislature and also convoke it. In order to avoid the possibility that he will refuse to call it up, there is a limit upon the length of adjournment; he must call it within those limits or be dismissed. **If the executive refuses, the people have the right to use force against him.** It is not necessary to have the legislature always in session, since it is not necessary to make laws continuously; but the executive must always remain at his post, since it is always necessary to enforce the law. During those times when the legislature is not in session, should a national emergency arise, the executive is given the power to deal with it. **This is the famous doctrine of "prerogative." Prerogative is defined by Locke as "the power to act, according to the discretion of the executive, for the public good without the prescription of the law, and sometimes**

even against it." Locke admitted that the use of executive prerogative could be dangerous; but he felt in view of the other safeguards his theory provided, any serious violation could be countered by the other branches of government, and by the people.

Criticism of Locke

In the *Second Treatise,* Locke tried to show that men can live amicably together without submitting to a ruler having absolute authority. This state of affairs can be attained through government by laws. Laws arrived at openly, and widely promulgated, make for a stable society; yet they are not absolute. If these laws eventually prove to be inadequate, they can be changed. Hobbes, on the other hand, assumed that the only alternatives were anarchy or despotism; either men faced a war of each against all, or they gave up their rights to an absolute monarch. But it was Locke's genius to see that the Hobbesian theory failed in an essential respect: by giving up their rights to an absolute sovereign, men were no more secure than they had been in the state of nature; for now they were subject to the whims and caprices of the monarch. Once again, they lived precariously—but this time the danger came not from their fellow men but from their ruler. Instead of exchanging, as Hobbes thought, anarchy for stability, they merely traded one form of chaos for another.

In perceiving that stability and self-government were not incompatible, Locke became the source of inspiration for democratic societies that have existed successfully now for more than two centuries. His arguments in one form or another have frequently been repeated in the struggle for self-government. Abraham Lincoln, for example, opposed those who wished to keep the suffrage as small as possible, with words that are almost a paraphrase of the *Second Treatise*:

> A majority held in restraint by constitutional checks and limitations, and always changing easily with deliberate changes of popular opinions and sentiments, is the only true sovereign of a free people. Whoever rejects it does, of necessity, fly to anarchy or despotism. Unanimity is impossible; the rule of a minority, as a permanent arrangement, is wholly inadmissible; so that, rejecting the majority principle, anarchy or despotism in some form is all that is left.

Locke's reasons for rejecting the Hobbesian doctrine depend in part upon his theory of human nature, but they also depend in part upon the construction of an entirely new theory about political relations among people, involving such notions as **"rights," "the law," "the proper end of government,"** and so forth. In rejecting the Hobbesian account that men always act egoistically, Locke was doubtless correct. But leaving aside this psychological question, which we have already discussed, what can be said for and against the political theory of Locke?

Two main criticisms have been directed against it: one against the doctrine of "rights," and the other against the notion of majority rule. Both of these doctrines, it is held, suffer from difficulties. Let us consider the question of rights first.

The main objection to Locke's doctrine of rights is that it is based on the idea of "natural rights," i.e., rights that men enjoyed in the state of nature before the emergence of organized society. The objection is that such a claim is incomprehensible, since it is difficult to know how rights could exist before there existed a government and a system of laws to grant them and to uphold them. Examination of the term shows that it does not have this kind of *descriptive* meaning; it makes a *prescriptive* claim that men *ought* to have these rights. This must cast some doubt on the validity of Locke's argument, which seems to be based on a belief that in a state of nature men do have these rights in some literal, descriptive sense.

Even if we agree with Locke's claim and accept that these are rights that men ought to have, there are still difficulties to be overcome. For example, the rights we feel men ought to have may be incompatible with the notion of "the public good." Locke held that the purpose of government is to preserve certain rights and at the same time work for the public good. But there may be cases where we cannot do both if we are the government. Consider the famous case of a man who shouts "Fire!" in a crowded theater, knowing that there is no fire. People may be stampeded in an effort to get out of the theater; some will be injured and others may be killed. If we accept the doctrine that a man has the "right" to free speech, we cannot penalize him for speaking freely. But the exercise of free speech is obviously in this case incompatible with the public good. Such a man is a menace to the general public, and in punishing him for his action, we do so on the ground that he has acted against the good of all. But it is clear that by so doing, we abandon the view that he has the absolute right to free speech.

Democratic philosophers who have puzzled about this question have, on the whole, been willing to abandon the doctrine of rights in such cases. They have agreed that men cannot have *absolute* freedom against the state; but, they argue, from this it does not follow that the state has absolute authority over men. A more moderate interpretation of "rights" is demanded. **Rights, in this view, are those areas that can be infringed only with majority consent—when the public welfare is genuinely at stake.** Otherwise, men may remain free to speak. This more moderate doctrine qualifies Locke's views of rights but still does not condone tyranny. **It holds that what is a right is a matter of degree.** Certain areas of human behavior can be interfered with only in times of great crisis; otherwise, they must be left untouched. This still allows men very considerable freedom within society, even if it does not allow them *absolute* freedom. In any case, freedom can never be absolute. Complete absence of control is not freedom but license. The notion of freedom is perfectly compatible with the existence of restrictions on our behavior. The real problem is what kind of restriction can be justified.

The second main criticism that has been directed against Locke's political theory concerns the notion of majority rule. In raising the question "Who should rule?," **Locke, unlike Plato and Hobbes, was on the side of the people as opposed to the few.** On the whole, this doctrine has had salubrious effects. The few traditionally have been the wealthy and the privileged, and in ruling they have worked for their own interests, or for the interests of a special class, against the interests of the majority. **But what Locke never realized is that the majority itself can become a tyranny; it can prove to be a despotism as fierce as any monarch in submerging the minority.** Democratic government is not merely government by majority rule, it is also government in which *minority* rights must be equally protected. Unless this latter provision is stressed, rule by the majority becomes despotic, and democratic government turns into government that in practice is indistinguishable from an oligarchy. Locke emphasized majority rule as one of the basic tenets of democracy; and in so doing, he was right. But at the same time, **no government can be a democracy without allowing for the protection of minorities, and it was Locke's great critic, John Stuart Mill, who completed democratic theory** by emphasizing the latter facet. We turn now to a discussion of Mill.

The political philosophy of John Stuart Mill

Every student of history has been struck, at one time or another, by the paucity of civilizations that have granted political liberty to their citizens. Freedom has indeed been a precious thing. It existed only feebly in the ancient world, not at all during the Middle Ages, and even today the societies that grant it are in the minority. Most attacks upon freedom traditionally have come from the "right," from societies that have been dominated by tyrants or by small groups of people. Liberty has also been threatened from the "left," from so-called "Communist" societies. These threats, although menacing, are obvious.

But some dangers to freedom are more insidious. They come from within democracy itself. One such is the power that the majority has in a democratic state. When this power is allowed to develop unchecked, it may lead to a form of tyranny as evil as any kind of despotism, **a tyranny of the majority over minority groups.** Mill's classic essay *On Liberty* can be regarded as an attempt to find a method for eliminating this threat.

Mill begins *On Liberty* by pointing out that he is talking about **civil liberty (i.e., the limits of the power of society over the individual)** rather than about freedom of the will. The question of **authority versus liberty,** like the problem of freedom of the will, is an ancient one. Originally, "liberty" was thought of in negative terms— as the protection that the subjects had against the authority of their rulers. Political thinkers conceived of the ruler as being necessary to the well-being of society, but at the same time as being dangerous to it. He/she was necessary to defend the society against external and internal enemies; but in preserving the peace, he/she might overstep his/her legitimate authority and become a tyrant. **The aim of early libertarians, therefore, was to set limits to the power of the ruler over his/her citizens.** This was to be done in two ways: (*a*) by a doctrine of rights, which, if infringed by the sovereign, justified rebellion against him/her, and (*b*) by constitutional checks upon him/her in certain important matters—such as the declaration of war.

However, with the development of democratic societies, political theorists refused to accept the position that the ruler's interest was opposed to that of the people. The ruler, in their view, was a representative of the people, and his/her authority was revocable at their pleasure. Since the rulers were delegates of the ruled, it was not important to limit their power; and indeed, to do so was equivalent to limiting the power of the people themselves.

Mill points out that although this standpoint is theoretically correct, a study of the actual development of the institutions within democracy has shown the practical **need for certain limitations being imposed upon the powers of the government.** "Self-government" does not express the true state of the case. **The people who exercise power are not the same as those over whom it is exercised.** Not only do they develop their own interests, but they are frequently influenced by pressure groups (such as lobbyists) to work against the welfare of the people. The notion of the limitation of the power of the ruler is thus still important, even though the rulers *theoretically* are accountable to the people.

Even more dangerous than the threat to freedom from the rulers, however, is the tyranny that the majority of people may exercise over minorities. **One of the basic elements of democracy is that it allows considerable latitude to its people in behaving as they wish, in developing interests that differ from those of the majority, and in satisfying such interests.** All of this can be summarized under the name of **"individualism."** Now the majority may develop **a kind of tyranny that prevents the development of individualistic behavior.**

This tyranny can work in two ways: (*a*) **through pressure upon the government** (or originating within the government) **to** adopt laws that operate against idiosyncratic or nonconformist or dissenting individuals, even though these individuals may be harmless (e.g., the seventeenth-century "witch hunts" in New England), and (b) merely by the pressure of public opinion. Even though no law may exist, public opinion against a nonconforming individual may be so strong as to deprive him/her of the usual benefits of the society. In the first case, the doctrine of rights can to a considerable extent prevent the formation of laws that infringe upon areas an individual may regard as sacred and therefore inviolable (such as free speech, etc.), but the threat to him/her comes from public opinion. And public opinion is notoriously susceptible to error; it may reflect ancient prejudices, be dominated by superstition and tradition. Consequently, Mill argues, public opinion ought not to be a law that individuals must conform to, even an unwritten law. It should be possible in a properly run democratic society for the individual both to have the protection of the law against the prevailing sentiments of society, as well as to act freely in the face of majority opinion where no laws, but only customs, exist. The problem that faces any democratic state can be put this way: some types of behavior by certain individuals obviously cannot be tolerated (e.g., criminal behavior), and yet all nonconforming behavior must not be suppressed, so that the problem is to find the legitimate extent to which the majority can interfere in the affairs of individuals or minority groups that do not conform to the behavior of the majority. As he writes:

Like other tyrannies, the tyranny of the majority was at first, and is still vulgarly, held in dread, chiefly as operating through the acts of the public authorities. But reflecting persons perceived that when society is itself the tyrant—society collectively, over the separate individuals who compose it—its means of tyrannizing are not restricted to the acts which it may do by the hands of its political functionaries. Society can and does execute its own mandates: and if it issues wrong mandates instead of right, or any mandates at all in things with which it ought not to meddle, it practices a social tyranny more formidable than many kinds of political oppression, since, though not usually upheld by such extreme penalties, it leaves fewer means of escape, penetrating much more deeply into the details of life, and enslaving the soul itself. Protection against the tyranny of the magistrate is not enough: there needs to be protection also against the tyranny of the prevailing opinion and feeling; against the tendency of society to impose by other means than civil penalties, its own ideas and practices as rules of conduct on those who dissent from them; to fetter the development, and if possible, prevent the formation of any individuality not in harmony with its ways, and compels all characters to fashion themselves upon the model of its own. There is a limit to the legitimate interference of collective opinion with individual independence: and to find that limit and maintain it against encroachment, is as indispensable to a good condition of human affairs, as protection against political despotism.

Mill's answer to the question "What are the legitimate powers which society has over the individual?" is as follows:

The object of this essay is to assert one very simple principle, as entitled to govern absolutely the dealings of society with the individual in the way of compulsion and control, whether the means used be physical force in the form of legal penalties, or the moral coercion of public opinion. That principle is, that the sole end for which mankind are warranted, individually or collectively, in interfering with the liberty of action of any of their number, is self-protection. That the only purpose for which power can be rightly exercised over any member of a civilized community, against his will, is to prevent harm to others. His own good, either physical or moral, is not a sufficient warrant. He cannot rightfully be compelled to do or forbear because it will be better for him to do so, because it will make him happier, because, in the opinions of others, to do so would be wise, or even right. These are good reasons for remonstrating with him, or reasoning with him, or persuading him, or entreating him, but not for compelling him, or visiting him with any evil in case he do otherwise. To justify that, the conduct from which it is desired to deter him must be calculated to produce evil to someone else. The only part of the conduct of any one, for which he is amenable to society, is that which concerns others. In the part which merely concerns himself, his independence is, of right, absolute. Over himself, over his own body and mind, the individual is sovereign.

Mill put certain limitations on this principle. For one thing, he assumed that the principle would not apply to children. Being immature, they must be guided. Similarly, certain "backward states" required paternal government. These states, if allowed self-government, would merely fall into chaos. The assumption throughout is that the principle should be applied only to mature and rational persons; but unlike Plato, who believed that only a specially trained few satisfied the requirement of rationality, Mill specifically states that in his opinion, in all modern nations all citizens have arrived at this state.

In order to show how the principle would operate in practice, Mill takes as a test case the suppression of opinion and discussion. He gives three reasons why it would be wrong to suppress any opinion. Let us consider each in turn:

First, it is wrong to suppress an opinion that the majority does not approve of because the suppressed opinion may be true. We all know of cases where the majority of people hold false beliefs; if the contrary belief is suppressed, we may never learn the truth—and this in the long run may prove harmful to us (an example of a widely held belief that was false was the belief that the world was flat). **A false opinion is frequently corrected through open discussion.** A wise person is one who will listen to all sides of a question, examine the evidence for or against each, before making up his/her mind as to which side is the true one. But if the contrary opinion to the received view is never allowed to be expressed, one will never get the chance to exchange falsehood for truth.

To deny others the right to express their opinions is to assume one's own infallibility. But no one is infallible, and if so, it is always possible that the opinion one holds in a given case is mistaken. Some might object to this point on the ground that in actual practice it is necessary for people to assume that they are not mistaken in pursuing a given course of action. If one believes that it is necessary to wage war against an aggressor, should one suspend his/her judgment? This would be impractical. Mill's answer to this objection is one of the famous remarks in the history of liberalism. He says:

There is the greatest difference between presuming an opinion to be true because, with every opportunity for contesting it, it has not been refuted, and assuming its truth for the purpose of not permitting its refutation. Complete liberty of contradicting and disproving our opinion, is the very condition which justifies us in assuming its truth for purposes of action; and on no other terms can a being with human faculties have any rational assurance of being right.

The second argument that Mill gives for not suppressing contrary opinion is this. Let us assume that the contrary opinion is mistaken and that we do in fact hold the true view. Nevertheless, even a true opinion can be held in different ways: it can be held openly by a mind that is always willing to change its point of view depending upon the evidence, or it can be held as sheer prejudice. Now when we hold the true opinion but are not willing to listen to contrary opinions, we hold it in the wrong way—as a prejudice. To hold an opinion in this way may be harmful, for **by reflecting upon all the arguments against it, and by thus being forced to think of ways of rebutting them, we actually come to understand our opinion more fully.** A person who fights for democracy but does not understand what he/she is fighting for could in other circumstances be fighting against it. He/she is merely reflecting the majority sentiments of the society he/she lives in without making any attempt to justify the validity of such sentiments. He/she thus may be fighting for democracy, but he/she may be fighting for it for the wrong reasons or, what is even worse, for no reason at all, except that his/her society commands him/her to do so. All this is an obstacle to future progress; **what we require in a democratic society is an enlightened individual, one who will be mature and responsible because he/she reflects upon the issues that face him/her.** If he/she does not consider the opposing opinion seriously, he/she cannot become such a person; and this is why we must

not suppress the opposite point of view without giving it a chance to be heard.

Mill writes on this point:

To abate the force of these considerations, an enemy of free discussion may be supposed to say, that there is no necessity for mankind in general to know and understand all that can be said against or for their opinions by philosophers and theologians. That it is not needful for common men to be able to expose all the misstatements or fallacies of an ingenious opponent. That it is enough if there is always somebody capable of answering them, so that nothing likely to mislead uninstructed persons remains unrefuted. That simple minds, having been taught the obvious grounds of truths inculcated on them, may trust to authority for the rest, and being aware that they have neither knowledge nor talent to resolve every difficulty which can be raised, may repose in the assurance that all those which have been raised have been or can be answered by those who are specially trained to the task.

Conceding to this view of the subject the utmost that can be claimed for it by those most easily satisfied with the amount of understanding of truth which ought to accompany the belief of it; even so, the argument for free discussion is in no way weakened. For even this doctrine acknowledges that mankind ought to have a rational assurance that all objections have been satisfactorily answered; and how are they to be answered if that which requires to be answered is not spoken? Or how can the answer be known to be satisfactory, if the objectors have no opportunity of showing that it is unsatisfactory? If not the public, at least the philosophers and theologians who are to resolve the difficulties, must make themselves familiar with those difficulties in their most puzzling form; and this cannot be accomplished unless they are freely stated, and placed in the most advantageous light which they admit of. The Catholic Church has its own way of dealing with this embarrassing problem. It makes a broad separation between those who can be permitted to receive its doctrines on conviction, and those who must accept them on trust. Neither, indeed, are allowed any choice as to what they will accept; but the clergy, such at least as can be fully confided in, may admissibly and meritoriously make themselves acquainted with the arguments of opponents, in order to answer them, and may, therefore, read heretical books; the laity, unless by special permission, find them hard to be obtained. This discipline recognizes a knowledge of the enemy's case as beneficial to the teachers, but finds means, consistent with this, of denying it to the rest of the world: thus giving to the *élite* more mental culture, though not more mental freedom, than it allows to the mass. By this device, it succeeds in obtaining the kind of mental superiority which its purposes require; for though culture without freedom never made a large and liberal mind, it can make a clever *nisi prius* advocate of a cause. But in countries professing Protestantism, this resource is denied; since Protestants hold, at least in theory, that the responsibility for the choice of a religion must be borne by each himself; and cannot be thrown off upon teachers. Besides, in the present state of the world, it is practically impossible that writings which are read by the instructed can be kept from the uninstructed. If the teachers of mankind are to be cognizant of all that they ought to know, everything must be free to be written and published without restraint.

The third reason for requiring that the opposite opinion to our own should not be suppressed without being heard first is that even if it is neither wholly true nor wholly false, it may contain elements of the truth. Political theories are extremely complex. A political theory we do not agree with may be mainly in error, yet it may contain elements of the truth within it, and if we do not hear such an opinion, we may lose the opportunity to discover even this much truth.

Criticism of Mill

As we have remarked previously, **Mill can be regarded as completing democratic doctrine.** Locke set down the main elements in democratic theory, such as government by promulgated law, the doctrine of "natural rights," and, most important of all, the rule by the majority of the people. Mill added to this framework the proviso that the minority must be protected against possible tyranny by the majority. Since he did not accept the doctrine of natural rights, he attempted to justify limitations on the power of the majority on utilitarian grounds. Roughly his argument is that **interference in personal matters will in the long run prove harmful to a democratic society. The development of individual initiative and a mature citizenry will both be prevented if the majority's likes and dislikes are allowed to become so powerful that they act as unwritten laws.** This doctrine, since the publication of the essay *On Liberty*, has been accepted by most democratic theorists; but it has also been attacked on the grounds that it is impossible to put into practice.

Mill held that the majority could legitimately interfere in the affairs of the minority only when minority behavior proved harmful to the fabric of society. But this raises the difficult problem: How can we tell when such behavior will or will not be harmful? Ultimately, these critics assert, the choice will rest with a majority decision, expressed through the framing of laws by an elected legislature. Thus, in the last analysis, minority safeguards will always crumble under attack by the majority. From a standpoint of realistic politics, the minority is only as safe as the majority will let them be; and if so, there is no area of human conduct that is (or even ought to be) immune from such interference.

Had Mill lived to answer this objection, he might have agreed with it in part. If the majority feels that an individual or group of individuals is behaving in a way that is harmful to society, it can pass laws that will restrict such behavior. Mill does not mean to deny the rightful authority of the majority in a democratic society. For example, it is necessary for the protection of the majority that we pass laws against the sale of adulterated food and drugs. But even in such cases, he would argue, the burden of proof is upon the majority to show that their interference is legitimate. They cannot justly interfere simply because they do not approve of an individual's conduct; they must show further that it is harmful to society. If this cannot be shown, the minority ought to be allowed to behave as it wishes. In practical terms, what Mill's philosophy reduces to is that **in any legal issue between an individual and the state, the burden of proof for showing that an individual's behavior is undesirable always rests upon the state, not upon the individual.** This presumption, once accepted (as it has been in Great Britain and the United States), will provide the individual with considerable security against majority interference, even if it does not guarantee him/her complete immunity.

The history of political philosophy can fruitfully be looked at in terms of the question "Who should rule?" Plato, Hobbes—and in fact most political theorists up to Locke—argued that individuals or special groups should rule. Locke, on the other hand, gave powerful arguments in favor of rule "by the people," where this is interpreted as rule by the majority. Mill, like Locke, believed that the majority should rule because on the whole they would be less threatening to the freedom of humankind than any single ruler or group; but even within democracy, checks must be put upon the rule of the majority to safeguard personal liberty. We now turn to a philosopher who, like Mill and Locke, wished to see the "people" rule—Karl Marx—but whose philosophy has had practical consequences that are inimical to freedom.

The political philosophy of Karl Marx

Karl Marx was born in Trier, Prussia, in 1818 and was reared in a comfortable, fairly conventional upper-middle-class atmosphere, which proved a far cry from the conditions of economic hardship in which he spent most of his mature years. He was sent to the universities of Bonn and Berlin and graduated with distinction, receiving the degree of doctor of philosophy. In the normal course of events, given this background, he might have been expected to pursue an academic career—and accordingly to have vanished into history in a cloud of cross-references and footnotes, as is the fate of most distinguished professors. But such was not the case. Even at that early date, Marx was regarded as being too radical for academic life, and consequently he chose to take a job on the *Rheinische Zeitung*, a left-wing newspaper that strongly opposed the policies of the government. When the newspaper was suppressed, Marx left Germany and went to live first in Paris and later in

Brussels—until the Revolution of 1848, when he returned to Cologne. When the revolution failed, Marx again departed from Germany, this time settling in London, which became his home for the remainder of his life.

In England, Marx renewed his friendship with Friedrich Engels, whom he had known in Europe and who had been his collaborator in the publication of the *Communist Manifesto* in 1848. Engels's father was a prominent manufacturer of cotton goods in Manchester and—as is so often the case with fathers who have radical sons—was highly conservative. Engels worked for his father, and with part of his income supported Marx, who at that time was living in incredible poverty. In 1870 Engels moved from Manchester to London, and with Marx he founded the International Workingmen's Association (sometimes known as the First International)—an organization designed to better the lot of working people. Marx died in 1883, and Engels—working from Marx's notes—completed the final volumes of *Das Kapital*, Marx's political masterpiece. Engels died in 1895.

Marx's political philosophy is a highly complex doctrine that contains at least three distinct elements. The first is a **metaphysics**, which Marx inherited from Hegel and in which **he attempts to prove that political, social, and economic events are to be understood in terms of certain general laws of history, called "the dialectic."** The second is an **economic theory**, in which Marx offers a **defense of socialism as opposed to capitalism;** and the third is an **ethic**, which stresses **human values as opposed to the values allegedly existing in material goods.** Let us consider each of these in turn, beginning with the metaphysical part of the doctrine.

Marx's metaphysics: the influence of Hegel. Georg Wilhelm Friedrich Hegel was, by all odds, the most important German philosopher of the nineteenth century. Like most young intellectuals of the period, Marx was greatly influenced by his writings, especially his writings on the philosophy of history. Later on in his life, Marx was severely to criticize Hegelianism, but he never really succeeded in shaking off its hold on him. Indeed, to a considerable extent, Marx's political doctrines can be understood only in the light of Hegel's metaphysics, as we shall now attempt to show. Roughly, the influence was this: **Marx believed that Hegel had found a general historical law, called the "dialectic," but he thought that Hegel's use of it was metaphysical rather than scientific.** Marx accepted the existence of the dialectic, but he attempted to make it materialistic by explaining the historical process in economic rather than metaphysical terms and by **applying it to classes rather than to nations. He thus tried to explain history in terms of the struggle between classes** instead of the struggle between nations, as Hegel had done.

As we have intimated above, the essential notion in Hegel's works—a notion that Marx utilized but applied differently—is what Hegel called the "dialectic." Hegel had borrowed the term from Plato but gave it a much broader signification. In Plato, "dialectic" is regarded as a certain kind of logical process. It is a method of argumentation, employing what modern logicians call the "method of the contrary case." It is used for the purpose of eliciting from someone to whom it is applied, information that he possesses but of which he may not be aware. Thus, by questioning a slave boy, Meno, who has never studied geometry, Socrates elicits from him certain theorems of Euclid, or again, by questioning Cephalus, Polemarchus, and others in the *Republic*, Socrates attempts to extract from them a true account of the nature of justice. The method operates as follows: Someone proposes a thesis about the nature of justice. For example, the *Republic* opens with Cephalus suggesting that "justice" means the same as "telling the truth and paying one's debts." The next step in applying the method is to find a contrary case to the thesis, i.e., a case that we would ordinarily say involved justice but did not involve telling the truth. This is called by Hegel the **"antithesis."** The reconciliation of thesis and antithesis produces a **synthesis** that itself becomes a new thesis at a more advanced level. By continually applying this method, by proposing **thesis and antithesis,** a true account of the nature of justice is finally arrived at—an account that **encompasses and reconciles** both thesis and antithesis.

To give an example of this process, taken from the *Republic*, consider the following: Cephalus proposes that "justice" means "telling the truth and paying one's debts." Socrates then produces a contrary case. He points out that if you have borrowed a weapon from a friend who subsequently goes out of his mind and demands it back, you would not feel it right or just to give it back to him. Justice in such a case requires that you ought not to pay your debt. If so, justice is sometimes compatible with not paying one's debts and

the thesis that "justice" means "paying one's debts" is false. We are thus forced to produce a new definition that will include both the original thesis and the contrary case. When found, this will be a **synthesis** of the original definition and the objection to it.

For Hegel, the term "dialectic" has much the same meaning that it has in Plato. **It is a logical process that proceeds from thesis to antithesis, and to a synthesis that combines them both.** But Hegel regards the dialectic as more than merely a logical process in the sense in which verbal argumentation is a logical process. For him, it is an **actual process that events in the world follow. All change, especially historical change, takes place in accordance with the law of the dialectic: a thesis is produced, it develops an opposition (its antithesis), a conflict between them ensues, and the conflict is resolved into a synthesis that includes both thesis and antithesis.**

Hegel, as we have mentioned, thought that history could best be understood by observing the development of nations in the light of the dialectic. A given nation can be regarded as occupying a position in the dialectic that is analogous to the position occupied in an argument by the thesis or hypothesis that the argument is supposed to establish. As the nation develops, it produces opposition to itself. An opposing nation may be regarded as its antithesis. Finally, the two conflict, and from the struggle there emerges a new civilization that is of a **higher order** than either of the previous ones. **It synthesizes what is of most value in each.** This new nation now becomes a new thesis, which in turn will develop its antithesis, and so forth, *ad infinitum*. Furthermore, according to Hegel, this is a process that is leading to perfection. It is through this process that a state progresses toward the realization of what he calls its "spirit." The end or aim of the development of the essential nature of every state is what he calls "the idea" or "the absolute idea." Thus, for Hegel, the dialectical process is a spiritual or metaphysical process.

Hegel believed that in discovering the dialectic he had discovered a *necessary law* of nature. It is not merely the case that nations sometimes oppose each other; but it is *logically necessary that by its very nature* every nation will ultimately breed its opposite, will conflict with it, and then proceed through the remainder of the dialectic. In short, **the course of history is determined by the dialectic, and nothing can alter this course.** People suppose that through social action they can change the course of history, but they are simply mistaken through a lack of historical knowledge. They are merely pawns of historical necessity—it is really the dialectic that controls the course of events.

Marx accepted Hegel's analysis of historical change as proceeding in accordance with the dialectic. But he did not like the metaphysical explanation of this process, and he thought that Hegel's application of the dialectic to nations was essentially superficial. Marx preferred a materialist dialectic; he preferred to explain the dialectical process of history in economic rather than metaphysical terms. The reason why nations change is that the classes within the nation begin to oppose each other. The history of the world should be regarded not as a history of the rivalry between states but, more fundamentally, as a history of the rivalry between classes.

Barnett Savery has put this point very well. He writes:

The Marxists explain the doctrine of opposites in the following way: everything contains two main opposing forces, one is called the thesis, the other is called the antithesis. These two forces destroy each other, but from the destruction arises a new situation which is called a synthesis. Eventually, this synthesis breaks down into its opposites—and we have a new thesis and a new antithesis. And then out of these opposing forces arises a new synthesis—and so on. The Marxists, as we shall indicate, make use of this idea in order to demonstrate that communism, as a society, is ethically superior to all previous existing societies.

The historical king-state society, according to the Marxists, broke down into its opposites—the king-rulers, on the one hand, and the dispossessed and slaves on the other hand. From the struggle between these opposites, a synthesis was formed, and the feudalistic society came into being. Feudalism, then, broke down into its opposing forces, the lords and the serfs; and this struggle was synthesized and modern capitalism was born. And, now, the Marxists claim that capitalism has broken down into its opposites; the employers, on the one hand, and the employees, on the other hand. The new society, according to the Marxists, will be Marxian socialism. The Marxists argue that each new society is ethically superior to the society that existed before. Feudalism, they claim, is superior to the king-state; capitalism to feudalism; and communism to capitalistic societies.

This aspect of Marxism indicates what is meant by the class struggle; it is the doctrine of opposites as it reveals itself in societies. The Marxists claim that they do not create the class struggle; they claim, rather, that they merely show its existence, and then make use of it in order to foster the growth of communism. The additional belief of the Marxists, that each distinctly new society is ethically superior to the old social forms, makes excellent propaganda for

Marxism. Undoubtedly, many people become adherents to communism because they believe that they are working for a world that is better than anything that has ever existed.

Let us show in somewhat more detail how Marx applied the dialectic to classes, and what inferences he drew from such an application. To begin with, Marx felt that every person belongs to a certain socio-economic group within the society. Such a group is called a **"class."** The system of classes that a given culture has is completely determined by the **economic means and conditions of production** in the culture. Thus, each period of economic development has a corresponding class system. For instance, during the period of hand-mill production, feudalism was the system of classes that prevailed. When hand-mill production was replaced by steam-mill production, capitalism replaced feudalism. Capitalism is an economic system with three main social classes: those who own or control the means of production, called by Marx the **"capitalists"**; those who are entirely dependent for their livelihood upon the earnings they get while working for the owners—the working class; and certain other groups, such as small business people or white-collar workers (lawyers, doctors, professors, etc.), who may not fit exactly into either scheme—the middle class.

Marx's Thesis Was That All Class Relationships Are Independent of People's Wills, and in Fact Are Really Determined by the Prevailing Economic System

People think they can choose the class they wish to belong to, but such opinions are merely self-deceptive. **Classes are really determined by the means of production,** and the class a person falls into will depend upon where one stands relative to the means of production. Since the means of production themselves follow the pattern of history, i.e., the dialectic, every such means will generate its own opposition and this will lead to a conflict. The conflict will itself engender new relations between people and the means of production, with a resulting change in the class arrangement of the culture. Classes being determined by their relation to the means of production, they, too, will be subject to the domination of the dialectic. The result is that history can be succinctly described as taking the course that class conflict takes.

To illustrate what Marx means by class conflict, let us consider a specific example, the rise of socialism due to class conflict within capitalistic society.

According to Marx, because of technological advances in a capitalist society, there will be a constant increase in the productivity of that society. This tendency toward an increase in productivity means that there will be a corresponding increase of wealth in the class that owns the means of production. At the same time, the conditions of life in the working class will become worse, and instead of having more money the workers will have less. Finally, in fact, most of the money in the society will be concentrated in the hands of the few who own the means of production. The intermediate classes will be wiped out, and capitalism will present a picture of two classes highly opposed to each other—a small but very wealthy class ("the bourgeoisie") and a large but indigent working class ("the proletariat"). Tension and hatred will develop between these classes, and finally a revolution will take place, one that will lead to a **classless society,** in which there is no exploitation of the worker. This is socialism as Marx pictured it. The steps of the dialectic are easily perceived in this picture: Capitalism presents a thesis—that one ought to work in order to realize a profit. The thesis, if followed, leads to a state in which a few own the means of production and everyone else is subject to the control of those few. But if followed, the thesis produces antagonism between the large, indigent class of workers and the small capitalist class. This is the stage of the dialectic called the "antithesis." Finally, an open conflict breaks out and the capitalist class is submerged. A new classless society arises (the "synthesis").

We may summarize Marx's metaphysics as follows: Marx accepted the Hegelian doctrine that world history follows a pattern of opposing forces, called the "dialectic." Hegel believed that the pattern primarily applies to nations, but Marx showed that it applies to classes. Classes are determined not by people's wills or inclinations but by the means of production existing in that particular culture. Classes produce their own oppositions, leading to conflicts and finally to an overthrow of the particular class system. In the case of capitalism, the overthrow will lead to a classless society, or socialism, in which the means of production will be controlled by the workers (i.e., everyone in such a society).

We have designated Marx's theory, as adumbrated above, a **"metaphysical" theory because it rests upon the thesis that all change takes place through conflict, and moreover, conflict of a curiously logical sort.** Marx himself, of course, believed that he had discovered a scientific law that applied to classes and that explained history. He thought this law was scientific because it referred to materialistic considerations (such as economic factors) in explaining the movement of events, whereas Hegel thought that nations were motivated by what he called "spirit." Marx rejected an explanation in terms of "spirit" as unsatisfactory and, instead, attempted to give a "hardheaded" account of the nature of change. But, as we have shown, his explanation, like Hegel's, may itself be charged with being metaphysical, **since it deduces the nature of change from purely logical considerations.** In terms of this doctrine, Marx predicts the coming of a classless or socialist society. But even though this prediction is based upon metaphysical assumptions, at least some of Marx's attack upon capitalism is based upon a careful descriptive account of how capitalistic societies have worked. This attack attempts, on economic grounds rather than on logical or metaphysical ones, to show that capitalistic societies will inevitably collapse. Let us turn now to Marx's economic theory to see how it reinforced his metaphysical views with regard to the prediction that capitalism must inevitably fail and give way to a socialist economy.

Marx's Economic Theory: The Attack Upon Capitalism

The basic notions in Marxian economic theory are **the labor theory of value, the theory of surplus value, and the concen-**

tration of capital, plus the coming of socialism as a result of that concentration. Let us begin with the labor theory of value.

The labor theory of value was not original with Marx. It was propounded by many famous economists who preceded him, among them, for instance, David Ricardo and Adam Smith. The point of the theory is to determine what is meant by "economic value." Marx's version runs something like this: There is a distinction between the **"use value"** of a commodity and its **"exchange value."** A commodity may be useful to us, but it may have no value if we try to exchange it for something else. For example, air has use value: we require it in order to live. But if we try to exchange it for a book, no one will accept it. This is because it is readily available to anyone who wants it. What makes a commodity have exchange value is that it can be obtained only at some cost. This cost is what Marx calls its **"economic value."** More basically, what makes a commodity costly is the amount of **labor power** that goes into its production. In order to save labor power, people will accept for exchange items that require labor power in order to be produced. Thus "economic value" is defined in terms of "the quantity of labor necessary for its production in a given state of society, under certain social average conditions of production, with a given social average intensity and average skill of the labor employed."

The Theory of Surplus Value

According to Marx, **the ordinary worker, lacking capital, is forced to sell his/her labor, and thus in a sense him/herself, as a commodity.** Roughly, the amount of money that an employer pays to the worker is an estimation of the economic value of the laborer regarded as a commodity that the employer must purchase. But the laborer normally produces items having much more economic value than is represented by the wages he/she receives. The difference between the amount of economic value he/she produces and the amount he/she receives for his/her work is called **"surplus value"** by Marx. The employer does not pay him/her for this—in fact, the employer takes the surplus value of a laborer's efforts and utilizes it in various ways, the most important of which is profit. Thus, according to Marx, workers actually produce the wealth through the amount of labor they contribute, but the capitalists take a considerable amount of it without rewarding the worker correspondingly. This is the source of their profit.

The theory of surplus value allows us to pinpoint the source of conflict between capitalist and worker. The capitalist wishes to accumulate as great a profit as possible. This will be possible only if he/she pays the lowest possible wages and sells his/her commodities for the highest possible price. On the other hand, the worker's demands are exactly the opposite: to receive the highest possible wages for his/her work and to buy produced goods as cheaply as possible. Thus, within capitalism we have a fundamental inconsistency, and strife between these classes is unavoidable.

The Concentration of Capital and the Coming of Socialism

According to Marx, capitalism as an economic system enjoins one to seek the highest possible profits from his/her investment. For the capitalist, this means engaging in constant competition with other business people, since profit depends upon the amount of goods that can be sold. Now in order to sell a large volume of goods, it is necessary to sell them as cheaply as possible. In effect, this means that one must constantly try to undersell his/her competitor. But since the cost of production is relatively similar for goods of similar quality, the only place where an employer, in the long run, can significantly cut his/her costs lies in his/her using the most inexpensive labor. As the power of the capitalist grows, this becomes even more important. For after freezing small business people out of business by underselling them, he/she will finally be left in competition with a few large-scale producers like him/herself. At that stage, in order to meet the competition and in order to acquire greater and greater profits, he/she will have to pay the worker less and less. He/she will demand a greater surplus of the worker's productivity. The result of this tendency, according to Marx, is that in the later stages of a capitalist society, the worker will become increasingly poorer and the capitalist increasingly richer. Tension is bound to develop between them when the worker realizes that he/she is being exploited (this realization is called "becoming class conscious")—and finally conflict will break out. As a consequence of this conflict, the worker will take over the means of production, and a new thesis will be inaugurated—the age of the classless society, or socialism.

Apart from the defects in capitalism that the above economic analysis indicates, there is an even more serious fault to be found with it. According to Marx, **capitalism engenders relations among people that are ethically immoral ones. Humanity disappears in the treatment of people by each other and is replaced by an inhuman drive for profits.** Thus, in arguing that capitalism is not a workable system, Marx is in part basing his contention upon an ethical theory, as well as upon economic and metaphysical doctrines. Let us consider briefly his views on morality in concluding this section.

Marx's Ethical Views

Marx maintains that **industry and technological discoveries develop much more rapidly than do the techniques for controlling them.** As he puts it:

> In our days everything seems pregnant with its contrary; machinery gifted with the wonderful power of shortening and fructifying human labor, we behold starving and overworking it. The newfangled sources of wealth, by some strange weird spell, are turned into sources of want. The victories of art seem bought by the loss of character. At the same pace that mankind masters nature, man seems to become enslaved to other men or to his own infamy. Even the pure light of science seems unable to shine but on the dark background of ignorance. All our inventions and progress seem to result in endowing material forces with intellectual life, and in stultifying human life into a material force.

Thus, even though industrial expansion should have made it possible for people to live more comfortably together, with greater security, exactly the opposite is taking place. The capitalistic system, in order to maintain profits for those who own the means of production, induces one war after another; children are forced into labor; the conflict between classes is intensified. All this, according to Marx, is due to two factors: to what he calls **"self-alienation"** and to what he calls **"fetishism."** Socialism will remedy both. "Self-alienation" is a term Marx uses to describe a person's plight in the modern industrial world. Instead of finding industry helpful, instead of finding that it improves people's relations with each other, exactly the opposite has occurred. **People are cut off from other people, are isolated and made fearful and insecure.** This is not merely alienation from the world but *self-alienation*; for it is a thing of people's own making. A person creates a highly technical world, but he/she cannot control it—and thus **he/she alienates him/herself from all those things that he/she prizes most and that this technology was designed to achieve for him/her: security, comfort, friendship, leisure, culture, and so forth. Self-alienation is accompanied by fetishism, the worship of the products of labor.** For instance, people produce motor cars by their labor; and once having produced them, people become ruled by such inanimate things. It is the *things* that are given value, not the *people* who create them. As Marx writes:

> The object which labor produces, its product, is encountered as an *alien entity*, a force which has become independent of its producer. The more the worker toils the more powerful becomes the alien world of objects he produces to oppose him, and the poorer he himself becomes.

The most terrible effect of capitalism has been to depersonalize the relations between people—to make people more like machines and machines more like people. It is this tendency that Marx is arguing against. Socialism, he feels, will not only remedy the economic affairs of people but introduce a new morality as well—a morality based upon human values, not upon machine values.

With these remarks, we conclude our exposition of Marx's political philosophy. Let us now turn, briefly, to some critical remarks.

Criticism of Marx

As we have pointed out, political philosophies may be classified according to how they answer the question "Who should rule?" As we have seen, Plato and Hobbes are advocates of the doctrine that a few should rule. Marx, on the other hand, like Mill and Locke, is unashamedly on the side of the many. **Marx's political philosophy can without distortion be interpreted as holding that in a capitalistic society a few will rule, i.e., those who own the means of production, and that this is basically wrong. In stressing that it is the majority that is important, Marx is firmly in the tradition of liberal and democratic philosophers.** Further, many contemporary thinkers are inclined to agree with **Marx's ethical outlook, which lays stress upon the importance of human values as opposed to the world of the machine that modern industry has created.**

The main criticisms of Marxist theory are aimed at its philosophy of history and at its economic theory. The Marxist conception of history has been attacked on two fronts. In the first place, it is argued that there can be no justification for any attempt to establish broad general laws of history. This may be a useful way of **understanding the past,** but it cannot provide any valid basis for **predicting the future,** as Marx tries to do. Marx sees historical development as an inevitable process that will ultimately lead in all states to the establishment of the classless society. There must be serious doubt about the validity of this kind of interpretation of history and of the claim that the process will stop at that point. The second criticism of his philosophy of history is leveled at the introduction of a **moral evaluation** of these stages of change. Each one, Marx tells us, is **ethically superior** to the one that precedes it, and the final stage, the classless society, is perfection. In other words, this is a theory of historical **progress** rather than of mere historical **change.** There must be some standard by which we evaluate this progress so that to speak in this way is to appeal to an absolute moral criterion that Marx himself will not admit the validity of in his other discussions of morals. For elsewhere he tells us that moral values are not expressions of "eternal truths" but are relative to the society in which they are held. The objective ideals of his conception of history are not compatible with his subjective view of social morality. This inconsistency lies at the very root of Marxism.

Marxist economic theory has been criticized by defenders of capitalism on empirical grounds, that is, by an appeal to facts that seem to disprove it. **According to Marx, the capitalistic system will inevitably produce periodic depressions and will finally culminate in the accumulation of wealth by the owners of the means of production, and in the increasing misery of the workers.** All this will lead to

revolution and to the development of a socialistic, classless society. Now, defenders of capitalism attack this thesis on two counts. **They point out that the prediction of increasing misery in capitalistic societies has not been confirmed.** In fact, the lot of the worker is better than ever. He/she works fewer hours, has more money, and in general lives on a higher standard than workers did a century ago. Instead of producing lower standards of living and instead of exacerbating the relation between employer and employee, capitalism has produced both higher standards of living and better relations between owner and worker. Its defenders also point out that **capitalism has shown itself amazingly inventive** in solving difficulties that appear within it. Such developments as the growth of trade unions, antitrust laws, and social security measures have all proved beneficial in contributing to the economic stability of capitalistic societies. For example, trade unions have thwarted the tendency to sell labor power more and more cheaply by fixing the rates for the use of labor time. Such measures as these, according to critics of Marx, will constantly be discovered by capitalistic countries, and hence the prediction of increasing misery will not be fulfilled.

The Marxian answer to both of these charges is the following: Although the standard of living in some capitalistic countries is higher than it used to be, this is not true of all capitalistic countries. Against the view that capitalism is imaginatively able to solve its problems, Marxists argue that many of the measures that are used are socialist measures. For example, deficit spending in a time of crisis is a socialist device for avoiding a depression; the growth of trade unions in order to restrict the size of the labor pool is likewise another instance of tampering with the normal development of capitalism. Marxists say that such devices as these are necessary in order to save the system from destroying itself.

At the beginning of the 1990s, political events in the so-called "Iron Curtain countries"—East Germany, Hungary, the former Soviet Union, Czechoslovakia, Romania, and what was called "Yugoslavia"—have had an enormous impact on the debate about Marxism. Three negative criticisms of the theory emerge from these events. First, it has been argued that the Marxist thesis that eventually the state will wither away and be replaced by a classless society has now been shown to be false. Since 1917 a large number of societies have been organized on so-called "Marxist lines," yet these have invariably been ruthless dictatorships in which human rights have been suppressed. Indeed, as recent events have shown, because such so-called "Marxist societies" failed to allow for democratic participation of the people in government, they became increasingly unpopular. In the late 1980s and early '90s, that unpopularity reached a boiling point and finally exploded, and the governments of these societies were overthrown and replaced by non-Marxist, capitalist, and democratically oriented governments—Hungary and Russia being prime examples. The Marxist notion that the dictatorship of the proletariat would lead to increased freedom has also been shown to be false, and indeed just the opposite has occurred. In a political sense, Marxism as a rubric to mobilize the majority of the people has failed. Instead, na-

tionalist, democratically oriented urges have been the driving forces behind these movements.

Second, it is argued, Marxism as a theory has always underestimated the driving force of nationalism and of ethnic rivalries and identifications. It is these, rather than the identification with one's economic class, that have motivated the changes in the countries mentioned above. The internecine conflicts that have risen in Yugoslavia, the Soviet Union, and Czechoslovakia have more to do with nationalist yearnings and tensions than with Communist ideals.

The third criticism is that Marxist economics, as practiced by these governments, has uniformly been unsuccessful in practice. All the former Communist countries, such as East Germany, the former Soviet Union, and Hungary, fell increasingly further and further behind in competition with the West. People in those countries endured an increasingly poorer standard of living. The Soviet Union, after three quarters of a century of planned economic activity, could not produce enough food to feed its population, while the capitalist, democratically organized nations, such as the United States, Canada, England, and much of Western Europe, have managed to produce more food and commodities of a higher quality than they can sell.

Some Marxist theorists respond to these charges by insisting that one cannot judge the merits of Marx's theory by these political events. They claim that the self-proclaimed Communist countries, such as the former Soviet Union, East Germany, etc., have never really followed Marx's precepts. They insist that better models of

Marxist theories are to be found in countries where socialism has taken the democratic political form envisaged by Marx—such as in the Scandinavian countries, in Israel, and in such Western nations as France and Italy, where socialist ideals have indeed been implemented.

Among philosophers today, these differing evaluations of Marxism have been vigorously defended and attacked. Some theorists now argue that Marxism is the most dangerous view ever put forth, while others would defend it and say that it has never been tested in its pure form. In between, there are many who would say that Marx is important mostly for his negative insights into capitalism—pointing out its faults in perceptive ways and also indicating some of the ways these can be eliminated or minimized—but would add at the same time that as an ideal, Marxism is neither practically possible nor desirable. The Marxist thesis that a new kind of social human being can be developed by changes in economic practice is from this perspective considered to be fanciful Utopianism. Still, something of Marx's yearning for a better world, and his vision of what this would ideally consist in, must be given serious consideration. How Marxist theory will eventually evolve will, of course, depend to a considerable extent upon how these political developments play out as we move into the twenty-first century.

Contemporary political theory

The political theories we have discussed, from Plato to Marx, have in their various ways importantly influenced political phi-losophy of the twentieth century. Nearly all these traditions continue to be represented in the literature of this epoch. We have philosophers who have defended private property and a minimal state apparatus, such as Karl Popper in his *Open Society and Its Enemies* (5th ed., 1966), Robert Nozick in *Anarchy, State and Utopia* (1974), and André Glucksmann in *The Master Thinkers* (1977). We have important works in a neo-Marxist tradition, such as Herbert Marcuse's *One-Dimensional Man* (1964) and *An Essay on Liberation* (1969), and we also have defenses of democratic forms of a welfare state, such as John Rawls's *A Theory of Justice* (1971). Because of the vast literature produced in this field in this century, we cannot even begin to discuss these widely divergent traditions. Let us confine ourselves, then, to John Rawls's 1971 book, *A Theory of Justice*, which is widely regarded as the most important book produced by an American political theorist in this century.

Rawls's defense of a form of liberal democracy has strong roots in such thinkers as Locke, Mill, and Kant. Like Locke and Mill, he believes that it is a condition of any form of legitimate government that it be democratic in principle. This entails that it must be a society that is self-governing, a community in which the people are free to choose their representatives and to be involved, in procedurally regular ways, in fundamental political policies. But, unlike Locke, Rawls does not believe that such a society must be committed to the defense of private property as a right. He believes that there are more important goals than the preservation of property, and in particular that a "good" society distributes its wealth in such a way that poverty is minimized. In this respect, Rawls is clearly influenced by the developments toward a kind of democratic socialism that one finds today in some Scandinavian countries and that was found in England under the Labour Government after the Second World War. Rawls thus takes the liberties Mill speaks about that protect the individual against government tyranny to be fundamental, but unlike Mill, *he is not a utilitarian.* He does not try to justify these freedoms on the ground that as political principles they will maximize happiness for the greatest number in the long run. On the contrary, Rawls feels that there are paradoxes built into the utilitarian scheme that no just society can tolerate. On utilitarian grounds, for instance, it would follow that a society could knowingly execute persons innocent of any crime if this turned out to be an effective way of deterring future lawless behavior. This is, in his view, a consequence of the principle of utility; and accordingly, it violates a basic principle of justice: that no innocent person should be the knowing victim of public policy.

If Rawls is a defender of a welfare form of democracy, and is a defender neither of property rights nor of utilitarianism, where does his view find its historical antecedents? The answer is that he finds them in the moral philosophy of Immanuel Kant. As we pointed out in Chapter 1, Kant argues for the objectivity and universality of certain moral principles. One of these is what he calls the "categorical imperative," which in one of its forms enjoins agents to treat each person as an "end in him/herself and never as a

means." The basic idea here is that a just society is one in which each individual, no matter what his/her station in life, must be treated equally before the law, be given due process, and be the subject of equal concern by society. It is this sort of *moral* principle that underlies Rawls's work. He is committed to a just society where "justice" means "fairness," and this is a society that cannot be justified on utilitarian principles but only on Kantian grounds.

Given this set of presuppositions, Rawls's main concern is to explain how such a society can be *economically* just. It is *politically* just because of its commitment to certain basic freedoms, but a society can be politically equitable in this sense and yet distribute its wealth in ways that are unfair. Here Rawls's outlook is tinged by the kind of moral fervor we find in Marx, who believes that unrestrained capitalism is *immoral* in the way it exploits workers while providing excessive profits and wealth for a small number in society.

Unlike Marx, Rawls does not object to a free society that exhibits differentials in wealth. What he objects to is a society where inequalities in wealth allow some persons to sink beneath a minimal level with respect to the material conditions of existence. One of the fundamental principles in Rawls's book is therefore what he calls the "difference principle." This holds that inequalities in certain basic goods of society will be allowed only when the distribution of primary goods also benefits the worst off in society. Thus Rawls might hold, for instance, that an advanced industrial society would be justified in restricting the amount of money wealthy persons could acquire. These restrictions would be lifted only when the wealth acquired by such persons also benefited those who were the poorest in society. Rawls's emphasis is thus on minimizing the differences in wealth among the members of a politically free society. Rawls is thus arguing for a form of mitigated egalitarianism—not of strict egalitarianism—where the wealth of society is concerned. In this respect, his idea of a good society is one that counteracts the natural inequalities deriving from birth, drive, talent, and circumstances, all features that tend to distribute wealth unfairly. The common good for him is measured in terms of certain basic benefits to individuals who otherwise would be economically disadvantaged.

Criticism of Rawls

Rawls has been subject to two different sorts of criticisms. The first is one that derives from a Platonic view of society. This holds that people are innately different in their abilities, creativity, and capacity for achievement, and accordingly make inequitable contributions to society. According to this view, a "just" society would not disregard these differences. It holds that persons who make more important and valuable contributions should be rewarded differently; that indeed they are entitled to a greater share of society's primary goods, *whether or not* their receiving such a share would benefit those who are worst off. This is the kind of argument developed by Robert Nozick, for instance, in his *Anarchy, State and Utopia*. Essentially, Nozick is working with a different conception of justice than Rawls is.

The second criticism of Rawls points out that the notions of equality of distribution of wealth and the principles of political freedom in certain cases may run into opposition with each other. Suppose some few persons in society have an enormous amount of inherited wealth, including vast landed estates. It might be in certain circumstances that their control of such vast properties might make it impossible for a large number of their citizens to live above the poverty level. A government might find that these persons not only control much of the wealth of their society but also control most of the organs of the state: the press, law courts, banks, and other institutions. There thus might be no democratic way that the economic situation could be corrected without suspending the free exercise of voting rights in that society. In such a case, one of Rawls's fundamental principles—freedom to vote—would have to be curtailed in order to bring about economic justice. It is thus felt that the theory embodies certain inconsistencies in that in the end it will have to give the government more power than a free society can allow. The result will be a move toward centralization and ultimately toward state control. Indeed, neo-Marxists like Herbert Marcuse argue that this is the only way to obtain economic justice; that the whole system of political liberties is only a smokescreen for the control of society by the wealthy. As interesting as these issues are, we shall have to leave them at this juncture; but we urge readers to look more deeply into these matters, since they go to the heart of present-day issues in democratic societies.

Applications

The previous discussion focuses upon political theories without much emphasis upon their applications. But like moral theories, political doctrines often arise from, and are constructed so as to apply to, practical situations. A good example of how theory and practice intertwine is to be found in the conception of punishment. Punishment, of course, may be applied in nonpolitical circumstances, for instance, when a parent spanks a child. But it also is a major problem for society itself, where the people who deserve punishment may be unknown to the punishing agents. In either case, the question that philosophical theory deals with is "What is the justification for punishing someone?" There are several theoretical answers to this question: (*a*) It is a matter of revenge. If A injures B, then B (or those protecting B) should exact revenge. "An eye for an eye, a tooth for a tooth" is one version of this doctrine. Normally, this would not be the motive for a parent's punishing a child, but it might still be personal; the members of a family might take revenge against somebody or some persons who have injured one of their members. (*b*) Most civilized societies, however, deny that revenge is a motive. A common reason that is given for punishing criminals is to deter or prevent future crime. Here the idea is that if a potential criminal realizes that punishment is likely to be swift and sure, he/she may decide not to commit the crime in the first place; or if he/she commits the crime and is punished, then he/she may be deterred from future crimes. The justification in such a case is that society is protecting itself by taking this sort of action against potential or actual law breakers. Utilitarians tend to give this sort of argument for punishment. Typically, they hold that the long-range effects of punishment will lead

to a situation in which the good for all is maximized over the long run. (*c*) A third sort of defense of punishment is, roughly speaking, "deontological," as we defined that term in Chapter 1. Here the argument is that duty requires that there be retribution against those who have committed offenses against society. The justification is simple: they have done wrong—violated a law, say—and therefore ought to be punished. Whether the consequences of doing so in the long run would be beneficial or not, the argument here is that such actions, being wrong, must be punished.

Let us see how these views appear in the following scenario. (I am indebted to one of my former students, David Barrett, for some of the material that follows.)

Suppose that in the year 1995 the United States Embassy in Beirut is attacked by terrorists who capture and then execute about forty of its personnel. (This is a *hypothetical* case, of course.) The President, after consultation with his advisors, decides to level the city of Beirut with low-power, tactical nuclear bombs, but then he changes his mind. The National Security Council is reconvened to reconsider its earlier decision.

The Secretary of Defense is strongly opposed to any change in the decision. Complicating the issue is the fact that our allies are aware of the earlier decision. The Secretary of Defense speaks as follows: "Mr. President, you can't seriously be reconsidering your previously stated position. The world is watching to see our resolve in this matter. You must not back down or compromise in any manner. It has been well chronicled, the great number of injustices and humiliations these terrorists and their sympathizers have wreaked upon this nation. No longer can we bear this insolence and repudiation of all that we believe and hold dear. They must now pay for the consequences of their treachery. They should rightly suffer for their total disregard of common morality and decency. It is they who began this provocation, not us, but we must not be lacking in zeal to pursue it to a just end.

"To those who would raise objections for the innocent people of Beirut, I can only reply: What of the hostages? What of their rights? What of their families? It would seem that these innocent people give their support and allegiance to a government that either tacitly supports terrorism or actually sponsors it. The Lebanese society as a whole bears the responsibility for this atrocity. How long will we in the world community allow such nations to stand defiantly breaking international law and the higher law of common decency and human rights?

"As to our allies, do we gain their respect with our 'patient tolerance' and slipshod sanctions? Far from it: they are watching us even now in this moment to see how we will respond. To them it will say volumes more than all of our rhetoric. A weak and morally feeble ally is no ally at all.

"As for international opinion, we can really not expect it to be realistically much affected at all. Publicly, we will be denounced; but privately, both friend and foe alike will know we will no longer be indecisive in rightly dealing with the wrongs aggrieved against us. Terrorism and barbarism will once again have consequences to be paid. As it stands now, our image is so poor that there is little we can do to improve it except to reestablish our credibility as the most powerful nation on earth. I urge you, Mr. President, to pursue the course we have plotted."

The Secretary of State then speaks to the Council: "Mr. President, no one here today does not share the good Secretary of Defense's outrage at the horrible events that have brought us here, but our anger and outrage must be tempered with good sense and practical consideration. The future of the whole world is at stake. Rash, wanton decisions will not do when so much is in the balance.

"I too feel that our resolve must be firm. But it should be a firmness that seeks justice, not a vendetta. The guilty should and must be punished, but we must be certain that we deal harshly only with the guilty. Our overreaction can do us and the whole world more harm than no action at all.

"We must ask ourselves whether or not the destruction of Beirut will help us obtain the justice we seek. I think so only if the complicity of the Lebanese can be proven, yet how will that serve our interests? Will the adding of more innocent victims be an aid to us?

"World opinion is now solidly behind us, but if we introduce nuclear weapons and cinderize this city, we will lose favor in the sight of the whole of humankind, becoming, in their eyes, guilty of a far more serious crime than those we seek to punish. Mr. President, we cannot allow the wrongs to go unpunished, but our response must be appropriate as well as decisive. For it to be any other way is to only mount tragedy upon tragedy."

Here the Secretary of State concludes his remarks.

The foregoing discussion may strike a familiar note to readers of the Greek classics. And it should, for it is based upon the famous Mytilene debate found in Book III of Thucydides' *History of the Peloponnesian War*. There the issue was whether Athens, a superpower, should wipe out the small state of Mytilene. Cleon argued that it should, and Diodotus argued against him. They gave reasons almost identical to those given by the Secretary of Defense and the Secretary of State in the previous scenario. Among the issues are: Should a whole society be held responsible for the actions of a few? What is the justification for any action against an enemy? We leave the analysis of the scenario to the reader, but all the themes we have mentioned are to be found in the discussion. The scenario is designed to show how different sorts of political theories can be brought to bear upon the issue of punishment. And with this application, we leave the subject of political philosophy.

Suggested further reading

Classical Authors

Aristotle. *Politics*. A great classic of political theory.

Hegel, G. F. W. *The Philosophy of History*. German idealism that influenced Marx.

Hobbes, T. *Leviathan*. A defense of absolute monarchy.

Locke, J. *Second Treatise on Civil Government*. A classic statement of democracy.

Machiavelli, N. *The Prince*. Advice to the ruler by a shrewd politician.

Marx, K. *Das Kapital*. Analysis of capitalism.

Mill, J. S. *On Liberty*. A defense of freedom.

More, T. *Utopia*. An attempt to work out a perfect society.

Plato. *Republic*. The most famous exposition of an authoritarian society.

Rousseau, J. J. *The Social Contract*.

Modern Authors

Baier, A. *Postures of Mind*. Minneapolis: University of Minnesota Press, 1985.

Barry, B. *Theories of Justice*. Berkeley, Calif.: University of California Press, 1989.

Benn, S. I., and Peters, R. S. *Social Principles and the Democratic State*. London: Allen & Unwin, 1959. A modern discussion of some of the major problems of political theory.

Clarke, S. G., and Simpson, E., eds. *Anti-Theory in Ethics and Moral Conservatism*. Albany, N.Y.: State University of New York Press, 1989.

Cohen, M., Nagel, T., and Scanlon, T., eds. *Marx, Justice, History*. 1980.

Dworkin, R. *Taking Rights Seriously*. 1978.

Foster, M. B., Jones, W. T., and Lancaster, L. W. *Masters of Political Thought*. 3 vols. London: Harrap, 1959. Good summary of the history of political thought, with many long quotations from the original texts; a very useful introductory work.

Habermas, J. *Philosophical-Political Profiles*. 1983.

Marcuse, H. *One Dimensional Man*. 1964.

Nozick, R. *Anarchy, State and Utopia*. 1974.

Plamenatz, J. *Man and Society*. 2 vols. London: Longmans, 1963. A detailed critical examination of the most important social and political theories from Machiavelli to Marx.

Popper, K. *The Open Society and Its Enemies*. 2 vols. London: Routledge & Kegan Paul, 1962. A discussion of the threat to democracy of the totalitarian implications of the theories of Plato, Hegel, and Marx.

Rawls, J. *A Theory of Justice*. 1971.

Sabine, G. *A History of Political Theory*. London: Harrap, 1963. An outstanding history of political thought.

Wallace, J. *Moral Relevance and Moral Conflict*. Ithaca, N.Y.: Cornell University Press, 1988.

CHAPTER THREE

Metaphysics

What is metaphysics?

Of all the branches of philosophy, none sounds more alarmingly abstract than metaphysics. In ordinary usage a theory or view is called "metaphysical" if it seems complicated beyond comprehensibility. Or, the term "metaphysical" is used as synonymous with "fanciful" or "imaginary."

Actually, metaphysics, in the ordinary Greek, meant simply "that which comes after physics." It has been speculated that the word entered the philosophical lexicon when the treatises of Aristotle, now called his *Metaphysics*, were found untitled among his papers. Since they appeared among the manuscripts after the work entitled *Physics*, they were simply called *Metaphysics*—*meta* being the Greek word for "after."

But there is another, a philosophical sense in which "metaphysics" means "after physics." Many of the early Greek philosophical writings were entitled *Concerning Nature* (the Greek term for "nature" being "physics"). These works usually dealt with what we would now consider physical science, but they were also speculations about the meaning and nature of the universe—that is, with questions that arise *after* the physical problems have been resolved, or that are concerned with what lies after or beyond the physical world of sensory experience.

Pluralism and monism

To explain this, let us consider an example of a metaphysical question with which the ancient Greeks were concerned. After developing a crude system of scientific "explanation" in terms of earth, air, fire, and water, they asked whether these were the fundamental elements of the natural universe, or whether something else accounted for the four elements and the events of nature.

Some of the early metaphysicians were **pluralists**, who held that **more than one** feature of the universe accounted for scientific knowledge of it; others were **monists**, who insisted that there was **one, and only one, basic feature.** What should be stressed is that the questions posed by the early metaphysicians were ones that arose *after* physical problems had been considered, and that these answers undertook to evaluate and interpret the physical theories in nonphysical terms.

Scope of metaphysics

Beyond these speculations, the metaphysician attempted to work out hypotheses that would account for (make intelligible) all scientific knowledge, as well as everything else that we may know or believe about the universe. These metaphysical explanations purport to encompass the most general and fundamental characteristics of the cosmos, both physical and mental (or spiritual).

In order to survey this vast and all-encompassing branch of philosophy, we will first consider some of the basic metaphysical problems that have persisted throughout the ages. Then we shall examine some of the most famous metaphysical systems in the history of philosophy. Lastly, we shall glance at some of the criticisms directed by certain philosophers at the value of metaphysical investigations.

The problem of permanence and change

The first metaphysical problem to be considered is one of the earliest in the history of philosophy, **the problem of permanence and change.** Beginning with the first philosopher we know of, Thales, Greek thinkers were impressed with two basic features of the world—**the occurrence of natural change, and the continuance of certain apparently permanent conditions.** The earliest theories attempted to account for both the persistent and the changing features by portraying the world in terms of certain stable, constant elements (or element) that consti-

tuted the "real," or permanent, aspect, while the rest was flux in the world of "appearance." The latter might continually alter, but the former always retained the same basic, unchanging aspects.

However, certain difficulties appeared that suggested that the changing and the permanent features of the universe were incompatible. On the one hand, it was pointed out, if everything changed, there could be nothing permanent; and on the other hand, if there was a permanent element of the universe, it could not change, could not account for alterations, and therefore could not be part of a system that involved change.

Heraclitus and Cratylus

The early Greek philosopher Heraclitus was the theoretician of change. **Everything alters and changes,** he insisted. One can never step twice into the same river, since it does not remain the same. The only permanence is not some "stuff" or substance that remains constant—but rather, the **principle or law of change.** Everything in the cosmos is in flux. It comes into being and it passes away. Only the universal principle that everything changes remains unaltered.

A later disciple of this philosophy of change, Cratylus, saw that if one took this theory seriously, no permanence would be left, not even the permanence of the law of change. If everything changes, even the words we use and the meanings they have must be in constant flux, so that we cannot even have a constant language with which to describe the world in which we live. So, Cratylus concluded, one cannot even step into the same river once, because by the time one steps into it, it has changed. In fact, if everything is constantly changing, one cannot even discuss anything, since by the time one finishes speaking, the speaker, the words, the meanings, and the listener have all altered. Hence all that Cratylus felt he could do in this world was wiggle his finger when he was addressed, to indicate that he had heard. But it would be futile to try to make the universe stand still long enough to make any response. Thus, if one took the notion of change literally, one could not make sense out of it, because there would be no lasting features that one could seek to understand.

Parmenides

If those who emphasized change as a fundamental characteristic of the cosmos encountered great difficulties, so did their opponents, who argued for permanence. Beginning with the early Greek philosopher Parmenides, an analysis was made of what could validly be said of the fixed, unchanging, and unchangeable features of reality. If the universe consists of some permanent, immutable base, Parmenides pointed out, then this constant element cannot alter, move, divide, separate, and so on, since any of these properties indicate change. Further, if the subject of investigation is some fixed being or reality, then this permanent element can have no properties other than **existence,** since any other properties suggest change or mutability. The sole truth that can be discovered about the permanent being is that it *is.*

Everything else in the world of flux, Parmenides claimed, cannot belong to the real world of permanent being. Anything that can alter changes from not existing to existing to not existing again. The permanent cannot change into anything without ceasing to be permanent. What is cannot change into what is not without passing out of existence. Hence, the permanent, the real, *is,* and cannot be part of reality or become part of reality. What is permanent must remain forever the same. It is what it is, and to become something other than this would involve the contradiction that it has become what it is not. The changing world is what the real, or permanent, world is not. The only property the fixed aspect of the universe has is **that it exists.** Thus the changing aspect cannot be part of existence, since it does not belong to the real, unchanging aspect and must therefore be nonexistent. As Parmenides concluded in a famous phrase, **"Being is, nonbeing is not,"** and only the unchanging belongs to the world of Being.

Zeno

As if Parmenides had not gone far enough in asserting what happens when one claims permanent features for the world, his disciple, the famous Zeno of Elea, went still further. Zeno (not to be confused with the Zeno whom we have already discussed as the founder of Stoicism) sought to show not only that the changing world has nothing to do with the real, permanent world, but that the concept of change itself is impossible. Zeno was not disputing that we experience change in the course of our daily lives—in seeing things grow, move around, and change qualities. Rather, he claimed that any attempt to explain change of motion would lead to contradictions and would thus compel acceptance of the Parmenidean philosophy that only the permanent and unchanging are real. The rest could be dismissed as an unfortunate illusion that we can only ignore.

ZENO'S "PARADOXES"

The arguments of Zeno, which still play a role in metaphysical discussions, are his well-known **paradoxes** concerning motion. By these he tried to show that starting with an ordinary situation in which we suppose something to be moving or changing, it could be shown that such motion cannot possibly occur. The most familiar of the Zeno paradoxes concerns Achilles and the tortoise. If Achilles can run ten times faster than the tortoise, and the tortoise has a ten-yard lead at the outset, then when Achilles has run ten yards to catch up to the tortoise, the latter has moved ahead one yard. When Achilles runs this yard, the slow tortoise has moved on one tenth of a yard. Each time Achilles reaches the position where the tortoise had been, the tortoise has moved on some small distance, so that Achilles will never catch up even though he moves so much faster.

Another of Zeno's paradoxes holds that for an object to move from one place to another, it first must move half of the distance involved. But to move half of the distance, it must move half of the half, and so on infinitely. Also, for it to move to each stage will take some time, no matter how slight. Thus, not only will the object go through an infinite number of distances, it will also require an infinite number of time intervals. Therefore, for an object to go from one place to another, no matter how small the distance, will require forever, and, according to the argument, in no finite time will it ever be able to traverse the distance.

The last of the Zeno paradoxes that we will mention here is the argument that for an object, like an arrow, to go from one place to another, it must move either where it is or where it is not. If it moves where it is, it will be standing still. If it moves where it is not, it cannot be there. Therefore, the object cannot move. A version of this argument is offered to show that it is impossible for a person to die. Someone dies either when he/she is alive or when he/she is dead. If he/she dies when he/she is dead, then he/she must have died twice. If he/she dies when he/she is alive, then he/she must be dead and alive at the same time. Therefore, he/she cannot die. (There is an amusing account that has come down to us of the Zenoist who was haranguing a crowd in ancient Athens about why nothing can move, and in the course of emphasizing his point with some wild gestures, he dislocated his shoulder. A doctor who was in the audience examined the shoulder and told the Zenoist that the circumstances were impossible, because he dislocated his shoulder either where it was or where it was not. If the former, then his shoulder was not dislocated, since it was still in the same place. If the latter, his shoulder could not be there to be dislocated. The patient, we are told, gave up his views at this point and demanded that the doctor fix his shoulder, no matter how it got there.)

Each of these arguments attempts to

show that when one tries to explain the commonsense fact of change or motion, one is led to the paradoxical conclusion that either nothing can move, or that if it does move, it takes an infinite time to traverse any distance. There is a vast literature analyzing Zeno's arguments, and propounding solutions to them. But in their day, regardless of one's opinions as to the ultimate merits of the reasoning, the paradoxes produced a crisis among both scientists and metaphysicians. The former were horrified to find that the best mathematical account of moving objects seemed to lead to such paradoxical conclusions. In Greek mathematics, there are ingenious attempts to construct different theories of motion in order to avoid the Zenoist conclusions. Among the metaphysicians, the problem became one of discovering some intelligible explanation of how the two basic features of change and permanence could be reconciled in a consistent theory about the ultimate nature of the universe. Heraclitus's views seemed to eliminate permanence as a characteristic of the world, and the arguments of Parmenides and Zeno appeared to show that change or motion could not be a real aspect of the world.

Democritus's Solution

One of the most important metaphysical theories in the ancient world was the **materialism of Democritus,** who tried to resolve the conflicts that had arisen between the theories of change and permanence by offering a new conception of the fundamental characteristics of the real world. **The basic features of the Democritean universe were both unchanging and unchangeable in one sense, and also constantly in flux in another.**

According to Democritus, the ultimate constituent of the real world was an indivisible physical unit, the atom (which originally meant "that which has no parts," or "that which cannot be divided"). Each atom had fixed characteristics of form, shape, etc., which remained permanently and perpetually the same. Thus the Democritean atoms had the immutable property that Parmenides had insisted must belong to the world of being.

But in addition to their unchangeable nature, the atoms were supposed to be in continual change of position, constantly moving through empty space. For all time, they fell through space, colliding with other atoms and being thrown into different courses and arrangements. Thus, although one could always describe the form and shape of each atom in the same manner, since it had a permanent character, one could also attribute to it a never-ending change of position, or a permanent impermanence of location.

With this compromise between the totally fixed and unchanging universe of Parmenides and Zeno, and the constantly changing one of Heraclitus, **Democritus believed he could develop a theory about the nature of reality that could account for all we know about the cosmos.** On the one hand, the eternal, immutable features of the atoms would provide a basis for the permanent features of the universe, a stable structure to which no changing properties could be attributed. The constant motion of the atoms, on the other hand, would account for alteration in an unchanging world. The world of atoms always remained the same; but the position and distribution of the atoms could be altered without affecting the permanent, stable characteristics. In this way, Democritus sought to explain apparent changes in terms of changing combinations of atoms—for example, the change of color of a leaf, the movement of visible objects. The changes we perceive do not actually take place in reality, but something else does, which does not alter the permanent structure of the universe but which produces, in conjunction with our atomic constituents, the apparent changes of our experience. Thus Democritus agreed with Parmenides to the extent of insisting upon the unchangeable nature of reality, and the illusoriness of apparent change, while at the same time claiming that a type of change (that of position) is a basic feature of the real universe and accounts for our experience of reality.

Aristotle's Solution

Another of the great metaphysical theories to resolve the problem of change and permanence was that of Aristotle. For him, neither experienced change nor permanence could be sacrificed in constructing an adequate theory of the fundamental characteristics of the world. Even the apparent changing qualities had to be taken seriously and not simply dismissed, as they had been in the writings of Democritus.

Accordingly, in Aristotle's analysis, one had to recognize two basic elements in any possible natural event. The first of these is that there must be **something that remains the same and yet is somehow subject to variation.** The other is that there occur **genuine changes of qualities.** Thus, for example, when an acorn grows into an oak, there must be some permanent feature that has at one time the qualities that we call an acorn, and later, those that we call an oak. Unless this were the case, we could not even properly describe it as a change, since there would be no relation between the former state and the latter. But if there is some fixed aspect, there must be another that changes, there must be something different between the acorn and the oak, or there would be no genuine alteration.

MATTER AND FORM

The two features, Aristotle said, are **matter and form.** Matter, in its pure state, would have no characteristics whatsoever. But matter is that which is capable of being "informed"—of assuming various forms. The **matter** of the acorn and oak (which is not really pure to begin with) has the potentiality of receiving different forms, of having one form at one time, and another at a later time. The **form** of the object at any given time is its **actuality, what it has become at that particular moment.**

Each and every object in this world thus has a permanent nature, which persists through its realization or acquisition of different forms. Each and every object can be understood only in terms of **both its matter and its form, and the process by which it grows, alters, or moves, that is, replaces one form with another.** The permanent aspect of an object (with one exception, which will be discussed later) never exists independently or without assuming some form. **The object always is in some state and is in process of reaching some other state.** Thus the **formal**, changing aspect and the **material**, permanent aspect of any object are always present and always constitute the basis for any explanation of what is occurring.

In the analysis of Aristotle and Democritus, an attempt was made to resolve the metaphysical problem of change and permanence. Each tried to develop some way of accounting for two of the basic features of the universe without being led into contradictory or paradoxical views. Each sought to construct a general explanation of the characteristics of the objects of the world that would provide a broad basis in terms of which all scientific information could be portrayed or understood.

The problem of permanence and change, like the other metaphysical problems that we shall examine next, is one of the persistent problems that any general system of the nature of the universe has to confront. Those who wished to construct a metaphysical framework in order to interpret or evaluate our knowledge and beliefs have found that the task centers around finding some consistent set of answers to the difficulties that have arisen from the beginning of philosophy. As we shall see, these problems are to some degree interrelated. The question that we shall consider next, the mind-body problem, in some measure involves the theory of permanence and change.

The mind-body problem

The mind-body problem has been a major concern of metaphysicians, especially since the rise of modern philosophy in the seventeenth century. In the form in which we shall discuss it, this problem has arisen as the result of certain views of the great French philosopher René Descartes. In spite of our increasing knowledge about the behavior of the mental and the physical world, this metaphysical question continues to plague philosophers.

Basically, the problem involves answering the questions **"What is the fundamental nature of mind and body?"** and **"How are mind and body related?"** An elementary consideration of what we know about mental and physical events might well lead one to suspect that the most general characteristics of each are different from the other, and yet that they seem to bear some relation to each other or have some influence upon each other.

Our scientific knowledge would seem to suggest that the physical world is inanimate, purposeless, yet determined or fixed in the order of events within it. The mental world, on the other hand, involves consciousness, planning, willing, desiring, etc. Yet, though these worlds may be different in many respects, our experience appears to indicate that they are interrelated or interconnected. When something happens in the physical world, this affects the mental world and may change one's thoughts, wishes, etc. Similarly, a desire that one may have can alter events in the physical world, as when one decides to strike a match. This decision, an event in the mental world, is then followed by a physical event of a match being struck and a flame being lit. Given the apparent differences between mental and physical events, and their apparent relationships with each other, various metaphysicians have tried to construct theories about the nature of mind and body and the connections between them.

Cartesian Theory

Descartes, who is often blamed for having created the difficulties that arose from this problem, asserted that mind and body are two totally different types of entity. They are different **substances.** From a careful scrutiny of the "clear and distinct" idea that he had of his own mind and of physical objects, he decided that the basic feature of the latter was its geometrical qualities (size, shape, and so on) and the basic feature of the former was **thinking.** In each case, these seemed to him to be the inseparable properties that accounted for all the other features of these two entities.

In his work *The Principles of Philosophy*, Descartes summed up his theory as follows:

> But although any one attribute is enough to give us knowledge of a substance, there is always one chief property of a substance that constitutes its nature and essence, and upon which all the others depend. Thus extension in length, breadth and depth makes up the nature of physical substance; and thought makes up the nature of thinking substance. For, everything else that may be attributed to bodies presupposes their extension, and is only a form of this extended thing; just as everything that we find in mind is only some form of thinking. Thus, for example, we cannot conceive of a figure except as an extended thing, nor of movement except as taking place in an extended space; and in the same way imagination, feeling and will occur only in a thinking thing. But, on the other hand, we are able to conceive of extension without figure or action, and of thinking without imagination

or sensation, and so on, as is quite clear to anyone who examines the matter carefully.

THINKING AND EXTENSION

Thus, according to Descartes, the **essential property of a mind is that it thinks, and the essential property of body is that it is "extended."** All of the forms in which bodies occur involve only various extensional features, never mental ones. Similarly, no form of thought involves extension. The realms of thought and extension are completely different. Then, if all this is accepted, how can mental events have anything to do with physical ones and vice versa, since the one occurs in space and the other is unextended thought with no physical properties whatsoever? To make the question more difficult, Descartes claimed in his physical theories that all physical action occurs by the impact of one extended object upon another. Since mental events are not extended, how can there be any impact or contact between that whose nature it is to occur in space and that which does not occur in space? How can an idea move a hammer, or a hammer strike upon an idea?

CONFLICTING EVIDENCE

In spite of the complete separation in his theory between mind and body, Descartes was impressed by the commonsensical and scientific evidence that indicated the reciprocal influence of mental and physical events. A pin jabbed into the physical, extended finger is followed by a thought or a pain in the unextended mind. But a studious examination of the medical and psychological evidence convinced Descartes that the mind is only aware of physical events in the brain. Various motions can take place in the body without being followed by mental events, unless the physical motions first cause movements in the nervous system and then in the brain. Similarly, just by producing certain physical motions in the brain, without affecting the rest of the body, one can stimulate thoughts. The example that most impressed Descartes was that persons who had lost a limb could be led to think that this "limb" was being moved, or pained, merely by stimulating parts of the nervous system. This sort of information led Descartes to the conclusion that there must be some kind of contact between the mental and physical worlds, and that the contact must take place in the brain.

On the basis of this conclusion, Descartes developed a theory that the interaction between mind and body took place in the pineal gland, which is located at the base of the brain. Here, presumably, some sort of impact occurred between the physical, extended brain and the unextended, thinking mind, which allowed physical events to lead to thoughts, and thoughts to alter the direction of the motions of extended objects.

When it was pointed out to him that his solution to this metaphysical problem was quite unsatisfactory, because he had still not explained plausibly how it was possible for mind and body to interact upon each other if they were really of two totally different natures, Descartes became more and more vague about the matter. He insisted that the fact of interaction was known to everybody; we experience it all the time. But how mind and body were united, he admitted, was most difficult to explain. The pineal gland theory actually produced more problems than it solved, since one could ask whether this gland was physical, and if so, how it could be next to something that did not occupy space. If it were mental, how could it be next to any part of the brain? And so on. In a letter written late in his life to one of his admirers, the Princess Elizabeth of the Palatinate, Descartes threw up his hands in despair and told her that the union of mind and body was best understood by not thinking about it, and that it was just one of those mysteries that had to be accepted without being comprehended.

The Materialistic Theory

Other metaphysicians were not willing to give up as easily as Descartes, and they suspected that the difficulties in the problem arose from the initial separation of mind and body in the Cartesian metaphysical system. If one refused to grant that mind and body were really different kinds of entity, then one would not have any trouble accounting for their interrelations. One way of avoiding some pitfalls of the Cartesian theory was to adopt a completely **materialistic metaphysics** and claim that both mental and physical events could be accounted for in terms of purely physical concepts and laws.

This type of theory, which was advanced in Descartes's time by his belligerent opponent, Thomas Hobbes, and in our own day by some **behaviorist psychologists,** maintains that **what we call mental events are really, like physical events, only various combinations of matter in**

motion. The physical movements that occur in the brain are what we call thoughts, and these are produced by other events in the material world, either outside our bodies or inside, and, in turn, can produce further physical motions in ourselves or outside of ourselves. Every idea—of pain, of perception, of memory, and so on—is nothing but a set of physical occurrences in our higher nervous system and brain. When we say that we have a sensation of yellow, for example, this is explained as the result of certain light waves stimulating the optic nerve, which in turn causes a certain pattern of motions in the brain.

The very simplicity of the materialistic solution to the mind-body problem makes it appealing. Moreover, the vast body of evidence accumulated about the physical basis of mental events by psychologists, psychiatrists, physiologists, and other scientists also makes this theory seem most plausible. Recent developments in the treatment of mental conditions, such as depression, disconnected thinking, and mood changes, by biochemical drug treatment strongly suggest some links between the biochemical condition of the nervous system and the mental condition of the individual. Various so-called "brainwashing" techniques also indicate that one's mental content and mental processes can be affected by physical stimuli such as sense deprivation and sleeplessness.

Work on "artificial intelligence" in computers, programming them to do intellectual tasks, suggests that physical events—the circuits in a computer—can resemble the mental processes in human beings.

All of these new developments make the materialist case strong, but they raise fundamental difficulties that have led many metaphysicians either to attempt to modify it or else to abandon it.

If one examines an idea and asks if this is actually the same as what we mean by a physical event, one discovers a problem. The experience of seeing or hearing something, and the bodily events that occur in the nervous system and the brain at the same time, do not seem to be identical. For instance, if a person were watching a television show, and a scientist were at the same time examining the viewer's brain, they each would see different things. The viewer would see a series of pictures, while the scientist would see a series of "readings" of various measuring devices. It is conceivable that our information about the physiology of the brain may reach the point where the scientist can tell what the viewer is seeing, that is, from the physical reactions in the brain, he might be able to construct the sequence of events that comprised the television show. Even so, it would still be the case that each of them would be seeing directly something else.

Computer experts like Marvin Minsky (of the Massachusetts Institute of Technology), who coined the term "artificial intelligence" in 1956, have been working on the possibility of designing self-repairing machines that, once in motion, could keep themselves active without human intervention. They are also working on computer programs that duplicate the way human beings deal with problems. This would involve duplicating not just logical or mathematical activities, but mixed logical and psychological ones as well. Computer programs already exist that can outdo humans in computation and in the solution of certain kinds of mathematical problems. And computer programs are being designed that come closer and closer to winning chess competitions, even against the best experts.

Around 1950 the English logician and computer expert Alan Turing raised the question "Can machines think?" He proposed that it might be possible to build a machine (now called a Turing machine) that would make exactly the same responses a human being would to various questions. If so, then would it not be fair to say that if the human respondent thinks, then the Turing machine also thinks?

All of this would suggest that many of the processes that we relate to what we call "intelligence" in human beings can be artificially created, and that there is artificial intelligence. If intelligence is the ability to solve certain kinds of problems through certain kinds of activities, and if the computer program does what human beings seem to do to reach this end, then isn't it fair to say that the computer program is intelligent? The investigation of this, and how to accomplish it, has become a scientific and technological subject in its own right. Various forms of what we take to be human mental activity are being duplicated in computer programs.

Philosophically, this has led to a new, modernized version of the materialist theory about the mind-body problem—put forth as neurophilosophy by Patricia Smith Churchland—using the latest biochemical and biophysical findings about how the higher processes of the brain operate as the way to explain mental actions

and to resolve the questions about mental life and mind-body interaction that philosophers have struggled with for centuries. Churchland identifies mind and brain, and insists that explanations of how the brain works account for mental events. She insists that brain processes are the mental processes. Hence scientific knowledge of how the brain operates will yield the knowledge we seek about mental events.

In 1991, an important study by Daniel Dennett, *Consciousness Explained*, appeared and has gotten a lot of attention. In it the author argues that the mind functions as a supercomputer, and *is* in fact a supercomputer. Dennett claims that the understanding of how the mind functions dissolves the consideration of the mind as different from the brain-computer. The brain-computer is an organic machine that uses effects of cultural inheritance to store and utilize information, and to solve problems.

CRITICISM

The materialistic theory, in its simplest form, denies any distinction between our mental life and the physical developments in our brain. Nevertheless, the critics stress the fact that one's immediate experience seems to belie this claim. One is aware of all sorts of sensations, feelings, etc., and not a series of physical occurrences in the brain. Even if the latter are the cause of the former, it still remains the case that they are different and distinguishable. Hence, the critics claim, the materialists cannot successfully reduce the mental world to the physical world simply by asserting that all mental events are actually nothing but a series of physical occurrences.

Another criticism of the materialistic solution to the mind-body problem is that if it were true, the materialistic theory itself, which presumably is a mental event in somebody's life, would turn out to be nothing but one more set of physical events in the brain. Similarly, any alternative theory would merely be some other physical event. In that case, how can one set of motions in the brain be said to constitute the truth, whereas others would constitute a falsehood? If any metaphysical theory is just a physical occurrence in somebody's head, why should one of these occurrences be taken seriously and the others discounted as wrong?

Finally, the materialistic solution also carries serious implications for ethics. If our thoughts are physical occurrences in the brain, they must be ultimately explicable in scientific terms; it must be theoretically possible to explain our thoughts in the same way as we explain events in the physical world, i.e., in terms of cause and effect. This leaves no room for evaluation of a situation, for consideration of its implications, for decisions reached after careful **thought.** In other words, such a theory must lead to an explanation of human behavior in terms not of **free choices** based on careful appraisal but in terms of **physical cause and effect, stimulus and response.** This is in fact the kind of explanation favored by the behaviorist psychologist, but its implication for ethics is that no such thing as a moral choice is possible. (We shall consider this problem in greater detail later in this chapter.) This would still seem to be the case whether one considers mental life as

coming from biochemical and biophysical processes in the brain and the nervous system, or whether one considers it as analogous to some computer programs. The former, in each case, may help explain the mental features. But, it can still be asked, is the former identical with our mental life? In an interesting volume, *Artificial Intelligence: The Case Against*, edited by Rainer Born, a group of philosophers have argued both against the reduction of mental states to physical states and against the possibility of creating artificial intelligence.

Epiphenomenalism

Because of such problems, a modified form of the materialistic theory of mind and body has been developed—**epiphenomenalism.** This view admits that our thoughts, feelings, etc., are not merely physical states in our brain. Instead, they are adjudged to be a by-product of the sequence of physical occurrences, something like the smoke given off by fire. The significant events that occur in the world are only those of matter in motion. But along with this, for reasons not yet known to us, each time there is a certain sort of physical situation in the brain, a thought occurs, which is caused by material events.

The epiphenomenalistic solution may overcome some of the difficulties in the simple version of materialism, but it does not do justice to our mental life. As we have just suggested, we take our thoughts seriously, are bothered by them, brood about them, seem to initiate actions on the basis of them. If they are nothing but a vague by-product of the material events that occur in our brains, bearing no actual relation to them, it is strange that they should play such an important part in our lives.

Idealism

If the materialistic theory in one form or another has its difficulties, the opposite alternative, **idealism, which insists that everything is basically mental rather than physical,** may be even less credible. When applied to the mind-body problem, this metaphysical theory (which will be considered later in this chapter) has the disadvantages of flying in the face of our commonsense beliefs and of being in apparent conflict with scientific evidence. Even before reflecting on these matters, we seem to be convinced that there are physical events that influence our behavior. Scientific data concerning the influence of, say, drugs and surgery on our mental life suggest that a mentalistic, or idealistic, approach to the mind-body problem is difficult to accept unless the arguments in its favor can far overweigh the initial conflicts with our ordinary beliefs.

The Theories of Malebranche, Leibnitz, and Spinoza

In the seventeenth century some interesting alternative theories were offered to resolve the problem of the relationship between mind and body, by some of the great metaphysicians of the period, Nicolas Malebranche, Gottfried Wilhelm von Leibnitz, and Baruch Spinoza. Malebranche, a Catholic priest, was a follower of Descartes, but much more consistent

than his mentor. Where Descartes accepted apparently conflicting theories in order to avoid denying or challenging our ordinary experience, Malebranche insisted on reaching a *consistent* conclusion, no matter how implausible it might be.

OCCASIONALISM

Malebranche's theory, which is called **"occasionalism,"** insists on the Cartesian distinction between mind and matter. Each is totally different—one is composed of nothing but ideas, the other only of extended events. (In fact, they are so different that Malebranche claimed that mind cannot even know body. All that mind can know are ideas. When we think of bodies, what we are thinking of is something called "intelligible extension," rather than physical extension. Malebranche found the sole evidence that bodies exist in the opening lines of the Book of Genesis, which proclaim that God created a physical world. Were it not for this, we would never even know that there are any material objects.) If these two realms are so distinct, Malebranche insisted, then there cannot be any interaction or connection between them.

What actually happens, according to Malebranche, is that although mental events have nothing to do with physical ones, whenever anything happens in one realm, God makes something corresponding occur in the other. The events in one are not the **causes** of events in the other, they are only the **occasions** of God's actions. Thus, when I hear the ring of the telephone, this is not due to the occurrence of sound waves, which are part of the physical world and have nothing to do with thoughts that I may have. Instead, when the events take place in the mechanism of the telephone, God produces a thought in me of ringing. Since one has nothing to do with the other, He might just as well have produced the taste of a pear in me, or the idea of the number 7. But, through the inscrutable wisdom of God, He has decided to order my mental life and the series of physical events so that when a specific event occurs in one, He makes something else occur in the other.

Criticism

No matter how peculiar Malebranche's theory may appear, it has the advantage that it avoids the difficulties of Descartes's speculations, and no experience can possibly disprove it. Descartes had insisted upon holding both to the complete separation of mind and body and to their interaction. By eliminating the latter, Malebranche is able to hold to the former without encountering contradictions. The theory can be made to account for literally everything. No matter what experiment one might devise to show that mind influences body, or body influences mind, it can always be explained in Malebranchian terms, as God producing a certain effect in one realm when something else happens in the other. On the other hand, no matter how consistent Malebranche's theory may be, it remains extremely unconvincing in light of our ordinary experience, which we naturally interpret in terms of some relation between mental and physical events. Moreover, Malebranche's conception of God as being constantly involved in producing all effects in this world—as engaged in producing sounds, tastes, smells, and motions in the physical world—is hardly in keeping with most "acceptable" concepts of the deity.

A further difficulty arises when we ask how God achieves these effects, how God acts causally on both mind and body. The source of the mind-body problem lies in the fact that physical substance and thinking substance cannot interact. The definition of substance that the Cartesians had used logically precludes the interaction of one substance with another. Two substances must by definition have nothing in common with each other. For if they have anything in common, they cannot be separate substances. Now, as Spinoza tells us, "If two things have nothing in common with one another, then one cannot be the cause of the other; for since there would be nothing in the effect that was also in the cause, everything that was in the effect would have arisen out of nothing." How, then, does God act causally on mind **and** body, on thinking substance **and** on physical substance? If God Himself is either thinking substance or physical substance, then there is only one of these substances that He can act causally on. The Cartesians, however, regarded God as neither, but as quite separate from both—in other words, as a third substance. On this account it is logically impossible for Him to act causally on either mind or body. This was one of the inconsistencies in Cartesianism, as developed by Malebranche, that Spinoza seized on, as we shall see.

LEIBNITZ

Leibnitz's theory of the relations between mental and physical events is not much more plausible than Malebranche's view. According to Leibnitz, every entity, whether characterized as mental or physical, is independent and constitutes a **monad**. Each monad is determined or fixed in its properties according to its nature. Everything that can possibly happen to a monad follows from its own essential characteristics and not from the influence of any other entity.

"Preestablished harmony"

What accounts for the apparent relationships between different monads—in Leibnitz's theory—is that though they have no influence on each other, there is **a preestablished harmony** between the monads. They have been so constructed that events occurring in one are harmonious with the others. In the example used earlier, monads of the telephone and of my mind are such that when certain physical occurrences take place in the former, I hear a ringing sound. This is not owing to the fact that the telephone caused me to hear anything, but rather, that our monads are in perfect order. Mine is so set that at a given time, I have the idea of a certain sound, and at just that time a physical clapper is beating on a physical bell in the telephone. The following illustration may clarify this theory: if there were two clocks that kept perfect time so that when one pointed to the hour the other rang a bell, it might be the case that this is because the clocks have some connected mechanism (**Descartes's theory**); or that some outside intervention makes one ring when the hands on the other reach a certain point (**Malebranche's theory**); or that the clocks had been made perfectly at the outset, and although they had no relation whatsoever to each other, they each kept perfect time (**Leibnitz's theory**). Thus each monad is so created by God that it is in perfect harmony with every other for all eternity, and the events in the career of one are bound to be in perfect accord with the others. Brutus did not kill Caesar because of anything Caesar did; instead, each monad was so constructed by God that at the same moment that Brutus's monad had certain thoughts, and performed certain actions, Caesar's was such that he was in a certain locale, and dropped dead.

Leibnitz's theory, like Malebranche's, overcomes the difficulties in Cartesian metaphysics by giving up any claim that there is a relationship between mind and body. Also, like Malebranche's, Leibnitz's view, though it may not contain any inconsistencies, is incredible from the point of view of our ordinary, common experience.

SPINOZA

The last of these seventeenth-century accounts of the mind-body problem that we shall consider is somewhat different. Spinoza decided that the difficulty in the Cartesian theory came from its total separation of mind and body and, as we have seen, the total separation of both from God, although this difficulty had not been appreciated by the Cartesians. To overcome this, he did not wish to adopt the materialistic or idealistic solution of subordinating one of these realms to the other; instead, he insisted that they were both aspects of the same thing. This theory, sometimes called the **"dual-aspect theory,"** claims that **mind and body are**

both attributes of one and the same entity, which Spinoza named God, substance, or nature.

If the mental world and the physical world are both aspects of the same entity, then what is the relationship between one and the other? According to Spinoza, there is no influence between one and the other, but there is a **parallelism,** so that for everything that happens in one realm, a corresponding event occurs in the other. This is due to the fact that the physical and mental worlds are really two different ways of looking at the same thing, God or nature. Hence, **Spinoza contended that the logical order of the mind is identical with the physical order of nature.** For every thought there is a corresponding physical event, and vice versa. Thus the ringing of the telephone that I hear and the physical motions that are taking place in the mechanism are not two different things but are two different aspects of the same thing, or two different ways of looking at the same thing, as it occurs in God or nature.

Spinoza's metaphysical solution may not lead to the same kind of unbelievable views as those of Malebranche or Leibnitz, or the inconsistencies involved in Descartes's view; however, it led to certain conclusions regarding the nature of God, which most of his contemporaries found completely unacceptable. (Some of these will be considered in the chapter on the philosophy of religion.) As a result, it was not until the time of the nineteenth-century German metaphysicians that Spinoza's views were treated seriously.

The theories regarding the relationship between mind and body illustrate the difficulty the metaphysician has in trying to develop an explanation of this fundamental feature of our experience. The first metaphysical question that we considered dealt with the general character of the universe, and the second, with the relationship between two of the basic features of it. Before examining some of the major metaphysical theories that have attempted to account for all of the chief characteristics of the cosmos as we know it, we shall look at one further problem that metaphysicians have debated throughout history—**the free will problem.**

The problem of free will and determinism

The problem of free will deals primarily with the human element in the universe— whether or not is it the "captain of its fate" to any degree. In our experience of our own behavior and own decisions, we find two opposing features. The first of these is our awareness of our own freedom, of our own ability to decide for ourselves, to deliberate about what to do in various situations, and to come to our own conclusions about what to believe and what to do. On the other hand, the second element is that we discover that in many cases what we believed at the time to be a free decision had been influenced by various personal and social factors, so that we did not actually decide the question "freely." The more we learn about the workings of human nature, the more we come to realize that a great deal of what we do and think is the result of our upbringing, our education, our environment, our biological nature, etc. Hence metaphysicians have been concerned with the problem of **whether, in view of the information at our disposal, human beings can be said to be free agents, or whether their activities and thoughts are determined completely by the many influencing factors that impinge upon them.**

Complexities

In most of our judgments about people we assume that, in some sense, they chose freely to do what they did, or to believe what they do. We punish, condemn, or blame individuals for making certain choices and decisions, and insist that they ought to have done something else, and that if they had, they would then be deserving of rewards and praise. Much of the basis for our legal system presumes that people can be held responsible for what they do, because, to some degree or extent, they could have done otherwise.

At the same time that we conduct ourselves morally and legally on the basis that human beings are free agents, and can make decisions of their own free will, we are being made more and more aware that this sort of assumption is very often erroneous. We are shown many forceful indications of the way in which human nature can be guided and influenced by propaganda, advertising, parental training, and so on, so that individuals are often more victims of circumstance and determinations beyond their control than responsible agents. Psychiatrists testifying at criminal trials have tried to show that the defendant cannot be held morally responsible for actions that resulted from determining factors beyond the control of the individual, so that it is meaningless to

hold that the person freely decided to commit the actions for which he/she is being tried.

This conflict between our ordinary assumption of human freedom and our often grudging recognition that this is not always the case has been brought sharply to public attention in discussions about the culpability of soldiers who are captured in war and who aid the enemy. Some of those who have been tried had evidently performed actions that were not in the best interest of their country, and actions that have been declared criminal in military codes. But were the soldiers in question responsible for what they had done? Can they responsibly be judged morally guilty? When it is made clear that they had been subjected to all sorts of pressures, direct and indirect, that either forced them to perform the actions or altered their conscious moral framework so that they "chose" to perform the actions, can they then be considered free agents?

We are much less inclined to judge harshly when it is revealed that someone's actions were involuntary. If people are compelled to commit actions by direct force, we do not hold them responsible. If torture, coercion, and threats result in actions that in ordinary circumstances we would judge wrong, we are willing to excuse this behavior because extraordinary circumstances prevented the person from deciding and acting as a genuinely free agent.

We often apply the same criteria to personal factors that prevent due deliberation and decision. If someone commits certain actions when under the influence of alcohol, narcotics, or extreme emotional stress, we are willing to take these conditions into account, and again conclude that the individual was not a free agent who can be held morally responsible. Thus, we distinguish between types of crimes and degrees of guilt according to whether there are mitigating factors that might have influenced or determined one's behavior at the time the deeds were committed.

The striking evidence of the effects of "brainwashing," and of psychological "conditioning" in general, creates a problem of judging to what extent we can ever hold people responsible as free agents for what they have done. When we learn that there are methods, some relatively simple, by which their attitudes and outlooks can be altered so that they can be made to "wish" to perform certain actions that are condemned by society, are people so conditioned actually responsible? Even if some soldiers voluntarily aided the enemy, were they actually free agents if they had first been subjected to influences that controlled their attitudes toward events and the choices they made?

The problem of judging the extent to which our so-called "voluntary" choices and actions really are voluntary, in the sense of being completely free, becomes even more difficult to decide when further evidence about human psychology is considered. The findings of modern psychoanalysis seem to indicate that our attitudes, our standards of judging, and even our choices have been determined by a host of conditioning processes. Our parents, our social group, our teachers, our employers all influence us, so that when we are acting voluntarily, we may actually be making the choices that we must make, given the factors that influenced our development.

By pursuing this sort of discussion, one can discover more and more areas in which our "voluntary" behavior can be shown to be the product of various influences. Even though we may be able to choose our actions, the framework in which we choose—the one that determines which of several alternatives we will select—may be something entirely beyond our control. We may not be responsible for this framework, and hence are not really free agents. The framework has been imposed upon us by all sorts of psychological, social, biological, and other factors.

In view of all this, the metaphysical problem of free will seems to revolve about determining how far a belief in human freedom is consistent with our experience, our knowledge, and our views about human nature. **On the one hand, there is a point of view that insists there actually is no human freedom—the view called "determinism." As against this, there is the claim that in some manner, and to some degree, there is some free element in human behavior.**

The Arguments for Determinism

Although most of the familiar evidence for determinism consists of scientific findings about human behavior, long before the rise of modern science forceful arguments were constructed to support this position. In fact, the area in which perhaps the greatest battles were fought between determinists and those who believed in free will was that of theological controversies. In many religious traditions, a form of **di-**

vine determinism has been advocated, claiming that God Himself is the sole causal agent in the universe and determines all actions, human and natural.

The Religious View

One form of divine determinism has argued that since God is all-powerful and all-knowing, He is able to control everything that occurs and to know beforehand (predetermine) everything that takes place. If there were any event, whether a human thought or the movement of a leaf, that God did not know in advance, then there would be a limitation on divine power. Since (in this theory) such a limitation is unthinkable, prior to the creation of the world God must have known all that would take place in the future. This being the case, He must have known every choice that we would ever make in the course of human history. Thus, **everything that anyone does is predestined and predetermined by God's prior knowledge and prior decisions**.

If one claims that God is the ultimate cause of whatever takes place, and that God has foreknowledge of everything that occurs, but that we are still able to choose freely, the theological determinists—like the great American Calvinist Jonathan Edwards—have argued that this is a spurious form of freedom. We may think that we are choosing freely, but our choices in fact have been determined in advance, so that we cannot actually make an original decision. Even though we may engage in elaborate deliberations about what choice to make, the ultimate decision is fixed, since God already knows it. Though we willingly make the choice that God ex-

pects, our willingness is merely another item that God controls, has foreseen and foreordained.

THE METAPHYSICAL BASIS

In addition to the theological argument for determinism, there is a metaphysical basis for this view, deriving from the maxim **"Every event must have a cause."** If one accepts this principle, then not only physical events but also mental events, such as our decisions, must have causal explanations. To apply the principle to everything except human wishes seems entirely unjustified and arbitrary.

If we accept the causal maxim as applying to the physical world because we feel that there must be some explanation of where the physical order comes from and why it functions as it does, then the mental world, and especially the world of our deliberations and choices, seems also to require a causal explanation. Why should I choose this instead of that? Why should I want this instead of that? How did I come to develop this sort of a mental outlook instead of some other? All these are perfectly reasonable questions. The answers appear to require a deterministic theory about our nature, our character, and our behavior, a theory that will account for one's performing certain acts and not others. Even if one insists that one's choices and decisions are due to factors within one's own nature, one is conceding that some sort of causal or deterministic explanation is possible.

In David Hume's account of causality (discussed in Chapter 5), the same kind of patterns of constant conjunction, or regular sequence, can be found with regard to our volitions as well as other things. How people will choose, or what they will want, can be predicted with considerable accuracy. Not only can trained scientists, such as psychologists and psychiatrists, discover laws of human volition so that they can predict the probable course of human affairs on the basis of certain concomitant events, but even in the more "practical" world of business, there seem to be reliable clues about human volition. Manufacturers are often able to foretell with impressive accuracy how many people will buy their product, given certain stimuli in the form of advertising, etc. If this sort of prediction were not possible, it would be extremely risky to manufacture anything save items that are necessary to the preservation of human life. Thus, even if we do not observe the force that makes people decide as they do (and, as Hume pointed out, we don't observe the force that makes physical actions occur either), we find that there are patterns of **constant conjunction between our voluntary decisions and other events, and that these patterns provide adequate clues for making reasonable or probable guesses about the future course of human choices, within a limited range of accuracy.**

Apart from the theological and metaphysical arguments for determinism, of course, the strongest and most convincing evidence at the present time is the almost overwhelming mass of scientific information about the factors that influence or determine human behavior. So many discoveries have been made in psychology, physiology, neurology, pharmacology, biochemistry, and biophysics, etc., that we appear to be fast approaching the determinist's dream of being able to predict *all* human behavior, not only the actions a person will perform but his/her thoughts and feelings as well. It may soon be the case that a thorough examination of the biological and psychological characteristics of an infant may enable scientists to write his/her autobiography before he/she lives his/her life, although they would probably have to write it in conditional terms, such that *if* certain things happened in the world around him/her, *then* he/she would have certain thoughts and feelings, make certain decisions, and perform certain actions. Most of us would prefer to think that this grim prospect is more science fiction than science.

In the face of the scientific evidence now available about the laws of human motivation, and the ways in which human attitudes can be affected, the case for determinism appears to be extremely strong. Anyone nowadays who would want to argue that human beings are really free agents, in spite of all the knowledge we have to the contrary, would be hard pressed to discover an area of human behavior in which there is not already some information indicating that there are influencing or determining factors that account for the actions and volitions of people.

Arguments for Free Will

Regardless of the apparent strength of the arguments and evidence for the deterministic theory, the opponents of this view have been able to formulate perhaps equally powerful arguments and to point out that there are experiences and attitudes of human beings that would make no sense at all unless people were free agents. First of all, the libertarians claim, everybody is aware of his/her own freedom. Even if someone can predict the choices I am going to make, when I make these choices, I feel that I am free. The proponents of free will insist that no determinist arguments can eliminate or account for the actual experience of freedom that we all sometimes have when we make our choices. (Of course, the determinists can point out that even if one grants that we have this experience, it in no way denies that in spite of how we may feel about it, our volitions are nonetheless determined.)

FREE WILL AND SCIENCE

In recent years the libertarians have also tried to enlist the support of a discovery in modern physics. This discovery is the **Heisenberg uncertainty principle,** which asserts that there is a fundamental indeterminacy in our knowledge about physical particles. If the position and velocity of a particle are to be experimentally determined, it is found that all experimental methods of so doing will give us the position accurately at the expense of error in the velocity determination; or they will give us the velocity accurately at the expense of error in the determination of position. It is not possible to determine both quantities without uncertainty.

The interpretation that has been made of this scientific law in relation to the free will question is that **there is an element of indeterminacy in nature.** This is taken to suggest that there is a degree of freedom of action on the most basic level of physical existence, and by analogy, that such freedom occurs on higher levels, such as

the human one. But the Heisenberg principle is actually irrelevant to the main issues involved in the argument between the libertarians and the determinists. It may show that a certain formulation of complete determinism is no longer adequate or in keeping with present-day physical theory. But this does not indicate in the slightest that because we may never be able to discover all the determining factors in the physical world, therefore human volitions are free. The Heisenberg principle has not led to any conclusion concerning the indeterminacy of our knowledge above the level of particle motions, which, in fact, are predictable in large numbers but not in individual cases. Indeterminacy on the lowest level of physical action certainly does not show that free will is involved or that any decisions have been made by the particles to act the way they do. Hence no serious analogy between the results of modern physical science and the basis of human volition seems possible.

The free will case is stronger when it points to those features of our moral and legal judgments that make sense only if human beings are in some sense free agents. Some opponents of theological determinism, and now of scientific determinism, have argued that most religious views of the world are silly or trivial if people cannot make free choices. The whole point of God's condemning people for original sin, and His later offer of salvation for people if they accepted or believed in certain principles, seems to require a free participation from a person's point of view. Otherwise, the theological drama, at least of the Judeo-Christian-Islamic tradition, becomes a puppet show in which we are trapped rather than a message that we can do anything about.

FREE WILL AND WILLIAM JAMES

This argument when conducted on the ethical level becomes, perhaps, more forceful. As William James insisted in his essay "The Dilemma of Determinism," there are two striking features of our moral experience that are intelligible only if we assume that people are free agents. The first of these is the occurrence of remorse. Over and over again people express the view that they regret that they did, or believed, certain things, and they wish that they had done or believed otherwise. If human actions or thoughts could not be otherwise, then what possible point can there be in regretting what might have been, especially since nothing else could have occurred?

Besides the fact that regret or remorse would be meaningless if we were not in some sense free, James also pointed out that our attribution of responsibility to people, and our punishing them for not exercising it properly, make no sense if we are all completely determined. We do not condemn and punish determined physical objects like stones and cars for the things they do, because we do not think that they are responsible free agents. Why, then, do we punish people if they also could not have done otherwise? If we punish them because we are determined by all sorts of factors to behave in this fashion, then punishment loses all moral significance and becomes only an indication of the influencing factors that determine the punishers. If we punish people in order to alter the factors that condition their

behavior, then are we, the judges, free in our decision to punish or merely determined by other factors? If the latter, then punishment is nothing more than inflicting the standards of the group in power on the minority, and has no moral or ethical significance. If the former, then the libertarian has made his/her point, by showing that someone must be assumed to be free in order that morality shall be meaningful.

A last form of argument that can be cited in favor of the free will theory is that arguments about the question assume that people are able to judge and decide these matters freely, according to the evidence. If the determinist's theory is true, then instead of propounding arguments, he/she ought to find out what factors produce philosophical decisions, and then employ these, whether they be wooden clubs, alcoholic beverages, drugs, etc. But the fact that he/she continues to use argumentation suggests that he/she, too, suspects there is some element of freedom in human behavior. Also, if one takes determinism seriously, anyone who believes in free will is determined to accept that theory, so what possible good could reasonable discussion accomplish?

Conclusion

The metaphysical problem of the freedom of the will, which has been argued for centuries, may indicate the role of the metaphysician more clearly. In trying to work out a general account or explanation of the elements of our experience, we find that there is **overwhelming evidence suggesting that human beings are completely determined** in what they do and think. On the other hand, some of the presuppositions that we employ in our moral life seem to require that we accept **some degree of free agency on the human level.** The libertarian may be able to show that complete determinism is incompatible with certain aspects of our experience and belief, but when he/she tries to specify in what our freedom may consist, he/she seems to be unable to find any type of human behavior for which there is no scientific evidence of its source. The metaphysician, faced with these two poles of explanation, is obliged to develop some general theory about the nature of the universe that can account for the evidence on both sides of the question.

Types of metaphysical systems

Having considered some examples of the kinds of problems that metaphysicians deal with, we shall now turn to some of the major metaphysical theories that have been constructed in the history of philosophy. Since their number is large, we shall consider only some of the basic ones, first of antiquity and then of more recent philosophy, that is, since the Renaissance. It has been claimed that all of the kinds of metaphysics are actually merely permutations of the views of Plato and Aristotle. Since that is in some degree the case, we shall start our survey with them.

Plato's Metaphysics

In a later discussion of the theory of knowledge, we shall see how some of the basic elements of Plato's metaphysical theory developed from his attempt to work out an explanation of what true knowledge we have and what it is about. Fundamentally, Plato's picture of the universe is that the real, stable, permanent part is the world of ideas, or forms. The world of ordinary experience is an illusory, transitory, unimportant sequence of events that take place in the physical world, the realm of appearance rather than of reality.

The relationship between the supersensible world of ideas and the visible, but only apparent, world of material things is set forth in Plato's dialogue entitled *Timaeus.* Both realms are described as if they were eternal. But the world of ideas is responsible for, or is the cause of, whatever order occurs in the material world. This is due not to any direct action by the ideal world, which does not appear to involve any sort of change or activity, but rather to some kind of agent who is able to introduce some shadow or copy of the real world into the chaos of the material or sensible universe.

On the one hand, there is a world of perfection, which is the permanent realm of ideas, comprising the meanings or definitions of things. On the other hand, there is some amorphous, incoherent "something" that is able to some extent to receive various aspects of the forms. But in order to explain how one of the realms comes in contact with the other, Plato conceived of an agent, called the **"Demiurge,"** who is able to exist on the borderline of both worlds. The Demiurge tries to impose the various forms on the chaotic material world, introducing triangularity, circularity, brownness, and so on, until there is some sort of order in the visible world. But the material world is not able to support or sustain these unchangeable ideas, and so it can only partake of them for limited periods of time. Hence there is bound to be the constant flux of the visible world as the temporary order it receives from the world of ideas dissipates.

LATER DEVELOPMENTS

Later Platonists in antiquity emphasized more and more the creative agency of the world of forms, changing it from a static world of perfection into the source of all power and reality in the universe. In the process of the absorption of Platonic metaphysics into Christian theology, the ideal world was finally made into the divine creator not only of the temporary order in the universe but of the physical universe itself as well. Thus, from Plotinus in the third century A.D. to St. Augustine 150 years later, there was a movement to transform the ideas into active agencies and, finally, into the divine power itself, which creates the physical world out of nothing and organizes it according to the divine pattern of the forms.

MIND-BODY-SOUL

The human world, in Platonic metaphysics, is conceived of as a borderline condition, somewhat akin to the position of the Demiurge. A person is part of the physical world in that he/she has a **body,** receives sense impressions, and so on. But at the same time, he/she has an immaterial **mind,** which is capable of knowing forms. He/she also has a directing agency, the **soul,** which is portrayed as a chariot rider, guiding and being guided by two horses, mind and body. The former wants to soar into the heavenly realm of the ideas and to contemplate them. The latter wants to

immerse itself in the affairs of physical life. The human soul is caught between these two opposing forces, trying to steer but trapped in its prison house, the body.

Somehow, in these circumstances, what the soul is able to accomplish in bringing about harmony remains afterward—after its liberation from bodily life. In terms of this metaphysical picture of human nature, we are supposed to be able to rid ourselves of complete determination by bodily needs. Most people, at present, have no freedom, because their lives are completely fixed by their physical requirements. One's soul, however, can liberate itself from this bondage and direct one's human life in terms both of one's physical circumstances and of one's intellectual desires. Then, after the end of bodily existence, the soul can soar upward to the eternal, perfect world of ideas.

THE INFUSION OF MYSTICISM

This side of Plato's metaphysics, though possibly not so intended by its author, has led to an otherworldly and mystical view, which is usually part of what is called **"Platonism."** (As the term is ordinarily employed in philosophy, it is a serious question as to whether Plato was himself a Platonist.) By stressing that aspect of Plato's theory (i.e., that which deals with the desire of the soul to escape from its prison house in the body), many Platonists have insisted that whatever is valuable in the universe is to be found only in the ideal world, not in the physical world. Somehow, they have insisted, we can enter into the higher metaphysical realms only by rejecting completely all material concerns and by contemplating the eternal characteristics of the perfect world of forms.

NEOPLATONISM

In the extension of Plato's views known as "**Neoplatonism**," the metaphysical theory propounded by Plotinus, the otherworldly point of view is distinctly emphasized. The Neoplatonists maintained that, metaphysically speaking, one could become part of that level of the universe with which one was concerned and which one understood. Thus one could change one's fundamental nature by renouncing interest in the physical world and by being concerned instead solely with the ideal world. If one finally reached the point of being able to contemplate the idea of ideas, the one, a mystical union would take place between oneself and the one. We are told that Plotinus was so convinced of this otherworldly and mystical side of Platonism that he tried to avoid showing even enough interest in his physical life to take a bath, and instead devoted himself to his studies and to contemplation so as to achieve this mystical union.

Aristotle's Metaphysics

In contrast to the dual nature of Plato's universe of the world of ideas and the shadowy world of physical things, Plato's student, Aristotle, constructed a metaphysical system devoted primarily to explaining **the natural world as the real world.** Starting from the conviction that the natural world we are all acquainted with in our daily life can be accounted for,

made intelligible without appealing to some metaphysical realms beyond human experience, he constructed a theory based on what he regarded as the fundamental characteristics of nature. Besides those that we discussed earlier (matter and form), **Aristotle also included the notion of purpose.**

TELEOLOGY

All the objects of our experience consist of formed matter moving or changing in a pattern that is usually purposeful, or **teleological, i.e., the motions or changes occur in order to achieve some goal.** As indications of this, Aristotle pointed to persistent patterns of development. Acorns always grow into oak trees, never into anything else. Children grow into adults. Stones always fall down until they reach a state of rest on the surface of the earth. In all these instances the motions or changes seem to be directed toward the achievement of specific results, which appear to be the same, or nearly the same, for all members of the group or species.

Further, the examples one can think of that violate this claim of fixed purposeful direction of change or motion actually constitute evidence for a more general thesis, that there is purposefulness that pervades all natural events and explains the course of nature. The instances in which objects do not change or move to accomplish an end are those in which objects have been interfered with by some outside agency. The acorn that is eaten by a squirrel, the stone that moves upward instead of downward, the child who fails to grow up because he is killed in his youth—all are instances of violent or, as

Aristotle would call it, **unnatural interference** with the object. But when the object is left to develop naturally, we note that it tends in a certain direction in order to arrive at some final result, which seems to be the same for all members of the same species.

The way in which this natural purposefulness, or teleology, exhibits itself is through the forms that objects tend to acquire in the course of their development. Every object in its natural history seems to be trying to realize or obtain a certain form proper to it, and its actions are all directed toward this goal. The acorn, for instance, normally goes through a series of developments, culminating in its losing its original form and taking instead the form of an oak. When it achieves a certain size, it seems to have reached the goal toward which its changes were tending. The stone when it falls to the surface of the earth also appears to have completed a series of changes that result in achieving its desired form, a resting place.

MATTER AND GOAL

Put in most general form, the Aristotelian contention is that every object in this universe, with the exception of God, is composed of some form of an underlying stuff called "matter." The matter of each kind of object has the potentiality for acquiring a form proper to the object, called its "end," or "goal." The process of change or motion is the actualizing of the potentiality of the object. There is a natural tendency or teleology that leads each and every object to seek the achievement of its natural goal, or final form. The alterations that every object undergoes cannot be understood except in terms of the purposes involved.

PURE FORMS

There is a **relative goal** for every object, that of realizing the form proper to its species. There is also an **ultimate goal** of every object, that of realizing a state of complete rest from which it will be absolutely impossible to change. But everything, insofar as it is composed of matter, always has some potentiality, some capacity for change, movement, or alteration. Hence, only by becoming **pure form** entirely devoid of matter would it be possible for an object to arrive at this final state.

As we look around the universe, we observe that to varying degrees different species are able to achieve some aspect of permanence, or immutability, or rest. The closest approximation to this state, Aristotle thought, is to be found in the heavens. The stars and the planets, as far as he could tell, change in only one respect, that is, they change only their position. Their shape and size remain forever constant; they neither decay nor grow. The only manner in which they appear to seek for their ultimate form is in their continually circling around the sky. In their movement, they always seem to repeat the same orbit, indicating that they are so close to complete rest that all that separates them from this goal is the regular, circular movement in which they engage in their unending quest for the state of being pure form.

However, compared to the near-perfect state of the celestial objects, those on the surface of the earth are much further removed from the achievement of the ultimate goal. All living things approach it only to the degree that the species remains forever the same, even though the individual members change, and finally decay and die. Since Aristotle was not an evolutionist, he regarded the form of the species as forever constant. Hence, it is through reproduction of the group, he claimed, that living things participate in "the eternal and the divine." But humans can come closer to the ultimate state than any other organism. They are able to accomplish this through **contemplating pure form.** To the extent that we can manage to reach such **pure thought, our minds acquire or realize a state of form alone, a conception of perfection.**

THE UNMOVED MOVER

Since, in one way or another, every object in the world aims to achieve a state of pure form, there must be an actual entity that is this goal of all change or motion. This object is called the **unmoved mover,** because, although it itself undergoes no change (since it contains no matter at all and, hence, has no potentiality), it is the reason why everything else in the universe moves. All things—from lowly stones to people and heavenly bodies—go through the kind of developments they do because of a natural tendency or desire to become like the unmoved mover. Thus it is out of love for the perfection of pure form that the natural world goes endlessly about its movement, alteration, and change. In Aristotle's metaphysical scheme, the perfect being, the unmoved mover, does nothing, and plays no part in the activities of the world, but only serves it by being its purpose and goal. This teleological universe, in which everything in nature happens purposefully and can be accounted for in terms of the relative and final ends being pursued, also has a frustrating aspect. Although all natural objects, except the unmoved mover, undergo change in order to actualize their potentialities, they are bound to fail because they never can become pure form. Even the heavenly bodies, so close to achieving perfection and rest, never do so; instead, they revolve forever in their circular orbits. The world, thus, is seen by Aristotle as an eternal series of processes, always pursuing the same goal and never arriving at this end.

Epicurean Metaphysics

In sharp contrast to the Aristotelian conception of the universe explained entirely in terms of purposeful action is **the materialistic view** of Epicurus. This theory, originally proposed by the early Greek philosopher Democritus and best known through the *De Rerum Natura* by the Roman poet Lucretius, portrays **a universe containing nothing but variously shaped atoms moving through empty space.** The conception of the indivisible atom as the fundamental feature of the universe, having no purpose, no qualities except its size and shape (and possibly weight), suffices, the Epicureans claimed, to account for all that we know about the world.

PHYSICAL THEORY

The permanent aspect of the universe is the physical atom, uncreated and unchangeable. The Epicureans considered the atoms as solid particles incapable of being broken down into smaller units and occurring in an unlimited number of sizes and shapes. There are, according to this theory, cube-shaped atoms, pyramid-shaped atoms, hooked atoms, spherical ones, and so on. Every object in the world is nothing but a combination of atoms distributed in empty space. This includes living things, and even the human mind, as well as inanimate objects like stones and tables. Though the atoms are eternally the same, their combinations alter, and hence the objects that we experience may change and disappear, but the atoms themselves never do.

Movement is a fundamental feature of the atom, which never had a beginning but has been going on for all time. In the original theory of Democritus, the atoms all fall downward at different rates of speed. Because of the varying velocities, the faster-moving atoms overtake the slower ones, and a collision occurs. Owing to their differences in shape, the colliding atoms are sent off in various directions, causing other collisions, and so on. As a result, all sorts of atomic combinations are formed and later broken up. **This version of metaphysical atomism is completely deterministic** in that from the initial position of atoms in the universe, and from the directions in which they are moving, it is possible to predict exactly the entire future course of the movements of all atoms. Hence every event in the world, including thoughts, volitions, and all mental events, is completely determined solely by the locations and motions of the basic physical particles.

INDETERMINACY

However, Epicurus, for various ethical reasons, was oppressed by the thought of a totally fixed universe, and therefore modified the ancient atomic theory by introducing an indeterminable element into the atomic world. According to him, besides moving straight downward and colliding, the atoms also occasionally have a "gentle swerve," which alters their course. The swerve, supposedly, occurs for no discoverable reason, but whenever it takes place, it disrupts the fixed, determined character of the atomic universe and prevents us from accurately predicting what will happen in the world.

Both the determinist and indeterminist versions of atomism are examples of a completely materialistic metaphysics. According to both Democritus and Epicurus, **everything in the entire universe can be accounted for solely in terms of the notions of matter and motion.** All physical action can be explained in terms of the "fortuitous concourse of atoms." Mental events, it is claimed, can also be characterized as the result of the collisions of a very fine type of spherical atom, called a "soul atom." Living things possess these atoms, whereas inanimate objects do not. When living things die, what happens is that the soul atoms depart from this particular combination.

PURPOSELESSNESS

Totally unlike the Aristotelian theory of the cosmos, Epicurean metaphysics portrays a world that is completely purposeless. It does not seek for causal explanations of natural events in the end or purpose toward which they are aiming; the explanation for why anything happens can only be in terms of the **prior events in the atomic world.** On both the cosmic level and the level of human events, nothing occurs in order to achieve any goal, but solely because certain atomic collisions have taken place. Man's habit of regarding the world as made for him/her, and the events in it as part of a plan in which he/she plays a central role, is condemned as an erroneous point of view. As far as our hopes, wishes, desires, thoughts are concerned, they have nothing to do with the actual course of events. Things have to happen because of the patterns existing in the world of atoms, not because we or anyone else want them to occur, nor because of any advantages that might result from their occurrence.

This completely materialistic metaphysics also rules out as important or relevant to the world's affairs the thoughts and ideals of humankind. These are only the results of atomic events within us, and rather than being guiding clues to the nature of events, or bases for comprehending the universe, they are merely the effects of certain material causes. The worlds of Platonic ideas, of Aristotelian purposes, are nothing but illusory visions taking place in the human brain and hence not deserving of serious consideration or of serving as the basis for our highest hopes.

The Epicurean vision of a purposeless, material cosmos is one of the great metaphysical systems. In spite of its sharp rejection of man's spiritual hopes and goals, this theory has contributed an all-encompassing scheme that provides a way of accounting for our experience. It has also served as an antidote to some of the grandiose metaphysical systems by returning people to an examination of the material world as a way of understanding their ex-

perience. It is quite understandable that during the great religious era, the Middle Ages, Epicureanism was almost totally neglected, but in the beginnings of modern science, in the sixteenth and seventeenth centuries, there was a strong revival of interest in ancient atomic metaphysics.

Stoic Metaphysics

The last of the major classical metaphysical theories that we shall consider is that of the leading opponents of the Epicureans, the **Stoics.** Like the former, they held to a materialistic conception of the world. But the Stoics also contended that the **material world was pervaded by a dynamic force, which acted not mechanically but purposefully,** in order to maintain a universal rational pattern throughout all nature.

MATTER AND REASON

The fundamental elements of the Stoic cosmos are **matter and reason,** which are found everywhere. **Matter** is not a series of atomic units but a continuous amorphous stuff, which is pervaded by a rational force that gives it its characteristics. Physical objects, according to this theory, represent various states of tension of matter owing to the action of the rational forces that exist throughout the physical world. The dynamic quality of these rational forces brings about all the changes that take place.

The element of **reason** is sometimes called **the soul of the universe, sometimes the rational seeds within it, sometimes universal reason, or sometimes God.** It is conceived of as a cosmic power that organizes and governs the entire universe, not from outside but from within. As a totality, it is the guiding principle of the world; and considered individually, it is the rational element, or seed, within each separate thing that governs or directs it.

STOIC DETERMINISM

Since in Stoic metaphysics, everything that happens, happens for a reason, and the reason is the plan of the cosmic rational element, there is complete determinism in nature. But this determinism is not the result of previous developments in the physical world; rather, it is due to the purpose of the cosmos, the end result toward which universal reason works. Everything must be as it is because its occurrence is rationally dictated by the all-pervasive reason in accordance with its rational purpose. Thus, **every event is rational and necessary in this completely rational world.** For anything different to take place than what does, there would have to be some reason. But there cannot be any, since universal reason directed the occurrence of what does happen, and hence this must be the sole rational possibility.

FATALISM AND OPTIMISM

This theory of the Stoics leads to **a complete fatalism and a cosmic optimism.** The fatalistic view results from recognizing that **everything that happens must happen and there is nothing we can do about it.** Since the causal agency is beyond our control or influence, instead of brooding about the course of events past, present, and future, we ought to accept the prevailing state of affairs—**what occurs must occur.**

The only area in which anything can happen that is not necessary is in the realm of thought. One can either accept or reject, in the mind, the course of events. The person who acquiesces in the universal law of nature and of reason can be at peace with the world. On the other hand, the person who cannot or will not accept this fatalistic view is unhappy and at war with the world. He/she spends his/her life disturbed at what happens and wishing it were otherwise. Since it cannot be, all that results is unhappiness, while the course of nature remains the same.

The optimistic side of the Stoic metaphysical outlook arises from **equating the necessity and rationality of what occurs with its goodness.** Since universal reason directs the activities of the world, they must be directed in order to achieve some cosmic purpose. This purpose would only be the goal if it were **the right goal** for the entire universe. No matter what happens, it is the result of the necessary actions guided by the universal reason pervading all of nature—therefore, this must be the best of all possible worlds.

The optimistic claim leads to the view that the universe can be judged only as a whole and in terms of the direction in which it is moving. To regard a part as significant, and to evaluate it, is to miss the essential point that the purpose of universal reason is expressed and worked out throughout the entire cosmos. Thus one who cannot understand how a basically good universe can contain such awful events as earthquakes, famines, plagues, and wars does not realize that the entire material world is interrelated and inter-directed. Even the parts of the whole that we may not approve of represent some aspect—a necessary one—of the rational scheme of things. If the parts are seen in terms of the larger context, then one, supposedly, will accept them as required features of this best of all possible worlds, and not as defects.

Stoic metaphysics, then, represents a combination of a pure materialism and a type of teleology. Nature is conceived of as entirely physical and also as pervaded by some rational cosmic force. As a result, instead of arriving at a deterministic, purposeless picture of the world, as the Epicureans did, the Stoics make their determinism the consequence of the universal guiding spirit, and the physical events that occur are necessary and good parts of a necessary and good world, moving toward the most reasonable, and hence best, of all possible conclusions.

Cartesianism, Modern Metaphysics

Turning from the ancient metaphysical systems, which form the basic patterns of the later ones, we shall next consider some post-Renaissance theories. With the beginnings of modern science, and the realizations that the older accepted systems of thought, especially medieval Aristotelianism, were no longer adequate to account for man's new knowledge, philosophers sought new metaphysical theories that might be more appropriate to this new situation.

The philosophy of Descartes provided this kind of metaphysics. (In calling it "new," this is not to ignore the fact that much of Descartes's fundamental outlook was based upon certain theories in the Platonic tradition, especially those of the great Christian Platonist, St. Augustine.) It is from the views of Descartes that most of the metaphysical systems of the last three centuries begin, trying to improve upon them or to overcome what they regard as difficulties in the Cartesian system.

THE THREE SUBSTANCES

In Descartes's metaphysics, as we have seen, there are three basic components in the universe, called "substances"—**God, mind, and matter.** Everything else is a modification, or particular example, of these. God is the creative substance, who has made the other two. The mental substance has, as its essential property, that **it thinks,** whereas the essential property of matter is that **it is extended.** Everything that happens in either the material or the mental realm is entirely dependent on the will of God, which orders and controls them.

The physical world is conceived of as a vast world machine, which operates according to God's constant laws. God constantly conserves and controls a physical order in which various portions of extension move others by contact, producing the regular world that modern science describes. According to Descartes, everything that is extended is part of this machine, including all of the animal world, which he thought of as a series of smaller machines, operating entirely by mechanical principles, but, possibly, more complicated than inanimate objects.

The only aspect of the created world that is not part of the world machine is—

mind. Mind is completely unextended, and hence not in contact with the material world. Mind engages in mental activities like thinking, willing, and the like. As we have seen earlier in this chapter, one of the gravest problems in Cartesian metaphysics is to explain satisfactorily how the mental world and the physical world can be in any way related and how God can be said to act causally on either of them.

Descartes's mechanism, **in denying completely any purposeful tendencies in the physical world,** provided a satisfactory metaphysical basis for the new physical theories of such scientists as Galileo. But at the same time, the sharp division of the created world between the mental and the physical substance gave rise to many difficulties in constructing a consistent theory of the entire universe. Also, the Cartesian conception of the overpowering role played by God seemed to tend toward a kind of mysticism rather than providing a basis for scientific knowledge. If all power rested in God alone, then neither aspect of the created world—mind or matter—could have any causal efficacy. Any account of natural events would ultimately reduce to saying, "It happens because God so wills." Hence, instead of employing mental or physical terms, the end result would be to convert all questions into divine mysteries, which mortals can never comprehend.

Because of problems that appear to arise out of Descartes's rigid separation of the basic components of the universe, various metaphysicians sought to construct theories that would modify the Cartesian conception by simplifying its fundamental conceptions. On the one hand, some philosophers felt that by eliminating the material substance from the metaphysical system, a more satisfactory theory could be developed. Others insisted that the solution lay in denying the mental or spiritual components of the Cartesian world and in working out a more advanced form of mechanism. Thus, out of the original Cartesian metaphysical theory two divergent kinds of metaphysics have developed, one **mentalistic,** called "idealism," and the other a **modern form of materialism.**

Idealism

The metaphysical meaning of **idealism** has little to do with the ordinary meaning of the word. Instead, its philosophical usage relates to **a theory that holds that the most important element in the nature of reality is mind or spirit.** After Descartes, some philosophers developed a Cartesian system without the notion of a physical substance. The full flowering of this kind of theory appears in the metaphysical views of the Irish philosopher Bishop Berkeley (discussed more fully in Chapter 5).

BISHOP BERKELEY

Berkeley's contention is that there is no such entity as a physical world, or matter, in the sense of an independently existing object. Instead, all that we ordinarily call physical objects are actually collections of ideas in a mind. A table is the set of perceptions that I have when I touch, look, and so on. But this is not to say that things are really different from what they appear to be. **Berkeley insisted that all that we** can ever know about objects is merely the ideas we have of them. **The appearances we experience are the very objects, and the appearances are sensations or perceptions of a thinking being.**

Mind and God

But what accounts for the series of ideas that occur and for the regularity of the patterns? According to Berkeley, ideas themselves are only passive effects of something, unable to produce or cause any further ideas. We, the perceivers who are aware of the ideas, are able to influence or affect only a very small number, if any, of the ideas that we have. Whether we will it or not, when we open our eyes, we perceive certain ideas. When our finger is pricked, even though we may not enjoy it, or wish it, we experience a painful sensation, and so on. Therefore, Berkeley claimed, the order of ideas must be due to some mind other than ours, a mind that constantly perceives all the ideas and at various times makes us perceive the particular group of them that constitutes our experience. **This universal mind that always perceives is God.**

Further, according to Berkeley's theory, **mind is active, and is an agent,** while **ideas are only the passive effects of mental activity.** In fact, the only sort of power that can produce anything exists solely in mind, either in the finite spirits, which are ourselves, or in the infinite mind of God. **The entire, magnificent world of nature, with its wonderful scientific harmony, is nothing but an expression of the ideas in the divine mind.** As Berkeley suggested, **the natural world was presented to us as a kind of sign language for interpreting God's mind.**

Thus the cosmos, in Berkeley's metaphysics, consists of spirits, or minds, some finite and one infinite, which are all active agents. In addition, there are the passive effects—ideas—which have the degree of permanence that they exist as the constant perceptions in the mind of God. They also, at various times, are the experiences of human beings. These ingredients, mind and ideas, Berkeley claimed, provide a completely adequate basis to account for all our knowledge about the world, whereas a metaphysical system including another independent ingredient—matter—would create all sorts of difficulties and problems.

SOLIPSISM

The Berkelian theory, which its author called **"immaterialism"** (the world conceived without matter), led to further extensions—**subjective idealism and solipsism. The latter view is that the universe, as far as one can ever tell, is nothing but myself, my mind, and its ideas.** This view develops from Berkeley's argument that the only things that we can know to exist are those that we can experience. This theory eliminates any other mind but my own, and any other objects but my ideas, and leaves the universe nothing but the sequence of thoughts that occur in me.

J. G. FICHTE

Besides the implausibility of solipsism, there is the problem in such a view of accounting for the origin or cause of one's ideas. In order to work out a more satisfactory theory of idealism, the German metaphysician Johann Gottlieb Fichte—

at the end of the eighteenth century—constructed his theory of **subjective idealism.** This view differed from Berkeley's and the solipsist's by insisting that mind is a continuously creative and evolving entity, somehow generating the various features of the world that we know.

Before expounding his theory, Fichte pointed out that there were two major metaphysical outlooks: **materialism**—the view that everything is to be accounted for in terms of material causes; and **idealism**—the view that the explanation must be in terms of mental causes. Neither of these theories can be proven or disproven, and each can develop arguments against the other. The philosopher who wants to meditate on metaphysical matters first must decide which outlook he accepts, and then proceed to construct his theories.

Ego and non-ego

Having made his choice for the idealistic outlook, Fichte envisaged the universe as the outpourings of the fundamental substance, called the **"ego."** From this source, he claimed, two aspects emerge, **the self that I am aware of, and the non-ego, the things that I regard as other than myself.** Both of these depend upon, arise from, are intelligible in terms of the underlying creative agent behind the scenes. Thus, by the time one develops any awareness or consciousness of the meaning of nature of one's experience, it is already in the form of **object** (the outside world) and **subject** (oneself). The subjective idealist comprehends this two-sided world in relation to a mental source or agent who created it, or who provides the grounds or foundation for making it understandable.

The person of idealistic tendency tries to probe beyond and behind the immediate features of his/her world in the quest for some explanation for them. The characteristics of the so-called "physical world," as we know it, and of our individual mental worlds, as we are conscious of them, are both known as effects of something. The entity that could account for both the objective and subjective aspects of our experience must lie behind both. Thus the ego of Fichte's metaphysics is not simply the mind of the solipsist, transformed into a creative agent who generated the entire universe. Instead, the ego is more impersonal, a creative agency from which each individual mind is derivative. Each person, and the world that he/she is aware of, are an expression of something more general, of the creative activity of the ego. In his efforts to avoid criticism from orthodox religious quarters, Fichte sometimes stated his theory so that he almost gives the impression that he is talking about the traditional notion of God, rather than a transcendent, superpersonal mind, as the source of all aspects of the universe.

OBJECTIVE OR ABSOLUTE IDEALISM: HEGEL

Perhaps the most famous modern metaphysician is Fichte's successor, Georg Wilhelm Friedrich Hegel, whose views dominated metaphysical thought throughout the nineteenth century and who has become somewhat of a villain for many twentieth-century philosophers. The abstruse complexities of his writings have made Hegel a professional joke, so that when somebody wrote a book entitled *The Secret of Hegel's Philosophy*, a reviewer pointed out that the author had kept the secret very well. Perhaps it is not possible to make complete sense out of the entire Hegelian scheme. In this brief sketch, we shall not attempt to enter into much of the involved structure of Hegel's system, but only to indicate a few of the central themes.

World and the absolute

One of the main Hegelian contentions is that everything in the universe can be understood only in terms of an **objective or absolute mind,** which has been evolving throughout the world's history into a transcendent, self-contained being. As we saw (see page 84–5), each stage in the world's development is the expression of the inner struggle of the absolute to achieve complete self-realization. In the process of evolving, it has been striving toward a stage of complete understanding and intelligibility.

Hegel claimed that the earlier phases of the history of the absolute could not explain or account for the events of nature and history. Every attempt to construct a system that would provide a complete account of the source, the nature, and the meaning of the universe, proved to be incomplete or unsatisfactory. (In Hegel's terms, each of these attempts contains contradictions, or contradictory elements.) The absolute itself was constantly striving to overcome this predicament by rendering itself, through its expression, the world, intelligible and consistent. Hence the world that has appeared in the historical realm has represented a successive series of approximations on the part of the absolute toward realizing its goal of making itself a complete, comprehensive,

and rational foundation of the totality of world experience.

To clarify this, let us consider Hegel's picture in terms of the evolution of the world. The universe commenced as a series of discrete particles, providing no explanation of how they were related, why they were here, and so on. Any attempt to describe this almost chaotic state of the universe would encounter difficulties, because any characteristics that were present in the world would be insufficient to describe the whole universe. Thus, if one asserted that squareness was a characteristic of the universe, this would be contradicted by other characteristics of the world. The absolute, in order to make itself more intelligible, synthesized the elements into a describable pattern—the physical system of the world.

Even so, this physical account was inadequate to explain why this takes place or to answer all the questions that could be asked. One could still find contradictory elements, or at least conflicting or apparent incompatible ones, in the attempt to work out a completely rational explanation of the world. So the absolute evolved to a higher stage, the chemical one, and then the biological one, and finally the human one. These stages represent the "march of reason through the world," the realization of a fuller expression of the absolute or objective mind, so that it can become a more consistent explanation of the universe.

The dialectic

In the Hegelian conception, this process of the absolute is a type of "logical" one, transformed in our experience into a historical one. The "logical" development is the famous Hegelian **dialectic, wherein each attempt to formulate something about the universe (a thesis) is contradicted by another formulation (an antithesis), and the conflict between the two is resolved in a proposition that incorporates the partial truth of both of them (the synthesis).** What is frequently presented as a conflict of thesis and antithesis is actually an example of two incomplete accounts that are then synthesized into a more general formulation. Thus the attempt to explain all physical processes quantitatively is opposed by the purely qualitative physical events, requiring an explanation that encompasses both.

The absolute is portrayed by Hegel as striving constantly to overcome, or resolve, this dialectic of thesis and antithesis by higher and higher syntheses until it will finally achieve complete self-realization in an all-encompassing synthesis, which will include all partial truths in one vast truth. At this point, the inner logical struggle will be over, as will the history of the world. Since each stage of dialectical ascent is expressed outwardly in terms of some stage in the development of the historical world, when the absolute reaches completion, so will the cosmos. The latter will then be a completely coherent entity, which can be entirely understood.

As the dialectical struggle goes on and the universe develops, so does our understanding of it. Until the world becomes completely intelligible, there can be only limited comprehension of its structure, since the developments themselves are not yet completely rational. The intelligence of any individual can reach only that degree of understanding and coher-ence that the absolute is then expressing. Therefore, the entire structure of the universe can be stated in a metaphysical system only when the absolute has reached full self-realization. At that point, thought and being will become identical, since full comprehension and the full state of the universe will be one and the same thing.

The Hegelian culmination

Hegel's **objective idealism** is the final culmination of transforming the Cartesian metaphysic into a theory where only mind is real, and only mental actions and effects can form a basis for accounting for the world of our experience. Moving from Berkeley's static world of ideas, as the persistent thoughts in the divine mind, to Fichte's creative ego, generating both the subjective and objective features of the universe, **Hegel completely objectifies thought and mind into the basic independent entity,** devoid of all personality and all subjective properties. **The Hegelian absolute mind becomes the real universe, manifesting itself outwardly as world history, and inwardly as the rational dialectical process, marching toward full self-realization.** Somehow the metaphysical system, when properly understood, is not just a description of the objective universe, but actually is the absolute, intellectually expressed.

Materialism

In contrast to the idealist's approach, the **materialists sought to develop a modified Cartesianism, eliminating mind, and possibly God, from the basic metaphysical scheme, and attempting to explain everything in terms of material events.** Beginning with Thomas Hobbes in the seventeenth century and continuing with the French materialists of the Enlightenment, the type of theory developed did not differ substantially from the Greek materialistic theories except in details.

IMPACT OF SCIENCE

Instead of employing the crude, speculative atomism of Democritus and Epicurus, the modern materialists tried to show in more elaborate terms, based upon the general discoveries and theories of modern physical science, that a purely materialistic account can be given of everything we know. Using first the physics of Descartes and of his contemporary atomist, Pierre Gassendi, and later the theories of Isaac Newton, the materialists tried to show that all events in the universe can be explained as the results of mathematically describable motions of extended, solid features of the universe.

The rapid growth of the physical sciences, of physics and astronomy, gave an initial appeal to the materialistic theory in the minds of a great many forward-looking thinkers, who had become exceedingly skeptical of previous metaphysical theories. The difficulties in a complete materialism seemed to arise in extending the already triumphant pattern of material explanation from physical things to living and thinking things. The beginnings of the social sciences in the eighteenth century, the development of modern chemistry in the nineteenth century, and the tremendous progress in biology and psychology in more recent times have all given greater authority to the materialist in his belief that even if it

has not yet been accomplished, it will soon be possible to account for all events solely in terms of physical concepts and laws.

But from the time of Descartes, certain problems in developing a complete materialism arose. The Cartesian metaphysic contains a materialism about the natural world, both animate and inanimate, but also recognizes that this cannot be extended to the mental world. In order to extend it to the world of living things, Descartes had to claim that animals are really "automata," small machines. Since Descartes's day, the materialists have tried to make good the claim that all living processes, like digestion, growth, reproduction, can be explained in a purely mechanical fashion, and that similar kinds of explanation can be offered for the events of one's mental life.

Biology

As a result, there has been a running battle between two opposing groups of theoretical biologists, the **vitalists** and the **mechanists.** The contention of the latter is that it is gradually being shown that various processes of animals and plants can be explained in physical and chemical terms, and that there is no reason to suspect that this cannot ultimately be done with all biological questions. On the other hand, their opponents claim either that it is already the case that one has to abandon purely materialistic concepts and introduce certain other ones, like "life-force," which cannot be reduced to physical or chemical notions, or that this will occur. Without such nonmaterialistic ideas, the vitalists assert, it will not be possible to give a satisfactory account of the information we already possess about the behavior of living things.

Psychology

Similarly, in psychological theory a battle has been, and is being, waged between those who believe that some sort of materialistic science of human behavior can be, or is being, developed and those who insist that the evidence indicates that this is not, or cannot be, the case. Here the issues involved are extremely complex, and much of the merit of each case will depend upon the future course of experimental research in establishing whether or not a satisfactory explanation of human and animal psychology can be developed along materialistic lines.

Physics

However, as modern physics moves further away from the simple mechanical conceptions of Newton's theory, the original materialistic metaphysic has begun to lose some of its force and appeal. If the picture of the physical world presented by the scientists is no longer one of simple physical particles in motion, as the cause of all physical events, then a theory about the basic characteristics of reality based on an outmoded scientific theory is not as acceptable. As scientific theorists move further away from a view that science provides accurate accounts of the intimate secrets of physical reality, to **a more empirical conception of science as a hypothetical model of what the world may be like, which suffices for predicting the future course of experience**, a materialism based on the developments in scientific research has become less attractive. Those who base their theories about the fundamental characteristics of the world upon an interpretation of our scientific knowledge have tended to adopt a **positivistic or pragmatic, or less materialistic, form of naturalistic theory than the classical forms of materialism.**

DIALECTICAL MATERIALISM

Although the type of materialism advocated by Karl Marx is discussed in detail in Chapter 2, it is relevant to say something about it here, before leaving this subject. **Marx's materialism is based on "standing Hegel on his head" and transforming the Hegelian idealistic pattern into a theory about the natural world.** Instead of attributing the dialectical scheme to some absolute or objective mind, **it is in nature alone that the processes of overcoming contradictions take place.**

Everything in the universe is interpreted as being the result of physical forces in operation. But these forces, rather than operating merely in a mechanical pattern, proceed in a dialectical fashion, achieving or evolving more and more consistent and coherent features. All the processes of nature can be explained as dialectical processes of this type, but as we have seen (page 83), Marx emphasizes the economic aspect of his dialectical materialism. The human world, which is, of course, the chief concern of the theory, **represents a type of materialistic being whose way of existence is determined by the material factors involved in one's attempts to produce sufficient material goods for one's survival.**

Economic theory

Each type of economy that has evolved in history contains conflicting, or contradictory, elements (a thesis and an antithesis) that have been resolved in a synthesis, a new type of economy, which in turn has involved new conflicting elements, and so on. The conflict between slave and master, serf and lord, has finally given rise to the present material system of production—capitalism. **At each stage, the entire culture—the intellectual and artistic forces—is an expression of the then existing materialistic base, which determines and accounts for human societies.**

The "synthesis" of communism

According to Marx, the present form of material life, based on a capitalistic economy, contains a final conflict that is to be resolved, a conflict between the producer, the worker, on the one hand, and the employer, the owner of the means of production, on the other. This will ultimately be synthesized in an economy in which this separation between employee and employer disappears, and with it all conflict. At this point, the Hegelian dream of the complete realization of the absolute will take place in the natural world instead, with the elimination of all contradictions, and the achievement of a totally rational social order—for Marx, a Communist society.

Naturalism

The last type of modern metaphysics that we shall consider is **naturalism.** In this theory, it is claimed that all the features of the universe can be explained or accounted for in **natural or experiential terms.** Materialism is a restricted form of naturalism in which only basic physical concepts, of matter and motion, are thought requisite in order to explain everything. **Naturalism can allow for the employment of any of the concepts that arise from our study of nature and experience, and not merely the concepts of physical science.**

The naturalists contend that beginning with the Cartesian system, an artificial division has been imposed upon our conceptions of the world that has continually engendered unsatisfactory results. After Descartes completely separated mind and matter, metaphysicians have tried to undo the damage by eliminating either mind or matter, or tried to reduce one category to the other, with unfortunate consequences. Instead, it is suggested, one should recognize that both are aspects of our experience, and ought to be interpreted in these terms.

THE INFLUENCE OF SCIENCE

There have been many different types of naturalist accounts of the universe, usually modeled on the prevailing scientific motifs of the time. The basic natural or experimental conceptions have been, by and large, drawn from the dominant scientific discoveries of the time, in physics, biology, etc. In the nineteenth and twentieth centuries, the most common expressions of naturalism have usually tried to work out consistent accounts of all of our knowledge about the world in terms of biological and psychological themes, especially in the light of the evolutionary aspect of the natural and human world brought to the fore in nineteenth-century geology, biology, history, psychology, etc. Such philosophers as Henri-Louis Bergson, Friedrich Nietzsche, William James, John Dewey, and others have attempted to construct general theories about the nature of reality in purely naturalistic terms, extending the insights provided by these sciences into metaphysical theories.

EXPERIENCE

In the most common versions of naturalism, the fundamental category is taken to be experience itself. Out of this, two aspects are distinguished, the objective and the subjective. These are not separate entities, the external world and the mind, but, rather, ways of looking at, or regarding, **certain relationships or processes that take place in experience.** On the basis of these aspects, further discriminations, or selections, are made, ones that encompass other aspects in terms of scientifically organized patterns, human values, purposes.

The evolving, developing character of experience becomes the basis for regarding the describable or understandable world, both objective and subjective, as **determinate to some degree.** Future possibilities are open as to what further natural properties, orders, and tendencies may appear. Hence there is also a degree of openness in naturalistic explanation, that **any attempt is always an approximation of the characteristics of the universe rather than a fixed and final description** that is bound to be correct for all times and all places.

Some naturalistic theories develop some of the suggestive leads of Stoic metaphysics in conceiving of the natural and experiential order as having a dynamic, emergent feature, which brings forth new facets in nature in the course of time. Such a natural dynamism would account for, these naturalists believe, the evolutionary character of our natural knowledge without appealing to any supernatural agency. It would also provide a basis for the belief in both the openness of natural developments, or their indeterminacy at any given moment, and the need for revising one's estimates of the fundamental nature of the universe.

Some criticisms of metaphysics

These metaphysical theories attempt in one way or another to present some **general system that will account for the manifold characteristics of the world, our knowledge of it, and our beliefs, hopes, aspirations, and other aspects of our "subjective" nature.** For over two thousand years, metaphysicians have debated as to which of these theories is more satisfactory, more plausible. After all this time, though many of these systems may appear as interesting speculations, there seems to be no general agreement among philosophers as to which of them is true, or at least truer than the others. Moreover, each school of metaphysicians appears to be able to show that there are serious difficulties in the views of all the others, but does not seem to be able to develop a satisfactory justification of its own views.

Because of this confusion, some philosophers have thought that the fundamental problem is that there is something wrong with metaphysical reasoning itself.

If this be the case, the question is not the truth or plausibility of the theories, but rather what is wrong with the entire metaphysical enterprise, and why is it bound, by its very nature, to lead to unsatisfactory results? We shall consider the answers to these queries by two of the most famous critics of metaphysical reasoning and system construction, David Hume and Immanuel Kant, who both claimed to have discovered the basic limitations that prevent any successful solution to any metaphysical problem.

Hume's Criticism of Metaphysics

Hume's criticism of metaphysics derives from his empirical and skeptical point of view, and is summed up in the famous concluding passage from his *Enquiry Concerning Human Understanding*. There he asked:

> When we run over libraries, persuaded of these principles [that is, Hume's empirical principles], what havoc must we make? If we take in our hand any volume; of divinity or school metaphysics, for instance; let us ask, Does it contain any abstract reasoning concerning quantity or number? No. Does it contain any experimental reasoning concerning matter of fact and existence? No. Commit it then to the flames: for it can contain nothing but sophistry and illusion.

The basis for the book-burning crusade is **Hume's contention that the only meaningful terms or ideas are either sense impressions or mathematical concepts.** Sense impressions are meaningful because they can be tested by experience and observation; mathematical concepts are meaningful because they express relationships between ideas that we can in-

tuitively see to be true and certain. No other concept can be meaningful, since we have no way of testing its validity. Hence the key notions of the metaphysicians—e.g., "substance," "reality," "mind," "matter"—actually are meaningless, since we are unable to define them in terms of anything that we know about. Therefore, the propositions that metaphysicians propound might sound impressive, but they have no significance.

MEANING AND EXPERIENCE

Further, the questions that the metaphysicians are seeking to answer are as meaningless as the concepts that they employ in trying to do so. They wish to find out what is the nature of reality, what is the cause of the world's characteristics, what is the relationship of matter and mind, what degree of freedom does the human will exercise, what is the role of God in the affairs of natural and human existence, and so on. But in terms of the sorts of relationships that we are capable of discerning in our experience, and in mathematics, none of these can be taken seriously. We would not even know what they are questions about, how one would go about answering them, or what a correct answer would look like.

Over and over again in his philosophical writings, Hume explained various metaphysical problems, and showed that when analyzed in terms of his empirical meaning-criterion, the questions dissolved into meaninglessness. If our knowledge about the world is restricted to what we experience, plus the inferences we make as a result of the constant conjunctions of events, and our own habit of expecting the future to resemble the past, then how can we possibly tell if there is any permanent structure to reality above and beyond what we are aware of? There is nothing in our experience that suggests that our impressions belong to some object outside of experience, or that they can be explained in terms of such an object.

THE CRITIQUE OF "SUBSTANCE"

The basic principle of metaphysical explanation up to Hume's time, the notion of a "substance," whether it be mental, physical, or divine, which is the fundamental element of the universe, Hume found completely unintelligible. If our ideas come to us from our sensations or our reflections, where does this notion come from?

> If it be conveyed to us by our senses, I ask, which of them; and after what manner? If it be perceived by the eyes, it must be a color; if by the ears, a sound; if by the palate, a taste; and so of the other senses. But I believe none will assert, that substance is either a color, or sound, or a taste. The idea of a substance must therefore be derived from an impression or reflection, if it really exist. But the impressions of reflection resolve themselves into our passions and emotions; none of which can possibly represent a substance. We have therefore no idea of substance, distinct from that of a collection of particular qualities, nor have we any other meaning when we either talk or reason concerning it.

Not only do we have no impression or idea of this thing called "substance," but when we look at what the metaphysicians say about it, we are further baffled. They say that a substance is something that can exist by itself, that is, something that can be conceived of apart from everything else, and requiring nothing else to account for itself. But if this means anything, Hume pointed out, it applies to every perception that we can have. Each idea in our mind can be thought of separately and can be distinguished from every other idea. When we conceive of the idea apart from all others, it seems to meet the metaphysicians' meaning of "substance."

But, the metaphysical philosophers might say, Hume has missed the whole point of what metaphysical explanations are about. A substance is something entirely different from a perception, and is that which accounts for why the perception has the characteristics that it does, and is that to which the perception belongs or inheres. When presented with this view, Hume observed: "We have no perfect idea of anything but of a perception. A substance is entirely different from a perception. We have, therefore, no idea of a substance."

As to the second point, that a metaphysical account in terms of substances is necessary to explain the existence or nature of our ideas or perceptions, Hume again disagreed. We have our perceptions; our impressions occur. Nothing seems to be required to explain or support their existence. As far as we can tell, they simply are, and any question about why they are, and why they are what they are, seems both uncalled for and actually unintelligible. So Hume concluded: "What possibility then of answering that question, Whether perceptions inhere in a material or immaterial substance, when we do not so much as understand the meaning of the question?"

When one looks further into these matters, Hume found, it only becomes worse. The concept of matter, and the physical world, as really composed of extended solid stuff in motion, Hume found as unintelligible as Berkeley did before him. If the qualities of immediate experience—e.g., color, sound, taste, smell—are excluded from being features of the material world that supposedly exists independently from us, then, Hume insisted, we cannot possibly conceive of what this matter is like. All the qualities that the metaphysicians attribute to matter—extension, motion, and solidity—turn out to be just as subjective as the others, as Berkeley had earlier proved. But once "we conclude, that neither color, sound, taste, nor smell have a continued and independent existence," and "we exclude these sensible qualities," then "there remains nothing in the universe which has such an existence."

THE CRITIQUE OF IDEALISM

When one leaves the problems of the materialists aside and examines the claims of the idealists, who would explain everything in terms of mind, the same difficulties arise. The concept of mind is just as unclear as that of matter. If we search for some impression that gives rise to such an idea, we find that there is none. We are not aware of some entity to which all of our thoughts belong. Instead, we are acquainted only with the succession of our ideas. Hence we do not know of any mental substance, nor do we find any way in which our perceptions or thoughts might belong to it.

THE MIND-BODY PROBLEM

When one examines some of the specific problems that metaphysicians are concerned with, it appears that their concepts make no sense and that the difficulties are all of their own making. Consider, for example, the mind-body problem, which had been so much debated in the hundred years between Descartes and Hume. The question of how a mental event can be related to a physical event, and vice versa, is a difficulty only if one first introduces the concepts of mental and material substance and then asks how, if these two are entirely different, there can be any necessary connection between what happens in one and what takes place in the other. If one eliminates the meaningless concepts of the two substances, and the equally unintelligible idea of a necessary connection between events, then what is left? Only the question of whether it is possible that certain events that we call mental, such as tastes and smells, can be constantly conjoined with others that we call physical, such as the movements of exended objects? The answer, Hume insisted, is yes. We experience this sort of conjunction all the time, between the taste of a pear and the shape of a pear, between the sound of C sharp and the striking of a certain key on the piano, and so on.

If it is pointed out that the mere fact that these constant conjunctions occur does not explain how the physical event produces the mental one, or vice versa, Hume could easily reply, "So what?" In no other case, whether it be of two constantly conjoined physical events, like a hammer moving and pushing a nail, or two conjoined mental events, do we ever discover how one produces the other. No **causal relationship** can ever be **observed**, even in the material world (see page 224). Thus the special case of conjunctions between mental and physical events raises no new problem, unless it is complicated by the introduction of some meaningless metaphysical notions.

FREE WILL AND NECESSITY

Similarly, Hume contended, if one examined the free will controversy, one would find again that there was no real problem. The difficulties have been due entirely to metaphysical notions introduced by the philosophers rather than to any grave, intricate matters concerning the notions of liberty and necessity. Thus Hume claimed:

> If I be not much mistaken, we shall find, that all mankind, both learned and ignorant, have always been of the same opinion with regard to this subject, and that a few intelligible definitions would immediately have put an end to the whole controversy.

All that anybody ever meant by necessity, or necessary connection, is that two events have been constantly conjoined, and that when we see one of them, we automatically expect or predict the occurrence of the other. In this sense, there is as much necessity in human actions as there is in any other aspect of the universe. Everybody has always been aware that there exists a constant conjunction between our motives and our voluntary actions. If we examine human behavior, both at the present time and in past history, we find that there have been regular

sequences, which have been repeated over and over again, of a certain motive followed by a certain action. Thus, Hume argued, in the ordinary meaning of "necessity," there is a necessity in human behavior.

LIBERTY

On the other hand, if one analyzes what people mean by "liberty," one will find that there is, and always has been, agreement that there exists liberty in human actions.

> For what is meant by liberty, when applied to voluntary actions? We cannot surely mean that actions have so little connection with motives, inclinations, and circumstances, that one does not follow with a certain degree of uniformity from the other, and that one affords no inference by which we can conclude the existence of the other. For these are plain and acknowledged matters of fact. By liberty, then, we can only mean **a power of acting or not acting, according to the determinations of the will;** that is, if we choose to remain at rest, we may; if we choose to move, we also may. Now this hypothetical liberty is universally allowed to belong to every one who is not a prisoner and in chains.

But in this common meaning of "liberty" there is no conflict between saying that human actions are necessary, in that they are regularly conjoined with certain motives, and saying that human beings possess liberty, in that they can act as they wish, so long as they are not constrained. The wishes people have can still be their own desires and also be conjoined with other factors. Thus, Hume insisted, as soon as one turned from the metaphysical constructions to a consideration of the problem in ordinary terms, the entire question, which had been so long debated, disappeared.

Philosophers had complicated the issue either by seeking to establish that every event, including human volitions, has a cause, in the sense of something that necessarily produces the occurrence of the event; or, on the other hand, by claiming that there could be an uncaused event, in the sense of an event that takes place without the influence of any other event in the universe. But since we can never tell from our experience whether events are necessarily produced by others, and, at the same time, every event we know of stands in some kind of relation of constant conjunction with some other occurrences, there really is no opposition of alternatives such as the metaphysicians had proposed. Thus, once this problem had been clarified, everyone could agree that, in an ordinary sense, **human beings are both free agents, in that they can do as they please when not constrained, and at the same time their actions are necessary, in that there are laws of human behavior.**

These examinations of metaphysical problems led Hume to the conclusion that there was no point in trying to answer the questions. Instead, he sought to show both why they are meaningless quibbles and why it is that supposedly sane and intelligent people discuss them at such great length. **The study of metaphysics, for Hume, becomes the study of metaphysicians.** This type of investigation constitutes an inquiry into the possible causes of this strange kind of human aberration, which has manifested itself in so many philosophers from ancient Greece to the eighteenth century. Many of Hume's comments on metaphysics are really research in the pathology of the metaphysical mind in operation.

According to one account Hume offered, one can discover psychological explanations for why certain people get snared into searching for solutions to metaphysical problems. In a case study that he presented of the Aristotelian philosopher, Hume first showed the series of mental steps involved by which the imagination of such a person creates the notions that he disputes about. Then, in comparing this sort of behavior to normal thinking, Hume believed that there must be some sort of metaphysical idiosyncrasy that leads these unfortunates astray, into a wilderness of their own invention.

What happens is that the metaphysician, like any good philosopher, notices that there is something peculiar about some of the things that ordinary people believe. For example, practically everyone believes that he/she perceives a connection between objects that are constantly conjoined. But the metaphysician sagely observes that this simply is not the case—each object is entirely distinct and separate, and it is only as a result of people's habit of association that they arrive at a contrary conclusion. The metaphysician, having begun by realizing that we do not see any necessary connection between events, nor the power that produces them, then sets off on a wild-goose chase, searching for this causal agency behind the scenes, seeking for some explanation for our ordinary experience.

They [the metaphysicians] have sufficient force of genius to free them from the vulgar error, that there is a natural and perceivable connection betwixt the several sensible qualities and actions of matter; but not sufficient to keep them from ever seeking for this connection in matter, or causes.

If the metaphysician were normal, he/she would accept his/her discovery calmly. He/she would realize that ordinary people are wrong, but that this is not terribly important. One can continue to live normally by recognizing, in theory, that we can only know the individual events of our experience, and also realizing that in practice we are led, naturally, to associate constantly conjoined events. The metaphysician goes astray by insisting that if the ordinary view of the causes of events is wrong, some other answer must be true. Then he/she is tormented forever, looking for his/her answer. "For what can be imagined more tormenting, than to seek with eagerness what forever flees us; and seek for it in a place where 'tis impossible it can ever exist?"

But fortunately for the forlorn metaphysician, Hume suggested, nature offers him/her some consolation. After he/she has invented his/her terminology and used it long enough, he/she begins to think that he/she is talking about something. The terms, which to begin with "are wholly insignificant and unintelligible," come to satisfy the metaphysician just because he/she uses them all the time. (Hume suspected that these people imagine that the strange words they use have some secret meaning, which might be discovered by deep reflection.) Merely by talking to each other and themselves, Hume claimed, the metaphysicians think that they are saying something and that they have found the answer to their quest.

By this means these philosophers set themselves at ease, and arrive at last, by an illu-sion, at the same indifference, which the people attain by their stupidity, and true philosophers by their moderate scepticism. They need only say that any phenomenon which puzzles them arises from a faculty or an occult quality, and there is an end of all dispute and enquiry upon the matter.

The sort of inventive imagination that metaphysicians exhibit, Hume suggested, is also found in the beliefs of children and in the fictions of poets. But, Hume observed, in concluding his study of the metaphysician, "We must pardon children, because of their age; poets, because they profess to follow implicitly the suggestions of their fancy: But what excuse shall we find to justify our philosophers in so signal a weakness?"

Kant's Criticism of Metaphysics

The great German philosopher Immanuel Kant (1724–1804) took the metaphysical quest more seriously than had Hume. Kant felt that what was wrong with this intellectual enterprise was not some psychological defect in some philosophers but a basic problem in the nature of what human beings could possibly know. Thus, from an investigation at the fundamental level, Kant thought, it would be possible to discover what certain knowledge we could attain, and thereby also to discover the limitations that would prevent the uncovering of any metaphysical truths.

MENTAL FACULTIES

Kant began his study of human knowledge, in his *Critique of Pure Reason*, agreeing with the empiricists' claim that our knowledge begins with experience. However, as he stated at the outset, "although all our knowledge begins with experience, it does not follow that it arises from experience." It is also the case, Kant argued, that what we know is the product of our own thinking faculty. **Our contacts with the experiential world supply the content of our knowledge, but our faculties supply the form in which we know it.**

A PRIORI KNOWLEDGE

What Kant was primarily concerned with was to discover not what knowledge we derive from experience but what *a priori* knowledge human beings could possess—that is, **knowledge that is universal and necessary** and independent of experience. He believed that in both mathematics and the study of nature (physics)—owing to the role played by the mind—there was some information that had to be true of all possible experience. But he wanted to discover whether there could be any *a priori* metaphysical knowledge, necessary and universal knowledge that was neither mathematical nor physical and that went beyond ordinary experience.

ANALYTIC AND SYNTHETIC KNOWLEDGE

The types of *a priori* knowledge fall, Kant claimed, into two groups: **analytic** and **synthetic.** The former consists of propositions of judgments whose truth can be determined without reference to any experience, but solely on the basis of the terms employed. For example, the propositions "A red rose is red" and "All bodies are extended," Kant asserted, are necessarily and universally true solely because of the definitions of the terms involved. This is the same point that we saw Hume making

about mathematical concepts. Such a proposition is true because what is predicated of the subject is already contained in the definition of the subject (see page 142). It requires only the principles of logic to discover that these judgments are **analytic *a priori* truths.**

But, in the case of **synthetic *a priori* knowledge, the predicate of the judgment must contain some information not contained in the subject.** The judgment must be the result of a **synthesis** of two quite separate notions, one being the subject about which the other, the predicate, is asserted. **Thus the analysis of the concepts included in the judgment would not suffice to reveal whether it was true.** But, Kant admitted after studying Hume, our ordinary empirical information, such as "This piece of paper is white," though synthetic, in that the predicate contains a concept not included in the subject, is not *a priori*, that is, is not universal or necessary or independent of experience. (It could be false that this paper is white, and even if true, it does not have to be true at all times and places.) Therefore, **a synthetic *a priori* judgment would have to contain some information not purely of a logical nature, and yet not depend on empirical or experimental information for its truth** (since, according to Hume, that would always render it less than completely certain, universal, or necessary).

In both mathematics and physics, Kant thought, there were judgments of precisely this character. Even the elementary proposition that $7 + 5 = 12$, he insisted, was a truth that was not merely true because of the definitions of the terms involved, but, rather, was one that contained more information in the predicate than was included   .

in the bare concepts of "7" and "5." In combining these two concepts into another one, which is their sum, a kind of intuition must take place that introduces something new in the conclusion.

> That 5 should be added to 7 was no doubt implied in my concept of a sum 7 + 5, but not that that sum should be equal to 12. An arithmetical proposition is, therefore, always synthetical, which is seen more easily still by taking larger numbers, where we clearly perceive that, turn and twist our conceptions as we may, we could never, by means of the mere analysis of our concepts and without the help of intuition, arrive at the sum wanted.

Similarly, in geometrical truths, Kant claimed, one finds the same sort of synthetic element, as for example in the proposition "A straight line is the shortest distance between two points," where the concept of "straight lines" does not include the notion of its being the shortest, and yet the statement is a necessary and universal truth. And in physics, he contended, it is also the case that there are propositions, like "Every event has a cause," that are synthetic and are also *a priori*.

INTUITION

The general problem of understanding what we can know, especially what we can know that is necessarily true, requires answering the question "How are synthetic *a priori* judgments possible?" (Kant took it for granted that there were such judgments.) The first level of his explanation is the claim that the very order or form of our experience has an *a priori* character that arises from the mind and not from the outside world. In order to

have a recognizable, discussible experience, it must of necessity fall into a pattern. We find, for instance, that we neither do have, nor can conceive of, any possible experience except in spatial and temporal terms. Thus, it appears to be required that there be a formal character to everything that we are aware of, and, in view of Hume's arguments, that experience itself cannot supply any necessary reason for the features it has. Therefore, Kant claimed, there must be some forms of all possible experience, or, as he called them, the **forms of intuition,** which we impose upon everything that we are in contact with. We can be certain, in advance of any experience, that two sorts of *a priori* characteristics will be present in any awareness that we may have, that it will have temporal and geometrical features, and that the truths of mathematics will apply to everything that we discover about the world of experience.

Besides the forms of intuition, Kant believed, there must also be principles or concepts by which we organize the general content of any possible experience in order to recognize it as a coherent datum. Otherwise, the argument goes, we would merely have the awareness without any means of discussing or describing it. Hence it must be the case, in Kant's theory, that since we are capable of attaining organized and intelligible information about the world, **we must have within ourselves the organizing principles.** Our minds structure and interpret the observations of our senses. (The objects of our experience cannot supply these factors, for once again, if Hume is right, there are no necessary features in the experiences themselves.)

CATEGORIES

These further conditions that are imposed upon the data of our sensations are those that are needed in order for us to be able to make any judgments at all. **Every judgment is a synthesizing of two concepts into a connected proposition.** This requires that the mind employ a certain formal apparatus in putting together what it is aware of, an apparatus such that its judgments must have certain **quantity** (that they be about "all" or "some" or "none" of something) and that they have some **quality** (positive or negative). Further, there must also be a general conceptual scheme by which the types of items that we are acquainted with are ordered and related. This last part of the intellectual framework consists of what are called the **"categories,"** which Kant listed in four groups of three, involving such notions as causality, substance and accident, possibility, etc. These are the "original pure concepts of synthesis, which belong to the understanding *a priori*, and for which alone it is called pure understanding; for it is by them alone that it can understand something in the manifold of intuition, that is, think an object in it."

Thus, Kant's theory is that **the world of our experience, the so-called "phenomenal world," is the product both of something that we are presented with and of the *a priori* conditions supplied by the mind.** The mind is viewed as something like **a vast blank form, which determines the kinds of answers that can be given but not the specific content, which only experience can determine. The forms of intuition, the logical functions of judgment, and the categories fix the necessary conditions of both experience and knowledge, but the actual content arises only from something independent of us.**

TRANSCENDENTAL INQUIRIES

This theory is much like claiming that we look at everything with a complex set of colored glasses that we cannot remove. We perceive the phenomenal world, the world of appearance. But what we experience has two parts. The form of the world of appearance is determined by the glasses, and hence is "necessary and universal." On the other hand, the content of the phenomenal world is not in any way conditioned or determined by the glasses. Only the way in which we will have to see and interpret it is. We can investigate both the content and the form. Science studies the former, and what Kant called "critical philosophy" can examine the latter, by **transcendental inquiries,** that is, investigations that seek to find out from our experience and our judgments what the necessary features of these must be in all cases.

CRITIQUE OF METAPHYSICS

Having claimed to have gone beyond Hume, by showing how we are able to attain necessary knowledge about the world, Kant then went on to agree with his predecessor that metaphysical knowledge about the general characteristics of reality is impossible to attain. When we try to expand our knowledge either inward or outward, we come to a complete impasse. If we seek inside ourselves for what is the cause of, or the basis of, our mental machinery of forms and categories, we are unable to discover anything.

Similarly, when we try to move beyond the phenomenal world to the realm of things-in-themselves, we are again unable to proceed.

The difficulty that prevents us from developing any metaphysical knowledge is that we have no way of determining if our mental apparatus is applicable to anything beyond the world of possible experience, the phenomenal world. We possess no concepts, no forms of intuition, no logical schema that we have any reason to believe apply to the self or to the **things-in-themselves,** the real objects that may exist behind the world of appearance. The *a priori* conditions that we can uncover are exclusively conditions of an experienceable world, not of one that may exist in another realm.

Our forms of intuition, first of all, restrict us to what can be experienced in a spatial and temporal context, namely, empirical objects. Our logical forms and our categories are organizing principles within this context. They constitute a set of necessary rules for thinking about items within, and, as far as we know, only within, the phenomenal world. Hence the necessary conditions that allow us to acquire *a priori* knowledge about the world of appearance cannot be extended to tell us about a possible transempirical world unless we can discover some means of determining whether the metaphysical realm can and must be thought of in the same way as the phenomenal one.

The metaphysicians who try to build some sort of bridge from what we know must be true of the phenomenal world to what must be true of the **noumenal** (that is, nonempirical) world always get into trouble. There simply is no basis for any inference, either from the content of experience or from its necessary conditions, to any metaphysical conclusion at all. To make this point, Kant examined what he regarded as the stock claims of the metaphysicians, and tried to show either that they committed some elementary logical fallacy in reaching their conclusions or that they arrived at completely contradictory results.

ANTINOMIES

As soon as the philosopher takes the *a priori* conditions of pure thought as objective conditions of the universe, all sorts of errors occur. The arguments built upon such an assumption to establish the nature of the mind or self necessarily commit certain logical errors, in order to move from some purely logical considerations to some claims of objective fact. The arguments that attempt to establish the nature of the noumenal world, the real world of things-in-themselves, result in what Kant called "antinomies," **conclusions that can be both proven and disproven.** Thus, reasonings that purport to prove that the world is finite, has a beginning in time, and so on, can be attacked by showing that just as good arguments can be constructed to establish the denials of these contentions. Hence we have no way of telling which of two contradictory views on these metaphysical questions is more likely to be true, or even plausible.

With regard to the ultimate metaphysical basis of experience, Kant claimed that all the evidence put forth actually established nothing at all. Although we shall later consider Kant's criticisms of the arguments for the existence of God, it can be stated here that Kant insisted that all the proofs that there must be some being whose nature accounts for the fundamental characteristics of the universe turn out, on careful inspection, to be inconclusive. Once again, the metaphysician tries to reason beyond his/her experience and conceptual framework—and, as a result, achieves nothing.

All in all, Kant concluded, **the metaphysical enterprise, in its traditional sense, is doomed to failure.** The summit of our understanding consists solely in our being able to discover the conditions that regulate our knowledge of the phenomenal world. But any attempt to go beyond this, to employ the necessary features of our judgments about experience, to discover the constituents of the real world, always ends in disaster. We can never tell if the noumenal world is spatial and temporal, but only that the world of appearance must be. We can never tell if the noumenal world contains substances, causally related events, and so on, but only that the sense world must be so interpreted. Hence any effort to discuss and reason about the realm of the self, the thing-in-itself, or God, becomes, for Kant, only an unfortunate dialectical illusion. The metaphysician who does not see this will merely waste time meandering around in a maze of his/her own construction, arriving at all sorts of odd and incompatible results.

Conclusion

As a result of the criticism of metaphysics propounded by David Hume and Immanuel Kant in the eighteenth century, and revived in many forms in the present day, many philosophers have accepted the judgment that the sort of knowledge sought by the metaphysician is not attainable. They have either developed Hume's critique into the modern form of positivism (see pages 290–95), insisting that metaphysics is a disease to be treated, not a discipline to be investigated, or they have followed Kant and held that our knowledge cannot transcend the categories that we employ in thinking about our experience. Therefore, some of the latter thinkers have suggested (as Kant did in his *Critique of Pure Reason*) that one ought to abandon the traditional investigation and transform metaphysical research into "categorical analysis," the study of the necessary conditions involved in knowing anything.

Others have refused to abandon the quest for metaphysical truths, for information about the "real nature" of things. Some metaphysicians reject critiques of their undertaking while proposing new solutions to the old metaphysical questions. (One of the most famous of these philosophers in the twentieth century is the late Alfred North Whitehead.) But by and large, metaphysical interests have diminished in contemporary thought and are just beginning to show some slight signs of revival in the English-speaking world.

Suggested further reading

Classical Authors

Allen, Reginald. *Greek Philosophy from Thales to Aristotle.* New York: Free Press, 1966. An anthology of source material from the Greek authors with excellent introductory discussions.
Also:
Berkeley, George. *Three Dialogues Between Hylas and Phi-*

lonous, ed. by R. M. Adams. Indianapolis: Hackett, 1979.

Descartes, René. *Meditations on First Philosophy*, trans. by Donald Cress. Indianapolis: Hackett, 1980.

Hume, David. *A Treatise of Human Nature*. Oxford University Press, 1975.

————. *An Enquiry Concerning Human Understanding*. Oxford University Press, 1978.

Kant, Immanuel. *Prologomena to Any Further Metaphysics*. New York: Barnes & Noble, 1978.

Plato. *Timaeus*, trans. by H. D. Lee. London: Penguin, 1972.

Modern authors

Blanshard, Brand. *The Nature of Thought*. 2 vols. London: Allen & Unwin, 1939. A modern statement of the case for idealistic metaphysics.

Born, Rainer, ed. *Artificial Intelligence: The Case Against*. New York: St. Martin's Press, 1987.

Churchland, Patricia. *Neurophilosophy: Toward a Unified Science of Mind-Brain*. Bradford, Mass.: MIT Press, 1986.

Collins, James. *History of Modern Philosophy*. Milwaukee: Bruce, 1970. An excellent examination of modern metaphysical systems, by a leading Catholic thinker.

Copleston, Frederick. *A History of Philosophy*. New York: Image Books/Doubleday, 1993. A very detailed, comprehensive history of philosophy. Volumes I–VI cover the period from ancient Greece to Kant.

Dennett, Daniel. *Consciousness Explained*. Boston: Little Brown, 1991.

Guthrie, W. K. *A History of Greek Philosophy*. 2 vols. Cambridge, England: Cambridge University Press, 1977.

James, William. "The Dilemma of Determinism." In *Essays in Pragmatism*. An important examination of the problems of free will and determinism.

Minsky, Marvin. *The Society of Mind*. New York: Touchstone Press, 1988.

Pratt, J. B. *Matter and Spirit*. London: Macmillan, 1926. On the various theories about the relationship of mind and body.

Russell, Bertrand. *The Problems of Philosophy*. Oxford University Press, 1967. An examination of some of the traditional problems by one of the leading empiricists of the twentieth century.

Santas, Gerasimos. *Socrates*. London: Routledge & Kegan Paul, 1982.

Sprague, Elmer. *Metaphysical Thinking*. Oxford University Press, 1978. An attempt to make metaphysics relevant to modern ways of thinking.

Taylor, A. E. *Elements of Metaphysics*. London: Metheun, 1956. A statement of traditional metaphysical problems by one of England's last traditional metaphysicians.

Vlastos, Gregory. *Socrates, Ironist and Moral Philosopher*. Ithaca, N.Y.: Cornell University Press, 1991.

CHAPTER FOUR

Philosophy of religion

The branch of philosophy called the **"philosophy of religion"** is not necessarily concerned with either justifying or disparaging any particular claims of any particular religion. Rather, the interest of this aspect of philosophy is **to examine the intellectual questions that arise in considering religious views.** These questions are usually either special problems connected with the **theory of knowledge as applied to religious knowledge, or metaphysical problems** involved in efforts to construct a satisfactory and consistent explanation of certain concepts employed by various religions.

Philosophy and religion

The age-old concern of humankind with religious questions, many of which antedated the earliest beginnings of philosophy, has led various thinkers to inquire into the meaning of the claims made by different religions, the evidence upon which these claims are based, the standards that can be employed in evaluating their merits, and whether these claims can be made part of a general theory about the nature of the universe. Some of the philosophers who have raised these questions have been interested in showing the plausibility or reasonable-

ness of certain religious views. Others have sought to disprove, or render doubtful, certain religious views. Some have regarded the problems involved neutrally, merely trying to ascertain whether any special kinds of knowledge and concepts are involved in religious matters, and whether any special standards need be employed. Thus, for some philosophers, the philosophy of religion has involved an attempt to find a rational justification or explanation of their religion, for some it has been an attempt to justify or explain the grounds or basis of their disbelief, and for others it has been merely an attempt to examine another area of human interest and experience.

In this section, we shall explore some of the problems of the philosophy of religion and some of the major theories that have been offered, including some views that have been used to justify or explain some of the major religious beliefs in the Judeo-Christian-Islamic tradition, and some of those that have been advanced in favor of atheism. We shall first deal with the problem of religious knowledge.

The problem of religious knowledge

Various religions purport to possess some special and vitally important knowledge about the nature of the world and of man's role in it. But there is a wide divergence of claims among different religions and religious persons as to what this information is and what assurance we have that it is true. If one examines the kind of information involved in religious knowledge and the kind of evidence for it, certain problems arise that indicate that religious knowledge is of a radically different sort from that which we find in other fields of human experiences, especially in the various fields of scientific investigation.

The Problem of Revelation

In many religions, the sort of information that is regarded as crucial consists of reported revelations of the word of God. If one asks, how did human beings discover this knowledge, and what guarantee do they have that it is true, one finds some remarkable differences between revealed knowledge and our ordinary knowledge. With regard to our knowledge about historical questions, scientific ones, and the like, we can give answers to these queries, which, though they may be open to serious difficulties, present a basis for general agreement that does not seem to apply to our religious knowledge. No matter what theory of knowledge one holds to, one would usually agree that it is at least highly probable that water is composed of hydrogen and oxygen, and that Julius Caesar was assassinated. But the same type of agreement does not hold for religious information.

Well, then, what is the difference? In our scientific and historical information, even if we cannot agree as to the ultimate basis for it, or the standards for evaluating its fundamental truth, at least there is, by and large, no serious disagreement as to what constitutes probable evidence. The appeal to experimental data, to records, to public experience is sufficient to establish what we call "the facts in the case." This will not settle the issues outstanding in epistemology but, except in special cases, will suffice to dispel any disagreement in the realms of our scientific and historical knowledge.

But when one turns to religious matters, these methods no longer appear to be applicable. If one asks whether the Bible contains religious information, this is no longer a scientific or historical question. There are historical problems about when the various books of the Bible were written, who wrote them, and the like, but these are different sorts of problems from whether the Bible is a source of religious knowledge. The historical questions can be investigated by the standard techniques of historians and, within limits, can be given answers with a fair degree of probability. But how can the other sort of problem be solved?

Investigating the history of Palestine two and three millennia ago may show that various statements in the Bible reporting historical facts, such as the location and description of Solomon's palace, seem, to the best of present-day historical knowledge, to be true. But even if every historical fact in the Old and New Testaments could be confirmed by careful examination of ancient records, archaeological findings, and so on, the question would still remain, how can we tell if the Bible contains any *religious* information?

Scientific and Religious Knowledge

Some people might suggest that this is an absurd question, since the Bible says clearly that it is not a mere record of some events in the history of ages gone by, but is also, and far more important, a statement of the word of God. So all that one has to do to answer the question is to read the book. But anyone can write a book, and record in the text that this book contains religious information. The crucial question is whether this claim is true. And merely by reading the book this cannot be ascertained. The fact that the book contains a sentence asserting that it contains religious knowledge can be established; but the *truth-value* of the sentence, the problem at issue, cannot be.

No historical investigation can establish that any particular person has had any religious information or that any book contains it. All that historical inquiry can tell us is that certain people and certain books have made the assertion that they possessed religious knowledge. We may become reasonably assured that the historical personage, Moses, lived at a certain time, that he performed certain acts recorded in the Bible, and that he asserted that he had received certain important religious truths from God. But whether Moses was correct in his assertion is not a question that can be answered by historical investigation.

If one asks what differentiates the Bible from other ancient historical records, like the writings of Herodotus, the Greek historian, it is not a question of historical fact, but, rather, that one of these documents is supposed to be a source of religious information, while the other is not.

But the point of this discussion is that the difference indicates something peculiar about religious information. The standards that we apply to determine historical information and scientific information do not help us to determine if some particular book, or a certain person, possesses some religious information. What seems instead to be involved in the case of religious knowledge is **some element of belief, faith, or religious experience.**

Religious knowledge does not seem to be a type of our ordinary empirical knowledge in that we cannot examine and evaluate it in the same manner. Claims about plant life outside the solar system, cures for cancer, or anything else dealing with events within the world of our experience, can be discussed and examined by certain standards that we call scientific. But the merits of various reported items of religious information can be discussed and examined only in terms of certain beliefs, faith, or religious experience, even if the belief is that these reported religious truths have no religious significance at all.

To clarify this point, we might consider a hypothetical example. If some mountaineers climbing Mount Everest discovered a document purporting to contain the word of God, how would we test whether the work did in fact contain religious information? An examination of the mountain climbers, the mountain, and the document would all involve certain scientific tests and standards, and would give us some reasonably reliable information about the people in question, the place where they made their discovery, and the nature of the document. But such an examination would not decide whether the document was the word of God, since this is not a feature or quality of a document that one can test chemically, historically, or in any other empirical fashion.

Those who accepted this hypothetical document as a statement of some important religious information might offer as reasons for their view that there were certain extraordinary features of the work that led them to this conclusion, certain extraordinary signs, or even miracles, that led them to distinguish this document from ordinary ones. In this case, they would be asserting that above and beyond the available scientific information, there was certain special information that enabled one to see, or realize, that there was a special significance to this document.

Others might claim that there were certain general theories about the nature of the universe which led one to conclude that the views appearing in the hypothetical document contained genuine religious information. Here again, the basis for judging the information to be religious would not be simply observable and scientifically testable features but, rather, **some metaphysical or ethical views that one had arrived at independently of the document.**

Lastly, one might state that certain beliefs, or personal experiences, convinced one of the religious nature of the document. No appeal would be made to special conditions or signs outside of oneself, or to any general reasonings that one could explain to others. Instead, the basis for accepting the document as a religious one would be one's personal conviction, belief, faith, or religious experience that this document revealed the word of God.

Natural and revealed religion

These varying responses reflect some of the major explanations that have been offered to explain the basis of, and warrant for, religious knowledge. These explanations can be divided, roughly, into the traditional distinction between **natural** and **revealed** religion. The contention of those who attempt to provide a **natural** basis for religious knowledge is that there are special events, facts, or other *reasons* that provide a foundation for religious conviction. On the other hand, the contention of revealed religion is that fundamental religious truths are known to us only by revelation, faith, or personal experience. This distinction is not to suggest that there is any necessary opposition between revealed and natural religious knowledge. In fact, the claim of a great number of theologians has been that much religious insight can be gained by natural procedures—for example, through recognizing certain signs or through reasoning—but that other religious truth can be gained only by faith or revelation. They have contended the two types of religious knowledge supplement, or complement, each other.

Since those claims regarding natural religious knowledge often involve the presentation of evidence, and argument about the nature and existence of a divine being, much philosophy of religion has dealt with an examination and evaluation of the merits of this sort of religious knowledge, and of the kind of support advanced in its favor. Therefore, we shall examine these claims, especially those regarding the natural evidence offered for the existence of God.

Natural Religion: The Argument from Design

Throughout the ages, those who believed that it is possible to discover religious knowledge by natural procedures have attempted to develop various proofs of the existence of God to show that the most fundamental religious knowledge—that there is a divine being—can be demonstrated by acceptable arguments. Among these arguments is one called the **"argument from design,"** which is probably familiar to almost everybody in one form or another. This argument purports **to establish the existence of God from an examination of and induction from information that we have gained about the universe.** In fact, since the beginnings of modern science, various versions of the argument from design have been presented that **attempt to prove the existence of God from the latest findings in the physical and biological sciences.**

Hume's argument

One of the classical statements of the argument from design appears in David Hume's *Dialogues on Natural Religion.* One of the characters, Cleanthes, states it as follows:

> Look around the world, contemplate the whole and every part of it: you will find it to be nothing but one great machine, subdivided into an infinite number of lesser machines, which again admit of subdivisions to a degree beyond what human senses and faculties can trace and explain. All these various machines, and even their most minute parts, are adjusted to each other with an accuracy which ravishes into admiration all men who have ever contemplated them. The curious adapting of means to ends, throughout all nature, resembles exactly, though it much exceeds, the productions of human contrivance—of human design, thought, wisdom and intelligence. Since therefore the effects resemble each other, we are led to infer, by all the rules of analogy, that the causes also resemble, and that the Author of nature is somewhat similar to the mind of man, though possessed of much larger faculties, proportioned to the grandeur of the work which he has executed. By this argument *a posteriori*, and by this argument alone, do we prove at once the existence of a Deity and his similarity to human mind and intelligence.

The central claim of the argument from design is that our studies of nature reveal an orderliness and a pattern in the features of the physical, chemical, and biological aspects of the world. The more that nature is studied, the more impressed one becomes with the intricate relationships within its parts and with the general plan of the universe. The order and design of nature resemble greatly the order and design of human artifacts, such as houses and watches, in which each part is perfectly adjusted to each other in order to achieve some purpose or end of the whole object. Since the effects of human planning are so much like the effects that we discover in the natural world, the argument runs, we can therefore infer, or induce, that the causes that produce the effects in each case are alike. In the case of human achievements, the cause is thought, wisdom, and intelligence. Therefore, there must be some kind of intelligent deity who is the author or cause of the effects in the universe. Since the amount of design or order in the natural world and its complexity far exceed human ingenuity, the cause of this must also be of greater wisdom.

Even in ancient times, with the extremely limited information then available about the many kinds of regularities and patterns in the natural world, many were struck with the force of the argument from design. But after the beginnings of the scientific revolution in the sixteenth and seventeenth centuries, one finds more and more elaborate appeals to scientific findings as the basis for concluding that there must be some divine being or power who organizes and directs the complex order of nature. In our own day, there have been various attempts to show that the amazing unfolding of the secrets of nature by contemporary scientists has strengthened the evidence that there is some sort of intelligent guidance to the world scheme. Some years ago a great French biologist, Le Comte de Nouy, published a work entitled *Human Destiny*, in which he argued that the intricate relationship found in biochemistry relating to the development of living organisms, and the general evolutionary history of plants and animals, suggest a plan that could not have occurred by accident but must instead have had some overall direction and director to account for its orderliness. Another version of this argument has been presented by the Jesuit Teilhard de Chardin in his *The Phenomenon of Man*.

In spite of the apparent force of the argument from design in terms of our evergrowing knowledge about the natural world, various thinkers have found many difficulties involved in this type of reasoning, which, if examined closely, may well vitiate entirely the seeming strength of the argument as a proof of the existence of God. Perhaps the best presentation of these difficulties occurs in a work already cited, Hume's *Dialogues Concerning Natural Religion*.

Hume's Criticisms of the Argument from Design

All his life, David Hume was concerned with the merits of various arguments that purported to establish the existence of a divine being. In his early notebooks and letters, he continually reflected about the problem, pointing out flaws or fallacies involved in the arguments of various religious writers. In various works, Hume made some incisive criticisms of the reasoning employed by some of the religious philosophers. Possibly because of its currency in his day, one of his major undertakings was a thoroughgoing critique of the argument from design. He worked on this, off and on, for about twenty-five years, perfecting his famous *Dialogues Concerning Natural Religion*. Some of his friends urged him to abandon his work, to destroy what he had written, because it was too dangerous and irreligious. For long periods of time he set it aside. Then, when he knew that he was dying, he completed the work and made plans to ensure its publication after his death. He tried to induce the economist Adam Smith, his good friend, to guarantee to have it printed after he died, but Smith was unwilling, either because he feared the consequences to himself or because he did not see what would be gained by making public such seditious material. Similarly, Hume's printer, also an old friend, refused to agree to publish the book. Finally, a nephew of the Scottish philosopher, who apparently had nothing to lose, published the work anonymously three years after Hume's death. The publication of the *Dialogues* in 1779 brought to light one of the most important documents in the philosophy of religion, one that has been studied and argued about ever since.

In the *Dialogues*, the argument from design is examined and dissected from almost every possible angle. Hume begins his attack by criticizing the analogy between human productions and nature. The works of man and those of nature do not resemble each other sufficiently so that we can have any strong reason to suspect that they have similar causes. As the skeptic in the *Dialogues*, Philo, puts it:

> If we see a house, Cleanthes, we conclude, with the greatest certainty, that it had an architect or builder because this is precisely that species of effect which we have experienced to proceed from that species of cause. But surely you will not affirm that the universe bears such a resemblance to a house that we can with the same certainty infer a similar cause, or that the analogy is here entire and perfect. The dissimilitude is so striking that the utmost you can here pretend to is a guess, a conjecture, a presumption concerning a similar cause.

Critique of the Analogy

We have experienced the relationship between human planning or design and the achievements that result from this. In case of nature, we have no experience of the cause, but only of the effect. The natural effects do not so resemble the man-made ones that we can be certain that similar kinds of causal factors must be operative in both. For all we know, there may well be numerous causes of order and design other than thought.

For aught we can know *a priori,* matter may contain the source or spring of order originally within itself, as well as mind does; and there is no more difficulty in conceiving that the several elements, from an internal unknown cause, may fall into the most exquisite arrangement, than to conceive that their ideas, in the great universal mind, from a like internal unknown cause, fall into that arrangement.

In fact, it is the height of human vanity to rush headlong to the conclusion that since in the tiny part of the cosmos occupied by man the same factors that occur to bring about planned human achievements appear similar to the natural effects around us, that therefore these same factors are the dominating principles of the governance of the entire universe about much of which we have no information at all.

Hume concludes this first general criticism of the kind of analogical reasoning involved in the argument from design by observing through his skeptical spokesman:

> And will any man tell me with a serious countenance that an orderly universe must arise from some thought and art like the human because we have experience of it? To ascertain this reasoning it were requisite that we had experience of the origin of worlds; and it is not sufficient, surely, that we have seen ships and cities arise from human art and contrivance . . .
> . . . Can you pretend to show any such similarity between the fabric of a house and the generation of a universe? Have you ever seen nature in any such situation as resembles the first arrangement of the elements? Have worlds ever been formed under your eye, and have you had the leisure to observe the whole progress of the phenomenon, from the first appearance of order to its final consummation? If you have, then cite your experience and deliver your theory.

Up to this point, Hume's criticism of the argument from design has been that **its fundamental contention that there is a great resemblance between the effects of human planning and natural effects, and that therefore the cause of human artifacts, namely thought, must be like the universal causal agency, is not convincing.** We have learned from experience that human effects result from design, but we have no such experience with natural effects and how they happen to arise. The defender of the argument in the *Dialogues*, Cleanthes, retorts "that it is by no means necessary that theists should prove the similarity of the works of *nature* to those of *art* because this similarity is self-evident and undeniable." For the sake of the argument, Hume temporarily accepted this claim in order to show that even if there were a strong resemblance between human and natural works, there would still be basic defects or disabilities in the argument to establish the existence of a divine being.

Cause and Effect

The basic principle employed by those who believe the argument from design is that **like effects prove like causes.** The more like the effects are, the more like are the causes. But even if we assume that there really is a close similarity between natural and human effects, then Hume showed that we would still have no grounds for coming to the traditional religious conclusions about the nature of God.

First, by this method of reasoning you renounce all claim to infinity in any of the attributes of the deity. For, as the cause ought only to be proportioned to the effect, and the effect, so far as it falls under our cognizance, is not infinite, what pretensions have we, upon your suppositions, to ascribe that attribute to the divine being?

Not only would the argument from design, if valid, prevent us from telling if God is infinite, it would also prevent us from concluding that He is perfect.

Secondly, you have no reason, on your theory, for ascribing perfection to the Deity, even in His finite capacity, or for supposing Him free from every error, mistake, or incoherence, in His undertakings . . . At least, you must acknowledge that it is impossible for us to tell, from our limited views, whether this system contains any great faults or deserves any considerable praise if compared to other possible and even real systems. Could a peasant, if the *Aeneid* were read to him, pronounce that poem to be absolutely faultless, or even assign to it its proper rank among the productions of human wit, he who had never seen another production?

But were this world ever so perfect a production, it must still remain uncertain whether all the excellence of the work can justly be ascribed to the workman. If we survey a ship, what an exalted idea we must form of the ingenuity of the carpenter who framed so complicated, useful, and beautiful a machine? And what surprise must we feel when we find him a stupid mechanic who imitated others, and copied an art which, through a long succession of ages, after multiplied trials, mistakes, corrections, deliberations, and controversies, had been gradually improving? Many worlds might have been botched and bungled, throughout an eternity, ere this system was struck out; much labor lost, many fruitless trials made, and a slow but continued improvement carried on during infinite ages in the art of world-making. In such subjects, who can determine where the truth, nay, who can conjecture where the probability lies, amidst a great number of hypotheses which may be proposed, and a still greater which may be imagined?

Anthropomorphism

If one takes seriously the similarity between human and natural effects, and the principle that like effects have like causes, then the result will be to conclude that the author or authors (since there is no reason for limiting the cause of nature to one agent on the basis of this argument) of nature are much like human beings. The more alike one insists that the effects are, the more human, or **anthropomorphic,** one will have to paint the portrait of the deity, until one is driven to a picture of God totally at variance with all religious traditions. On the other hand, if one denies that the causes—that is, God and man—are really alike, then one has no basis for drawing any conclusion about the nature of a divine being by means of the argument from design.

At best, Hume insisted, the evidence about the order and design in nature allows one:

> To assert or conjecture that the universe sometime arose from something like design; but beyond that position he cannot ascertain one single circumstance, and is left afterward to fix every point of his theology by the utmost license of fancy and hypothesis. This world, for aught he knows, is very faulty and imperfect, compared to a superior standard, and was only the first rude essay of some infant deity who afterward abandoned it, ashamed of his lame performance; it is the work only of some dependent, inferior deity, and is the object of derision to his superiors; it is the production of old age and dotage in some superannuated deity, and ever since his death has run on at adventures, from the first impulse and active force which it received from him.

One can go on endlessly inventing possible explanations in keeping with the basic claim of the argument from design, that there is a similarity between the order in nature and the order in human productions. Any explanation, hypothesis, imaginative theory that accounts for the occurrence of the degree of order that we find in nature is equally satisfying if one accepts the argument from design as a valid argument for establishing that some sort of designer or designers of the universe exist.

Other Possible Analogies

As if he had not gone far enough in showing that the basic analogy is not really a sound one, and that if it were, one would be led to conclude either that God was just like a human being or that an unlimited number of hypotheses were equally plausible, Hume offered another and perhaps more devastating assault on the argument from design. Starting with the same evidence about the order in nature—he reasoned—**totally different kinds of analogy can be equally well established that will yield totally different kinds of conclusion.** Not only do some aspects of the natural world resemble the effects of human activities, but some also resemble the effects of the biological activities of animals and plants. One finds many similarities between the development of living organisms and natural events. The organic and functional relationships in the biological world can also be found in other aspects of nature.

One who accepts the argument from design asserts that the world:

Resembles the work of human contrivance; therefore its cause must also resemble that of the other. Hence we may remark that the operation of one very small part of nature, to wit, man, upon another very small part, to wit, that inanimate matter lying within his reach, is the rule by which Cleanthes judges the origin of the whole; and he measures objects, so widely disproportioned, by the same individual standard. But to waive all objections drawn from this topic, I affirm that there are other parts of the universe (besides the machines of human invention) which bear still a great resemblance to the fabric of the world, and which, therefore, afford a better conjecture concerning the universal origin of this system. These parts are animals and vegetables. The world plainly resembles more an animal or a vegetable than it does a watch or a knitting-loom. Its cause, therefore, it is more probable, resembles the cause of the former. The cause, therefore, of the world we may infer to be something similar or analogous to generation or vegetation.

Like the vegetable world or the animal world, the entire natural world may possess some inner principles of development and of order. There are sufficient similarities among biological entities to provide a theory of the cause of natural order different from the claim that there must be an intelligent designer of nature. Instead, there might merely be some sort of **inner self-regulation and growth,** as one finds in carrot seeds, that orders the direction of their development.

If one were to say that there is no evidence to support such an explanation, Hume was perfectly willing to agree, *but* he also maintained that, by the same token, there is no evidence for the argument from design. All that we know is the evidence of patterns or regular orders in nature. What we see around us resembles to some extent the effects of human produc-tions, but it also resembles still more the effects of biological organization. The crucial point is that:

> We have no data to establish any system of cosmogony [a theory about the origins of the universe]. Our experience, so imperfect in itself and so limited both in extent and duration, can afford us no probable conjecture concerning the whole of things. But if we must needs fix on some hypothesis, by what rule, pray, ought we to determine our choice? Is there any other rule than the greater similarity of the objects compared? And does not a plant or an animal, which springs from vegetation or generation, bear a stronger resemblance to the world than does any artificial machine, which arises from reason and design?

Materialist Hypotheses

In fact, if the only information that we have to judge by is the character of the events that we see, one could also offer a completely materialistic and mechanistic interpretation of nature. One could develop a hypothesis like that of the ancient Greek philosopher Epicurus, to the effect that the cause of natural events is nothing but the blind motions of solid, material atoms, moving through space, and occasionally colliding, without plan or reason. The small portion of the universe that we are able to observe has obvious features of order or organization. But, from what we can tell about, we have no more basis for assuming that the cause of this order is like the cause of the order in a ship or a watch, or in an ant or an onion, or *even* the order due to pure chance. If one threw several thousand small pieces of iron into the air, in falling they would exhibit some sort of pattern or design, which we would say was due not to any ordering principle but, rather, to accident or chance. Hume suggested that we cannot be certain that the so-called organized universe is not also the result of some blind cosmic accident. We cannot even be sure that there is an agency that is responsible for the order in the world; hence we certainly cannot conclude that the agency is an intelligent one.

Critique of Religious Traditionalism

As a final feature of his critique of the argument from design, Hume pointed out that the analogical reasoning employed in the argument **does not provide a basis for any conclusion about the moral attributes of the designer of nature**, even if one concludes that there is such a designer. The conception of a moral, just, good deity does not follow from the comparison of natural and human effects. If the designer is supposed to be like the human designer, then we would have no reason to suppose that there is any special moral quality belonging to the author of nature. When one examines the product, i.e., nature, and observes all its unpleasant features, e.g., hurricanes, earthquakes, the wars of one part of nature upon another, can we conclude that the planning was that of a just and good intelligence?

After accumulating evidence of the unpleasant features of nature, Hume made his criticism in the form of an analogy to show that if one merely contemplated the character of the object presented to us, one would be hard-pressed to believe that it was designed by either a very wise or a very good planner.

Did I show you a house or palace where there was not one apartment convenient or agreeable, where the windows, doors, fires, passages, stairs, and the whole economy of the building were the source of noise, confusion, fatigue, darkness, and the extremes of heat and cold, you would certainly blame the contrivance, without any further examination. The architect would in vain display his subtlety, and prove to you that, if this door or that window were altered, greater ills would ensue. What he says may be strictly true; the alteration of one particular, while the other parts of the building remain, may only augment the inconveniences. But still you would assert in general that, if the architect had had skill and good intentions, he might have formed such a plan of the whole, and might have adjusted the parts in such a manner as would have remedied all or most of these inconveniences. His ignorance, or even your own ignorance of such a plan, will never convince you of the impossibility of it. If you find any inconveniences and deformities in the building, you will always, without entering into any detail, condemn the architect.

When this point is applied to a consideration of the world we know, the question can be asked:

Is the world, considered in general and as it appears to us in this life, different from what a man or such a limited being would, *beforehand*, expect from a very powerful, wise, and benevolent deity? It must be strange prejudice to assert the contrary. And from thence I conclude that, however consistent the world may be, allowing certain suppositions and conjectures with the idea of such a deity, it can never afford us an inference concerning his existence.

Thus, given the unfortunate, unpleasant, and undesirable events that one witnesses, one is unable to infer that the design of the cosmos is benevolent, just, or good. This is not to deny that if we knew the nature of the cause of the world's order, we might be able to explain satisfactorily these apparent ills. But if all our knowledge of this cause is supposed to result from an induction or inference from our observations, then, Hume insisted, we have no basis for judging that there is any moral guidance to the course of nature. In fact, Hume claimed, some other hypotheses are more plausible, such as that the directing force or agency in the world has no moral or immoral character, or possibly that there are two radically different directing forces in the universe, one good and the other bad. (This latter theory is often called the **Manichean** view.)

Conclusions

Hume demonstrated that the argument from design is based on an unsound analogy, which, if it were sound, would lead to the conclusion that the deity is much like a human being, that many other theories are at least as likely, if based solely on experience, and that the evidence is insufficient to allow us to infer that the directing force or agency is infinite, perfect, or even moral. Hume finally concluded his criticism by admitting that the argument from design, if not a valid argument, is still to some extent convincing. The order in nature, in spite of all that has been said, suggests, if it does not prove, **"that the cause or causes of order in the universe probably bear some remote analogy to human intelligence."** Beyond this, we have no way to extend the argument in order to establish anything about the characteristics of this cause or these causes, or to develop any hypotheses about how they are related to us and our problems. As Hume had indicated earlier, beyond this "one simple, though somewhat ambigu-

ous, at least undefined, proposition," one can construct endless possible theories of nature. Unfortunately, if we are restricted only to what we can observe, we have no standards for evaluating or judging which of the many hypothetical possibilities may be the more probable.

Thus, in his masterful analysis of the argument from design, Hume showed that this attempt to establish the existence and nature of a divine being was most inconclusive, and the more plausible or reasonable the argument might be made, the less it would tend to prove that there is any kind of divine agency or guidance similar to that taught by the various major religious traditions. Moreover, if our religious knowledge is to be derived from scientific knowledge, we would be able to find little or nothing that would lead us to conclude that there is some deity who governs the universe and who is concerned in governing in our interests or in terms or certain ends in which we are, or may be, involved.

If Hume's analysis of the argument from design is sound, as many thinkers since have found it to be, then those who attempt to discover some kind of natural evidence or reasoning upon which to base religious knowledge will have to turn elsewhere. Other philosophers, therefore, have produced two different types of argument to establish the existence of a divine being, the **cosmological (or causal) argument** and the **ontological argument**.

The cosmological (or causal) argument

This argument, like the argument from design, begins from the facts of our experience, from what we observe. We see things move, change, and so on. In order for these events to occur, **there must be either a cause in the sense of a prior event, or a reason for the occurrence of the event.** As we trace back from effects to their causes, either we can continue indefinitely, or there is some ultimate cause that requires no further causal explanation. **This ultimate cause is what is meant by God.** In order to rule out the alternative of an indefinite or unlimited succession of causes, it is argued that if it were possible to trace back the causal sequence indefinitely, then there would be no beginning to the series. If there were no actual beginning, then there could be no succession, since each cause must follow after its predecessor. If there is no first element to the causal sequence, then there could be no second, third, and so on. Therefore the conclusion is that **there must be a first cause** of events, and this first cause is what is called God. Thus, from the experience we have of caused events we can prove the existence of a supreme being, or a first cause.

Aristotle, Maimonides, and St. Thomas Aquinas

This argument, often called the cosmological argument for the existence of God, has been employed for a long time by philosophers and theologians. In one form or another it is in the proofs offered by Aristotle, by Maimonides, by St. Thomas Aquinas, and many others. Sometimes it is employed to establish that there must have been a first cause in the history of the universe, that is, a first event, from which all the others have followed, like the Big Bang in the cosmology of most present-day physicists. Others have used it to claim that there must be an ultimate explanation for the events in the universe, whether the cosmos had a beginning or has been eternal. Their contention has been that to account for the occurrences in the world, an explanation has to be made, and an explanation for that, and so on. Unless there is some ultimate explanation, they assert, there can be no other explanation, and nothing can be accounted for.

Although this argument has been subjected to severe criticism, it is still accepted as valid and decisive by many philosophers of religion. In the form in which it occurs in the *Summa Theologica* of St. Thomas Aquinas, the cosmological argument is regarded as conclusive evidence for establishing the existence of a supreme being by the Roman Catholic Church. One finds, however, that with non-Catholic thinkers the argument has lost ground since the criticism of it by David Hume and Immanuel Kant.

Some Criticisms of the Cosmological Argument

If one agrees with the arguments Hume presented regarding the theory of knowledge (see discussion on pages 222–34), then the main premise and the conclusion of the cosmological argument lose their force. Hume maintained that if his claims as to what we cannot know are legitimate, then we are unable to establish that any particular being, whether it be God, or anything else, must, of necessity, exist.

> I shall begin with observing that there is an evident absurdity in pretending to demon-

strate a matter of fact, or to prove it by any arguments *a priori*. Nothing is demonstrable unless the contrary implies a contradiction. Nothing that is distinctly conceivable implies a contradiction. Whatever we conceive as existent, we can also conceive as nonexistent. There is no being, therefore, whose nonexistence implies a contradiction. Consequently there is no being whose existence is demonstrable.

Thus, according to Hume, no valid argument can establish the existence of a supreme being or of anything else. Since we can always conceive what it would be like for any describable object to exist, to be part of the temporal and spatial world, or not to exist, then no demonstration that a specific entity must exist can be decisive. The denial of the conclusion of the demonstration cannot be disproven; and hence nothing has actually been established by any reasoning that purports to establish that some particular being must exist.

CRITIQUE OF CAUSALITY

Further, Hume argued that we cannot prove or establish the fundamental premise of the cosmological argument, that every event must have a cause. If what is meant by a cause is something that produces an event, or something that explains or accounts for an event, then we cannot even tell whether it is the case that events have been produced by something or can be accounted for. We can only determine what events occur in regular sequences with other events in our experience. But, in Hume's analysis, is there any reason to conclude that the sequence of constantly conjoined events must have a first term, or that there must be some ul-

timate explanation of the entire sequence? We can trace back the succession of events indefinitely, but why must we conclude that it has to have had a beginning?

> In such a chain, too, or succession of objects, each part is caused by that which preceded it, and causes that which succeeds it. Where then is the difficulty? But the *whole*, you say, wants a cause. I answer that the uniting of these parts into a whole, like the uniting of several distinct countries into one kingdom, or several distinct members into one body, is performed merely by an arbitrary act of the mind, and has no influence on the nature of things.

Thus, **it is Hume's contention that the observable succession of events that we consider causes and effects requires no ultimate beginning, since it can be conceived indefinitely, forward or backward.** The entire causal chain requires no explanation; it can be regarded as merely an arbitrary fact of our experience, or an arbitrary act of the mind as it structures that experience, that we see events occurring in some orderly fashion instead of occurring completely helter-skelter.

Finally, Hume argued, even if the cosmological argument were valid, it would still not establish what its supporters claim. If there had to be some first cause, **why could this not be the material, physical world rather than God?** If one answered that there has to be some explanation for where the world comes from, or why it has the properties it has, then Hume would retort that exactly the same is true of God. If one is willing to accept as a final explanation of the universe that God is its first cause, then an explanation that **the material world is its own cause** should be just as satisfactory.

Kant's Critique of the Cosmological Argument

The great German philosopher Immanuel Kant, following after Hume's analysis of the problem of knowledge and applying Hume's conclusions to the problem of the existence of a supreme being, made a series of criticisms of the arguments for the existence of God in his *Critique of Pure Reason*. With regard to the cosmological argument, Kant contended that it contains invalid assumptions that prove nothing.

The first of these assumptions, Kant wrote, is that from contingent events we can infer that there must be a necessary cause of their existence. **The principle of causality, that every event must have a cause, applies, as far as we can tell, only to the world of sense experience.** But, in the cosmological argument, this principle about empirical knowledge is used to carry us beyond the world of sense experience to something that is supposed to transcend it. This extension, Kant insisted, is unjustified and illegitimate. We have no basis for assuming that the principles we employ in the analysis of our experience can be made to apply to anything beyond experience.

THE ATTACK ON "FIRST CAUSE"

Further, Kant pointed out, we have no justification for inferring that there must be a first cause. **The principles that we follow with regard to the use of reason do not support the argument in question, since we have no rational means for arriving at the end of our quest for causes and explanations, nor have we any way of determining when the series of causes and explanations have been completed.** Therefore, we can never be justified in claiming that we have found the first cause.

Basically, what Kant considered to be at fault in the cosmological argument for the existence of a supreme being is that it attempts to reason **beyond all possible experience, as well as beyond the limits for which we have any guarantee that our rational faculties are reliable.** By illegitimately extending principles—whose only known application and warrant is the realm of actual experience—to questions that transcend all possible experience, one creates these proofs and comes to conclusions about the necessary existence of some of our concepts. But once one has left the limits of the application of reason, all sorts of arguments can be constructed and things proved, and all sorts of paradoxes and dilemmas created. In this realm, we have no standards as to what is valid argumentation, and hence no way of determining when we have successfully established anything at all. All that we can do is recognize that all arguments that transcend possible experience, whether they be about God or anything else, are entirely speculative, and fruitless, and prove nothing of which we can be certain.

The criticisms directed against the cosmological argument by Hume and Kant derive from their theories of knowledge. To the extent that the basic views of most modern philosophers are built upon claims of either of these thinkers, the cosmological argument has found slight support in recent years. A great many philosophers assert that the argument is not conclusive and fails to establish the existence of a supreme being.

The ontological argument

Another argument that has been employed to prove the existence of God is the **ontological** argument. This proof tries to establish that **solely from the definition of a supreme being, it follows that He must necessarily exist.** No knowledge about the world is required in order to develop this argument, and hence it is considered **as a purely *a priori*** demonstration. It has been a favorite of many of the great metaphysicians, such as St. Anselm, Descartes, and Spinoza. Apparently, they have preferred it above all other arguments for the existence of God for what to most non-metaphysically inclined persons may appear to be its most obvious defect, namely, that the argument bears no relation to our experience, but only to a concept or idea of a supreme being.

St. Anselm

The classical form of the ontological argument appears in the writings of the famous medieval thinker St. Anselm. He contended that anyone who understood what was meant by the term "God" or "supreme being" would see that such an entity must exist. God is that being than which none greater can be conceived. Since I can comprehend this definition, I can conceive of God. Moreover, I can conceive of God not only as existing as a concept in my own mind but also as **existing in reality,** that is, **independently of my ideas.** Since it is greater to exist both as an idea and as a real thing than merely to exist as an idea, **God must exist both in reality and as an idea.** By definition, God is that than which none greater can be conceived. Hence God must exist in reality, or else something greater than God can be conceived (that is, an entity possessing all of God's properties, *plus* real existence); this, by the very definition of God or the supreme being, is impossible.

Spinoza

A briefer though probably less convincing presentation of the ontological argument appears in the *Ethics* of Baruch Spinoza, although it is worth remembering that the meaning Spinoza gives to "God" is very different from its customary meaning, as we have seen (pages 113–14). The eleventh proposition of Book I reads: **"God, or substance, consisting of infinite attributes, of which each expresses eternal and infinite essentiality, necessarily exists."** The evidence offered for this proposition is: "If this be denied, conceive, if possible, that God does not exist: then His essence does not involve existence. But this is absurd (that is, it is contrary to the definition of God). Therefore God necessarily exists."

Descartes

A more discursive version of the argument appears in Descartes's *Meditations*. There he reasoned:

> But now, if from the simple fact that I can draw from my thought the idea of anything it follows that all that I recognize clearly and distinctly to pertain to this thing pertains to it in reality, can I not draw from this argu-

ment and a demonstration of the existence of God? It is certain that I do not find in me the less the idea of him, that is, of being supremely perfect, than that of any figure or of any number whatever; and I do not know less clearly and distinctly that an actual and eternal existence belongs to his nature than I know that all I can demonstrate of any figure or of any number belongs truly to the nature of that figure or that number: and accordingly, although all that I have concluded in the preceding meditations may not turn out to be true, the existence of God ought to pass in my mind as being at least as certain as I have up to this time regarded the truths of mathematics to be, which have to do only with numbers and figures: although, indeed, that might not seem at first to be perfectly evident, but might appear to have some appearance of sophistry. For being accustomed in all other things to make a distinction between existence and essence, I easily persuade myself that existence may perhaps be separated from the essence of God and thus God might be conceived as not existent actually. But nevertheless, when I think more attentively, I find that existence can no more be separated from the essence of God than the essence of a rectilinear triangle can be separated from the equality of its three angles to two right angles, or, indeed, if you please, from the idea of a mountain the idea of a valley; so that there would be no less contradiction in conceiving of a God, that is, of a being supremely perfect, to whom existence was wanting, that is to say, to whom there was wanting any perfection, than in conceiving of a mountain which had no valley.

Essence and Existence

In each of these presentations, the same basic theme occurs. From an examination of our concept of God as a perfect being, or that being than which none greater can be conceived, we can see that one of the elements of this perfection, one of the ingredients of the very definition of God, must be His existence. Hence, unlike any other concept whose definition does not entail that it must exist, or does not include existence as one of its properties, the concept of God includes in its very nature that **God is an existent being.** Thus, merely from the idea of God, we can tell that He must necessarily exist, in the same way that from the definition of a triangle, we can tell that the sum of its interior angles equals 180°.

Before considering some of the many criticisms that have been leveled against this metaphysical argument for the existence of God, it should be pointed out that some philosophers who employed the argument did not do so as a means to establish a fact (namely, that there is a God) but, rather, to explain **the nature of divine being.** Descartes, for instance, did not offer the ontological argument as a disproof of atheism but introduced it only after he believed he had already established the existence of God by other means, by an argument of a causal type. Then, if one already accepted the fact that God exists, the value of the ontological argument was that it made clear what sort of a being God is, as distinguished from all others. God, alone, of all the objects we know of, is such that the concept or idea of Him includes the idea of necessary existence, whereas no other thing that we can conceive of includes within itself, or within the definition of it, its necessary existence. **This showed, for metaphysicians like Descartes and Spinoza, that God alone is the cause of Himself, is a self-existent being.**

Criticisms of the Ontological Argument

Ever since the original presentation of the ontological argument by St. Anselm in the

Middle Ages, philosophers have attempted to show that there is something peculiarly wrong with this form of reasoning. The earliest critique was sent to Anselm by a contemporary of his, Gaunilon, a monk of Marmoutier, who wrote in defense of the "fool," whom Anselm had claimed could say, but could not believe, that God does not exist, since as soon as he understood what the concept of God was, he would see that it followed from his definition that He exists. In order to demonstrate what was wrong with the ontological argument, Gaunilon pointed out that if this sort of reasoning were legitimate, one could also show that all kinds of unreal or imaginary objects must also exist. For example, if one could imagine that there is a perfect island somewhere beyond the point where any explorer could possibly go, it follows that if this island is perfect, or is that island than which none greater can be conceived, then, according to Anselm's argument, the island must exist. If it did not, then it would not be perfect, or be that island than which none greater could be conceived. But since by definition it is perfect, and no greater island can be imagined, then from that concept alone, we can be sure that it must actually exist. By indicating that one could develop all sorts of ontological arguments about all sorts of ideas, Gaunilon sought to show that the argument contained elements that are absurd and contradictory. (Anselm, in his own defense, claimed that the ontological argument applied only to God, since no other concept could be that of a perfect object.)

ST. THOMAS AQUINAS

Another kind of criticism was made by St. Thomas Aquinas, who claimed that the error of the ontological argument was that it assumed we could know the nature of God, that He is a perfect being, before knowing whether He exists. Actually, **His nature can be learned only after one knows His existence, and not vice versa.** In fact, the ultimate knowledge of God, the final understanding we can come to, according to St. Thomas, is the definition of God as He is conceived in the ontological argument. Hence, **first we must establish His existence** by other means, then study His properties; and, at the end of this investigation, we may know enough to define God, that is, to be able to employ St. Anselm's argument. Until then, according to St. Thomas, the ontological argument is only an uninteresting hypothetical observation that if God is a perfect (that is, a necessarily existent) being, then God necessarily exists.

KANT

Perhaps the best-known criticism of the ontological argument is that of Immanuel Kant in which he undertook to demonstrate why **existence is not the kind of property that can be part of the definition of any concept.** The idea or conception that we have of anything involves a series of properties or predicates (e.g., that it is square, green, heavy). But can existence be such a predicate? If we conceive of something, and then conceive of it as existing, is our idea of the thing any different? In his famous illustration, Kant pointed out that the idea of one hundred thalers and a real one hundred thalers contain the same monetary elements. The idea that I have in my mind is something that can be broken down into one hundred one-dollar bills, into coins, etc. Its economic value is the same, whether I am merely thinking of it or whether I have the money in my pocket. One does not change the concept involved whether one merely thinks of it or whether one thinks of it as existing. As applied to the argument for the existence of God, **the force of the concept or idea of God or a perfect being is not increased by thinking of it as existing or by merely thinking about it.** Hence no bridge can be built from the idea of a perfect being to the actual existence of such a being. We can prove either something trivial or nothing at all by means of the ontological argument. Either it is shown that we can define the term "God" in such a way that the proposition "God necessarily exists" can be derived from the definition (which only shows an interesting but metaphysically unexciting fact about this definition, but nothing about what objects may or may not exist in the universe), or nothing is shown, since the idea of a being than which none greater can be conceived is the same whether we are thinking of this object as something in our minds or whether we are thinking of it as a real independent object.

Conclusions

Although many thinkers believe that the existence of God can be established by means of rational or natural evidence, other philosophers maintain that no satisfactory rational evidence can be adduced to prove God's existence. Some of the latter believe that no satisfactory proof is possible because the object in question does not happen to exist. Others

have concluded that the difficulties involved in all the proofs are due to the nature of the subject, which is perhaps beyond our rational capacities. These thinkers have claimed that the problems involved in finding rational or natural evidence establishing the existence of God may indicate that one must seek another type of evidence entirely and abandon the quest by means of reason.

Atheism

If there are no valid proofs for the existence of God, then three completely different conclusions seem possible. **The first of these is simply the outright denial that there is any divine being.** This atheistical conclusion does not, of course, follow as a logical consequence from the unsatisfactory nature of the proofs. The fact that adequate rational evidence cannot be found to establish that something exists neither shows that it does exist nor shows that it does not exist. In fact, most of the criticisms that have been leveled against arguments purporting to prove the existence of God are equally cogent when leveled at the use of similar arguments to prove the nonexistence of God. Therefore, the atheist attempts to claim too much for the criticisms that have been leveled against arguments for the existence of God if he claims that they prove that God does not exist.

Agnosticism

A conclusion that may be more in keeping with the evidence is that of the **agnostic, who contends that there is not sufficient rational evidence to establish either the** existence or the nonexistence of a supreme being. Therefore, he declares that he simply does not know (which is the literal meaning of "agnostic") and that he will withhold opinion until such time as there may be more decisive evidence to support one side or the other.

Fideism

Besides these irreligious or nonreligious conclusions, there is also a religious conclusion that has recognized the inadequacy of the proofs for the existence of God. This is called **fideism, a view that our religious knowledge is not, and ought not to be, based upon rational or natural information, but solely on faith.** The general contention of the fideists has usually been that **religious knowledge is beyond the limits of a person's rational faculties and understanding.** Hence what human beings must do in order to obtain religious knowledge is first to recognize the hopelessness of accomplishing this by rational means, and then seek knowledge of God by **faith alone.**

Fideism represents a combination of a complete skepticism about the possibility of human knowledge, at least in the area of religious knowledge, and an appeal to knowledge through faith, unsupported by rational evidence. In fact, the fideists have portrayed the attempts by human beings to comprehend God by their reason and their sense information as an impious and dangerous example of human vanity, trying to measure the divine world by the puny standards of people's imagination, understanding, and experience. Heresies have resulted, the fideists charge, from this human presumption and rashness,

from a person's insistence on making his/her mental conceptions of the universe the measure of all truth. In order to avoid this, one should recognize, as Hume said (possibly with tongue in cheek, since he was more likely an agnostic than a fideist), that "to be a philosophical skeptic is, in a man of letters, the first and most essential step toward being a sound, believing Christian."

In nearly all leading religious traditions in the Western world, there has been fideistic theorizing, usually by religious or mystical thinkers, who have regarded the attempt to comprehend religious knowledge by means of reason as a most dangerous trend. On the other hand, some of those who have made out the best case for the fideistic viewpoint have apparently been nonbelievers who felt that this was the easiest or safest way to state their doubts. This rejection of rational evidence for religious knowledge appears in such religious thinkers as Pascal and Kierkegaard, and such irreligious thinkers as Hume and Voltaire. In both the religious and the irreligious philosophers who have asserted the irrationality of religious belief, very similar arguments occur.

What this appears to indicate is that the nature of fideism is such that it is based upon a skeptical theory of knowledge that leads either to a religious or to an agnostic conclusion, both of which are compatible with the philosophical arguments employed. If one is convinced that we have no rational evidence, and can have no rational evidence, regarding either the existence or nature of God, then what follows? The fideists claim that *because* of the lack of evidence, one ought to believe by faith alone. But one could just as well arrive at the conclusion that because of the lack of evidence, one ought to suspend judgment and reach no conclusion at all. The arguments indicate that neither the fideistic nor the agnostic conclusion is the correct one. The argument would be compatible with either one or the other.

PASCAL

Perhaps this point will be clarified by a passage from the great seventeenth-century French scientist and religious thinker Blaise Pascal. After gaining fame as a scientific prodigy, Pascal suddenly withdrew from the world of affairs, retiring to the stronghold of an extremely pious religious group, the Jansenists, at the convent of Port-Royal. In an unfinished work, *Les Pensées*, he set down the reasoning that led him to his religious outlook. The work, as we now have it, is a series of comments on various themes about people, their understanding and their destiny. In one of the longest of these comments, Pascal discussed the relationship between skepticism and religious belief. The passage begins:

The main arguments of the skeptics . . . are that we possess no certainty concerning any principles apart from faith and revelation, except insofar as we perceive them naturally within ourselves. But this natural intuition is no convincing proof of their truth; because we have no certainty, apart from faith, as to whether man was created by a good God, or a wicked demon, or chance, and these principles are true, false, or uncertain depending upon our origin. No person is certain, apart from faith, whether he is awake or asleep . . . [and so, the skeptics have shown that everything we know is uncertain. But, on the other hand, we find ourselves drawn by nature to believe all sorts

of things. We are torn between an intellectual skepticism which renders everything doubtful, and a natural dogmatism which inclines us toward believing many things. . . . R. H. P.]

What then shall man do in this state? Should he doubt everything? Should he doubt if he is awake, if he is being pinched, or if he is being burned? Should he doubt whether he is in doubt? Should he doubt his own existence? We are not able to go as far as that; and I put it down as a fact that there never has been a completely thoroughgoing skeptic. Nature sustains our feeble reason, and prevents it from raving to that extent.

Should he then assert that he is in possession of certain truth—he who, when pressed at all, can show no title to it, and is compelled to let go his hold upon it?

What a chimera then is man! What a novelty! What a monster, what a chaos, what a contradiction, what a prodigy! Judge of all things, imbecile worm of the earth; depositary of all truth, a sink of uncertainty and error; the pride and trash of the universe!

Who will unravel this mess? Nature refutes the skeptics, and reason refutes the dogmatists. What then will become of you, O men, who try to discover by your own natural reason, what is your true condition? . . .

Know then proud man, what a paradox you are unto yourself. Humble yourself, weak reason; be silent, foolish nature; learn that man infinitely transcends man, and learn from your master what is your true condition, of which you are ignorant. Hear God.

This powerful passage from Pascal stresses our complete uncertainty, and our complete inability to understand anything. But, Pascal insisted, we are not able to rest in skepticism or agnosticism but find ourselves impelled to believe. Since we cannot justify our beliefs rationally, we are therefore compelled to turn away from the unsatisfactory quest for knowledge by means of rational evidence, to knowledge based on faith alone. The skeptic or agnostic shares with Pascal the rejection of all knowledge supposedly based on natural or rational principles, but does not take the next step he proposed, that of pure belief. Instead, the skeptic or the agnostic has no belief, or has suspended judgment on all questions for which there cannot be satisfactory evidence. No argument or evidence can be given for determining which is the better or truer path, that of the fideist or that of the agnostic, but both start out from the same skeptical basis. Hume's comment that skepticism is the starting point for true Christianity may be correct from the fideistic outlook, but it was also the starting point for the irreligious and agnostic outlook of Hume and Voltaire.

Revelation

Another conclusion that is often drawn from the criticism of the arguments for the existence of God, sometimes as part of a fideistic theory, is that **religious knowledge cannot be based upon natural evidence, but is, instead, based upon revealed knowledge.** The contention here is that the philosophers who debate the merits of rational arguments miss the point. There is another source of knowledge that is the basis for our religious knowledge, and if one accepts this source, one will not be interested in whether a particular argument advanced by a philosopher or a theologian happens to be valid.

Those who advocate this conclusion usually insist that religious knowledge is of a different order from natural knowledge, and that the philosophers of religion have frequently failed to make this distinction. Hence they have dealt only with natural religion, which may well be as unsatisfactory as Hume and Kant thought. But there is another area of religion, revealed religion, which is unaffected by the criticisms that have been leveled against natural religion.

Revelation is to be found either in certain documents that are accepted as the word of God or in certain experiences that are taken as communications or contacts with a divine being. The philosophers of religion may raise various questions about how one recognizes that certain knowledge is revealed, or how one distinguishes private experiences that are illusory from those that are said to be genuine. The believer in revealed religion can retort that he/she is as assured of the revealed character of this knowledge as of the knowledge itself. Even if he/she cannot prove by rational means that certain information is genuine revelation (which would be a problem in natural religion), he/she has access to certain knowledge and to certain assurances that settle these questions as far as he/she is concerned.

In the last hundred years, another view about religious knowledge has developed, one based on human needs and the special character of human religious experience. The American philosopher and psychologist William James (who will be discussed at length in Chapter 7) examined the varieties of religious experience as reported by religious persons. He sought to show that such experience was not reducible to variants of sexual or abnormal psychological experiences, but formed a distinct kind of human experience. In his essay "The Will to Believe,"

James argued that some people want to believe whether there is adequate evidence or not. The effect of believing for such people can be momentous in their lives, and so should not be denigrated just because these believers cannot prove or substantiate what they believe. Pascal and Kierkegaard, as well as James, insisted that believing is different from knowing. One believes in spite of the lack of knowledge, if believing is of sufficient importance.

The German Jewish philosopher Martin Buber tried to portray the special character of religious experience in his various works. In *Tales from the Hassidim*, he set forth the attitude of a religious community, the Hassidim of Central Europe. Readers all over the world who never heard of the group have been struck by the way the religious features of the group's activities leap from the page as the believers express their religious views through dancing. It is irrelevant to Buber's picture that these believers do not offer evidence for their beliefs. They are immersed in them. In a later work, *I and Thou*, Buber sought to show how the experience of animate, sentient, and spiritual characteristics of the human world appear in human affairs. One recognizes various elements of experience as having an I-thou relationship with oneself. These elements are not things but personalities. Above and beyond this, one has a spiritual awareness of an everlasting thou, whether one can characterize this in any traditional religious or theological terms.

More recently the Rumanian scholar Mircea Eliade has tried to show the religious nature of human beings, their craving for some transcendental and sacred element, as opposed to the secular and profane aspects of experience. Eliade has examined the history of religions from the primitive to the most sophisticated to exhibit how the sacred and the transcendental are manifested in different cultures and belief systems.

Neither James nor Buber nor Eliade offered answers to the philosophical problems about the evidence concerning the nature and existence of God. Instead, they stressed the role of religious experience and belief in human affairs, and insisted on its special and important function in many human lives. Their views and findings are compatible with a wide range of religious and irreligious theologies, even with Nietzsche's claim that God, as a supernatural being, is dead, or with deist or theist views we will describe below. Religious beliefs may result from human needs but are not explained or explained away by these needs.

The problem of the nature of God

Another question dealt with by philosophers of religion is that of **the nature of God**. By and large, this is a metaphysical question in which the attempt is made to develop a theory compatible either with our general information as given in certain religious traditions, our scientific knowledge about how the world operates, or with our rational understanding of the character of the various aspects of our experience. Theories about the nature of God range from different forms of scientific atheism, contending that God is a figment of the human imagination invented for various psychological, sociological, economic, and other reasons, to very elaborate metaphysical theories purporting to explain the characteristics of the divine will, the divine intelligence, and the like.

Atheism

Atheism is the theory that either **there is no God, or if there is, He cannot in any way affect human existence.** To support this contention, evidence is offered consisting of our knowledge of the physical world and human behavior, or some sort of materialistic or naturalistic metaphysics, or insoluble difficulties that confront those who affirm the existence of God.

In modern times, the increased understanding of the operations of the natural and human world has led many thinkers to claim that all problems can be resolved by natural rather than supernatural concepts, and that supernatural concepts can themselves be explained in natural terms. This view is perhaps summed up in the attitude of the mathematician Pierre-Simon de Laplace, who, when he was explaining to Napoleon his theory of how the astronomical universe came into existence, was asked where God fitted into his scheme. He replied, "I have no need of such a hypothesis." The atheistical contention is that the questions that formerly were answered in terms of God can now be answered in terms of scientific knowledge.

In addition, the atheists contend, we now have information that explains why people hold religious beliefs and this information suggests, if it does not show, that the role played by religious belief in human history has nothing to do with the actual existence of a God. Psychological

theories developed by Friedrich Nietzsche, Sigmund Freud, and others suggest that religious beliefs have arisen because of certain human needs, a human desire to feel secure in such a vast cosmos, and the like. Thomas Paine, Karl Marx, and others have drawn attention to the role played by religious belief in securing certain institutions and keeping classes in social and political power. Some psychologists like James Leuba and Freud tried to establish a connection between sexual problems and religious convictions. In this manner, the atheists have claimed that God as an actual entity does not exist but is only a construction of the human mind, invented to meet certain needs.

PHILOSOPHICAL BASIS OF ATHEISM

A more philosophical basis for atheism is given by **any metaphysical theory that provides an adequate rational comprehension of what we know about the world by means of a system containing no supernatural concepts. A materialistic or naturalistic metaphysics** that attempts to account for our knowledge and experience in terms of a cosmos containing **nothing but material or natural objects** has been advanced as a rational justification of atheism. If one can satisfactorily account for everything without requiring the concept of a divine being, then, the atheist asks, why should we have need of, or believe in, such a being?

As part of the philosophical justification for atheism, some philosophers have pointed out that no consistent or satisfactory theory of the nature of God explains how a divine being can have the properties usually attributed to divinity and yet have anything to do with the human world. From ancient days, in the views of Epicurus, down to such present-day thinkers as Bertrand Russell, philosophers have argued that there are paradoxes and contradictions involved in the notion of an all-powerful God, in the notion of a just God who governs an unjust universe, in the notion of an eternal, unchanging deity who acts and creates the universe, and so on.

Pantheism

Another theory of the nature of God, which its opponents have regarded as merely another form of atheism, is **pantheism. This is the view that God is not a separate being, but is either the entire natural order or an aspect of the entire natural order. Either the universe as a whole is God, or the power or force that pervades the whole of the cosmos is God. God is everywhere, and is everything, or is in everything.**

SPINOZA

Perhaps the most famous presentation of pantheism is the metaphysical system of Spinoza. As we saw in the previous chapter (pages 113–14), he sought to establish that **God and nature are one and the same substance;** that everything that exists or takes place in the world is an aspect, modification, or attribute of God; and that everything can be explained or accounted for by showing the manner of its derivation from God or nature. Every physical or mental event in the universe was interpreted in Spinoza's great metaphysical system as an aspect of one of the two known attributes of God or nature, **thought or extension**.

According to the Spinozistic view, God has no personal qualities, since He is not a being independent of, or separate from, the universe. Those views that describe the divine being as having properties analogous to those of human beings were dismissed as being merely anthropomorphic and having nothing to do with the true nature of things. The proper attitude toward the universal divine nature is what Spinoza called **"the intellectual love of God," the appreciation of the divine character of everything, through understanding the nature of reality.** Thus, through comprehending the structure of the universe, by means of grasping the vast scientific system that determines the various specific events of the cosmos, one is expressing the intellectual love of God, and recognizing the pantheistic character of the world.

Deism

This theory of the nature of God maintains that **there is a divine being or divine power** separate from the physical world, which it has created or started, but that this divine being or power exercises no direct influence or force on events occurring within the universe as it now exists. With the development of modern astronomical and physical systems in the seventeenth century, many thinkers saw that these scientific views suggested a picture of the universe as a self-contained mechanism, like a clock, and each successive state of affairs could be completely explained in terms of the previous state of the mechanism. In these terms, they developed the conception of the nature of God called **"deism"** to account for God's relations to this mechanical cosmos. God was pictured as the "perfect watchmaker," who had created or regulated this mechanism according to the best rational principles, and then, having set the machine in motion, no longer played any role in the affairs of the natural world.

The deist theory finds no place for the relationships believed to exist between man and God by most religious traditions. Since God takes no active part in the affairs of the world, there is no point to prayer or supplication. In fact, assuming complete wisdom on the part of God, some of the deists claimed that this must be the best of all possible worlds, and that prayers to bring about certain changes in the world actually constituted a form of dangerous blasphemy against the perfectly ordained and ordered system of the universe.

Theism

The theory of the nature of God that best fits most religious traditions in the Western world is that called **"theism."** This is the view that there is a God, or there are gods, who stand in some kind of **direct or personal relationship with human beings.** Either the theistic conception of divinity can be **polytheistic**, that is, that there are many gods, e.g., the theism of Greek mythology; or it can be **monotheistic**, that is, it can limit the conception of divinity to one God, as is the case in the Judeo-Christian-Islamic traditions. But in either the polytheistic or the monotheistic conception of God, there are several further questions about the nature of God that have to be resolved.

THE NATURE OF GOD

One of these is whether the God or gods are finite or infinite in power, knowledge, and other attributes. In ancient Greek polytheism, each of the deities was limited as to what he or she was able to accomplish. In the conception of God in the Judeo-Christian-Islamic tradition, the deity has usually been portrayed as all-powerful, unlimited in what He is able to do. However, there have been several philosophers of religion, even within this tradition, who have thought that the only way of reconciling the conception of the divine nature with the evils that occur in this world was to portray God as lacking complete or absolute power or knowledge.

THE ETHICAL PROBLEM

Another question that has been much discussed by theists is the relationship between the divine nature and the standards of goodness, justice, morality, and the like. As the problem was put by Plato long ago, is something right because the gods will it, or do they will it because it is right? The question at issue is whether the standards of value are only the arbitrary pronouncement of God or the gods, or whether there are some universal standards of value that even the deity accepts and obeys. On the one hand, there are theistic theories that conceive the nature of God as coeternal with certain eternal truths, such as the ultimate standards of value and truth, which God accepts and employs in His relations with the world.

On the other hand, there are theories, sometimes called **voluntaristic,** that assert that the power of the deity is totally unlimited and that it is within this divine power that God makes various things true or good. Anything that God wills is, by the very fact that God has willed it, necessarily right and just.

As is evident, the range of possible theistic theories is very large. Conceptions of the number and character of the divine being can be adjudged in terms of their consistency and their coherence with our general understanding of the world. Most theistic theories have been developed in terms of how they fit in with certain religious traditions, which begin with what they believe to be certain knowledge about God and his relation to the universe. The theistic philosophers' achievements can then be evaluated according to how well they fit in with the view of God held by these traditions.

In the Judeo-Christian-Islamic tradition, there has been a long history (dating back from the Book of Job, the Epistles of St. Paul, the philosophy of Philo Judaeus, and other works) of attempts to develop a theistic point of view in harmony with the picture of the divine nature as revealed in Scripture. Those who were concerned with working out an intelligible and rational conception of God that was compatible with our other knowledge about the world, and who were also believers either in Judaism or Christianity, tried to construct philosophically acceptable forms of theism. The conceptions of the nature of God (or the gods) of Plato, Aristotle, and the Neoplatonists have been studied, modified, and combined in order to present a rationally satisfactory version of theism that is also consistent with the Judeo-Christian-Islamic God's nature.

Philosophers and theologians within the three traditions of Judaism, Christianity, and Islam tried, especially during the Middle Ages, to work out acceptable rational explanations of the fundamental beliefs of their religions. Some like Averroës, Maimonides, and St. Thomas Aquinas based their explanations on Aristotelian and Neoplatonic philosophy. Where they could not reconcile Aristotle's views with their basic religious beliefs, they insisted that some knowledge of the nature of God and God's relations with the world could be known only by faith and not by reason.

CRITICISMS OF THEISM

Alongside the history of attempts to construct a rational theology, usually in theistic terms, there has been as long a history of either cynical opposition or attacks from mystics and fideists. Powerful objections have been made that the proposed theory does not meet the requirements of a rational mind. Various religious thinkers have tried to show that we cannot rationally know anything at all about the nature of God. (Some of the most extreme of the mystics and the fideists have presented a theory called **"negative theology,"** maintaining that God is beyond any of the classifications or categories that man can conceive. No statements that we can make can apply to God except negative ones that tell us what He is not. Thus our sole knowledge about the nature of God is in negative terms, telling us, for example, that "God is not an animal.")

The theistic conception of God, since it best corresponds to the various revealed religious traditions, has of course been of great concern to philosophers of religion. Within nearly every Christian, Jewish, and Islamic group, there have been many attempts to develop a theistic theory that is consistent with the group's concept of God. In terms of such a theory, each group has tried to construct a satisfactory rational defense of its religion.

Fundamentalism

Others, like Sir Isaac Newton, have held the view that both nature and Scripture were presentations of God's message to man, which was to be learned scientifically or through the study of God's revelation as presented in the Bible and/or the Koran. Newton, in his *Principia Mathematica*, offered a version of the argument from design to show what we could know of God scientifically. In his *Observations on the Prophecies of Daniel and St. John*, Newton sought to show what we could know of God and His plans for mankind from the Bible.

A rising movement of Bible scholars, starting with Spinoza, developed what was called the "Higher Criticism of the Bible," a study of the work in terms of its history and development, which questioned whether we have an accurate text and whether it is a divine text or one written by human beings in certain historical situations. If the latter, the Bible would provide information not about God but about man at an early stage of human history. This, the Higher Critics said, would account for the many discrepancies that people have found in the text and for the claims that are counter to now accepted scientific findings.

At the end of the eighteenth century and the beginning of the ninteenth century, a view was set forth that would now be called **"fundamentalism."** It insisted that the Bible is the Word of God, that the Bible that we possess is inerrant in all matters, and that the meaning of the Bible can be ascertained by literal reading of the text. This view presupposes that we know God exists, that He does not change, and that He communicates His will to mankind through a text that he has preserved for us through all of the vicissitudes of history.

Fundamentalism was especially important in the United States as a way of opposing Darwinism as an explanation of man's nature and destiny. In the early part of the twentieth century, it appeared as an anti-intellectual way of opposing new scientific knowledge. In the post–Second World War era it has become a serious and growing view in Judaism, Christianity, and Islam. Its adherents take the developments in the modern world—the return of the Jews to Palestine, the rebuilding of Jerusalem, the Cold War, the emergence of Islamic republics—all as evidence that the prophecies in the divine books are being fulfilled and that our knowledge of God and His plans comes to us by literally interpreting what has been set down in holy writings.

Some fundamentalists take this way of knowing God and about God in most scholarly fashion. They learn the requisite ancient languages, study Biblical archaeology and Biblical history to grasp the literal meaning of the texts and to predict the future course of events in terms of the prophecies in the texts. Their opponents remain skeptical in view of the disagreements among fundamentalists about what the literal meaning of a given text is, and in view of the predictions made by fundamentalist readers that have not been fulfilled. They would suggest that either the text is errant or the literal interpreter is. In either case, other means would be required to learn about God and His message.

Conclusion

In view of the age-old concern of humankind with religious problems, this area of human experience constitutes a subject matter for philosophical analysis. The philosopher—in examining the problems of religious knowledge and metaphysical theories about the nature of God—is not necessarily concerned to argue for or against any particular religious belief or theory. Rather, his/her interest is to analyze it, to raise questions about it in order to understand it rationally.

Although much philosophizing about religious questions has been of an apologetic character, that is, has been aimed at rendering various religious beliefs intellectually acceptable, it is just as likely that careful rational examination may result in doubts that an intelligible theory is possible. The philosophy of religion is committed to developing evidence neither for atheism nor for religious belief. Instead, **its crucial concerns are to examine the knowledge-claims that are made in this area,** to see if there are standards in relation to which they can be justified, and to evaluate and interpret these claims within the framework of rational understanding. It is always possible that the best conclusion one may be able to reach is a fideistic or skeptical one—that no defensible rational comprehension can be gained in the area of religious knowledge, and that no satisfactory rational interpretation or explanation can be made.

We may best follow the attempts to understand the special character of religious experience and its effect on human affairs, rather than seeking arguments for or against various religious-knowledge claims. With the present rise in religious activities all over the world, we may better profit from examining the role religion is now playing and why it is again a very vital force in the human world, than by reexamining *ad nauseum* the arguments for the existence of God, and the various theological conundrums that have bedeviled philosophers for two millennia.

Suggested further reading

Classical Authors

Hume, David. *Dialogues Concerning Natural Religion.* Indianapolis: Hackett, 1980.

Kierkegaard, Søren. *Training in Christianity.* Oxford University Press, 1941. An exposition of the fideist point of view by one of the most important modern theologians.

Nietzsche, Friedrich Wilhelm. *The Philosophy of Nietzsche.* London: New English Library, 1966. Contains several works of Nietzsche in which his atheism is set forth.

Pascal, Blaise. *Pensées.* London: Penguin Books, 1966. One of the classical presentations of the problem of the nature of religious knowledge.

St. Anselm. *Proslogium.* The classical statement of the ontological argument.

St. Thomas Aquinas. *Basic Writings.* Selections from St. Thomas's writings, covering his most important theories.

Voltaire. *Candide.* London: Penguin Books, 1968. A brilliant satire concerning the problem of evil.

Modern Authors

Buber, Martin. *I and Thou*. Boston: Scribners, 1984.

Copleston, Frederick C. *Aquinas*. London: Penguin Books, 1967. A good critical discussion of the views of this philosopher by a modern Thomist.

Eliade, Mircea. *From Primitives to Zen*. New York: Harper and Row, 1978.

Hannay, Alastair. *Kierkegaard*. London: Routledge & Kegan Paul, 1982.

Hester, Marcus, ed. *Faith, Reason, and Skepticism: Essays by W. P. Alston, Robert Audi, Terence Penelhum, and R. H. Popkin*. Philadelphia: Temple University Press, 1992.

Hick, John. *Classical and Contemporary Readings in Philosophy of Religion*. Englewood Cliffs: Prentice-Hall, 1969.

James, William. *The Varieties of Religious Experience*. A classic in the psychology of religious behavior and attitudes.

Penelhum, Terence. *God and Skepticism*. Dordrecht, Netherlands: Reidel, 1983.

Plantinga, Alvin, and Wolterstoff, Nicholas, eds. *Faith, Rationality, Reason and Belief in God*. South Bend, Ind.: University of Notre Dame Press, 1984.

Sandeen, Ernest. *The Origins of Fundamentalism*. Chicago: University of Chicago Press, 1970.

CHAPTER FIVE

The theory of knowledge

One of the most important branches of philosophy is **epistemology** (theory of knowledge). Philosophers have attempted to discover the means by which our knowledge is acquired, the extent of our knowledge, and the standards or criteria by which we can judge the reliability of knowledge-claims.

We tend to be well satisfied with what we think we know about the universe and do not ask how we obtained our knowledge or question its reliability. Occasionally we are shocked to discover that what we thought was certain is proved dubious or false. If this happens often enough, we may become suspicious of all claims to certainty.

Suppose, for example, that someone whom we trusted told us that all the news in our daily newspaper was false. We might—in consequence—begin to distrust our friend, or distrust the newspaper, or distrust ourselves. We would certainly begin to think about the kind of evidence we would need to help us to discover what the truth of the case was. We would begin, in fact, to ask the sorts of questions that have led philosophers to develop a theory of knowledge.

Perhaps the most fertile source of material for developing a theory of knowledge has been the history of human opinions. No theory or doctrine has been so absurd that there has not been someone who believed it and argued for it. The history of science is replete with theories that have been thoroughly believed by the wisest men and were then thoroughly discredited.

Repeatedly, people have attempted to impose their beliefs on others and to punish those who rejected them. The early Greek philosopher Anaxagoras was exiled from Athens for saying that the moon was a stone. In the twentieth century, a teacher in Tennessee was punished for teaching the Darwinian theory of evolution. In the last fifty years, there have been many martyrs whose "crimes" were that they challenged the "infallible wisdom" of the rulers of their society.

Philosophers are concerned to determine the basis of all knowledge-claims and to agree upon standards for judging these claims. If so much of what had been taken as certain has instead proved false or doubtful, then how can we ever be certain?

René Descartes: the problem posed

The great French philosopher and mathematician René Descartes (1596–1650) posed the problem in a most striking form. Descartes lived in a rapidly changing world, one marked by almost continuous religious conflicts between the Catholics and the Huguenots, and by intense controversy between the advocates of Aristotle's views about the nature of the physical world, and those who supported the new theories of Copernicus, Kepler, and Galileo. The fact that there were new theories suggested that there were other methods of seeking after knowledge than those that had been employed by the Greeks and by everyone else since that time; this encouraged philosophers to begin to inquire into the nature of these methods and the validity of the knowledge they led to. Descartes, trained in Aristotelian philosophy, set out to study the world for himself. After extended investigation, he came to suspect all accepted views that claimed authority merely because they were ancient and honored. When he returned to Paris in 1628, he found that the most independently thoughtful of his contemporaries were similarly agitated by the conflict between the older ideas, which they felt they could no longer accept, and the new theories. Most of them despaired of finding certainty and turned to **skepticism**—a view that doubts whether any of our beliefs can be supported by adequate or sufficient evidence. Descartes, however, did not surrender to skepticism. He had an intense desire to be certain, to be so certain that no discovery could ever shake his beliefs again. He left Paris, a desperate man in quest of certainty. In his retreat in Holland, he tells us, he inquired into everything he knew to see what, if anything, he could accept as reliable knowledge.

Descartes felt that he could be certain only of that which could never be false or doubtful. Most of what we accept, Descartes thought, could not meet this standard—despite our certainty, it still might be false. He determined to test the knowledge that he like anyone else ordinarily would accept—knowledge derived from our sense experience. The results of his test (if he is right) are so devastating that philosophers have been compelled ever since to investigate the problem of the foundation of knowledge.

Descartes's Test

Before examining some of their theories, we must first consider Descartes's test. He begins his *Meditations on First Philosophy* (1640) by writing:

> It is now some years since I detected how many were the false beliefs that I had from my earliest youth admitted as true, and how doubtful was everything I had since constructed on this basis; and from that time I was convinced that I must once for all seriously undertake to rid myself of all the opinions which I had formerly accepted, and commence to build anew from the foundation, if I wanted to establish any firm and permanent structure in the sciences . . .
>
> Now for this object it is not necessary that I should show that all of these opinions are false—I shall perhaps never arrive at this end. But inasmuch as reason already persuades me that I ought no less carefully to withhold my assent from matters which are not entirely certain and indubitable than from those which appear to me manifestly to be false, if I am able to find in each one *some reason to doubt*, this will suffice to justify my rejecting the whole. And for that end it will not be requisite that I should examine each in particular, which would be an endless undertaking; for owing to the fact that the destruction of the foundations of necessity brings with it the downfall of

the rest of the edifice, I shall only . . . attack those principles upon which all my former opinions rested.

That is, Descartes feels that there is no need to test *every* opinion that he formerly held—an "endless undertaking"—but will instead consider general types of belief. **If there is any reason for doubt, then the entire category ought to be treated as doubtful and unreliable.** The first category to be treated is those opinions which we derive from sense experience.

All that up to the present time I have accepted as true and certain I have learned either from the senses or through the senses; but it is sometimes proved to me that these senses are deceptive, and it is wiser not to trust entirely anything by which we have once been deceived.

RELIABILITY OF SENSE DATA

Descartes assumes that everyone is familiar with the phenomenon of being deceived by his senses. One may see something at a distance that turns out to be quite otherwise when seen close up, or see things differently when they are in water from when they are out of it, e.g., when one is rowing, the oar appears to be bent. Since this sometimes happens, Descartes suggests we cannot really be certain that we are not always mistaken. If one grants that this is sometimes the case, but objects that in most cases we can be quite certain that our senses are not deceiving us, Descartes presses his test:

But it may be that although the senses sometimes deceive us concerning things which are hardly perceptible, or very far away, there are yet many others to be met with as to which we cannot reasonably have

any doubt, although we recognize them by means of the senses. For example, there is the fact that I am here, seated by the fire attired in a dressing gown, having this paper in my hands and other similar matters. And how could I deny that these hands and this body are mine, were it not perhaps that I compare myself to certain persons, devoid of sense, whose brains are so troubled . . . that they constantly assure us that they think they are kings when they are really quite poor or that they are clothed in purple when they are really without covering, or who imagine that they have an earthenware head or are nothing but pumpkins or are made of glass. But they are mad, and I should not be any the less insane were I to follow examples so extravagant.

Perhaps; but Descartes is beginning to shake our assurance. Can we be certain that we are not also subject to delusions? If his test has not already led to some doubt, Descartes raises another, more troubling problem:

At the same time I must remember that I am a man, and that consequently I am in the habit of sleeping, and in my dreams representing to myself the same things, or sometimes even less probable things, than do those who are insane in their waking moments. How often it has appeared to me that in the night I dreamed that I found myself in this particular place, that I was dressed and seated near the fire, whilst in reality I was lying undressed in bed! At this moment it does indeed seem to me that it is with eyes awake that I am looking at this paper; that this head which I move is not asleep, that it is deliberately and of set purpose that I extend my hand and see it; what happens in sleep does not appear so clear nor so distinct as does all this. But in thinking over this I remind myself that on many occasions I have in sleep been deceived by similar illusions, and in dwelling carefully on this reflection I see so manifestly that there are no certain indications by which we may clearly distinguish wakefulness from sleep that I am lost in astonishment.

And my astonishment is such that it is almost capable of persuading me that I now dream.

The problem thus posed is troublesome. How can we be certain that everything we see and do is not part of a dream? Any means that we employ as a check might, for all we can tell, also be parts of the dream. People have dreamed that they have pinched themselves to see if they are dreaming. Descartes concludes that no matter how we feel about it, there is no guarantee that our sense experience is not part of a dream. Therefore, we have grounds for suspecting the reliability—that is, the accuracy—of the information we acquire through our senses. But even if it is all a dream, one might ask, are not some aspects of the dream trustworthy? Accordingly, Descartes proceeds with his test:

> Now let us assume that we are asleep and that all these things, e.g., that we open our eyes, shake our head, extend our hands, and so on, are but false delusions; and let us reflect that possibly neither our hands nor our whole body are such as they appear to us to be. At the same time we must confess that the things which are represented to us in sleep are like painted representations which can only have been formed as the counterparts of something real and true, and that in this way those general things at least, that is, eyes, a head, hands and a whole body, are not imaginary things, but really exist. For, as a matter of fact, painters, even when they study with the greatest skill to represent sirens and satyrs by forms the most strange and extraordinary, cannot give them natures which are entirely new, but merely make a certain medley of the parts of different animals, or if their imagination is extravagant enough to invent something so novel that nothing similar has ever before been seen, and such that their work represents a thing purely fictitious

and absolutely false, it is certain all the same that the colors of which this is composed are necessarily real.

Descartes, at this point, seems willing to admit that even if it were possible that the particular content of our experience might be a dream, still the dream itself must be based on something. All the objects that we are acquainted with—ourselves, chairs, tables, trees—might be part of a vast delusion or dream, but at the same time, the fantasy seems to be based on *something*. But on what? Descartes suggests that the particular objects that we experience, talk about, live with, may be part of a **continuous dream world.** We may invent in our dream the objects that populate it. But our invention, if it is such, follows certain patterns and has certain fixed properties. Elephants are always bigger than butterflies, and squares never have round corners. Descartes concludes from these considerations that the actual items of our experience may be illusions, and the studies we make of them (e.g., astronomy, botany, physics) may also be illusions if their objects are figments of our imagination that exist only in our dreams. Still, the world of our dreams—if we assume for the sake of the discussion that everything we experience is part of a dream world—has some order and is constructed according to certain geometrical and numerical patterns. "For whether I am awake or asleep, two and three together always make five, and the square can never have more than four sides, and it does not seem possible that truths so clear and apparent can be suspected of any falsity or uncertainty."

THE QUESTION OF DEITY

But lest anyone think that the test is over and we at last have something that we can rely on, Descartes raises a final and more devastating reason for doubting even the knowledge of which we are most certain:

> Nevertheless I have long had fixed in my mind the belief that an all-powerful God existed by whom I have been created such as I am. But how do I know that He has not brought it to pass that there is no earth, no heaven, no extended body, no magnitude, no place, and that nonetheless, I perceive all these things and they seem to me to exist just exactly as I now see them? And, besides, as I sometimes imagine that others deceive themselves in the things which they think they know best, how do I know that I am not deceived every time that I add two and three, or count the sides of a square, or judge of things yet simpler, if anything simpler can be imagined? But possibly God has not desired that I should be thus deceived for He is said to be supremely good. If, however, it is contrary to His goodness to have made me such that I constantly deceive myself, it would also appear to be contrary to His goodness to permit me to be sometimes deceived, and nevertheless I cannot doubt that He does permit this.

Having suggested the most harrowing possibility of all, that the world is commanded by a deity who deceives humanity, Descartes prepares to conclude his test. If, notwithstanding all our efforts, we cannot avoid being misled, then how can we trust *anything*? If when I add two and three, I am compelled to make a mistake that I am incapable of detecting, how can I avoid mistaken conclusions? Once the possibility of systematic deception is admitted, all appears lost, and even our most "reliable" information seems dubious. Hence Descartes concludes:

> At the end I feel constrained to confess that there is nothing in all that I formerly believed to be true, of which I cannot in some measure doubt, and that not merely through want of thought or through levity, but for reasons which are very powerful and maturely considered; so that henceforth I ought not the less carefully to refrain from giving credence to these opinions than to that which is manifestly false, if I desire to arrive at any certainty in the sciences.

DOUBT

Descartes's test appears to have ended in disaster. If we inquire into the truth of our opinions, seeking evidence that would guarantee the impossibility of these beliefs being false, we find that such evidence appears to be lacking. Instead, reasons can be offered that suggest, whether plausibly or not, that **our most cherished and firm beliefs could be false.** Sense illusions, and fantasies due to insanity or drunkenness, cast some doubt on the reliability of our sense information. We may merely be "seeing things." The possibility that the whole of experience may be part of a dream leads to further doubts as to whether we are in fact seeing a world that exists, or even whether there is any world outside of our imagination. Lastly, the possibility that an evil genius is deceiving us leaves us entirely without assurance in the foundations of our knowledge.

DESCARTES'S PURPOSE

The purpose of Descartes's test it not to promulgate science-fiction fantasies but to illuminate a crucial problem. We are willing to take for granted a great deal that *might* be false or uncertain. In showing the difficulties that exist in establishing acceptable views, Descartes does not wish to convert us to skepticism and total doubt, make us unwilling to accept an opinion for fear that it might prove false. Instead, he undertakes to find a satisfactory basis for our knowledge, a basis so certain "that all the most extravagant suppositions brought forward by the skeptics would be incapable of shaking it."

The Problem

Let us now examine theories that Descartes and other philosophers have formulated about the nature of our knowledge, the foundation for it, and the extent of it. In order to make clear what their theorizing has been about, it is first necessary to understand **the nature of the problem of knowledge.**

When we say we "know" something, what sort of claim are we usually making?

POPULAR USAGE

In ordinary discourse, we use the verb "to know" loosely. When we say that we "know" something, we usually mean we are sure that something is true, as when two people dispute about the Davis Cup Final of 1984 and one says, "I *know* the U.S. won"—with complete assurance. Without help from Descartes, it is clear that when we use the word "know" to express personal conviction, our claim may in fact be groundless. We are all acquainted with extremely opinionated people who are in fact—extremely mistaken.

There are still less positive usages of "know," as when people use the word as equivalent to "believe," "think," and the like. When lay persons say they "know" that the Salk polio vaccine is effective, they in fact mean that they "think so," having perhaps heard that this is the view of some authoritative persons. If one is asked if Smith is going to be at the party, and the answer is "Yes, I know that he is," this may merely be a convenient way of saying "I believe he is; at least, I heard him say that he was planning to be there." One is not expressing complete assurance, but only a conviction. One would hardly be willing to guarantee the accuracy of such a statement on the mere basis of having heard Smith's plans. Clearly, Smith may have to change his plans, or something may happen to prevent his attendance.

Of course, the word "know" may be used to express what is nothing more than a hunch, or a hope, or a pigheaded opinion. The gambler who "knows" the next number on the roulette wheel is merely guessing or acting on a "hunch." Politicians who during election campaigns "know" who will win, and who "know" what will happen to the country if they are wrong, are only expressing their hopes and fears. Similarly, the person who "knows" that Italy has a better soccer team than Brazil when Italy has lost all its games, and Brazil has won all, is simply expressing a fanatical loyalty that transcends, and is indifferent to, mere facts.

The problem of knowledge: a closer look
The Philosophical Sense

But the popular usages of "know" are hardly what philosophers have been debating. "Knowledge" of that order could not survive Descartes's test. Philosophers have been concerned to find out if we can really "know" anything in the sense of possessing information that is not open to question. "Knowledge," in this usage, is sharply distinguished from opinion. Many skeptics have claimed that people's "knowledge" only expresses opinions that may or may not be true. Against this, some philosophers have insisted that there is obtainable information that is not mere opinion but that is beyond question true. **It is the quest for this type of certain knowledge that has given rise to the problem of knowledge.**

To illustrate this usage, an anecdote may be helpful (a story that our informant insists is true). A philosopher and a friend were driving in a car. At an intersection the car was struck by another one, which had apparently driven through a red light, since the light facing the car with the philosopher and friend was green at the time of the accident. The friend owned the car and sued the person who had struck him. The latter, at the trial, insisted that the light was green for him and red for his accuser. In fact, he insisted that he *knew* he was right. (This was probably the use of "know" in the sense of "hope," or "believe.") To corroborate his friend's story, the only other witness, the philosopher, was put on the stand. The lawyer for the plaintiff asked the philosopher about the color of the light, and the witness answered that it seemed to be green. The lawyer asked him to be more precise—did he *know* the color of the light? The philosopher said that he did not *know*, but it *looked* green, and he thought it was *probably* green. The more

the lawyer pressed the philosopher-witness for a positive answer, the more the latter insisted that he did not *know*, he merely had an *opinion* that might be wrong. The jury and judge, faced with the absolute assurance of the defendant and with the uncertainty of the philosopher, could only decide against the philosopher's friend. The rub was that the philosopher insisted on using "know" in the strict sense in which one who knows is *absolutely certain*—by Descartes's standard. In fact, our law courts usually avoid the philosopher's difficulties by seeking to establish the defendant's guilt "beyond reasonable doubt," without seeking *absolute* assurance that a person *must* be guilty and cannot *possibly* be innocent.

The philosophers who have sought to discover what sort of knowledge, in this strict sense, we possess—and what sort of evidence we can adduce, and what standards we judge it by—have offered various theories about the nature, source, and basis of our knowledge. We shall now consider some of these theories. The first group makes positive claims to the effect that human beings can discover **absolutely certain knowledge, knowledge that under no circumstances can be false, and that this knowledge can be acquired through the use of our rational faculties.**

Ancient Greek philosophy

The Sophists

One of the oldest positive theories of knowledge was developed in the early days of Greek philosophy. In the fifth century B.C., a group of wise men appeared in

Athens called the **Sophists.** They were **extremely doubtful about the possibility of discovering anything that was really true.** Instead, they taught their followers how to "get along" in the world *without* certain knowledge. They taught their followers how to win disputes; how to speak well and convincingly; and generally, how to succeed. Their underlying theory developed from two remarks of two of the leading Sophists. Protagoras, perhaps the greatest of the Sophists, said, **"Man is the measure of all things."** And Gorgias, another great Sophist, proclaimed, **"Nothing exists, and if it did, no one could know it, and if they knew it, they could not communicate it."** From these statements the Sophists developed the view that knowledge in the strict sense is unattainable and, therefore, that man should not bother to seek what he can never find. Instead, the Sophists insisted on following Protagoras's dictum that everyone should "measure" matters according to his nature and needs, since man alone is the measure of all things.

SOCRATES AND PROTAGORAS

Thus the Sophists proposed that man should accept the fact that all his alleged knowledge is only relative to man's outlook. Since no one, according to Gorgias's statement, can know any truth, or report it if he did know it, the Sophists solution was to train for success. In one of Plato's dialogues, entitled *Protagoras*, Plato describes a meeting between Socrates and Protagoras, the great Sophist. A friend named Hippocrates tells Socrates that Protagoras is in Athens and that they must rush to see him. When Socrates asks

why, Hippocrates answers that he must become a student of the great Sophist and acquire his wisdom. Socrates asks his friend what he expects to learn. Hippocrates is unable to answer clearly, and they go to see Protagoras to find out what he can accomplish. Socrates tells Protagoras that his friend Hippocrates is a well-to-do Athenian who desires to achieve political eminence, and "who is desirous of making your acquaintance; he would like to know what will happen to him if he associates with you." Protagoras answers, "Young man, if you associate with me, on the very first day you will return home a better man than you came, and better on the second day than on the first, and better every day than you were on the day before."

Socrates is baffled and inquires, "When you say that on the first day on which he associates with you he will return home a better man, and on every day will grow in like manner—in what, Protagoras, will he be better? and about what?" The great Protagoras answers, "You ask questions fairly, and I like to answer a question which is fairly put. If Hippocrates comes to me he will not experience the sort of drudgery with which other Sophists are in the habit of insulting their pupils; who, when they have just escaped from the arts, are taken and driven back into them by these teachers, and made to learn calculation, and astronomy, and geometry, and music . . . but if he comes to me, he will learn that which he comes to learn. And this is prudence in affairs private as well as public; he will learn to order his own house in the best manner, and he will be able to speak and act for the best in the affairs of state."

CRITICISM OF SOPHISM

Socrates worried about such "schools for success" (which resembled many present-day educational institutions). What troubled him was that people like Protagoras professed they did not possess genuine knowledge and yet presumed to instruct people in worldly success. The students and the teachers might, after all, be doing the wrong thing, since they did not have any positive knowledge. Learning "how to get away with it," Socrates thought, was not wise, unless one was sure that it was *right* to get way with it. Being able to speak well, to convince people, to be a leader, was not enough, unless one also knew what to speak *about,* what to convince people *of,* and *where* to lead them. Otherwise, Socrates argued, the results of such skills might be disastrous.

What was dangerous about the Sophists, Socrates thought, was that neither they nor their students had any knowledge; hence the blind were leading the blind. But with the skills for success the Sophists had mastered, they became public menaces, unless they knew what was *right.* This they could be sure of only if they had genuine knowledge, which could not possibly be false. If the Sophists prevailed upon people to accept their views, they might well follow them down a road to utter ruin, if the opinions were wrong.

Plato

Socrates was convinced that one could act only on the basis of the truth. In various dialogues, Plato, in his presentation of the conversations of Socrates, tried to construct a theory of knowledge—what

knowledge was available, how we could obtain it, and why it was true.

Plato's view, put briefly, was that knowledge consists in the apprehension of those aspects of the world that never change, never alter. Plato believed that the world contained such constituent elements, which he called "ideas," or "forms." What, then, are "forms," and why does knowledge consist in the apprehension of them rather than of changing things?

The problem may appear clearer if we consider a series of statements: (*a*) "Rover is a dog," (*b*) "Fido is a dog," and (*c*) "Spot is a dog." If Fido and Rover and Spot are all different animals, what are we saying about them? We are saying that they have something in common, and that each animal falls into a common classification (e.g., being a dog). But what does the general term "dog" refer to? If we were asked what "Rover" referred to, we could simply point to that dog. But what would we point to in order to show what "dog" referred to? If we pointed to Rover, and then to Fido, and then to Spot, would that make clear what the general term "dog" referred to? We might be indicating that they all had tails, or spots, or all said "Woof."

Plato suggested that our ordinary statements include the use of general terms, and that in order for our ordinary statements to be meaningful, one must know what these general terms signify. To do this, Plato insisted, one must do more than merely point to various particular things. Those things would only be, at best, *examples* of things that fall into general classifications, but would not themselves be the classifications.

The *Euthyphro*

In one of Plato's dialogues—the *Euthyphro*—Plato made this point forcefully. The dialogue is a discussion between Socrates, on his way to the courthouse, and a priest of Athens, Euthyphro. The latter tells Socrates that he is going to court to have his father tried for murder. When Socrates asks for details, we see that it is extremely doubtful whether Euthyphro's father is actually guilty; but Euthyphro insists that he should accuse his father because that is the holy thing to do in this case. Socrates asks him, what is holiness? Euthyphro responds, it is doing what I am doing. Socrates responds that Euthyphro's act may be an *illustration* of holiness; but to determine if the act is holy, one must know the meaning of the general term "holiness." When Euthyphro attempts to make clear what "holiness" means, Socrates shows him that his definition is inadequate. Finally, Euthyphro gives up, because he says, each time he puts his words down, they get up and walk away.

Universals

To prevent the words from marching off, Plato claimed, we must discover the meanings of our general terms. If we employ these terms to classify items in our experience (e.g., to point out that we call this a "dog" and that a "cat") by virtue of the fact that they fall into certain classifications, then these remarks can only be meaningful if we know the meaning of the general terms, also called **"universals."** The general terms seem to refer to something different from the items of our experience, since they are the means for saying things about items in our experience. We call Rover a "dog" by virtue of certain characteristics. Plato's thesis is that only if we know what is required for something to be a dog, can we tell that Rover falls into this classification.

How can one discover what these general terms, or universals, mean, so that one can tell if a certain item falls into some classification? Plato argued that, first of all, we could *not* know these universals (or, as they are sometimes called, **"forms," or "Platonic ideas"**) through our ordinary sense experience. All that we discover by these means are *particular instances*, which keep changing all the time. Rover grows, sheds his hair, moves around, and so on. In these circumstances we cannot know the general nature or characteristics by virtue of which Rover is a dog. Our sense experience does not reveal universals, or forms, but only particular examples. Therefore, if we are to know Platonic ideas, it must be by some other means.

Socrates' theory of universal forms

In a dialogue entitled *Meno*, Plato portrayed Socrates as claiming that **we cannot acquire knowledge through learning.** He argued that in order to learn something, we must discover a truth that we did not previously know. But in that case, we could not recognize it. Thus, if one were taught something that one did not already know—such as the truth in Euclidean geometry that the area of a rectangle is equal to the height multiplied by the length of the figure—Socrates claimed that one could not tell that this proposition was true when one learned it unless one already knew it to be true. In brief, the Platonic thesis is that **one cannot learn what one does know since one already knows it.** And one cannot learn what one does not know, since if one doesn't know it, one cannot recognize it as a truth when one learns it. Therefore, learning is impossible, and any knowledge that we can have we must already have.

Recollection

Socrates concluded that we do not *learn* anything—we remember what we already know; **all the knowledge of forms, or universals, is already in our minds.** Our sense experience can, at best, only have the incidental effect of jarring our memory, and bringing to our conscious attention information that is within us, but of which we have not yet become aware.

THE *MENO*

To demonstrate this theory of knowledge by recollection, Socrates, in the *Meno*, talks to a slave boy, who reveals that he has never been taught any mathematics. He is then asked to solve the following problem: If there is a square whose sides are each one inch long, how long are the sides of a square whose area is double that of the original square? The slave boy answers twice as long, that is, two inches long. Socrates shows him that that is incorrect by getting him to figure out the area of this new square (the height times the length), or two inches times two inches. Hence, the new square is four times the area of the original one. Without ever indicating the answer, but only by criticizing whatever the slave boy says, Socrates finally leads him to discover the right answer—a square built upon the diagonal of the original square. The fact that the slave boy, who had never studied or been taught mathematics, could recognize the right answer and be completely sure of it, and could find the right answer without being told, is offered as evidence that he must already, in some sense, have known the answer.

The Source of Knowledge

If we gain our knowledge through recollection, as this theory holds, where does our knowledge of universals, or forms, or Platonic ideas, come from? According to the argument, it cannot come from experience or from education, since it is already within us. But when and how did it come within us? According to Plato, since we have never acquired the forms in our lifetime, they must have already been with us when we were born. To account for the fact that infants do not seem to know very much, we are told that the soul (which Plato believed must have existed prior to one's birth, in order to contain the Platonic ideas) forgets its knowledge of forms at birth and must somehow regain consciousness of the knowledge that is already there.

The philosopher-king

With this much of Plato's theory of knowledge before us, we may ask again, how can we gain knowledge of universals, or forms? How can one jar one's memory to recall the Platonic ideas and thus come to possess real knowledge? An answer to this question is presented in Plato's great dialogue, the *Republic*. As we saw in Chapter 2 (pages 60–63), in the course of outlining the nature of the ideal state, Socrates is asked how this new and better world might be achieved. He answers: "Until philosophers are kings, or the kings and princes of this world have the spirit and power of philosophy, and political greatness and wisdom meet in one . . . then only will this our state have a possibility of life and behold the light of day." To show how one might become a philosopher, Socrates discusses the problem of how the intended rulers of his society may come to possess true knowledge and to employ it in guiding the republic.

Kinds of Knowledge

There are, according to Socrates' account, two main types of information that we can possess—**visible or sensible (i.e., acquired through the senses) and intelligible.** The **visible or sensible information** is divided into images or shadows, and opinions. The lower level of our visible information is a vague, blurred conglomeration of patterns; the higher level is the clear patterns—with identifiable objects and coherently organized images. But none of this constitutes knowledge, because none of it is indubitable—it is not understood in terms of the forms, or universals. Hence all that we can report is how it *seems* to us, what it *appears* to be.

The **intelligible information,** on the other hand, deals with Platonic ideas, and it is here that knowledge is possible. The lowest level is the use of Platonic ideas as hypotheses without understanding their nature. If squares have certain properties, then we can draw certain conclusions about geometrical relationships. One assumes, but still does not know, the nature of these universals. The highest level, complete knowledge, occurs when one knows the Platonic idea, in the sense of being fully aware of it in one's mind, and understanding its nature.

THE ALLEGORY OF THE CAVE

This division, and the road to complete knowledge, are further explained by Socrates by means of a tale that is sometimes called **"the allegory of the cave."** It begins:

And now, I said, let me show in a figure how far our nature is enlightened or unenlightened: Behold! human beings living in an underground den, which has a mouth open toward the light and reaching all along the den; here they have been from their childhood, and have their legs and necks chained so that they cannot move, and can only see before them, being prevented by the chains from turning round their heads. Above and behind them a fire is blazing at a distance, and between the fire and the prisoners there is a raised way; and you will see, if you look, a low wall built along the way, like the screen which marionette players have in front of them, over which they show the puppets.

I see.

And do you see, I said, men passing along the wall carrying all sorts of vessels, and statues and figures of animals made of wood and stone and various materials, which appear over the wall? Some of them are talking, others silent.

You have shown me a strange image, and they are strange prisoners.

Like ourselves, I replied, and they see only their own shadows, or the shadows of one another, which the fire throws on the opposite wall of the cave.

True, he said, how could they see anything but the shadows if they were never allowed to move their heads?

And of the objects which are being carried in like manner they would only see the shadows?

In such a world, Socrates claimed, "the truth would be literally nothing but the shadows of the images." But what would happen if the prisoners were suddenly released and no longer took the shadows for the real objects?

At first, when any of them is liberated and compelled suddenly to stand up and turn his neck round and walk and look toward the light, he will suffer sharp pains; the glare will distress him, and he will be unable to see the realities of which in his former state he had seen the shadows; and then conceive someone saying to him, that what he saw before was an illusion, but that now, when he is approaching nearer to being and his eye is turned toward more real existence, he has clearer vision—what will be his reply?

Obviously, he will be confused when, emerging from the cave of the visible world, he first sees the forms.

And if he is compelled to look straight at the light, will he not have a pain in his eyes which will make him turn away to take refuge in the objects of vision which he can see, and which he will conceive to be in reality clearer than the things which are now being shown to him?

True, he said.

And suppose once more, that he is reluctantly dragged up a steep and rugged ascent, and held fast until he is forced into the presence of the sun himself, is he not likely to be pained and irritated? When he approaches the light his eyes will be dazzled and he will not be able to see anything of all of what are now called realities.

This state of being blinded by real knowledge will not last long. Socrates claimed:

He will require to grow accustomed to the sight of the upper world. At first he will see the shadows best, next the reflections of men and other objects in the water, and then the objects themselves; then he will gaze upon the light of the moon and the stars and the spangled heaven; and he will see the sky and the stars by night better than the sun or the light of the sun by day.

Certainly.

Last of all he will be able to see the sun, and not merely reflections of him in the water, but he will see him in his own proper place, and not in another; and he will contemplate him as he is.

Plato stated the essence of the allegory by having Socrates interpret it in terms of his theory of knowledge:

The entire allegory, I said, you may append, dear Glaucon, to the previous argument; the prison house is the world of sight, the light of the fire is the sun, and you will not misapprehend me if you interpret the journey upward to be the ascent of the soul into the intellectual world according to my poor belief, which, at your desire I have expressed—whether rightly or wrongly God knows.

Making of a Philosopher-King

It is necessary to escape the jail of the cave (i.e., the world of visible information) and turn upward to the world of intelligible knowledge, to find the forms, or universals, that are within us, and to grow accustomed to contemplating them, so that we may at last achieve real knowledge.

To achieve this goal, Socrates outlined a scheme of training for would-be philosopher-kings, so that they would arrive at the knowledge of Platonic ideas. What must be done is to bring about "the turning round of a soul passing from a day which is little better than night to the true day of being." Those who genuinely desire knowledge must be trained to discover the forms or universals in their minds. But if, as had been previously claimed by Socrates, learning is not really possible, then the "education" of the future philosopher-kings must be a peculiar process, one that does not actually *teach* them. Instead, what will be done is to train them to *recollect* the knowledge that is, and always has been, within them.

THE USE OF REASON

The first step is to lead them to realize the inadequacy of sense information, as well as to notice the recurrence of certain oddities in the visible world. By observing the changing quality of the same object in the world of shadows, one begins to wonder. The fourth finger, for example, is large when compared with the little one, but small compared with the middle finger. Is the fourth finger large, or is it small? When one ponders such a problem, Socrates claimed, "these intimations which the soul receives through the senses are very curious and require to be explained." The eye sees the object as large and also as small. To explain this, according to Socrates, the mind seeks to understand what "largeness" and "smallness" mean. Thus the mind has begun the search for universals, or Platonic ideas.

ARITHMETIC

Having started the future philosopher-king on his journey toward understanding and knowledge through the use of reason rather than the senses, Socrates proposed a second, more lengthy and difficult step. This stage consists of training the mind to deal with abstractions, to reason about universals, or forms. To do this, the student is to be trained first of all in **arithmetic.** Here, instead of looking at shadows, he must look inward at his ideas and learn to deal only with thoughts and meanings rather than with visible objects. Socrates held that "arithmetic has a very great and elevating effect, compelling the soul to reason about abstract numbers, and rebelling against the introduction of visible or tangible objects into the argument." In learning to do sums "in his head," instead of counting his fingers and his toes, the student will be liberated from the cave and will catch a glimmering of the forms within him.

GEOMETRY

After one has become skilled in arithmetic. Socrates proposed to teach the would-be philosopher-king **geometry,** since "the knowledge at which geometry aims is knowledge of the eternal, and not of anything perishing and transient." Geometry will lead one to discover necessary truths about universals, such as lines, squares, triangles, and circles. When one discovers such truths not from looking at pictures or diagrams but solely from ideas, then one will have acquired knowledge that can be demonstrated and that is unchangeable. The pictures or diagrams may change, but the geometrical truths, depending only on the ideas, or the meaning of the terms, will not change.

SOLID GEOMETRY AND ASTRONOMY

From geometry the course of study proceeds to **solid geometry**. It is clear from what Plato says about this that very little research had been done in this field in his own day. However, he is convinced of the need to advance research in this area and to encourage his philosopher-kings to come nearer to the abstract forms by proceeding from a study of two-dimensional figures to a study of those of three dimensions. This is a necessary preliminary to a study of **astronomy,** a study of the movements of solid bodies. The heavenly bodies may be the most perfect of **visible** things, but because they *are* visible, they are greatly inferior to the true realities, the true objects of knowledge. But a study of their movements must be undertaken by the intellect rather than by the senses, so that such a study will again lead our philosopher-king toward the unchanging, eternal truths.

HARMONICS

The last stage of this course of studies is the study of **harmonics.** Just as the study of astronomy will help the philosopher-king to come nearer to abstract thought by starting from those things that are visible, so will a study of harmonics, by starting from those things that are audible. Again, the emphasis is not on a study of sounds themselves but on the relationships between them.

THE DIALECTIC

The would-be philosopher-king is finally ready for the last and most important step—complete liberation from the shad-

ows of the cave through the study of **dialectic.** Through this study one is not merely aware of, or familiar with, the forms or universals—now one **knows and understands** them. Now one is able to recall completely the true, indubitable knowledge within oneself.

In what does the study of dialectic consist? Socrates pointed out that one could only answer this question accurately if one has already reached complete understanding. Negatively, the difference between the study of mathematics and that of dialectic can be briefly indicated; and positively, its general characteristics can be stated. But the actual content of dialectic is what each person would know when he finally obtained real knowledge, "when a person starts on the discovery of the absolute [i.e., forms, or Platonic ideas] by the light of reason only, and without any assistance of sense, and perseveres until by pure intelligence he arrives at the perception of the absoute good." Then "he at last finds himself at the end of the intellectual world."

Mathematics and Dialectic

The difference between dialectic and the various branches of mathematics is that the latter are based upon assumptions and hypotheses that the mathematician takes for granted without examining them to find out why they are true. The forms, or universals, are employed, but the mathematician assumes their characteristics without being able to explain what their nature is or why they have it. Thus, for example, in arithmetic, it is assumed that when equal quantities are added to equal quantities, the results are equal (e.g., if A = B, and C = D, then A + C = B + D). When Socrates asked the mathematicians what "equality" meant, and how they knew that assumptions like these were true, he discovered they did not know but had accepted a great many hypotheses from which they developed their subject matter. In the dialogue *Theaetetus*, in a discussion with one of the greatest of the Greek geometers, Socrates showed that the man did not understand the basic concepts and had never questioned or examined the basic assumptions of the subject. To this extent, then, mathematics is only what Socrates called "dreams about reality."

If, on the other hand, one examines one's hypotheses and assumptions and concepts until one has arrived at full and complete understanding of them, then one will be involved in the study of dialectic. **Mathematical studies prepare one for this understanding** by providing some facility in dealing with forms, or universals. But the last step, that of **understanding and grasping the nature of Platonic ideas, is the work of the dialectic.**

> Then dialectic, and dialectic alone, goes directly to the first principle, and is the only science which does away with hypotheses in order to make her ground secure; the eye of the soul, which is literally buried in an outlandish slough, is by her gentle aid lifted upward; and she uses as handmaids and helpers in the work of conversion, the sciences which we have been discussing (i.e., the various branches of mathematics).

The way to obtain complete and true knowledge, according to Plato, is, first, to give up any reliance upon sense information and turn instead to examining the intelligible world through the aid of one's reasoning power only. When one turns away from the sensory world, one begins to discover the forms, or universals, in one's own mind. To become used to examining the world of ideas, one first learns to manipulate and relate various ideas in the light of several assumptions and hypotheses—those of the different branches of mathematics. When one is finally able to examine and understand the forms, or universals, and grasp their nature, then one has arrived at real knowledge, full recollection of the Platonic ideas that are within oneself, and have always been there.

Appearance and Reality

To the question "What would one know upon acquiring this type of knowledge?" Plato replied that one would know the real world and not merely the "shadows" or "images." The Platonic ideas, for him, are not mere items in one's mind—they are real things, which exist eternally, without change, apart from the visible, physical world. **Just as sense information is considered illusory by Plato, so are the objects that we encounter in our sense experience.** The real, the important, the valuable objects of this world are those that we discover when we have real knowledge. Thus Plato conceived of the universe as divided between **appearance and reality,** and our information about it as divided between **opinion and knowledge.** We can only have opinions about the world of appearance, but our souls can have true knowledge about the real world, the world of Platonic ideas.

Plato claimed that we can possess knowledge in the strict sense, that is, knowledge of which we can be absolutely certain, but such knowledge is different from the sort of information in which we are usually interested. Knowledge in this strict sense can be obtained about universals, or Platonic ideas, but only through the arduous means of forcing one's "memory" through an extended study of mathematics. When one becomes aware of the Platonic ideas, the experience of knowing them makes one completely certain—that is, incapable of being wrong. But such knowledge, which seems to be guaranteed solely by the experience of having it, is nevertheless limited. What we know thereby is, according to Plato, **the real world, the world of forms (or universals). The visible world can never really be known.** The forms that it partakes of, and that are copied in the shadowy appearances always before us, can be known; but we cannot know, in this strong sense of "know," the world of shadows, since they are not the forms but merely reflections of them, often inaccurate ones. Our best knowledge—actually, our only complete and true knowledge—is that discovered through the study of dialectic—our knowledge of Platonic ideas. Mathematics, the next highest, is not yet complete knowledge, but it does deal with the forms. (Sciences like physics—Plato thought—could not involve true knowledge, since physics would be a study of the world of shadows, the changing world of appearance.)

Descartes's theory of knowledge

If we turn from Plato to a much later theory of knowledge, that of René Descartes, we find another **positive theory claiming that we are capable of discovering absolutely certain knowledge.** Descartes's views about the nature, source, and basis of our knowledge in many ways resemble those of Plato.

The Quest for Certainty

At the beginning of this discussion, we examined Descartes's test for the reliability of our knowledge and saw the devastating results he achieved in showing that *all* of our ordinary information—including scientific and even mathematical information—is open to challenge. Descartes's point in proposing such a catastrophic test was not just to introduce doubts about everything: "I did not imitate the skeptics, who doubt only for the sake of doubting, and pretend that they are always uncertain. On the contrary, my purpose was only to obtain good ground for assurance for myself, and to reject the quicksand and mud so that I might find the rock or clay." Descartes was seeking an absolutely certain basis for all knowledge. He felt that such a foundation could be secure only if one had first used his test in order to eliminate anything that might possibly be false or doubtful. Descartes writes:

> I shall go on setting aside everything which might, in the slightest degree, be supposed to be doubtful, just as if I had found out that it was completely false; and I shall continue to follow in this path until I find something which is certain, or at least, if I am unable to do anything else, until I have learned that it is certain that there is nothing in the world that is certain.

THE CERTAINTY OF EXISTENCE

In this manner, Descartes carried on his test in search of some information that would be indubitable and certain. If he could find such knowledge, he could use it as a starting point for justifying the entire structure of human knowledge. After having cast doubt on our sense information, our scientific information, and on mathematics, Descartes continued his quest until he found exactly the kind of certainty for which he sought.

> I was convinced that there was nothing in the entire world, that there was no heaven, no earth, that there were no minds, nor any bodies. Was I not then also convinced that I did not exist? Not in the least. It was certain that I myself existed since I convinced myself of something (or just because I thought of something). But there is some kind of a deceiver, who is very powerful and very cunning, and who always uses his ingenuity in order to deceive me. Then, for certain, I exist also if he is deceiving me, and let him deceive me as much as he wishes, he can never make me be nothing as long as I think that I am something. So that, after having considered this well, and having carefully examined everything, we have to arrive at the definite conclusion that this proposition: "I am, I exist" has to be true every time that I utter it, or that I mentally think about it.

"I think, therefore I am." The only piece of information that Descartes found **had to be true** was **I exist."** Whenever I think about it or try to conceive, according to Descartes's test, how it could possibly be false, I realize that in order to think about it, or in order to perform the test, **I must be.** No matter what the alleged "deceiver" may do, no matter how hard he may try to deceive me, he cannot deceive me into thinking that I am, if in fact I actually do not exist. If I think, Descartes insists, then I can be absolutely positive that I exist. As soon as I try to conceive of any condition under which **"I think, therefore I am"** (or in its famous Latin form, *Cogito, ergo sum*) may possibly be false, I am completely assured that I exist. Any attempt to doubt or deny this is still another thought that confirms and assures me that I must exist in order to think. No matter how hard I try to disprove the statement "I think, therefore I am," as soon as I *think*, the truth of the statement has been demonstrated again.

Perhaps one way of underlining Descartes's point is to consider the following story. A famous American philosopher, Morris Raphael Cohen, was reported to have engaged in a discussion with a student after class. Professor Cohen had been teaching Descartes to his class and had developed all the reasons for doubting that have been outlined earlier in this discussion. Then he sent the students home to read Descartes's *Meditations*. The next day, according to the story, a very haggard student, unshaven, eyes bloodshot, came to Professor Cohen after class and said that he was very worried. He had been up all night studying and thinking about the assignment, trying to decide whether he really existed. "Professor Cohen," he said very anxiously, "tell me, please tell me, do I exist?" Professor Cohen considered the question and then answered, "And who wants to know?"

In any case, Descartes was convinced that he had finally discovered a truth that "was so certain and so assured that all the most extravagant arguments brought forward by the skeptics were incapable of shaking it." He hoped that by examining this one absolutely certain truth, it might be possible to discover a rule or criterion by which to judge the truth of other statements.

> I am certain that I am a thing that thinks; but then do I not also know what is required to make me certain of a truth? Certainly in this fundamental knowledge, there is nothing that convinces me of its truth, except the clear and distinct perception of that which I assert, which would not, indeed, be sufficient to assure me that what I say is true, if it could ever happen that something which I conceived so clearly and distinctly could be false. And, therefore, it seems to me that I already am able to establish as a general rule that all things which I conceive very clearly and distinctly are true.

Descartes's contention is that by inspecting the one truth ("I think, therefore I am"), we can discover a rule or criterion about *all* truths. Why am I so certain that "I think, therefore I am" is true? According to Descartes, the only feature of this statement that convinces me that it is true is that I clearly and distinctly see, or understand, what is being said. If this **clarity and distinctness** are the only conditions that produce my conviction, and they are not *general* conditions that all truths must have, then I might be mistaken in this case. If clarity and distinctness are not the standards or criteria of truth, and they are all that indicates that "I think, therefore I am" is true, then that assertion may actually be false. Therefore, the argument concludes, **clarity and distinctness must be the marks of truth, the distinguishing characteristics by which you can tell the true from the false.** Hence the general rule can be formulated, "Whatever is clearly and distinctly conceived is true."

CLARITY AND DISTINCTNESS

But what are these characteristics of clarity and distinctness? In a somewhat baffling section of his *Principles of Philosophy*, Descartes gave as clear and distinct an explanation of what clarity and distinctness are as one can find in his works. The section reads as follows:

> What a clear and distinct perception is. There are even some people who, in their entire life, perceive nothing so accurately as to be able to judge of it properly. For the knowledge on which a certain and uncontestable judgment can be formed, ought not only to be clear, but distinct as well. I call that clear which is present and apparent to an attentive mind, just as we say that we see objects clearly when, being present to the perceiving eye, they operate on it with sufficient strength. But the distinct is that which is so precise and different from everything else that it contains nothing within itself but what is clear.

At first glance, this explanation may not seem to help very much; but by careful consideration, it may aid us in grasping Descartes's point. Apparently, an experience or a thought is clear if it is **so forceful that we cannot avoid being aware of it.** The illustrations Descartes offered of a clear idea fall roughly into two types — one of **vivid sense experiences,** such as toothache, and the other of **thoughts,** such as mathematical ideas or mental activities like thinking, wishing, and so on. In both types, the mind is made aware of something **either mental or sensory.** But, as we are told soon afterward, while an idea can be clear without being distinct, the reverse cannot occur. An idea that is clear but not distinct is an experience that is so vivid or forceful that we cannot avoid being aware of it; but at the same time, we are not certain of *what* we are experiencing. The example that Descartes employed in this connection was that of the toothache. The experience is clear. One is forced to be aware of it. Nevertheless, one is not certain of *what* the ache is or *where* it is. One cannot tell whether the pain is in the tooth or in the mind. (In terms of Descartes's theory of the relation of mind and body, which was examined in Chapter 3 [see pages 105–7], he was convinced that the pain could not be in the physical tooth but only in the mind.) What is lacking here is an ability to distinguish what the experience is from anything else in the world. If one could accomplish this, that is, **so define the experience that it could not possibly be confused with anything else, then it would be distinct as well as clear.** On the other hand, any idea that we could so define would of necessity also be clear, since in order to be able to distinguish it from anything else, we would have to be intensely aware of the idea.

EXTENSIONS OF CERTAINTY

Pursuing further the notion of clear and distinct ideas, Descartes asked what else is true besides the truth that I am a thinking being. In the course of this investigation, he developed a theory about the universe we can know with complete certainty, a theory that in the end would provide further justification for his criterion of true knowledge. In order to complete this discussion of his theory of knowledge, we shall briefly state the remaining argument of his *Meditations*.

INNATE IDEAS

When I examine my ideas in order to find which of them are clear and distinct, Descartes claimed, I discover that most of them are either unclear or indistinct, and that either they come from experiences I have had, or they have been invented by myself. These include ideas such as those of the sun, of mermaids, of the Cathedral of Notre Dame in Paris, and of goblins. In addition to such ideas, Descartes insisted that there is another type called **"innate ideas,"** which can neither come from experience nor be constructed or invented in my imagination. As we shall see shortly, these innate ideas are the ones that are really clear and distinct.

God

The kind of ideas that Descartes believed must be innate are those of **mathematical objects,** like the idea of a circle, and also, and most important for his argument, **the idea of a perfect being, God.** These ideas have properties that do not appear in our experience. No circle that we see is perfectly round. But the one that we can think about is. We ourselves are not perfect enough, Descartes claimed, to invent the sort of perfection that appears in some of our ideas, especially that of God. We are merely finite, temporal creatures, and yet we have an idea of an infinite and eternal God. How then, Descartes asked, can we create concepts of properties that we discover neither in our experience nor in ourselves? From such reasoning, he concluded that mathematical ideas and the idea of God must be of a special category, called "innate," which must be implanted in us by some agency other than ourselves and other than the events of our lives.

Developing the concept of a perfect being, Descartes concluded that this idea can only be caused by something that had at least the same perfections as the idea itself exhibited. The idea is that of "a substance that is infinite, eternal, immutable, independent, all-knowing, all-powerful, and by which I myself and everything else, if anything else does exist, have been created." I do not have properties like these to make use of in inventing an idea, and in my experience I never see anything with such perfection. Therefore, the idea of a perfect being must come from something that is at least as perfect as the idea. Hence, Descartes reasoned, there must be a God who has created me and who has implanted in me the idea of a perfect being.

FURTHER CERTAINTIES

Having now established two truths, "I think, therefore I am" and "God exists," Descartes searched for still further certainties. "It seems to me that I have now found a road that will lead us from contemplating the true God (in whom all the wonders of science and wisdom are contained), to knowledge of the other objects of the world." The first stage along this road is to realize that if God is a perfect being, then He is incapable of deceiving human beings. Fraud and deception, Descartes insisted, are imperfections and hence cannot be characteristics of a perfect being.

This discovery—on the basis of the clear and distinct idea of God—that the perfect being cannot be a deceiver guarantees to Descartes that God is not, and cannot be, the evil demon he had envisaged earlier.

If God is not that, then a great deal of the information that had earlier been considered suspect can now be considered reliable. All that is needed is to find out what God, the nondeceiver, wants and makes us to believe is true. Since God cannot deceive us, we can place complete faith in the knowledge He gives us.

From an analysis of our rational faculties, Descartes found that the only **judgments we are forced to make** are those regarding clear and distinct ideas. We are compelled to assent to any clear and distinct ideas and to believe that whatever is clear and distinct is true. Since the all-powerful God forces this upon us, we cannot be mistaken when we believe that something that we clearly and distinctly conceive is true, because God cannot be a deceiver. On the other hand, we can withhold our judgment with regard to matters that are unclear and indistinct. God does not force us to come to any conclusions in this area; if we do, it is *our* responsibility, not His. Therefore, with respect to such ideas, we have no guarantee that what we believe is true. **The faculty of judgment functions reliably in relation to the clear and distinct innate ideas that God has implanted in us.** But since we are imperfect creatures, we insist on using our faculties beyond this range, and judge matters about which we have no assurance. Therefore, we make mistakes when we misuse our faculties. But we cannot make mistakes when we use them as God intends and forces us to do.

Some examples may help here. According to Descartes, God has given us clear and distinct mathematical ideas. When we examine our ideas of "2" and "3" and "5," we find that it is clear and distinct that 2 + 3 = 5. Since God has given us the idea and the judging faculty, and has forced this belief upon us, and since He cannot be a deceiver, then 2 + 3 = 5 must be true. But when we see a group of color patches that look like some people walking, it is not clear and distinct that these are people, that this may not be part of a dream—hence we are not forced to judge that what we see is "some people." If we judge in this case, it is at our own risk, since we have no divine guarantee.

> . . . I have found the source of falsity and error. And certainly there cannot be any other than that which I have explained, since as long as I restrain my will within the limits of my knowledge it makes no judgment on any matters except those which are clearly and distinctly conceived by the understanding, I can never be deceived. Every clear and distinct conception is certainly something, and therefore cannot come from nothing, but must necessarily come from God—God, I say, who is supremely perfect, and cannot be the cause of any error. Thus, we must conclude that such a conception or judgment is true.

The argument for objective reality

Of what, then, can we be certain? We can be certain of our own existence, of God's and of God's guarantee that whatever is clearly and distinctly conceived is true. On this basis, Descartes claimed, we can be positive that the entire realm of mathematical knowledge is true, since it deals only with clear and distinct innate ideas. This knowledge is true whether I am awake or asleep, since it is clear and distinct in either case, and God would not deceive me. But this mathematical knowledge only gives me truths about concepts in my mind. Is it possible that I can also be certain that there is a world outside me, and that certain things are true about it?

By an elaborate argument that we shall not examine, Descartes sought to establish the reliability of our natural belief that there is a world outside our minds, and that our experience consists of ideas that come from this world. The basic reason offered is that since the belief in an external world is a natural one, God would be deceiving us unless it were true. Since God cannot be a deceiver, there must be an external physical world. The properties that we can safely attribute to it are those that we find in our clear and distinct ideas of bodies—namely, that they are extended, that geometrical and arithmetical truths apply to them, and so on.

Although Descartes began with the most extreme doubts about knowledge and belief, he concluded with an extensive theory about the degree of certain knowledge we can possess, claiming that we can be absolutely certain of our own existence, of God's, of God's not deceiving us, and hence of all clear and distinct knowledge, including all mathematical knowledge, which can also be applied to physical objects as well as to mental ones. On the basis of clear and distinct innate ideas, we can possess a wealth of certain knowledge. However, regarding matters that are not clear and distinct, such as our sense experience, we can never have complete certainty. We can know the laws of physical bodies insofar as they are mathematical relationships, but we cannot know with any certainty the indistinct or unclear features of the world (e.g., its colors, sounds, smells), which may be, for all we can tell, illusions or dreams. The world of innate ideas, the clear and distinct ideas that God implanted in us, provides all the certainty we can have, but it is *absolute* certainty. The method of doubt, and testing of our information by questioning it, enables us to distinguish what is certain from what is not. When we are done, Descartes claimed, we have a vast amount of certain knowledge about our clear and distinct ideas, some of which can be applied to the eternal world, giving us the basis for certain knowledge of nature. If we avoid judgments based on unclear and indistinct ideas, we will never make any mistakes.

Rationalist theories of knowledge

Theories of knowledge like those of Plato and Descartes are called **"rationalistic"** because they assert that by employing certain procedures of **reason alone** we can discover knowledge in the strongest sense, knowledge that can under no circumstances possibly be false. Usually such rationalistic theories (and both of the theories presented here do so) maintain that we cannot find any absolutely certain knowledge in sense experience but have to seek for it only in the **realm of the mind.** Both Plato and Descartes claim that the true knowledge is already within us in the form of innate ideas, which we do not acquire but are born with. It is further maintained by rationalists that what we know as certain by various rationalistic procedures *is* the real world. The world that cannot be known with certainty is

generally judged to be an illusory or unreal or unimportant world.

Criticism of Rationalist Philosophy

The claims of the rationalists to have discovered such certain truths have met with objections. Opponents have challenged philosophers like Plato and Descartes, denying that we ever actually possess such certainty or that there are any "Platonic ideas," or "innate," "clear," and "distinct" ideas. (In fact, a seventeenth-century French skeptic wrote some large books offering hundreds of reasons why the statement "I think, therefore I am" may not be at all certain.)

SKEPTICAL CRITICISM

Skeptical opponents of the rationalists suggested that what philosophers like Plato and Descartes were offering as certain knowledge was really nothing more than their personal fantasies. The vast range of opinions that rationalistic philosophers presented as indubitable truths have made many people extremely suspicious. The alleged certain knowledge might well be mere beliefs taken much too seriously by those who held them. The world of "Platonic ideas" or of Descartes's "innate ideas" is neither visible nor tangible. The evidence for the existence of such worlds has not struck all philosophers with the force and conviction that it had for Plato and Descartes. Hence many thinkers of a skeptical turn of mind have rejected rationalist claims of complete certainty.

This opposition to the doctrine of certain knowledge is grounded in the development of human knowledge, and the revolutions in thought that have occurred throughout history. When we examine critically the matters that were regarded as assured truths in Plato's day and compare them with our modern knowledge, it is difficult to understand how the science of dialectic can lead to certain truths already existing in the mind. The advance of scientific knowledge and the changes in scientific theory over the centuries have made many thinkers reluctant to consider anything an absolutely certain and permanent truth.

Rationalists like Plato and Descartes might claim that the development of scientific theory does not really discredit their theories, since science deals only with the visible world, which can never, according to them, be known with absolute certainty. The certain knowledge of the rationalists deals with a different realm entirely—the real world of "pure ideas"—and this world never changes, nor does our knowledge of it change. When one has grasped a truth about this "real world," it is true for all time.

But the opponents argue that, first of all, there has been a conflict of opinion among the rationalists as to what is true about the real world. The history of philosophy from Plato to Descartes does not inspire confidence in the claims of any particular rationalist—almost every truth that has been asserted with complete assurance by one philosopher has been disputed by another who, with just as much assurance, has advanced contrary claims. Almost every truth concerning the real world that has been held by a rationalist to be self-evident has proved to be open to some question or doubt. When one examines the alleged "self-evident," "absolutely certain" truths of such rationalists as Aristotle, St. Augustine, Descartes, and others, one sees that these propositions are actually very much open to question.

Even in an area of human knowledge that various rationalists have used as a model—mathematics—there is some basis for disputing claims of absolute truth. The history of mathematics indicates that developments and changes have taken place in our mathematical knowledge, and that some theorems that were regarded as true have had to be modified or discarded. Even today mathematicians disagree as to which branches of the subject, and which theorems, are really certain. No doubt there has been less diversity of opinion here than in any other area of human inquiry, and hence mathematics has always served as the model for the complete assurance relationalist philosophers have sought. But the fact that disputes and revisions are possible tends to support the doubters, and in any case, as we saw in Chapter 1 (see page 6), not all knowledge is analogous to mathematical knowledge.

NON-EUCLIDEAN GEOMETRIES

In particular, an important modern development has made most theoreticians of mathematics doubtful of rationalist claims. In the early nineteenth century it was discovered that various alternative systems of geometry could be developed in which different theorems would be true. If one replaced the axiom of Euclidean geometry that stated that one, and only one, line could be drawn parallel to another line through a given point, with another axiom that stated either that *no* line could be drawn parallel to another line through a given point, or that an *unlimited* number of lines could be drawn parallel to a given line through a given point, then perfectly consistent systems of geometry could be constructed. But these alternative systems of geometry, the so-called **"non-Euclidean geometries,"** contain theorems that are not true in Euclidean geometry. If one asks which of these geometries contains the truths about the real world, there does not seem to be a satisfactory answer. Each of the geometries is as logical, as consistent as the others. The theorems in each seem as true as those in the others. To call one set of theorems absolutely true and the others not true appears to be completely arbitrary and indefensible. Thus the development of alternative systems of geometry has cast grave doubts on the claim that mathematics contains a unique set of absolutely certain truths about the real world.

CERTAINTY AND PROBABILITY

Besides the conflict of theories, and the developments in science and mathematics, one of the major reasons for doubting the claims that human beings can possess "certain" knowledge has been the question of **whether we ever need or use absolutely certain knowledge.** The information that we employ for ordinary purposes, the critics point out, is not indubitable. We manage to live our lives without truths that under no possible conditions could be false. With the aid of scientific information about the visible world that may someday prove false or inadequate, we resolve the questions that confront us. Plato and Descartes pointed out the dangers of basing our actions upon information that may not be completely reliable; nevertheless, the opponents claim, for all ordinary purposes, all that we seem to possess and employ is *probable* knowledge. If there really is "certain" knowledge, it does not appear to be required for the ordinary purpose of life, nor does it even seem to be sought by people in the quest for answers to their questions.

Empirical philosophy

Owing to doubts about the rationalist theory of knowledge, many philosophers have searched for a theory of knowledge that would be consistent with ordinary human behavior. Instead of seeking absolutely certain knowledge about an alleged real world, they have tried to discover where we do *in fact* get our information from and what degree of reliability it *actually* possesses. Rather than rejecting the data we acquire through our senses in favor of some completely certain knowledge about a nonvisible realm, **these philosophers have begun with our sense experience as the source and basis of what we know, and have tried to construct an account of knowledge in terms of sense experience.** This type of theory, which attempts to explain knowledge in terms of sense experience, is called **"empiricism."**

The Social Context of Empiricism

The empirical approach to the problem of knowledge has usually developed in countries where the dominant interests have been practical and worldly ones. Thus empiricism has been the prevailing theory of knowledge in England, and to some extent and in various forms in the United States, but has played a relatively minor role in the intellectual history of other countries. The modern theory of empiricism grew out of the philosophical struggles in seventeenth-century England, at a time when that country was rapidly developing, commercially and industrially. People were just beginning to realize the possibilities that lay in controlling and utilizing the physical world. The great English scientists such as Robert Boyle, Robert Hooke, and Isaac Newton were developing the basis of our modern scientific and technological world.

In such an atmosphere, many philosophers came to regard the age-old quest for absolute knowledge as fruitless; information offered by the leading British scientists seemed to be useful and important. Over and over again, one finds the scientists of the time proclaiming that their aim is not to discover the real, indubitable truths of the universe, but **only to develop probable hypotheses about the world around us.** With the tremendous advances that resulted from this new knowledge, some philosophers felt that one had to abandon the search of the rationalists and work out a theory of knowledge more in keeping with the **actual achievements of the scientists.**

So in seventeenth-century England one finds a few brave thinkers striking out along new lines to discover a theory of knowledge in keeping with the new knowledge discovered by the practicing scientists of the time. These philosophers in quest of a different point of view were,

by and large, not professional philosophers but men of affairs who were not concerned with the classical problems that baffled philosophers, or over which philosophers had disputed over the centuries. Starting with Sir Francis Bacon (1561–1626), who was Lord Chancellor under King James I, the leading lights of the "new philosophy" in England were, almost without exception, men removed from the ivory towers of the academic world, men who gained their fame in the world of practical affairs.

John Locke

Bacon was the first important proponent of the empirical approach in seventeenth-century England. Later in the century, John Locke (1632–1704), a medical doctor by profession, tried to work out **an explanation of our knowledge in terms of sense experience** in his *Essays Concerning Human Understanding*. In this work, Locke argued that **our knowledge comes to us through our senses and that we have no innate ideas.** Systematically, he attempted to show how various concepts or ideas come from or are built up from different kinds of experience, starting from the simple sense awareness of one quality, such as yellow, to the most elaborate compounds of qualities, such as a city.

By examining the nature and origin of our knowledge in these terms, Locke believed that he could greatly aid mankind in realizing what sorts of things they could actually know about and what sort of assurance they could have.

If, by this inquiry into the nature of the understanding, I can discover the powers thereof, how far they reach, to what things they are in any degree proportionate, and where they fail us; I suppose it may be of use to prevail with the busy mind of man to be more cautious in meddling with things exceeding its comprehension; to stop when it is at the utmost extent of its tether; and to sit down in a quiet ignorance of those things, which upon examination, are found to be beyond the reach of our capacities.

Denial of Innate Ideas

When we examine our information, Locke insisted, we discover first that **we possess no innate knowledge.** There are no principles or ideas that we have any reason to believe we have prior to, or independent of, our sense experience. The examples that previous rationalists had offered of truths that were implanted in the mind, Locke claimed, are not actually known by all human beings. Neither children nor idiots are aware of these alleged innate truths. To say that these truths are in their minds, even though they do not know them, is nonsense. "To say a notion is imprinted on the mind, and yet at the same time to say that the mind is in ignorance of it, and never yet took notice of it, is to make this impression nothing."

The White Paper

Instead, Locke maintained, if people will look at their own observations and experience, they will realize that originally their mind was just a "white paper, void of all characters, without any ideas." All the many things that anybody knows about or thinks about come from **experience.** All of our information is based upon our experiences, either through our senses or by reflecting on what goes on in our

minds. Thus, according to Locke, there are just two sources of our knowledge: **one is sensation, and the other is reflection.**

Let any one examine his own thoughts, and thoroughly search into his understanding; and then let him tell me, whether all the original ideas he has there are any other than of the objects of his senses, or of the operations of his mind, considered as objects of his reflection; and how great a mass of knowledge soever he imagines to be lodged there, he will, upon taking a strict view, see that he has not any idea in his mind, but what one of these two have imprinted, though perhaps with infinite variety compounded and enlarged by the understanding.

Simple Ideas

In order to justify his empirical claims, Locke patiently tried to show how all our information derives either from experiences of reflection or of sensation. The most basic elements of our knowledge are what Locke called **"simple ideas." These are ideas that are not compounded of any other elements.** As examples of such simple ideas, Locke offered the experience of the taste of sugar, the smell of a rose, the whiteness of a lily, or the coldness of a piece of ice. These simple ideas are presented to us only in sensation and reflection. The mind has the power, we are told, to store up, to repeat, and to combine these basic ideas, once it has experienced them.

Certainty

In the course of his lengthy *Essay Concerning Human Understanding*, Locke tried valiantly to show how the various parts of our knowledge come from different experiences of sensation or reflection. A basic difficulty that he ran into, which has plagued empirical philosophers ever since, was that of showing which of our ideas are real, that is, which parts of our information "have a conformity with the real being and existence of things." We have a great many ideas in our minds that we do not believe relate to anything that actually exists in the world, such as our ideas of mermaids, unicorns, and the like. How do we tell just from the examination of our ideas which ones ought to be considered as real and which ones are only the result of our imagination, or of the mind's ability to combine various experiences it has had in the past? The answer Locke gives to this question enables him to work out a theory about the character and reliability of knowledge.

Primary and Secondary Qualities

Locke divided the sensations that we have into two groups—**the ideas of primary qualities and the ideas of secondary qualities.** The primary qualities are those items in our experience that must belong to the objects that we are experiencing, whereas the secondary qualities "in truth are nothing in the objects themselves, but powers to produce various sensations in us by their primary qualities." For example, according to Locke's account, size and shape are primary qualities, while the color that we see in objects is not. The color is the result of certain conditions—or, as he called them, "powers"—in the objects that act upon our minds so that we see colors when the actual objects that we are experiencing do not, in fact, have any color in them. The distinction that Locke was trying to draw is that between the **scientific description** of an object—

what properties scientists report an object has—and our **ordinary experience** of the same object.

> The particular bulk, number, figure, and motion of the parts of fire, or snow, are really in them, whether any one's senses perceive them or no; and therefore they may be called real qualities, because they really exist in those bodies; but light, heat, whiteness, or coldness, are no more really in them than sickness or pain is in manna. Take away the sensation of them; let not the eyes see light or colors, nor the ears hear sounds; let the palate not taste, nor the nose smell; and all colors, tastes, odors, and sounds, as they are such particular ideas, vanish and cease, and are reduced to their causes, i.e., bulk, figure, and motion of parts.

If, then, there are certain qualities, called "primary" ones, which we experience and which belong to objects, how do we get our ideas of objects? Locke claimed that when we observe that several **simple ideas constantly appear together and always seem to be conjoined, we presume that these ideas belong to one thing.** We are unable to conceive of these simple ideas existing without belonging to, or being attached to, some one thing. Thus, we suppose that there must be a substance, or a substratum, something that either holds all the qualities together or gives rise to them. When we experience the qualities together that we ordinarily call "gold" (the color, the hardness, and other qualities), Locke claimed that we also suppose that there is a "substance," or a "substratum," to which these qualities belong or from which they come, something that underlies all these qualities and holds them together. We can give no clear or precise notion of what these substances are except in terms of the qualities that belong to them. If one is pressed to give an exact description of a substance, all one can say, Locke pointed out, is that one does not know what it is, but one still finds that one must suppose that there is something that the various elements of our experience belong to. To make clear what the type of difficulty is that occurs when one tries to describe a substance, Locke compared it to the case of "the Indian before mentioned, who, saying that the world was supported by a great elephant, was asked what the elephant rested on? to which his answer was, a great tortoise. But being again pressed to know what gave support to the broad-backed tortoise, replied, something, he knew not what." On this rather vague and hazy basis, we attribute various elements of our experience to different substances, either as that to which they belong, in the case of primary qualities, or that by which they are caused, in the case of secondary qualities.

Kinds of Knowledge

But how much knowledge can we have by means of sensation and reflection, and how reliable will it be? The fourth book of Locke's *Essay* is devoted to trying to work out an answer to these questions. All of our knowledge deals with various ideas that we have acquired through experience in the course of our lives. Knowledge is the result of the examination of ideas to see if they agree or disagree in some respect. The first sort of knowledge is achieved by the inspection of two or more ideas to see if they are **identical or different.** Thus, for example, one can compare the ideas of "white" and "black," and see immediately that they are different. The second sort of knowledge about ideas deals with the coexistence of two or more ideas, that is, the discovery that **two or more ideas belong together.** This usually amounts to finding out that these ideas are parts of, or caused by, the same substance. A third kind of knowledge about our ideas is the discovery that two or more ideas are **related together in some manner.** The fourth and last type of knowledge is the discovery of whether or not any of our ideas are **experiences of something that exists outside of our minds, that is, if they are ideas of some real existences.**

> Within these four sorts of agreement or disagreement is, I suppose, contained all the knowledge we have, or are capable of: for all the inquiries that we can make concerning any of our ideas, all that we know or can affirm concerning them, is, that it is, or is not the same with some other; that it does, or does not, always coexist with some other idea in the same subject; that it has this or that relation to some other idea; or that it has a real existence without (here meaning "outside") the mind.

Intuitive Knowledge

If these are all the different kinds of knowledge that we can have, according to Locke, how much knowledge can we have of each type, and how certain will it be? The greatest degree of assurance that we can have is when our knowledge is intuitive, that is, when simply by looking at two or more ideas, we see immediately that something is true about them. "This part of knowledge is irresistible, and like bright sunshine, forces itself immediately to be perceived, as soon as ever the mind turns its view that way; and leaves no room for hesitation, doubt or examination, but the mind is presently filled with the clear light of it." This type of complete certainty, Locke claimed, we can have about truths like "white is not black," "a circle is not a triangle," and "3 = 2 + 1," which intuitively we see are true.

Demonstration

Unfortunately, not all of the agreements and disagreements between ideas can be known in this intuitively certain manner. Sometimes when we merely consider certain ideas together, we are unable to tell if they do or do not have something in common, and must, instead, first connect the ideas we are comparing with some others before we can come to any knowledge. This process Locke called **"demonstration."** When we go through several steps in order to reach a conclusion about the agreement or disagreement of one idea with another, we do not immediately see or recognize a truth. Instead, we discover the truth only indirectly. But, Locke insisted, the type of assurance we acquire through reasoning is just a string of intuitions. Each step in a proof is seen immediately by the mind to be certain, and so, if each part of a demonstration is certain, the conclusion will also be. However, it is often the case that in carrying out the chain of steps, we leave something out or do not notice that there is no intuitive certainty between some of the steps. Because of these sorts of errors, Locke pointed out, we cannot rely on demonstrative knowledge with the same degree of assurance that we have in simple intuitions.

"Sensitive" Knowledge

In a strict sense, Locke was willing to admit, only intuitions and demonstrations can give us knowledge we can be sure of. But, in addition to these two, there is another degree of assurance, which, though not as certain, is still relied on by nearly everyone, and hence ought to be included as a degree of knowledge also. This is what Locke called **"sensitive" knowledge, which assures us of the actual existence of particular things.** In spite of all the doubts raised by Descartes and the skeptics, we are still pretty sure that some of our experiences are of things that exist outside of our minds, while others are not.

> But whether there be anything more than barely that idea in our minds, whether we can thence certainly infer the existence of any thing without us, which corresponds to the idea, is that whereof some men think there may be a question made; because men may have such ideas in their minds, when no such thing exists, no such object affects their senses. But yet here, I think, we are provided with an evidence, that puts us past doubting: for I ask anyone, whether he be not invincibly conscious to himself of a different perception when he looks on the sun by day, and thinks on it by night; when he actually tastes wormwood, or smells a rose, or only thinks on that savor or odor? We as plainly find the difference there is between any idea revived in our minds by our own memory, and actually coming into our minds by our senses, as we do between any two distinct ideas.

Even though it may possibly be the case that nothing really exists outside of our minds, or that we may be dreaming all the time, or some other strange possibility, it is nonetheless true, Locke insisted, that there is a commonsense assurance that we all have by which we know about the existence of things outside of our mind. This type of assurance, though much weaker than that of intuition or demonstration, is our sensitive knowledge. It may be false, but it is sufficient for our ordinary purposes.

With these three degrees of assurance or certainty, how much are we actually capable of knowing? First of all, we can only know about those matters of which we can have ideas. But even regarding just the ideas that we can and do have, Locke observed, our knowledge is quite limited. We can "intuit" or "demonstrate" very little about the various ways in which ideas may agree or disagree. By means of sensitive knowledge, we can be sure only of the existence outside of us of some of the ideas immediately present to the mind.

We can be sure intuitively, Locke claimed, whether any two ideas are identical or different. With regard to the coexistence of ideas, our knowledge is, however, sharply limited. Our only way of judging which ideas belong together is by the conjunctions that occur in our experience. From these we cannot tell which of our ideas have to take place together. Thus our knowledge about coexistence is limited to what we have already experienced. This is especially the case, Locke pointed out, in relation to the coexistence of primary and secondary qualities, because "there is no discoverable connection between any secondary quality and those primary qualities which it depends on." Only through experience can we tell which objects will appear yellow to us, will taste sweet, and so on.

We are able to find out a great deal about the relation between different ideas, mostly in terms of mathematical ideas. Here, large bodies of knowledge have been developed. Locke believed that in addition to the mathematical disciplines, we can acquire a great deal of information about ethics and politics by examining the relations between ideas—for example, of the relations between the ideas of "government," "justice," "liberty," and the like.

The Limitations of Knowledge

In what is probably the most important area of knowledge, we are most severely limited. When we examine what we can know about the real existence of things, Locke was willing to admit only one case that we can be intuitively certain of, namely, our own existence. In addition, we can have demonstrative knowledge of God's existence. For anything else, we can have only sensitive knowledge, which extends only to the objects that are present to our senses. For those items for which we do not have even sensitive knowledge, we can never be sure whether they have real existence. All we can do is accept the limitations to our knowledge, and rest content in our ignorance.

Since our knowledge of coexistence and real existence is limited, Locke concluded that a science, in the sense of absolutely necessary and true information, is not possible for either the physical world or the spiritual world if all of our information is restricted to empirical elements that we have acquired from sensation or reflection. We can never discover, except from experience, what qualities occur together. But from our experience we never know enough to find out why these qualities have to occur together. We can never be absolutely sure that some things have to happen and that others cannot happen. Therefore, any sciences that man can develop about the world must always fall short of complete certainty and must be based only on his limited experience of the relationship between qualities previously experienced. Complete understanding of the natural world will, unfortunately, always be beyond the limits of our knowledge.

Thus, in Locke's empirical theory, knowledge is limited to the respects in which various ideas of ours agree or disagree. Perhaps if we can rely only upon experience, it may actually be the case that we cannot know *anything* about what goes on outside of the ideas in our minds. As Locke put the possibility:

> I doubt not but my reader by this time may be apt to think, that I have been all this while only building a castle in the air; and be ready to say to me, "To what purpose all this stir? Knowledge, say you, is only the perception of the agreement or disagreement of our own ideas: but who knows what those ideas may be? Is there anything so extravagant as the imagination of men's brains? Where is the head that has no chimeras in it? Or, if there be a sober and wise man, what difference will there be, by your rules, between his knowledge and that of the most extravagant fancy in the world? They both have their ideas, and perceive their agreement and disagreement one with another. If there be any difference between them, the advantage will be on the warm-headed man's side, as having the more ideas, and the more lively."

External Reality

In order to prevent his empirical theory of knowledge from ending in the above-suggested conclusions (i.e., that what we call

knowledge is just one man's opinion based on what goes on in his own mind), Locke attempted toward the end of his *Essay* to show that even with our limited information gained from experience, we have some basis for claiming that we know something about what goes on outside of our minds. His argument is that our knowledge of our own ideas is more than just our own imagination, and there is a conformity between our ideas and the real nature of things. How do we tell when our ideas really represent something outside of our minds? Locke's answer is first that we can be sure that all simple ideas represent something real. The mind, he insisted, is incapable of inventing simple ideas, since they cannot be formed from any other ideas that we already possess. "From whence it follows, that simple ideas are no fictions of our fancies, but the natural and regular productions of things without us, really operating upon us." If we cannot invent the simple ideas, then they must be the effect of something outside us. In the case of secondary qualities, we can be sure, Locke claimed, that these ideas are the results of some powers that external things have. In the case of primary qualities, these are not just ideas of ours but also properties of objects as well. With respect to mathematical and moral studies, in which all of our knowledge consists of either intuitive or demonstrative truths, Locke claimed that his knowledge was about real objects if there happen to be actual triangles, squares, or property and justice in the external world. From this, Locke concluded: "Wherever we perceive the agreement or disagreement of any of our ideas, there is certain knowledge: and wherever we are sure those ideas agree with the reality of things, there is certain real knowledge."

John Locke tried to work out a theory of knowledge that would show how all of our information comes from our experiences. If our knowledge is based on our sensations and reflections, Locke attempted to show, there are certain conditions under which we can be sure of what we know, and even sure that what we know applies to something outside of ourselves.

Conclusions and Criticism

In the course of working out his empirical theory of knowledge, and trying to show how knowledge derives from our sense experience, Locke revealed certain characteristics and difficulties of the empirical approach. In the first place, if all of our knowledge comes from experience, then a good deal of the knowledge that philosophers such as Plato and Descartes claimed that we have, or could have, would have to be considered as illusory or fictitious. The knowledge dependent upon Platonic ideas or innate ideas would have to be declared invalid, since such ideas do not appear in, or develop from, our sense experience. In general, an empirical theory of knowledge, Locke's work pointed out, would yield only limited results, in that those claims to knowledge that could not be justified in terms of our experiences would have to be discarded. All the beautiful pictures of what the world is "really" like, which previous philosophers had presented, would have to be rejected as imaginative daydreams or nonsense if they could not be derived from experience. On the other hand, if Locke is right and they are imaginative day-

dreams, then, of course, we should reject them.

Secondly, Locke's attempt to develop his theory of knowledge indicated that the empirical approach might engender certain difficulties. If all of our information is based upon the ideas that we acquire from experience, and our knowledge is about the agreement and disagreement of our ideas, how can we ever tell if our knowledge is actually about something outside of us? Locke claimed that we have to suppose that there is something called substance, or substratum, that our ideas, or at least some of them, belong to. By an examination of the nature of our ideas, he insisted, we can distinguish those that do in fact represent some actual features of this substance, or substratum, and hence discover some actual knowledge about the real world. But some of Locke's opponents pointed out that his "way of ideas" made such knowledge-claims difficult to support, since all we have to go on are the ideas in our mind. The supposition that there is anything outside of us to which we can attribute ideas seemed to have no justification if one adhered strictly to the empirical thesis that all of our knowledge comes from experience. The claim that by inspection of the ideas—and the agreements and disagreements among them—we can discover truths about the real world also seemed questionable. All our ideas appear to be on the same level: they are all in our mind. Then, the opponents asked, how can we tell which to take seriously, which to use as a basis for knowledge about the world, and which to discard as personal fancy or imagination? The attempt to work out these implications of the empirical theory of knowledge appeared in the works of two eighteenth-century philosophers, Bishop Berkeley and David Hume.

Bishop George Berkeley

George Berkeley (1685–1753) was born and educated in Ireland. While he was a Fellow of Trinity College, Dublin, in his early twenties, young Berkeley worked out his philosophical theories and wrote his two most important works, *A Treatise Concerning the Principles of Human Knowledge* (1710) and *Three Dialogues Between Hylas and Philonous* (1713). After failing to create much interest in his theories, he spent several years in such minor jobs as secretary and tutor. Then he became interested in founding a college in the New World, in Bermuda. In 1729 he went to America, living in Rhode Island for a couple of years. Although he never succeeded in his plan, he exerted significant influence on the development of institutions of higher education in America, especially at Yale, to which he gave money and a library, and at Columbia, whose first president was a disciple of Berkeley's. A few years after his return to England, Berkeley was appointed Bishop of Cloyne in Ireland and stayed there most of the rest of his life. One of his most intense interests in later life was trying to convince people of the virtues of tar-water as a cure for many of the ills of mankind.

Berkeley's Philosophic System

The philosophical theory that Berkeley offered was intended, he wrote, "to demonstrate the reality and perfection of human knowledge, the incorporeal nature of the soul, and the immediate providence of a deity: in opposition to skeptics and atheists." Part of the cause of these pernicious views, that is, skepticism and atheism, Berkeley charged, was due to the theories of John Locke and of many other philosophers before him. Locke and others had claimed that some of the ideas that we have are not reliable, while others give us true knowledge of real things. As soon as any doubts have been cast on the reliability of our sense information, "Then," Berkeley wrote, "we are insensibly drawn into uncouth paradoxes, difficulties, and inconsistencies, which multiply and grow upon us as we advance in speculation; till at length, having wandered through many intricate mazes, we find ourselves just where we were or, which is worse, sit down in a forlorn skepticism." What makes all the trouble, Berkeley insisted, is that philosophers refuse to believe what everyone else does, and persist in distinguishing the real nature of things from the experience of their senses. Even Locke, in separating primary and secondary qualities, and claiming that only the primary qualities really are qualities of actual substances, has developed a theory in which real things are different from the items of our sense experience. This sort of distinction leads to "skepticism and paradoxes" and leaves philosophers spending their lives "in doubting of those things which other men evidently know, and believing those things which they laugh at and despise." The dangerous effect of this is "that when men of less leisure see them who are supposed to have spent their whole time in the pursuits of knowledge profess an entire ignorance of all things, or advancing such notions as are repugnant to plain and commonly received principles, they will be tempted to entertain suspicions concerning the most important truths, which they had hitherto held sacred and unquestionable."

Thus Berkeley's thesis is that the theories of philosophers like Locke lead to paradoxes and doubts, which in turn produce a general skepticism. When the ordinary person sees what sort of odd theories the so-called "wise" philosophers advance, and sees that philosophers deny the most basic things that ordinary people believe, this will make him/her doubtful too. And finally, when philosophers have engendered this sort of skepticism, this will lead to doubts even about religious truths. Hence atheism will be the ultimate outcome.

Three Dialogues

In order to advance his claims by the most striking means, Berkeley wrote the *Three Dialogues*, in which a discussion takes place between Philonous ("lover of mind"), who represents Berkeley's views, and Hylas (which means "matter"), representing the opposition. The first dialogue begins with Hylas saying that he has heard that Philonous is an extreme skeptic in that he holds that there is no such thing as material substance in the world. Philonous says that he certainly holds that opinion, but that it is neither skeptical nor opposed to ordinary common sense, and that he will show that it is the philosophers who believe that there is something called "material substance," or "matter," who are really the skeptics.

(A skeptic, we are told, is "one who doubted of everything . . . or who denies the reality and truth of things." Hylas, then, accuses his friend Philonous of denying the real existence of sensible things, or of pretending to know nothing about them. A "sensible thing" is defined as a thing immediately perceived by the senses—that is, something seen, or heard, or felt directly in our immediate sense experience. Now Berkeley is ready to state his case.)

Does Matter Exist?

What do we perceive immediately by our senses? Only colors and shapes, sounds, tastes, odors, tangible qualities, and the like. Then what constitutes the reality of sensible things besides their being perceived? Hylas, the believer in some sort of material substance, insists that the real existence of sensible things is independent of their being experienced. They exist "distinct from, and without any relation to, their being perceived." Then, Philonous suggests, consider the case of heat. In Hylas's theory, heat must exist outside of the mind as something independent of our experience. But when we experience extreme heat, what we actually feel is great pain, and no one believes that material substance contains pain. Hylas protests, and says that one has to distinguish between the pain, which is in the mind, and the heat, which is in the material object. Just try, Philonous suggests, putting your hand near a fire, and see if you feel two things, heat *and* pain, or only one thing, pain. Hylas yields and is willing to admit that our sensible experience of extreme heat—pain—exists only in the mind and not in the object.

Philonous immediately shows him that the same reasoning applies to all the various degrees of heat, which are felt either as pleasant sensations of warmth or as pain, and that Hylas certainly does not believe that there is either pleasure or pain in material objects. Further, Philonous points out, if one hand is warm and the other cold and they are put into a bowl of water at room temperature, the water will feel cold to one hand and hot to the other. Hylas would not want to claim that both qualities, heat and cold, are in the same object, the water, at the same time. Hylas finally concedes "that heat and cold are only sensations existing in our minds."

Taste

But what about other qualities that we experience? Philonous shows Hylas that the same point can be applied to taste. Sweet and bitter tastes are experienced as different kinds of pleasure or pain. No one believes that sugar contains various pleasures, so that pleasant experience must be in the mind rather than in the sugar. At this point, Hylas suddenly thinks of a response to this sort of reasoning, much like a theory of Locke's, namely, that these qualities as perceived by us are pleasures and pains, but as they exist in external objects, they are something different. Philonous regards this new line of defense with complete scorn. We are talking about sensible things, that is, things that we immediately perceive by our senses.

> Whatever other qualities, therefore, you speak of, as distinct from these, I know nothing of them, neither do they at all belong to the point in dispute. You may, indeed, pretend to have discovered certain qualities which you do not perceive, and assert those insensible qualities exist in fire and sugar. But what use can be made of this to your present purpose, I am at a loss to conceive. Tell me then once more, do you acknowledge that heat and cold, sweetness and bitterness (meaning those qualities which are perceived by the senses) do not exist without the mind?

Poor Hylas is crushed and yields.

Other Sensations

Then the same point is raised in connection with odors, and Hylas admits that they are just pleasant or painful sensations, and vary with different observers. Therefore, they are only in the mind. But when Philonous continues this line of reasoning into the subject of sounds, Hylas balks. Sounds, the noises that we hear, Hylas is willing to admit, are only sensations that we have. But at the same time, he insists, there are sound waves that exist in the exterior physical world, apart from us. But, Philonous points out, this means that real sound, the sound waves, are never heard. Only noises are heard. The sensible thing that we perceive is noise. The sound wave we do not hear. So once again Hylas must admit that the sensible thing, the noise, exists in the mind; the "real" thing, the sound wave, is not a sensible thing and hence not relevant to their discussion. (The reader may be familiar with another version of this point, namely, "Is there any sound when a tree falls in a forest and no one is there?" What Berkeley is pointing out is that if we mean by sound, *experienced* noise, then the answer is no, if no one hears it.)

After this they go on to discuss colors,

with the same results. The colors that we experience differ depending upon lighting conditions, our own state, the type of optical devices that we employ, and other factors. No one would want to claim that the object had all the different colors that we see. Hylas tries to answer this by introducing the theory of light waves. The colors that we see may be in our minds, but there are real colors outside of us, in the sense of light waves. Philonous again points out that Hylas is admitting that the sensible colors that we perceive exist only in our minds, not outside of us in some material object.

To avoid the conclusion that Berkeley is aiming at, **that the objects that we perceive are only ideas in our minds and do not exist outside of, and independent of, the mind,** Hylas comes forth with Locke's theory of primary and secondary qualities. The secondary qualities—such as colors, smells, tastes—exist only in the mind. But the primary qualities—such as extension, motion, gravity—really exist in bodies. Therefore, some of our sense information is only of ideas in our minds, but some refers to the *actual* qualities of external, material objects.

Berkeley's Criticism of Locke

Berkeley then tries to show that if one is a *consistent* empiricist, one will not be able to maintain this theory of Locke's. If one admits that some of our sense experience consists of ideas that exist only in the mind, then one will have no basis for making an exception of the primary qualities. Exactly the same reasoning that convinces one that the secondary qualities are in the mind applies to the primary

qualities as well. Our experience of size, shape, motion, and so on, varies depending upon where we are, how we feel, and other factors. Thus the primary qualities appear to be just ideas in our minds, just as colors and sounds are, and no special reason can be given as to why we should regard our ideas of extension and motion as being real qualities in material bodies, if we admit that other qualities are only parts of our experience and exist in us.

To put his case another way, Berkeley points out that **all our experience consists of sensations.** Sensations belong only to sentient (i.e., capable of feeling) beings, not to inanimate objects. Therefore, we cannot attribute to material objects, which are not thinking beings, sensations, which, as far as we know, only thinking beings can have. Material objects do not have pleasures or pains, or sensations in general. If we admit that the sensible things we know are only sensations, then we cannot claim that they are unthinking, unfeeling material things.

But after all this, Hylas, like anyone else confronted with Berkeley's reasoning, is unwilling to give up.

> I acknowledge, Philonous, that upon a fair observation of what passes in my mind, I can discover nothing else, but that I am a thinking being, affected with a variety of sensations; neither is it possible to conceive, how a sensation should exist in an unperceiving substance. But then, on the other hand, when I look on sensible things in a different view, considering them as so many modes and qualities, I find it necessary to suppose a material *substratum*, without which they cannot be conceived to exist.

Thus, like John Locke before him, Hylas still finds it necessary to suppose that our sensations belong to something outside of us, something that we call matter.

Philonous responds by saying that we do not learn of this material substratum by our senses, which tell us only about sensible things, sensations, not something that exists apart from sense experience. Also, if we try to conceive of what this matter is like, we can think of it only in terms of our sensations, not as something unlike them, which exists apart from all experience. Finally, to make his point, Philonous challenges Hylas, "If you can conceive it possible for any mixture or combination of qualities, or any sensible object whatever, to exist without the mind, then I will grant it actually to be so."

Matter and Mind

Hylas thinks this is simple: "What more easy than to conceive a tree or a house existing by itself, independent of, and unperceived by, any mind whatsoever? I do, at this present time, conceive them existing after that manner." Philonous replies that this tree or house is being conceived by Hylas and is in *his* mind. Nothing can be thought of, or experienced, except by some mind that thinks of it or experiences it. Therefore, one cannot even imagine or conceive of what it would be like for something to exist outside of, or independent of, the mind. As soon as one imagines this, it is an idea in a mind.

Hylas still is unwilling to surrender. He admits by now that whatever is immediately perceived is an idea, and that ideas cannot exist outside of a mind. But why can't there also be something called "real things," or "external objects," that exist independently of the mind and are known or represented by our ideas? Why can't this be like looking at a picture of Julius Caesar (an idea) that represents Julius Caesar (a real, external object)?

But how do we ever find out about these alleged real objects? By our senses? No. Our sense information consists entirely of ideas, and so it cannot tell us about something that is not an idea. If one is an empiricist, and believes that all of our knowledge comes from the senses, then how can he/she accept this claim that we can know about something that is not part of sense experience? The example of the picture of Julius Caesar does not help, Berkeley argued, since we learned about both people and pictures from sense experience, but we do not learn about real objects from any of our sensations if all of our sensations are ideas.

If our ideas are said to represent these supposed real objects, then, Berkeley argued, this is a weird claim. The ideas are fleeting, changing, ephemeral, and the real objects are supposed to have a fixed and real nature. Ideas can be perceived, but the real objects cannot be. Thus the ideas cannot be like the objects they are supposed to represent. "Can a real thing, in itself invisible, be like a color; or a real thing, which is not audible, be like a sound? In a word, can anything be like a sensation or idea, but another sensation or idea?"

Philonous claims that he has shown that this notion of a real, material object makes no sense. This enables us to see that Hylas's views lead to skepticism. Hylas had originally asserted that the reality of sensible things consisted in their existence outside the mind. But Hylas has now been forced to deny that sensible things, our experiences, exist outside the mind. Hence he has been forced to deny that they are real. By his own definition of "skeptic," he has been shown to be a skeptic.

By this stage in the argument, Hylas has been reduced to complete doubt. His belief that there are real, external material objects has been destroyed. Now he is convinced that there are no real objects and that everything is just a dream. But Berkeley is at great pains to point out that this sad result is due to holding some of the views that Locke had formulated. As long as Hylas believes that there must be some real, material substratum that exists outside the mind, then he is forced to admit that none of our sense experience can belong to this matter. As long as he believes in the theory of primary and secondary qualities, he is led to the conclusion that all of our experience consists of secondary qualities that exist only in the mind. One of the reasons that Hylas has been forced to complete skepticism is that he, like Locke, was not completely an empiricist. He insisted on believing that there must be independent material objects that our sensations belong to. When he is shown that there cannot be such objects, he suddenly feels that then there cannot be *anything* in the universe, and that *everything* that he perceives must be illusory, since it cannot consist of objects existing outside of the mind.

What Berkeley has shown, up to this point, is that if one seriously accepts the empirical theory of knowledge, all that we can know is what we experience. What we experience are not independently existing material objects but, rather, a series of ideas. All that we can know about these ideas is what we perceive. Hence we cannot tell from what we see if they exist apart from minds that perceive them. In fact, as he has pointed out, we cannot even conceive or imagine, in terms of our experience, what it would be like for our sensations to exist apart from being thought of. Thus, in Berkeley's famous phrase, **"the existence of things consists of their being perceived,"** or, as he put it in Latin, *"esse est percipi"* (literally, "to be is to be perceived").

Berkeley's Positive Theory

Does this mean that if we rely on the information we gain from our sense experience, we can never be sure that things exist other than ideas? Does this mean that we cannot be sure that the chairs and tables in the room exist except when we perceive them? At this point in the discussion, Berkeley revealed that he had a radically different theory from that of Hylas, and hence did not concur in the complete skepticism to which Hylas had been reduced. Speaking through Philonous, Berkeley declared:

> I deny that I agreed with you in those notions that led to skepticism. You indeed said that the reality of sensible things consisted in an *absolute existence* out of the minds of spirits, or distinct from their being perceived. And pursuant to this notion of reality, you are obliged to deny sensible things any real existence: that is, according to your own definition, you profess yourself a skeptic. But I neither said nor thought, the reality of sensible things was to be defined after that manner. To me it is evident, for the reasons you allow of, that sensible things cannot exist otherwise than in a mind or spirit. Whence I conclude, not that

they have no real existence, but that, seeing they depend not on my thought, and have an existence distinct from being perceived by me, *there must be some other mind wherein they exist.* As sure, therefore, as the sensible world really exists, so sure is there an infinite omnipresent spirit, who contains and supports it.

Immaterialism

This explanation that Berkeley presented is a theory called **"immaterialism."** All that we can perceive is an idea. Ideas can belong only to minds and cannot have an existence independent of minds. Since the ideas that I am aware of do not depend upon my wishes, these ideas must have some kind of existence apart from my mind. But ideas can belong only to some mind. If I am not responsible for the ideas I perceive, and cannot invent and control all my ideas at will, then there must be some other mind that possesses, controls, and maintains the ideas. And so, Berkeley claimed, there must be some universal mind, or God, in whose thoughts the ideas are located. Thus the things that I perceive exist distinct from me in the mind of God and do not leap in and out of existence when I experience them. My house is always perceived by God. Hence, although the house is only an idea, it continues to exist whether I perceive it or not, since God always perceives it.

This thesis of Berkeley's has been summed up in a famous limerick by Ronald Knox.

There was a young man who said, "God,
I find it exceedingly odd
That this tree I see should
Continue to be
When there's no one about in the Quad."
Reply.

"Dear Sir:
Your astonishment's odd:
I am always about in the Quad.
And that's why the tree
Will continue to be
Since observed by
Yours faithfully,

GOD

Berkeley's Claims

Berkeley claimed that this strange theory, besides being a consistent empirical philosophy, was also the only theory of knowledge that was in agreement with ordinary commonsense beliefs. Other theories led to skepticism and to paradoxes, and ended up denying what everybody knew and was sure of. His view, on the contrary, combined the best elements of philosophical reasoning and common sense. Philosophers, like Locke and Descartes, had concluded that *"the things immediately perceived are ideas which exist only in the mind."* On the other hand, ordinary people believed that *"those things they immediately perceive are the real things."* Berkeley insisted that his theory, and only his theory, was in agreement with both the philosophers and ordinary folk, and did not lead to any of the skeptical or paradoxical conclusions that he had shown were involved in the theories of knowledge offered by previous thinkers.

Theories of knowledge had always distinguished things from ideas and had tried to learn how we discover any knowledge about things from our information about ideas. All that we are immediately aware of are ideas. If things are different from ideas, then how do we relate knowledge about ideas to something outside of our ideas? Berkeley, by reasoning astutely from the empirical claim that all of our knowledge comes from our experiences, which are ideas in the mind, showed that if things are different from ideas, we can never know anything about them. This reduced Hylas to his "forlorn skepticism."

In order to avoid this sad conclusion, that we can never know anything at all about what real things are like, Berkeley offered his theory of immaterialism. First of all, he insisted, things are only the ideas we have of them. It is the philosophers who have invented this strange unknown item called "an independently existing material object." Everybody believes that what he/she perceives (an idea) is a real thing. He/she thinks there is a tree in his/her garden because he/she sees it, touches it. It is his/her experience, his/her ideas, that give him/her his/her information about things. The real things of the world are only the ideas that we have. But then, Berkeley claimed, not only is the world the sequence of the ideas in *my* mind, but it is a real, continuously existing series of things, because the ideas that I perceive are also perceived by God, and hence it is still perceived. The information that I gain through my senses is accurate information about the ideas in God's mind and consists of true knowledge about real things. In terms of the various ideas that I have, I can develop sciences about the order and relation of ideas in God's mind.

Berkeley's Theory of Notions

However, as Berkeley saw, he had to hold that we have knowledge that does not come from our sense experience. Our knowledge about God is not derived from sense experience. Rather, Berkeley insisted, in addition to the ideas in our mind, there are also other items called **"notions." The basic notion is our awareness of ourselves.** We do not see ourselves as we perceive chairs and tables, as a series of sensory qualities, colors, shapes, and the like. What we are aware of, Berkeley claimed, is that we are active agents who think, will, act. This conception, or awareness, of the active spirit called "myself," or "me," gives us our primary notions. We also develop a notion of God as the omnipresent spirit who thinks and perceives all the ideas. It is through notions that we learn about the structure of the world. This accounts for all of our ordinary information and explains how we get our knowledge about the world of experience, or things, and why it is true.

In spite of Berkeley's high hopes that he had succeeded in solving all the difficulties that had arisen in earlier theories of knowledge, and had developed a theory that would be compatible with ordinary common sense, his contemporaries regarded his theories as fantastic. The immaterialistic conception of the universe was regarded with suspicion, and Berkeley's philosophy—if one rejected his world of spirits, with God always perceiving everything—seemed to terminate in the weird claim that everything is nothing but an idea in the mind, with no real existence outside the mind. It is said, for example, that once when Berkeley visited Dean Swift, he was left to stand on the doorstep, on the grounds that if his philosophical views were correct, he could enter through the closed door. There are other stories of similar reactions to his views. Some thinkers, who took Berkeley's arguments seriously, were willing to admit that he had made out a good case and had offered a series of proofs that might "admit of no answer"; but at the same time, they saw that Berkeley's reasoning also "produced no conviction."

David Hume

But one of the philosophers who came shortly after Berkeley pursued his reasoning to an even more disastrous and shocking conclusion, and thereby exposed some of the limitations of all empirical theories of knowledge. This was the Scottish skeptic David Hume (1711–76), who is probably the most influential philosopher of modern times. Hume grew up in Ninewells, near Edinburgh, and briefly attended the University of Edinburgh, leaving there at the age of fifteen. After a series of ill-starred attempts to enter various careers, he went to France to write a great philosophic work. By the time he was twenty-six, he had finished his *A Treatise of Human Nature*, which he thought would radically change the course of philosophy. Instead, when it appeared in 1739, it "fell dead-born from the presses," as Hume lamented, and elicited no great interest from any of his contemporaries. His later *An Enquiry Concerning Human Understanding* attempted to present his views in more popular form but still failed to get Hume the recognition he sought. Finally, his political writings and his popular *History of England* brought him fame, making him one of the best-known writers in the English language in the latter half of the eighteenth century. When he served as secretary to the British

Embassy in Paris in the 1760s, he was hailed by the French intellectuals as the most important writer of the British Isles. Hume's irreligious views made him a hero to the French skeptics and Enlightenment leaders. Back in England, he served briefly as under secretary of state and became a leading advocate of freedom for the American colonies. Hume's unorthodox views in religion and politics gained him great notoriety, so that by the time he retired he was generally known as the "gentle skeptic" and the "great infidel."

Hume's Theory of Knowledge

Hume's philosophy appears to have grown out of two strands. One, a deep interest in skepticism, with an extreme doubt that philosophers were capable of discovering the truth about any matter whatsoever. Two, a conviction that what was needed in order to uncover what knowledge, if any, we were capable of was an inquiry into what he called the **"science of man."** This science would examine the processes by which we think and try to find out how people form their views and come to believe what they do about the nature of events.

Psychology

Hume's greatest philosophical work, his *A Treatise of Human Nature*, claims at the outset to be the application to the mental world of the scientific method that Isaac Newton had so successfully employed in solving physical problems. What is to be examined is the mental nature of human beings, their psychology, in order to see the actual processes by which our alleged knowledge develops. All the sciences that we have, like physics, and disciplines like mathematics have been discovered by human beings; and so, Hume suggested, by understanding what human beings are like, we may find out something important about the nature of the knowledge that human beings possess. From the outset, Hume conceded that he probably would never be able "to discover the ultimate original qualities of human nature," but by examining our experiences, we may be able to find some general hypotheses about human nature that could be of the greatest value. This is what had earlier been done in developing a science about the physical world, and could have even more significant results in the mental world.

> We must therefore glean up our experiments in this science from a cautious observation of human life, and take them as they appear in the common course of the world, by men's behavior in company, in affairs, and in their pleasures. When experiments of this kind are judiciously collected and compared, we may hope to establish on them a science which will not be inferior in certainty, and will be much superior in utility to any other of human comprehension.

Impressions and Ideas

Hume begins by pointing out that everything that we are aware of can be classified under two headings, **impressions and ideas.** The difference between these two is the **"degree of force and liveliness,** with which they strike upon the mind." The impressions are more forceful and lively than the ideas. Also, there are **simple** impressions and ideas, and **complex** ones. The difference is that the simple ones "ad-

mit of no distinction or separation." Thus the perception of the quality blue is simple, whereas the perception of a blue *picture* is complex and can be separated into parts. When we examine our impressions and ideas, Hume claimed, we find a great resemblance between them. However, some of our complex ideas, we find, never appear as impressions, as, for example, our complex idea of a mermaid. But on careful inspection of our ideas and impressions, we find that in every case our simple ideas are just like our simple impressions, and that the impressions have always occurred first. Thus, our acquaintance with a simply quality like orange first occurred as a forceful and lively impression, and later occurred as an identical idea. As Hume pointed out, this law that simple impressions always precede the simple ideas that resemble them in our experience amounts to **a denial that there are any innate ideas, and also to the claim that all of our ideas come from experience.**

Memory and Imagination

Further, with regard to our ideas, we find that we have two different faculties, one called **"memory,"** in which we have present in the mind a series of ideas in a fixed order or sequence. The other faculty is called **"imagination"** by which we can arrange our ideas in any order we like. But in spite of this freedom of the imagination, we find that our ideas come in patterns. When we think of an idea, we have a tendency to think also of a resembling idea, or of an idea that was contiguous to it in time or space, or of an idea that is causally related to it. These patterns are the **associations of ideas.** We find that one of the principles of human nature is that there "is a kind of attraction (in other words, something like Newton's theory of Universal Gravitation), which in the mental world will be found to have as extraordinary effects as in the natural, and to show itself in as many and as various forms."

Hume's Analysis of Causation

The importance of this claim about the association of ideas is brought out when Hume investigates what constitutes our knowledge, and especially our information about what events are causally related to each other. Knowledge, according to Hume, consists of information that can be gained from the inspection of two or more ideas. If we look at two or more ideas, we can tell immediately whether they resemble each other, whether they are different, whether one is darker than another, whether one is larger than another. **This type of knowledge by immediate inspection of two or more ideas, Hume insists, is intuitive and certain.** It cannot be false, since it merely depends on bringing two or more ideas to mind in our imagination and then examining them. On the basis of this sort of knowledge, coupled with a series of demonstrations, we can develop an indubitable branch of knowledge like arithmetic.

But when we ask how we are to discover that two or more ideas are *causally* related, we find something very peculiar. This sort of information about what is going on does *not* merely depend upon looking at two or more ideas. If we examine a situation in which we frequently say

"This event causes that event" (for instance, the experience of seeing a rock striking against a window pane), do we actually perceive, as a feature of the impression, a part called the "cause"? There is no quality, such as green, that we find in every experience that we call a "causal sequence." Then, Hume suggested, perhaps the causal connection between events is a relation between the elements in an impression or between successive impressions. But when we examine a situation like that of the rock striking the window, we find that the elements, window and rock, are contiguous, that is, the rock at some moment is next to the window, and also we find that there are some motions of the rock prior to the shattering of the glass. But, besides the **contiguity** and **succession** of the events, is there anything else? Well, we feel that there must be more, some element or property by which the cause *produces* the effect. But all that we see, Hume pointed out, is only the contiguity of two things, and the succession of events. This point is well illustrated by a story of two children who were traveling on a train with their mother. The mother gave each of them a banana. As the first child bit into the banana, the train rushed into a tunnel. "Don't eat that banana!" he cried out in panic to his brother. "It makes you go blind." The contiguity and the succession were there. Why, then, do we not accept the causality? This is Hume's point.

Shall we then rest contented with these two relations of contiguity and succession, as affording a complete idea of causation? By no means. An object may be contiguous and prior to another, without being considered as its cause. There is a necessary connection to be taken into consideration; and that relation is of much greater importance, than any of the other two above-mentioned.

This crucial element in our reasoning about causally related events is not immediately evident. It does not seem to be one of the parts, or relations, that we discover in our impressions. But if the empirical theory of knowledge is accepted, our idea of necessary connection must derive from some impression or some feature of our impressions. Since the source of this basic idea is not located simply by examining and dissecting impressions, Hume felt that he might find the answer to his question by first finding out the answers to the two following problems: (*a*) "For what reason we pronounce it *necessary*, that everything whose existence has a beginning, should also have a cause?" and (*b*) "Why we conclude, that such particular causes must *necessarily* have such particular effects; and what is the nature of that *inference* we draw from the one to the other, and of the belief we repose in it?"

THE PROBLEM OF CAUSE

The mere asking of the first question is a bit startling. Everyone had taken for granted that every event has a cause and that everything that exists has a cause for its existence. But, Hume asked, why do we believe this? What evidence do we have for this causal principle? It is not intuitively obvious. When we look at the various impressions and ideas in our minds, we do not see as a feature of the impressions or ideas that they must have a cause. There is no connection between the ideas that we have of a new existent, (i.e., something that has just begun to exist) and the idea of a cause. This can be shown by the fact that since all ideas that are distinct can be separated by the imagination, anyone is capable of thinking of the idea of a new object without also thinking of its cause. Hence the two ideas are not linked together.

Then why do we think that every object that begins to exist must have a cause? Hume examined the various arguments that such philosophers as John Locke had offered to prove this causal assertion. Their proofs, Hume found, were inconclusive because somewhere in the proof they assumed the very claim they were trying to establish. For instance, in Hume's version of Locke's argument, the proof is that if things were produced without any cause, then they would have *nothing* for a cause. But *nothing* is not something and therefore cannot act as a producing agent. But, as Hume pointed out, this argument proceeds only by supposing that every object must have a cause, and then by showing that *nothing* cannot be a cause. And what has to be proven is the supposition that everything has to have a cause.

After examining the types of arguments presented by various philosophers and demonstrating their invalidity, Hume concluded, "Since it is not from knowledge or any scientific reasoning, that we derive the opinion of the necessity of a cause to every new production, that opinion must necessarily arise from observation and experience." The next question, then, should naturally be: "How does experience give rise to such a principle?" In order to answer this question, Hume found it was first necessary to solve his other problem—why do we think that particular causes must necessarily have particular effects, and why do we form an inference from one to the other?

ELEMENTS OF CAUSAL ANALYSIS

Our causal reasoning seems to involve three sorts of elements. One is a **present impression,** which we believe is connected with another item, some **idea** we have of a related event. The third element is the **connection or inference,** and this is what Hume was searching for. When a detective discovers a body—the present impression—he/she immediately reasons to the idea, some *cause* of death. If the body contains a bullet, the detective immediately infers that there must have been a gun from which the bullet came. It is this reasoning process, from impression to idea, that Hume was trying to analyze. The body does not appear with a sign on it announcing that it is the result of a gun having been fired. The detective, like anyone else, could have thought of an unlimited number of ideas instead of a gun. Then, Hume asked, why is it that although we do not see the cause, we think immediately of an idea that we think was necessary to produce the experience that we do have? Merely from an examination of the particular impression, no specific ideas have to be called to mind. The imagination is capable of thinking about any idea that one has. One could just as well think of the taste of a pear, instead of a gun. But one doesn't. The sort of inference the detective makes is like that any of us make. When we see one event, although it does not force us to think of any particular idea, we do in fact tend to think of something that we call the "cause" or the "effect" of the impressions we are having. When we hear a certain sound, we think of a piano being played, even though the impression, the sound that we hear, does not contain the visual element of the piano and the player.

Then how and why do we make this sort of inference? Hume asked. Not by reasoning, because just from the impression, no necessary conclusion follows. Any other ideas could be *thought* of. Then it must be due to something in our experience.

> We remember to have had frequent instances of the existence of one species of objects; and also remember, that the individuals of another species of objects have always attended them, and have existed in a regular order of contiguity and succession with regard to them. Thus we remember, to have seen that species of object we call "flame," and to have felt that species of sensation we call "heat." We likewise call to mind their constant conjunction in all past instances. Without any further ceremony, we call the one *cause* and the other *effect*, and infer the existence of the one from that of the other.

Constant Conjunction

Then what happens, according to Hume, is that in experience we are aware of two items occurring together, that is, constantly conjoined. When this has happened often enough in the past, we come to consider them as causally related, and when we experience just one of these items, we immediately infer that the other one must also exist. But why, to explore the problem further, should past experience have this effect upon us? If it were by means of a rational procedure, it would require that a principle like that of the uniformity of nature must be true, that is, "that instances, of which we have had no experience, must resemble those, of which, we have had no experience, and that the course of nature continues always uniformly the same." Thus, in order to prove from our past experience that when we hear a certain sound, someone is now playing the piano, we would have to presume that the same sort of experience we had in the past must be taking place in the present, and that the constant conjunctions that we discovered in the past continue in the present.

But is there anything that we can ever discover from our experience that gives us any guarantee that the principle of the uniformity of nature is true? No, Hume insisted, because no matter how uniform our experience has been in the past, it is always possible that the future will be different. We can examine our experience from now until doomsday and we will never be able to show that future events must be similar to previous ones, or that the apparent uniformity of nature up to any point in our experience is adequate evidence that nature will continue to be uniform in our future experience.

Uncertainty

Here Hume discovered something most peculiar. The principle of the uniformity of nature is involved in nearly all of our inferences as to what is going on in the world beyond what we immediately perceive. Almost all our interpretations of the impressions we have—the sounds, the colors, the smells—are based upon assuming that matters that were constantly conjoined in past experience are still conjoined in the present and will be in the fu-

ture. But if we are asked for evidence for this all-important principle, we find that we have none. We cannot demonstrate it, since it is always possible that when we wake up tomorrow, the universe will be radically different from what it has been until now. It is always possible that the constant conjunctions of items in our experience will be altered in the future, and that salt will taste sweet, that water will burn, and so on. No amount of observation and study of experience will help establish this principle, because all that we will learn thereby is that nature has been uniform, but we still cannot be sure that it will *continue* to be so. Thus, to make Hume's point more forcefully, even the best-tested scientific laws, such as the law of gravity, depend upon the principle of the uniformity of nature. We can never be sure, no matter how many objects have been tested to see if they gravitate toward the earth, that the law will be true in the future.

Human Nature

If the principle of the uniformity of nature is so basic to our information about the world, and if we can neither prove it nor offer sufficient evidence for it, then why do we believe it? Hume's answer is that the belief is due to a psychological custom or habit that people have, so that after they have experienced the constant conjunction of two impressions often enough, and one of the conjuncts occurs again in their experience, they are immediately led to think of the other as an idea in their imagination. But we think of the idea usually associated with the impression in a special manner. We could, since our imagination is free, think of *any* idea. But only the associated idea is thought of with "force and vivacity," or is believed in. Thus, when I hear a certain sound, I could, if I wished, conjure up any idea I wished—say, that of the taste of a pear. But naturally, Hume pointed out, I think of this idea of someone playing the piano, and I think of the idea with "force and vivacity." I believe that someone is actually playing the piano, whereas I do not believe that a pear is being tasted. The belief that occurs in one case and not the other is only the result of the different ways the two ideas are conceived. Only the associated idea (that is, associated in past experience) is thought of **forcefully.** Any other idea would merely be thought of.

What is it that makes us conceive some ideas forcefully and vivaciously? In order to explain this phenomenon, there must be some basic habit or custom of human nature so that whenever any impression is presented to us, the mind is not only led to think of the idea or ideas associated with this impression, but also led to think of the idea with some of the force and vivacity of the impression. Somehow the strength of the impression is carried over to the idea whenever the idea is one that has usually been constantly conjoined with the impression in the past. Thus, our reasoning about what goes on in the world beyond what we immediately see is due not to any rational procedures but, instead, to some basic quirk of human nature that makes us believe that "instances of which we have no experience, must necessarily resemble those of which we have." We do not **reason** that this has to be the case; rather, we find that we are so constituted that we automatically believe

certain ideas, or conceive of them more forcefully than others. Thus:

> 'Tis not solely in poetry and music, we must follow our taste and sentiment, but likewise in philosophy. When I am convinced of any principle, 'tis only an idea, which strikes more strongly upon me. When I give the preference to one set of arguments above another, I do nothing but decide from my feelings concerning the superiority of their influence. Objects have no discoverable connection together; nor is it from any other principle but custom operating upon the imagination, that we can draw any inference from the appearance of one to the existence of another.

If our reasoning beyond our immediate impressions, and our conclusion that particular causes have particular effects, are the result of this habit or custom by which certain ideas are automatically brought to mind, and certain strong feelings attach to them, which constitute our belief, then what is our idea of necessity that leads us to say that certain objects are necessarily connected? It is not one of the features of our impressions, since we do not perceive any necessity or power that makes events occur; we only perceive the succession of events. But when we have seen several similar instances of successions of impressions, we then begin to consider the events as necessarily connected. Thus the idea of necessary connection seems to be involved with something that occurs with the **repetition of resembling events.**

But what happens when the same sequence of impressions occurs repeatedly? If the sequences are similar, Hume pointed out, then we perceive approximately the same thing each time. If we do not perceive the necessary connection between events in one case, we will not perceive it any more from a hundred, since, if the cases are resembling, then the same qualities must be present each time. We do not see anything new after watching the same process over and over again that we did not see the first time. But what happens is that we have a different mental attitude than we did before, and it is this different mental attitude that constitutes our belief that events are necessarily connected.

> For after we have observed the resemblance in a sufficient number of instances, we immediately feel a determination of the mind to pass from one object to its usual attendant, and to conceive it in a stronger light upon account of that relation. This determination is the only effect of the resemblance; and therefore must be the same with power or efficacy, whose idea is derived from the resemblance. The several instances of resembling conjunctions lead us into the notion of power and necessity. These instances are in themselves totally distinct from each other, and have no union but in the mind, which observes them, and collects their ideas. Necessity, then, is the effect of this observation, and is nothing but an internal impression of the mind, or a determination to carry our thoughts from one object to another.

Denial of Cause

Thus "necessity" is something that exists in the human mind, and not as a quality or feature of objects, as far as we can ever tell. The necessity that we believe exists, that a glass window must break when struck with a hammer, is only, Hume insisted, a determination of the mind to think of one idea when experiencing a certain impression, and to think of that idea most forcefully owing to its constant con-

junction with the present impression. If we examined our impression of the hammer, and of the glass, we would not find any part or feature of the impression that was the necessity of the glass breaking. The necessary connection between these two events, the hammer and the broken glass, lies in the way the mind thinks about them and not in the events themselves. Hume asserted that we have a propensity to join our internal experiences to the external ones that occur at the same time. Thus, although the necessity occurs only as a mental determination upon experiencing certain impressions, we have a tendency to locate this mental event in the observed events and to think of it as occurring there with the events, even though it is actually taking place in our minds.

As Hume well realized, this analysis of our idea of necessary connection, and the nature of our causal reasoning, might sound strange and incredible. "I doubt not but my sentiments will be treated by many as extravagant and ridiculous. What! the efficacy of causes lie in the determination of the mind!" But odd as this analysis may seem at first reading, Hume insisted, it is the only way of making sense of the reasoning that we carry on about our sense experience. If we honestly examine what we perceive, we do not experience any necessary connections between the various items of our sensory world. We find no reason why one event must follow another. But we do discover that we have a mental determination to think of certain ideas that have in the past been constantly conjoined to the present impressions, and to think of them in a forceful and lively manner. Hence the only actual connection that we ever discover between events is a **psychological** one, a way in which we think, and not a physical one, an actual link between one event and another. Thus, all that we mean by the notion of cause is "an object precedent and contiguous to another, and so united with it in the imagination, that the idea of the one determines the mind to form the idea of the other, and the impression of the one to form a more lively idea of the other."

Application of Hume's Theory to Science

As startling as Hume's claim may be, he maintained that this was perfectly **in keeping with the actual achievements of scientific investigation.** What scientists are finding out are the constant conjunctions of events that occur in human experience, and the expectations that people have as to what will happen next, in view of how they think about these events. Thus, the scientific "fact" that alcohol boils at 80° centigrade under normal atmospheric conditions means, according to Hume, that it has been observed many times that a certain impression, called "alcohol boiling," has been constantly conjoined with another impression, of a thermometer reading of 80° centigrade. No one actually sees the temperature cause the alcohol to boil. But because these two impressions have been conjoined over and over again in the past, we have a determination to think of one as soon as we either see or recall the other, and to expect that they will be conjoined again in the future. We can prove neither that they are necessarily connected nor that the conjunctions observed in the past

will continue into the future. But owing to our mental determinations and habits, the observed constant conjunctions of events are taken as guides for future expectations and predictions. Our scientific information does not tell us about any necessary relationships in nature but, rather, about some regular sequences that have been observed to occur over and over again in the past. On the basis of this information about observed regularities, we expect and predict that similar regularities will occur under similar circumstances in the future. The expectations and predictions are based not upon finding some hidden connections in nature, but only upon certain **psychological habits of human nature** that lead us to think of certain ideas in a more lively and forceful manner after having experienced their constant conjunction in the past.

One might protest that this account of what scientific discoveries are about may fit some of the more elementary laws that have been observed, but that present-day sciences are much more complicated than mere compilations of various sets of regularities observed in human experience. Contemporary followers of Hume, however, many of them quite prominent scientific theorists, maintain that in spite of manifold involvements of sciences like physics and chemistry, they essentially conform to Hume's claim. The systematic organization of these sciences consists only in discovering the most general regularities in human experience, from which others can be derived. But even such sciences as atomic and nuclear physics can be conceived of as the discovery of certain basic regularities in a body of knowledge, on the basis of which predictions can be made, presuming that our mental determination to believe that the future will resemble the past proves to be the case.

Hume's Complete Skepticism

David Hume, starting out from an examination of our sense experience and how we organize it, concluded with **complete skepticism about the possibility of human beings knowing anything about the universe.** All that we are aware of is a series of impressions with no necessary relations to each other. From these we derive our ideas, which we associate together not on the basis of any actual properties of the impressions but because of our mental customs or habits. When we search for some object outside of us to which our impressions belong, we find no impression of something called a "body," or a "material object." When we search inside ourselves for something that contains these impressions and ideas, something called a "self," we find no such item in our experience.

The Nature of Experience

If all of our information about the world is restricted to what we actually experience, then we must recognize that what we experience is only a sequence of impressions unrelated to each other and, as far as we can tell, not attached to, or belonging to, either external objects or an internal object called the "self," or "mind." Even the spirits that Berkeley had claimed were "experiencers" who possess the experiences cannot be known through experience. The only basis that

we have for ordering or interpreting the sequence of unrelated experiences is our mental habits or customs. There is one habit that leads us to ordering our experiences causally, to relating the constantly conjoined sequences. We have other habits, Hume claimed, that lead us to believe that there are external bodies; that lead us to believe that there is some sort of continuous thing inside us that holds our experiences together, called a "self"; and that lead us to believe that there is probably some sort of intelligent ordering to our experience. These habits or customs give a kind of order and coherence to the sequence of impressions and ideas in our minds. Some habits yield one kind of order; others, another. Sometimes these habits even give us conflicting orders to our experience and lead us to believe something on the basis of one habit that we disbelieve on the basis of another.

"Normal" and "Abnormal"

With such a picture of human nature, what is meant by being "reasonable" is operating on the basis of the set of mental habits that we call "normal." The person who believes that fire will burn, that two plus two equals four, that the sun will rise tomorrow, that there are external objects that exist even when not experienced, and that there is some sort of internal continuity to his/her experience, called "him/herself," has the "normal" set of beliefs and is considered a reasonable human being. Someone else, operating with different mental habits and customs, who thereby has a different set of beliefs, is "abnormal" and "unreasonable." But which of the two has true knowledge?

Which of the two believes something that actually corresponds to what is going on in the world?

The Compulsion to Believe

As Hume pointed out, we can never answer these questions. Any beliefs that we have only show what mental quirks we operate by. There is no justification for believing one thing rather than another, except that we find that we have a strong feeling or tendency to do so. When we try to find a reason for, or evidence for, believing something, we discover that we can find none and can only report that our minds work in the curious manner that we think that the belief is true. The further we explore the bases for belief, the more we find out about the irrational and unjustifiable foundation of our mental behavior. But at the same time, we discover that no matter how little basis we may have for our beliefs, we also cannot avoid believing. No matter how skeptical we may become about the merits of, or the foundations for, what human beings believe, at the same time, our human nature prevents us from giving up these beliefs. We may not be able to tell if they are true, and may even have some good reason to suspect that at least some of our beliefs are false. But all the same, we are compelled to believe certain things—and to act and talk and live on the basis of that belief.

Thus, in theory, Hume became a complete skeptic when he concluded that the information about the world that we derive from our experience is based only on a peculiar set of mental habits or customs to conceive of certain ideas in a forceful and lively manner. But Hume, like everyone else, found that when he stepped out of his philosophical study, he was compelled to be a believer in the uniformity of nature, in the existence of external objects, in the continuous existence of himself, and so on. Even his belief in his own philosophy he found to be indefensible by reason; but it was at the same time a theory about human nature that he could not avoid accepting when it struck most forcefully upon him. Thus he advocated his views as the feelings he had on those occasions. He concluded the first book of his *A Treatise of Human Nature* by saying:

If the reader finds himself in the same easy disposition, let him follow me in my future speculations. If not, let him follow his inclination, and wait the returns of application and good humor. The conduct of a man, who studies philosophy in this careless manner, is more truly skeptical than that of one, who feeling in himself an inclination to it, is yet so overwhelmed with doubts and scruples, as totally to reject it. A true skeptic will be diffident of his philosophical doubts, as well as of his philosophical conviction; and will never refuse any innocent satisfaction which offers itself, upon account of either of them.

Nor is it only proper we should in general indulge our inclination in the most elaborate philosophical researches, notwithstanding our skeptical principles, but also that we should yield to that propensity, which inclines us to be positive and certain in *particular points*, according to the light, in which we survey them in any *particular instant*. 'Tis easier to forbear all examination and enquiry, than to check ourselves in so natural a propensity, and guard against that assurance, which always arises from an exact and full survey of an object. On such an occasion we are apt not only to forget our skepticism, but even our modesty too; and to make use of such terms as these, *'tis evident, 'tis certain, 'tis undeniable;* which a due deference to the public ought, perhaps, to prevent.

A Matter of Mood

Thus, for Hume, even the philosophy one believes in is a matter of taste and of habits and customs. With his habits and customs, even though he knew that he could not justify them, these are the beliefs he held at various times. If others have the same feelings, all well and good; if not, there is nothing that one can do except to point out that other people operate according to different principles and habits and propensities. For Hume himself, in those moments when the doubts about the reliability of human beliefs were paramount, he was a skeptic. At other moments, he was a normal believer, like anybody else, when the force and vivacity of certain ideas were foremost in his mind. Hume's "gentle skepticism" consisted in doubting everything when he felt he must and in believing all sorts of things, including his own theory about the nature of human beliefs, when he had to.

Summary of the empirical theory of knowledge

Beginning with John Locke, those philosophers who developed theories of knowledge maintaining that all knowledge comes from sense experience were led gradually to Hume's conclusion. If our only source of information about the world is the impressions that we gain through our senses, then a great deal of what we think that we know turns out to be illusion. What we gain through our senses are qualities such as colors, sounds, shapes. As Berkeley showed, there is nothing in our sense experience that shows us that these qualities belong to any so-called "material," or "external," objects. All that we see are the qualities themselves. As Hume showed, our experience does not contain any necessary relations or connections between the various items of our sense experience. Any connections that we impose upon our experiences are due not to what we see but to our mental habits or propensities.

The empiricist critique of rationalism

The empiricists, beginning with a grave doubt about how much the rationalist philosophers claimed we could know, concluded with a theory that proposed grave doubts as to whether we could really know anything, in the strict sense, at all. In turning away from magnificent realms of perfect knowledge (e.g., those that Plato and Descartes had conceived) and looking instead at the more familiar world of ordinary experience for information as to what actually took place, the empiricists found that only a very limited amount of information was available through this source, and our assurance about it would always be far less than perfect.

But at the same time, the empiricists could always insist that limited as their picture of human knowledge might be, it at least could not be accused of being fanciful. Plato's world of ideas could not be pointed to, or demonstrated, in the ordinary world of affairs. But the ingredients and elements that the empiricists perceived were the actual features of everyone's experience. One might not be sure what it was an experience of, or whether its properties would persist into the future, but at least the items were open to everybody's inspection.

Our information about our experience may never be more than merely probable, but, the empiricist claims, this probable information has been, and probably will always be, more important and useful to mankind than all of the alleged certainties of the rationalists. For all their claims of absolute certitude, the rationalists have not been able to agree as to what it is that is so certain. Many of their claims have had to be retracted. But, the empiricists maintain, the more tentative claims made upon the limited basis of human sense experience and human fallibilities are more open to correction and development, and to the test of further experience. As evidence for the empiricist's viewpoint, one can point to the fact that the area of the most obvious improvement in human understanding over the last few centuries has not been in our grasp of the so-called "real" world of Plato or Descartes but in the empirical sciences. Fully realizing the limitations of such understanding, in terms of Hume's analysis of our empirical knowledge, one can still point out that even if such information is uncertain, dependent on our senses and psychological habits, it is still the information that has most affected human life. Those who have developed the extremely complex picture of the physical world, from the nuclear particles of the atom to the grand picture of the solar and stellar universes, from the protein molecule to the latest medical

and psychological theories about the behavior of human beings, have, by and large, been seeking not for absolutely certain knowledge about the real world but for uniformities and regularities in the world of appearances. No matter how little faith various rationalist philosophers may have had in the merits of sense information, one cannot avoid being impressed, possibly even overimpressed, with the achievements of empirical research in the last three hundred years.

Summary

We began this discussion by raising the question of what human beings could know with certainty. In spite of our ordinary assurance, we found that to some degree nearly everything we claim to know is open to doubt. For this reason, philosophers have tried to develop a theory of knowledge to account for the source, basis, and certainty of our knowledge. **Some philosophers—the rationalists—have tried to find a completely certain foundation for our knowledge, in terms of certain procedures of human reasoning.** They sought for knowledge in the strongest possible sense, i.e., information that under no circumstances could be false. Usually, the rationalists found that such knowledge could not be discovered in sense experience, but only in some mental realm.

As a reaction against such rationalist theories, another approach to the problem of knowledge was developed, that of the empiricists. Beginning with John Locke, empiricists hoped to discover **a basis for our knowledge in sense experience.** But from Locke to Berkeley to Hume, they found that our sense experience yielded far less information about the world than we might have hoped for. Hume indicated that a thorough examination of what we in fact know from sense experience would lead to a most depressing skepticism about the possibility of any genuine knowledge. If we can believe Hume, it is only the curious psychological makeup of human beings that leads to our views as to what occurs around us. What we consider our knowledge is only a manner of organizing the experience that is thrust upon us.

The devastating results of the English philosophical tradition in the eighteenth century, especially the work of Berkeley and Hume, have inspired philosophers either to develop a more perfect form of an empirical theory of knowledge—as John Stuart Mill tried to do in the nineteenth century and as modern positivists have tried to do in this century—or to find some way of modifying or circumventing the conclusions of Berkeley and Hume in order to work out some compromise theory of knowledge, admitting the claims of the empiricists, yet trying to salvage some of the elements of the rationalistic theory of knowledge. Beginning with the great German philosopher Immanuel Kant (who said that Hume awoke him from his dogmatic slumbers), thinkers have attempted in many ways to construct a theory of knowledge that would guarantee the certainty of some of what we know, while at the same time accepting the force of Hume's skepticism.

By and large, philosophers have found that when they try to account for the assurance that ordinary mortals have in what they know, their task is extremely difficult. The attempt to construct an adequate theory of knowledge raises some of the most difficult problems that human beings have had to cope with. Whether anyone has succeeded in settling all these problems is still a matter in dispute. Possibly the trouble, as Bertrand Russell once suggested, is that no one has succeeded in developing a theory that is **both credible and consistent.** Some of the more believable theories appear to contain grave inconsistencies, and some of the most logical theories appear to be unbelievable.

Suggested further reading

Classical Authors

Berkeley, George. *Three Dialogues Between Hylas and Philonous.* Berkeley's best presentation of his argument, in dialogue fashion, discussing all the possible objections that Berkeley could think of.

Descartes, René. *A Discourse on Method.* The method of Cartesian doubt.

———. *Meditations on First Philosophy.* The best presentation of Descartes's theory of knowledge.

Hume, David. *An Enquiry Concerning Human Understanding.* The best summary statement of his views.

———. *A Treatise of Human Nature.* The most complete statement of Hume's theory.

Kant, Immanuel. *Critique of Pure Reason.* Kant's attempt to show that empiricism can lead to a more positive theory of knowledge.

Locke, John. *An Essay Concerning Human Understanding.* Locke's famous statement of his empirical theory of knowledge.

Plato. *Meno.* A short dialogue setting forth the problem of knowledge.

———. *Republic.* The most extended discussion of the Platonic theory of knowledge.

Modern Authors

Allison, Henry. *Kant's Transcendental Idealism.* New Haven: Yale University Press, 1986.

Burnyeat, Myles, ed. *The Skeptical Tradition.* Berkeley, Calif.: University of California Press, 1983. Articles by experts on various skeptical challenges and how they were answered from ancient times to modern ones.

Curley, E. M. *Descartes Against the Skeptics.* Cambridge, Mass.: Harvard University Press, 1978. Examination of Descartes's arguments.

Ewing, A. C. *A Short Commentary on Kant's Critique of Pure Reason.* Chicago: University of Chicago, 1987.

Goldman, Alvin. *Epistemology and Cognition.* Cambridge, Mass.: Harvard University Press, 1986.

Montague, William P. *The Ways of Knowing.* London: Allen & Unwin, 1925. A survey of various problems about knowledge.

Moore, G. E. *Philosophical Studies.* London: Routledge, Kegan Paul, 1922. Contains criticisms of some of the major theories of knowledge, plus examination of the problems by a major twentieth-century philosopher.

Popkin, Richard H. *The History of Scepticism from Erasmus to Spinoza.* Berkeley, Calif.: University of California Press, 1979. A study of the impact of the revival of skepticism on modern philosophy.

Popkin, Richard H., ed. *The Philosophy of the 16th and 17th Centuries.* New York: The Free Press, 1966. Selections of the major texts on the theory of knowledge from the period.

Russell, Bertrand. *A History of Western Philosophy.* London: Allen & Unwin, 1968. A lively anecdotal history, with interesting criticisms of many of the major theories of knowledge.

Stroll, Avrum. *Surfaces.* Minneapolis: University of Minnesota, 1988.

Stroud, Barry. *Hume.* London: Routledge & Kegan Paul, 1981.

———. *The Significance of Philosophical Scepticism.* Oxford University Press, 1984.

CHAPTER SIX

Logic

The definition of "logic"

As we have tried to demonstrate throughout this book, reflection is the very stuff of which philosophy is made. A person who behaves mechanically or habitually in everyday life is not a philosopher; he/she does not philosophize until he/she begins to reflect or speculate about him/herself, about his/her place in the scheme of things, about experiences and relations to others. For almost every type of such reflection there is a corresponding branch of philosophy. For example, when one thinks about the nature of his/her conduct, he/she is engaged in ethical speculation; when one reflects on the nature of the universe, he/she is involved in metaphysics. **Logic may be defined as the branch of philosophy that reflects upon the nature of thinking itself.** It attempts to answer such questions as "What is correct reasoning?" "What distinguishes a good argument from a bad one?" "Are there any methods to detect fallacies in reasoning, and if so, what are they?" It can be seen from these remarks that **logic is perhaps the most fundamental branch of philosophy. All branches of philosophy employ thinking; whether this thinking is correct or not will depend upon whether it is in accord with the laws of logic;** hence the need for a thorough grounding in logic.

In defining logic as the branch of philosophy that deals with the nature of thinking, certain important qualifications must be made. We have *not* intended to imply that logic is a branch of psychology or that logic deals with *all* types of thinking. **Logic differs from psychology in that it does not deal with all types of thinking, such as learning, remembering, daydreaming, supposing, and so forth, but only with that type of thinking called "reasoning."** Furthermore, while the psychologist is concerned with the mental processes of the thinker, the logician's interest is in the reasoning itself; he/she is concerned not with why people think in certain ways but with the formulation of rules that will enable us to test whether any particular piece of reasoning is coherent and consistent, i.e., whether it is **logical.**

In order to illustrate how reasoning differs from other types of thinking, such as remembering or daydreaming, it will be useful here to discuss an actual example.

Suppose I have agreed to meet a friend one hour hence at a place that is three miles away. Upon reflection I wonder whether I can be at the designated place in time for our appointment. I have only two means of getting there, since I do not own a car: either I must walk or I must take a bus. Now, as a result of previous military service, I know that I can walk at a maximum average speed of two and a half miles per hour. But since my destination is three miles away and since I must be there in exactly one hour, I cannot reach it in time by walking. Therefore, if I am to reach it on time, I will have to do it by bus. The next bus will pass my present location in fifteen minutes and then will take another thirty minutes to travel to the place where I am to meet my friend. Thus I conclude that I can keep my appointment by taking the bus.

Let us consider this example in closer detail in order to show why it is an instance of reasoning. To begin with, we have a certain problem: Can I arrive at the place of my appointment within an hour, given the means of transportation that are available? I first raise the question of whether I can keep the appointment on time by walking. I decide I cannot, and the reasons why I cannot are: the distance is three miles; I must be there in an hour; and I can walk only at a speed of two and a half miles per hour. In giving these reasons, I am supplying evidence for my conclusion that I cannot arrive there on time by walking. On the other hand, in supplying the following reasons— a bus will pass in fifteen minutes; it will take thirty minutes to arrive at the appointed place; and the appointment is scheduled for an hour hence—I am providing evidence for the conclusion that I can keep the appointment by taking the bus.

What is characteristic of reasoning, as may be inferred from the word itself, is that we produce reasons as evidence for a certain conclusion we wish to establish. As the above example makes clear, **reasoning is closely connected with inferring. The reasons we provide allow us to infer a certain conclusion.** If true, they serve the function of providing **evidence** for the truth of the conclusion. **Now logic is the discipline that attempts to distinguish bad reasoning from good reasoning, or (what is equivalent) good inferences from bad ones.** It attempts to formulate rules that can tell us whether the reasons we have given are "good" reasons for inferring the conclusion we wish to establish. Logic might be defined, without too great distortion, as **the science of "good reasons."**

It should be noted that the reasons we give in support of a conclusion are always expressed in **language**. Because this is so, **logic has sometimes been characterized as a discipline that deals with the relations between sentences, or "propositions," as the logician prefers to call them, since he/she is concerned not with interrogative or exclamatory sentences but only with those that make assertions. Inference is considered to be a process that allows us to establish the truth of a certain proposition, called the "conclusion" of an argument, from the truth of other propositions that constitute the evidence for the conclusion.** On this interpretation, one might define **logic as the branch of philosophy that attempts to determine when a given proposition or a group of propositions permits us correctly to infer some other proposition.**

Deductive and inductive logic

Philosophers have traditionally divided logic into two branches. These are called "deductive logic" and "inductive logic," respectively. Both branches are concerned with the rules for correct reasoning, or correct "argumentation," as philosophers frequently say. Deductive logic deals with reasoning that attempts to establish **conclusive inferences. To say that an inference is "conclusive" means that if the reasons given are true, then it will be impossible for the inference based upon these reasons to be false.** Such reasoning is called **"valid"** reasoning. Deductive logic is thus concerned with the **rules for determining when an argument is valid.**

Not all reasoning in daily life attempts to provide conclusive evidence for the truth of a given conclusion. Sometimes, by the very nature of the case, conclusive evidence cannot be produced. But very often for practical purposes we do not need conclusive evidence. We merely want the evidence to show that the conclusion we have arrived at is **well founded,** that it is more **probable** than some other conclusion we might have reached. It is easy to imagine situations in which it is important to make a decision even where conclusive information is not available. For instance, if we are the judge in a murder trial, we may wish to know whether a conclusion we have arrived at is **reliably inferred from whatever evidence we have on hand. Inductive logic** deals with cases such as these; it is not concerned with the rules for correct reasoning in the sense of "valid," or conclusive, reasoning; but rather, **it is concerned with the soundness of those inferences for which the evidence is not conclusive.** In particular, while deductive logic is concerned with inferences from the general to the particular (i.e.,

from assertions about the whole of a class of things to assertions about some of them), inductive logic is concerned with inferences from the particular to the general, and the inference of a general proposition from particular assertions can never be conclusive. Perhaps an example or two will help make the distinction somewhat clearer.

Suppose one wishes to establish the truth of the sentence "All Europeans are mortal." He/she can do this in two different ways: either by deductive reasoning or by inductive reasoning. Let us illustrate the former technique first. One may assert, as reasons in support of the above sentence, that the following statements are true: (a) "All Europeans are human beings," and (b) "All human beings are mortal." Now if both of these sentences are true, then it will be impossible for the sentence "All Europeans are mortal" to be false. In short, the truth of the sentences (a) and (b) provides conclusive evidence for the truth of the sentence "All Europeans are mortal." Here we have an inference from an assertion about **all** human beings to an assertion about **some** human beings, i.e., Europeans, and this, therefore, is an example of the use of **deductive reasoning.**

On the other hand, one may not believe that the sentence "All human beings are mortal" is true. After all, one could know this with certainty only after every human being had died—a difficult matter if one includes him/herself among the class of humans. So, in order to establish the truth of "All Europeans are mortal," one may wish to adopt a different procedure. One may wish to use as evidence propositions that are known to be true and to argue from the particular to the general. He/she may say (a) "Every European born before 1830 has died." (b) "Europeans are still dying." The truth of (a) and (b) makes it probable that "All Europeans are mortal" is true; but unlike the reasons provided in the deductive argument above, the truth of these reasons does not make it *certain* that all Europeans are mortal. It is still possible that (a) and (b) may both be true, and yet that someone alive today or who may be born in the future will be immortal. Hence, even though our reasoning is sound, and even though we have correctly inferred our conclusion from the evidence we have, it is possible (although highly improbable) that the conclusion may be found to be false at some future time. **Inductive logic is thus concerned not with valid inferences but with inferences that are probable, given as evidence the truth of certain propositions upon which they are based.**

Inductive logic has one of its most important uses in connection with science. The scientist employs deductive methods, and even intuitive guesses, in order to investigate the world, but it is inductive logic that is his/her most important tool. Some writers have in fact spoken of "scientific method" and "inductive logic" as if they were synonyms—a mistake, but one that is not far from the truth. Let us describe some of the major steps in scientific activity in order to show why inductive logic is essential to scientific inquiry.

The most rudimentary stage of scientific investigation consists of the description of individual happenings and occurrences. For example, Galileo described the rate at which a particular body accelerated when he dropped it. He then dropped other bodies and in each case measured their rate of acceleration. If we were to reconstruct his activity, we might say that he arrived at a number of true individual statements describing the rate at which particular bodies accelerated. He noticed, for instance, that body A when dropped accelerated at a rate of 32 feet per second per second; body B fell with the same acceleration, so did body C, and so forth. Now from the truth of such individual, or particular, propositions (i.e., propositions describing particular events) he inferred a general truth of nature, sometimes called a **"law of nature."** He inferred that *all* bodies when dropped will fall with an acceleration of 32 feet per second per second. From the standpoint of inductive logic, we might say that the individual propositions provided him with sound reasons for inferring the general conclusion that all bodies fall with a certain degree of acceleration.

Put most generally, we may say that **inductive logic is a theory about what reasons provide evidence for a given conclusion's truth when the reasons in question are not conclusive ones.** In practice, inductive logic thus coincides with what has been called **"probability theory."** Inductive logic is concerned with the **relation between the evidence and a conclusion drawn from the evidence.** The main question that such a discipline is concerned with is that which asks "When does the evidence make the truth of the conclusion more probable than not?"—or more exactly, "What is the probability that the conclusion is true, given the evidence in question?"

Because of the highly intricate nature of probability theory and of statistical analysis (which is based upon probability theory), in this section we shall confine our discussion of logic to **deductive logic.** It should be stressed before so doing, however, that logic in recent years has been one of the most actively pursued studies in the whole area of philosophy, and therefore, even our discussion of deductive logic alone must be severely limited.

Deductive logic: the syllogism

In this section, we cannot study all types of deductive reasoning. In order to introduce the reader to the study of deductive logic, we shall therefore restrict our discussion to one of the most famous types of deductive reasoning: **the syllogism.** Roughly, **a syllogism may be defined as an argument that contains two premises and a conclusion**—but we hasten to add that this is not an exact definition. Since the exact definition can be understood only after some technical terms have been defined, we shall postpone giving such a definition. Let us now consider some of these technical terms in order to begin a discussion of the theory of the syllogism.

The terminology of logic

Every syllogism must be composed of three propositions—no more and no less. The proposition that one is trying to prove or establish is called the **"conclusion"** of the argument, while the other two propositions provide reasons for asserting that the conclusion is true. These propositions are called the **"premises"** of the argument. Consider the following examples of a syllogism:

(a) All dogs are vertebrates.
(b) All vertebrates are animals.
(c) All dogs are animals.

Propositions (a) and (b) are the **premises** of this syllogistic argument, while proposition (c) is its **conclusion**. It should be noticed that the reasons in this case are **conclusive,** i.e., since they are true, it will be impossible for the conclusion to be false. In such a case, we say that the premises **imply** the conclusion, or equivalently, that the conclusion **follows from** the premises. What has been called "the theory of the syllogism" is the system of rules that enables us to tell when syllogistic arguments are such that their premises imply the conclusion, and when they do not. In short, by telling us which arguments are valid and which are not, the theory of the syllogism provides us with a technique for distinguishing good from bad reasoning.

It should also be noticed that each of the propositions that make up a syllogism contains four parts. For example, proposition (a) is composed of four words, "all," "dogs," "are," and "vertebrates." Proposition (b) is similarly composed of four parts, the words "all," "vertebrates," "are," and "animals." And likewise for proposition (c). Every syllogism must be composed of propositions having these four elements; they determine what is called the "standard form" of a syllogistic sentence. This form must be the following: The proposition must begin with what is called a **"quantifier."** The word "all" plays the role of a quantifier in each of the propositions in the syllogism we have examined above. Secondly, the proposition must contain a word which is its

subject. This is called the **"subject term."** The word "dogs" is the subject term of proposition (*a*). Thirdly, the proposition must contain a **"predicate term"**; in this case the word "vertebrate" is the **predicate.** And finally, it must contain a word that **connects or relates subject to predicate,** and this word is called the **"copula."** The word "are" performs this role in our sample syllogism above. In short, **a syllogism must contain exactly three propositions, all of which are in standard form, i.e., they must have a quantifier, a subject term, a predicate term, and a copula.**

A word of explanation about the use of these technical terms may assist the reader. **The subject term refers to that thing or entity about which we assert something. The predicate term designates that which is asserted of the subject. The copula will always take some form of the verb "to be"**—usually it will be either "are" or "is." **The function of the quantifier is to indicate the extent to which we refer to the members denoted by the subject term.** The usual word that is employed is "all," "some," "none," "no," or "nothing."

Throughout this section, in order to assist readers, we shall provide exercises that will serve as a check on their understanding of the subject matter. The answers to the exercises will be found at the end of this chapter. See pages 269–73.

EXERCISE 1

Identify the subject term, predicate term, copula, and quantifiers (if any):

1. Some mad dogs are happily married.
2. All bats are members of the class of rodents.
3. James is wicked.
4. Horses are man's best friend.
5. Some tables are not mahogany.
6. Nothing green is in the room.

Affirmative and negative propositions

In part depending upon the purpose for which they are used, and in part depending upon their grammatical structure, the sentences of the English language may be divided into various classes. Let us begin with a classification of these sentences that depends upon their grammatical form. We can thus distinguish (*a*) **declarative or indicative sentences,** (*b*) **interrogative sentences,** (*c*) **imperative sentences,** and (*d*) **optative sentences** from one another. If we turn to the uses of these sentences, we can distinguish (*a*) **assertions,** (*b*) **questions,** (*c*) **commands,** and (*d*) **wishes** from one another. Since it would take us too far astray to attempt to define the above uses of language precisely, or to attempt to delineate the grammatical structure of such sentences exactly, we shall here characterize them roughly. The point of these remarks is that, as we have already mentioned, **logic deals only with declarative sentences, i.e., with those types of sentences that are used for the purpose of making assertions.**

The reason why logic does not deal with all of the types of sentences above is that **only declarative sentences, which are used to make assertions about the world, can be either true or false.** An interrogative sentence is used to ask a question. If I say "Is the door open?" I am not making any claim about the door. I am not asserting or stating that it is open. As a result, what I say cannot be either true or false. For a sentence to be either true or false, it must make some claim about the world. It must assert that something is the case. For instance, if I say "There are twelve cars in the garage," I am making a claim about the number of cars in the garage. My sentence is thus either true or false. It is true if, and only if, there are twelve cars in the garage; otherwise, it is false (i.e., if there are either less than or more than twelve cars in the garage). Similarly, an imperative sentence is generally used for the purpose of issuing a command. If I say "Right face!" this utterance is neither true nor false. I am not making an assertion such as "He always obeys my commands," but rather, I am issuing a command. A command may either be followed or not followed; but whether it is followed or not, we do not say that a command is true or false, since it makes no declaration about the entities in the world. An optative sentence is a sentence used for the purpose of expressing a wish. If I say "Oh, would I were king!" I am again not making a statement such as "I am king." I am merely expressing the hope that I might become king, and this is different from asserting that I am or that I will be king.

Logic thus deals only with declarative sentences, i.e., sentences used for the purpose of making some claim or assertion about the world. This is why the logician prefers to use the term **"proposition,"** to distinguish such sentences from those he/she is not concerned with. In the case of arguments of a syllogistic type, such declarative sentences or propositions must always be of the subject-predicate form.

They must always be such that the predicate asserts something of the subject. Thus if I say "The table is brown," I am asserting that the color "brown" belongs to the thing called "the table." Or again, if I say "All cats are mammals," I am asserting that the property of being mammalian belongs to each and every cat.

The reason why logic deals only with declarative sentences is clear if one reflects upon the remarks we made earlier about the nature of logic. We pointed out that logic deals with correct reasoning. Correctness of reasoning is closely connected with truth and falsity, although it is not to be identified with them. The connection is this: **When one reasons correctly, if the premises of his/her argument are true, it will be impossible for the conclusion to be false.** Since other types of sentences are not capable of being either true or false, it would be impossible to define correct reasoning in relation to the truth of such sentences; and this is why logic restricts itself to those sentences that are used to make assertions.

Declarative or assertive sentences or propositions may be further divided into those in which the predicate affirms something of the subject, and into those in which the predicate **denies** something of the subject. We call the former "affirmative" and the latter "negative." An example of an affirmative proposition is "All lions are ferocious." The presence of a word like "no" or "none" or "not" or "nothing" indicates that the proposition is negative, as in "No teachers are wealthy" or "Some teachers are not wealthy," and so on.

When we describe a proposition as "affirmative" or "negative," we are speaking of the **"quality"** of the proposition. We shall see in the next section that quality must be distinguished from the "quantity" of a proposition.

Sometimes it is difficult to determine whether a proposition is affirmative or negative. The two propositions "Some Moslems are nondrinkers" and "Some Moslems are not drinkers" are equivalent in meaning; they both say that part of the class of Moslems is excluded from the class of those who drink. But the former is affirmative: it asserts that some Moslems belong to the class of nondrinkers; while the latter is negative: it denies that some Moslems belong to the class of drinkers. In the first case, the word "non" modifies the predicate; in the second case, the word "not" modifies the copula. Thus, from the fact that an adjective or noun is modified by such a word as "non," we cannot always infer that the proposition in question is negative. What determines a proposition to be negative is whether the word "not" or "no" modifies the copula. When it does, it is negative. Thus, such a proposition as "No dogs are feline" is negative because it denies that feline qualities can be asserted to dogs.

EXERCISE 2

Determine whether the following propositions are affirmative or negative:

1. James is very unhappy.
2. Lions are not untrustworthy.
3. She was not disinclined to come.
4. None but the lonely heart is filled with sadness.
5. Nothing tried, nothing gained.
6. He has been unwell for months now.
7. Some philosophers are intuitive.
8. No nonaddicts can understand the problem.
9. All non-S are non-P.
10. All except women may attend.

Universal, particular, and singular propositions

We have just pointed out that declarative sentences may be classified as either negative or affirmative. Such a classification is referred to by logicians as one of "quality." But there is another important classification of such sentences—into those that are **"universal," "particular,"** or **"singular."** This distinction is termed one of **"quantity."**

Whether a proposition is universal, particular, or singular depends upon whether we are speaking about *all* of the entities referred to by the subject term, about *some* of them only, or about a *single* individual. If I say "All film stars are wealthy," I am uttering a sentence whose subject term refers to each and every film star. This is why we say such a sentence is "universal" in scope. On the other hand, if I qualify my remarks by saying that "Some film stars are wealthy," I am not necessarily referring to each and every film star. I am referring to a certain set or group of them—this is why we term such a proposition as "particular." On the other hand, if I say "Paul Newman is wealthy," I am referring to one and only one person, and thus my judgment is said to be "singular."

In the theory of the syllogism, for purposes which we shall explain immediately, **singular propositions are always interpreted as "universal" ones.** This achieves considerable theoretical simplification, since it reduces the number of classifications of sentences according to their "quantity" to two: those that are universal and those that are particular. Singular propositions are regarded as universal ones for two reasons. First, because in such a proposition as "Paul Newman is wealthy," we are referring to *all* of Mr. Newman, not merely to a part of him. This being characteristic of universal propositions as well, it is natural to designate singular propositions as "universal." Secondly, singular propositions are regarded as universal for another reason. Syllogistic logic deals with the relations between classes of things. When I say that "All men are mortal," the terms "men" and "mortal" refer to classes of entities—the class of men and the class of mortals. On the class interpretation of the proposition, I am asserting that the class of men is included within the class of mortals. I am thus specifying a relation between the two classes, the relation of "being included within." On the other hand, when I say "Jack is an American," I am ordinarily suggesting that Jack is a citizen of the United States or, more accurately, a member of a certain group. The relation of being a member of a class is different from the relation of one class being included within another. Syllogistic logic would become much more complicated if it had to distinguish between such relations. In order, therefore, to deal with singular propositions, this sort of logical system interprets singular propositions as universal ones. Such a proposition as "Jack is an American" can be interpreted as saying that a class containing only one member, namely Jack, is included within the class of Americans.

When the subject class has no quantifier,

as in "Tenors love spaghetti," we are uncertain sometimes whether the proposition is to be interpreted as being universal or particular. **The rule in such cases is that "all" is intended unless "some" is clearly indicated.** Hence "Tenors love spaghetti" is to be interpreted as "All tenors love spaghetti." On the other hand, such a proposition as "Men have climbed Mount Everest" is to be interpreted to mean "Some men have climbed Mount Everest" rather than "All men have climbed Mount Everest."

EXERCISE 3

Determine whether the following propositions are universal or particular:

1. Fish are mammals.
2. Some dragons are fierce.
3. This table is brown.
4. That system is useless.
5. They are crazy.
6. Hardworking students are successful.
7. Albert Einstein was a genius.
8. Those tins seem heavy.
9. That bottle of aspirin is not full.
10. No human beings are infallible.
11. Some cats are not wise.
12. Men have climbed Mount Everest.
13. All police are not cruel.
14. All golfers are wealthy.
15. Some babies are small.

The four standard propositions of logic

According to the logical system we are now considering, **every declarative sentence will be either universal or particular, and either**

affirmative or negative. All syllogistic reasoning or argumentation will thus involve the use of these types of propositions. If we combine them in various ways, we can see that **there are four, and only four, possible types of propositions dealt with by logic.** It is assumed by logicians that much of the discourse in a natural language, such as English, can be translated into one or another of the four propositions of syllogistic logic. It is thus assumed that the type of logic we are considering is capable of dealing with numerous cases of reasoning that one might encounter in his everyday activities. The four types of proposition are:

(*a*) Those that are **universal and affirmative.**

(*b*) Those that are **universal and negative.**

(*c*) Those that are **particular and affirmative.**

(*d*) Those that are **particular and negative.**

(It will be recalled that singular propositions are interpreted as universal ones in this schema.)

Traditionally, logicians have given names to each type of proposition for purposes of convenience in discussing them. The names are the vowels **"A," "E," "I,"** and **"O."** Thus, **universal-affirmative propositions are called "A propositions"** (the name being derived from the initial letter of the Latin word *affirmo,* meaning "I assert"); **universal-negative propositions are termed "E propositions"** (from the initial vowel in *nego,* "I deny"); **particular-affirmative propositions are designated by the letter "I"** (from the second vowel of *affirmo*); while **particular-negative propositions** are de-

noted by the letter "O" (from the last vowel in *nego*). **The affirmative forms are A and I; the negative forms are E and O; the universal forms are A and E; the particular forms are I and O.**

EXERCISE 4

Determine whether the following propositions are to be designated as "A," "E," "I," "O," and also determine their quantity and quality, i.e., whether they are universal and affirmative, etc.:

1. No Americans are explorers.
2. All doctors are interested in medicine.
3. Some lawyers are golfers.
4. Muhammad Ali is no longer heavyweight champion.
5. Martin Luther King was a champion of freedom.
6. Some conductors are nonluminous.
7. All football players are excluded from the class of authors.
8. Some tennis players are not authors.
9. That paper was well read.
10. Each and every lion is ferocious.

The distribution of terms

As we shall show later, it is possible to develop a set of rules that enable the student, in a very simple way, to determine whether a syllogistic argument is valid or invalid. One of the basic notions involved in the statement of such rules is the notion of "distribution." It is very important, therefore, to understand the following section if the student wishes to be able to apply correctly the rules we shall develop later.

Distribution is a very simple idea. We say that **a term is distributed when the term refers to all the members of the class denoted by the term.** For example, if I say "All Englishmen are insane," the term "Englishmen" is distributed because I have referred to *all* Englishmen. On the other hand, if I say "Some Englishmen are wise," the term "Englishmen" is not distributed, since I am referring only to part of the class of Englishmen. Let us now see how all the A, E, I, O propositions distribute their terms. Since each of these propositions contains two terms, a subject term and a predicate term, we shall have to determine for each type of proposition whether one or none of its terms is distributed, or whether both are.

Distribution of Terms in the "A" Proposition

In an A proposition (i.e., a universal proposition such as "All lions are carnivorous"), the subject term is obviously distributed, since we are referring to *all* lions. But the predicate term is not distributed. We are not referring to all carnivorous things when we say that "All lions are carnivorous." We are merely saying that the class of lions is included in the class of carnivorous things; but we are not speaking about *all* carnivorous things, and hence the predicate term is not distributed. This can be seen if we were to reverse the subject and predicate terms in a true A proposition. If I say "All lions are carnivorous," the proposition is true; but, on the other hand, if I say "All carnivorous things are lions," the proposition is false. This shows us that we were not referring to all carnivores in the proposition "All lions are carnivorous." For this reason, as we have said, the predicate term is not distributed.

Distribution of Terms in the "E" Proposition

Both the subject and predicate terms are distributed in the E proposition (a universal-negative proposition, e.g., "No dwarfs are blond"). Here we are saying that the class of dwarfs is entirely excluded from the class of blonds. We are thus referring to all dwarfs and to all blonds and are saying that both classes are disjoint.

Distribution of Terms in the "I" Proposition

Both the subject and predicate are undistributed in the I proposition (i.e., a particular-affirmative proposition: "Some birds are black"). Here we are asserting that the class of birds and the class of black things have a common member. But we are not speaking about *all* birds and about *all* black things, but only about some in each class. Hence both subject and predicate are undistributed.

Distribution of Terms in the "O" Proposition

In the O proposition (i.e., a particular-negative proposition: "Some paths are not steep"), we find the subject term to be undistributed and the predicate term to be distributed. It is easy to see that the subject term is undistributed, since it refers merely to part of a class; but why is the predicate term distributed? This is because we are saying that some paths are excluded from the entire class of steep things. In short, we are speaking about the whole class of steep things, and thus the predicate term is distributed.

We may summarize our results as follows:

Both universal propositions distribute their subject terms, but the A proposition does not distribute its predicate, although the E proposition does. Both particular propositions do not distribute their subject terms, and the I proposition does not distribute its predicate, although the E proposition does. The following diagram may help to make this somewhat easier to understand:

Distribution of terms in A, E, I, O propositions

Type of proposition	Subject term	Predicate term
A	Distrib.	Undist.
E	Distrib.	Distrib.
I	Undist.	Undist.
O	Undist.	Distrib.

EXERCISE 5

Indicate which terms are distributed and which are undistributed in the following examples:

1. All Americans are good swimmers.
2. No conductors are overpaid.
3. Some swans are not black.
4. Some swans are beautiful.
5. Jane is a model.
6. All Iowans are nonfarmers.
7. Some Nevadans are not farmers.

Middle, major, and minor terms

In order to comprehend the rules for determining when a syllogism is valid, one must understand three pieces of logical terminology: (*a*) the distinction between affirmative and negative propositions, (*b*) the meaning of the term "distribution," and (*c*) what is meant by the "middle term," "major term," and "minor term" of an argument. We have already, in the preceding sections, discussed (*a*) and (*b*). We shall therefore now proceed to explain (*c*), i.e., what is meant by **"middle term," "minor term,"** and **"major term."** After that we shall be in a position to lay down the rules for assessing the validity or invalidity of a syllogistic argument.

As we explained near the beginning of this chapter, a syllogism can roughly be characterized as an argument containing two premises and a conclusion. We are now prepared to make this characterization more exact, and in so doing, we shall also be explaining what such terms as "minor term," "major term," and "middle term" mean. Since a syllogism contains two premises and a conclusion, it is composed of three propositions of the subject-predicate form. It thus contains six terms, i.e., three subject terms, three predicate terms. Consider the following syllogism as an example:

All idiots are happy.
All football players are idiots.
Therefore, all football players are happy.

It will be noticed that there are three *different* terms among the six terms that occur in the three propositions making up the argument. Each of the three different terms (i.e., "idiots," "happy," "football players") occurs twice. **Now by the "middle term" we mean the term that appears in both premises. The middle term does not appear in the conclusion, since each term is used twice and only twice.** In the foregoing example, the word "idiots" is the middle term, since it occurs in both premises. **By the "major** term" we mean the term that occurs as the **predicate of the conclusion.** The major term is also found in the first premise of our sample argument. In the example above, the word "happy" is the major term. **The phrase "major term" is applied to the predicate of the conclusion, since it is the term designating the class with the largest extension.** In the argument above, we are saying that the class of football players is included in the class of idiots; the class of idiots is included in the class of happy people; hence the class of football players is included in the class of happy people. The word "happy" thus refers to the largest class, and this is why the predicate of the conclusion is called the "major term." **The subject of the conclusion, on the other hand, is called**

the **"minor term."** The minor term also occurs, it will be noticed, once in the premises, as well as being the subject of the conclusion. In the example we have selected, the term "football players" is the minor term.

As a further matter of terminology, we should mention that the **major premise is that premise which contains the major term,** while the **minor premise contains the minor terms.** Each premise, of course, contains the **middle term.**

It is frequently convenient for purposes of exposition to let certain letters stand for the corresponding terms. Traditionally, logicians have designated the letter "M" to stand for the middle term, "S" for the minor term, and "P" for the major term. Our argument could thus be symbolized, using the above letters, as follows:

All idiots are happy.
(All   M   are   P   )
All football players are idiots.
(All   S   are   M   )
Therefore, All football players are happy.
All   S   are   P   )
The form of the argument put symbolically is:
All M are P
All S are M
———————
Therefore, All S are P

EXERCISE 6

Identify the middle, major, and minor terms of the following syllogisms; also, designate the premises as major and minor:

1. All men are fallible.
   I am a man.
   Therefore, I am fallible.

2. Some politicians are ignoble.
   No one who is ignoble is wise.
   Some politicians are not wise.
3. All singers are temperamental.
   No truck drivers are temperamental.
   No singers are truck drivers.
4. All S is M.
   No M is P.
   No S is P.

Rules for determining validity and invalidity

We are now ready to state and discuss the rules for determining when a syllogistic argument is valid or invalid. It will be understood, of course, that no argument can be both invalid and valid. If it is valid, then it cannot be invalid, and conversely. The rules we are about to lay down are such that if one cannot prove by them that an argument is invalid, then he/she can assume that the argument is valid. In short, **if a syllogistic argument does not violate any of the five rules we are about to give, it is a valid syllogism. If it violates any of the rules, then it is invalid.**

These rules can be divided into two sets: those that refer to the **quantity** of a proposition (i.e., **rules of distribution**) and those that refer to the **quality** of a proposition (i.e., whether it is **affirmative or negative**).

Rules of quantity
Rule 1: The middle term must be distributed at least once.
Rule 2: If a term is not distributed in the premises, it must not be distributed in the conclusion.

Rules of quality
Rule 3: No conclusion can follow from two negative premises.
Rule 4: If either premise is negative, the conclusion must be negative.
Rule 5: A negative conclusion cannot follow from two affirmative premises.

Before discussing each of the above rules, it is important to mention to the reader that **the above rules apply only to syllogistic arguments.** Therefore, before applying the rules to an argument, one must first check to make sure that the argument is of the syllogistic form or can be expressed in syllogistic form (i.e., it must have two premises and a conclusion, three and only three terms, each of which is employed twice in the argument; and finally, the middle term must appear in both premises). If an argument satisfies the above conditions, then one can apply the five rules we have stated in order to determine whether such reasoning is valid or invalid.

We turn now to a detailed discussion of the rules.

RULE 1:   **The middle term must be distributed at least once.**

The following syllogism violates the rule:

All men are human beings.
All women are human beings.
Therefore, all women are men.

The middle term in the above argument is "human beings." Since it is the predicate term in both premises, and since both premises are A propositions, neither premise distributes its predicate. Thus the middle term is undistributed. The error or fallacy in the argument is this: even though it is true that all men are human beings and that all women are human beings, it does not follow that they cannot both belong to the same class, i.e., human beings, and yet be different from each other, since at no stage does the syllogism assert that either men or women constitute **the whole class** of human beings. In short, **the two premises are not connected**

by the middle term. This fallacy is called the **"fallacy of the undistributed middle."**

At this point, it is necessary to mention explicitly a distinction we hinted at earlier. It is very important to distinguish between the **validity of an argument** and the **truth or falsity of the premises and conclusion of the argument.** It is possible for the premises of an argument to be true (as in the above example) and yet for the argument to be invalid. Or again, all the premises of an argument may be false, and yet the argument may be valid. Validity depends upon *how* one reasons. To say that reasoning is valid is not to say that the premises one employs are true. **It is to say that if they are true, and if one's reasoning is valid, it will be impossible for the conclusion to be false.** The following examples will illustrate the distinction between validity and truth:

If   1 is greater than 2, and
If   2 is greater than 3,
Then 1 is greater than 3.

It will be noted that both premises and the conclusion are false; yet the argument is valid; for *if* the premises were true, it would be impossible for the conclusion to be false, as can be seen from the following example:

If   3 is greater than 2, and
If   2 is greater than 1,
Then 3 is greater than 1.

On the other hand, it is important for the reader also to realize that simply because an argument has true premises and even a true conclusion, it may not embody valid reasoning.

We cite here an example of an argument violating Rule 1 in which both premises and the conclusion are true. But since the argument does not distribute its middle term, it is invalid:

All Texans are mortal
All Americans are mortal.
Therefore, all Texans are Americans.

RULE 2:   **If a term is not distributed in the premises, it must not be distributed in the conclusion.**

The following syllogism violates this rule:

All cats are mammals.
No dogs are cats.
Therefore, no dogs are mammals.

The fallacy involved in the violation of this rule is sometimes called **"illicit process,"** or **"illicit distribution."** It should be noted that the term "mammals" is distributed in the conclusion but not in the major premise. This is because the major premise is an A proposition and does not distribute its predicate; but the conclusion is an E proposition, which does. **The error of "illicit process" is one in which the conclusion attempts to give us more information than is contained in the premises.** The premises do not tell us about *all* mammals, but the conclusion does. The argument would be valid if, and only if, we could infer that *all* mammals are cats; but this statement goes beyond our information, which is merely that all cats are mammals.

RULE 3:   **No conclusion can follow from two negative premises.**

The following syllogism violates this rule:

No dogs are cold-blooded.
No cold-blooded things are capable of barking.
Therefore, no dogs are capable of barking.

When we have two negative premises, we fail to establish any connection between the terms of the argument. For example, in order to show that no dogs are capable of barking, we have to show that dogs belong to the class of cold-blooded things; but this would be to assert an affirmative premise, i.e., All dogs are cold-blooded—which contradicts the information given us in the premises. Hence, no conclusion follows.

RULE 4: **If either premise is negative, the conclusion must be negative.**

The following syllogism violates this rule:

All headhunters are primitives.
Some Australians are not primitives.
Therefore, some Australians are headhunters.

It should be noted that the above argument satisfies all the other rules we have discussed. The middle term is distributed; no term is distributed in the conclusion, which is not distributed in the premises; and at least one premise is affirmative. Nevertheless, the argument is invalid, since the premises are true and the conclusion is false. The fallacy consists in inferring that because some Australians are excluded from a certain group, some must belong to the group. This does not follow, **since even though we only assert that some are excluded from a group, all may be.**

RULE 5: **A negative conclusion does not follow from two affirmative premises.**

The following syllogism violates this rule:

All men are mortals.
All mortals are fallible.
Therefore, some fallible things are not men.

Again, this syllogism satisfies the previous rules. It distributes the middle term, "mortals," and it does not contain a distributed term in the conclusion that is undistributed in the premises. Likewise, it violates neither of the two rules of quality we have just discussed. **But again, it commits a fallacy, since we go beyond the information given us when we infer that some fallible things are not men.** We know, on the basis of the two premises, that all men are fallible. But we cannot conclusively infer *either* that there are some fallible things that are not men, or that there are not some fallible things that are not men.

EXERCISE 7

Determine whether the following syllogisms are valid or invalid. If invalid, state the fallacy they commit.

1. All accountants are tennis players.
   All youngsters are tennis players.
   All accountants are youngsters.
2. All plants are substances.
   All animals are substances.
   All plants are animals.
3. All poets have creative imagination.
   No poets are good business people.
   No good business people have creative imagination.

4. Some modern poetry is interesting.
   Everything interesting has value.
   Nothing that has value is worthless.
   Some modern poetry is not worthless.

5. All Buddhists are vegetarians.
   George Bernard Shaw is a vegetarian.
   George Bernard Shaw is a Buddhist.

6. Some Moslems are nondrinkers.
   All Arabs are Moslems.
   Some Arabs are Moslems.
   Some Arabs are nondrinkers.

7. All football players are well paid.
   Some teachers of philosophy are not football players.
   Some teachers of philosophy are not well paid.

8. Some bus riders are alcoholics.
   Some train riders are not alcoholics.
   Some bus riders are train riders.

9. No Russians are democrats.
   Some democrats are not fascists.
   Some Russians are not fascists.

10. Some teeth are not white.
    All white things are beautiful.
    Some beautiful things are not teeth.

Translating ordinary into logical sentences

We have presented the formal theory of the syllogism. In terms of the five rules given, every syllogistic argument can be shown to be either valid or invalid. It is easy to apply these rules once discourse has been put into the standard A, E, I, O propositions of logic, but there is difficulty in applying the rules directly to examples of reasoning in everyday life. Generally, such reasoning does not take place in propositions having neat logical forms of the sort we have discussed. Logicians are thus faced with the problem of translating ordinary English into the standard, and somewhat artificial, propositions of logic—since it is only when sentences are in such standard form that arguments containing them can be determined to be valid or invalid by the methods we have outlined above.

In this section, therefore, we shall give some rules for translating irregular sentences of ordinary discourse into the standard A, E, I, O propositions of formal logic.

RULE A: **Clearly identify the subject and predicate of the English sentence.**

Consider the following: "Seldom have sailors had such acclaim." The subject here is not "seldom" but "sailors." The sentence should be transformed to read: "Sailors have seldom had such acclaim," or if we introduce the appropriate part of the verb "to be" as copula, "Sailors are persons who have seldom had such acclaim." Another example is: "All take great risks who put their eggs into one basket." This again should be rendered so that the subject and predicate are clearly indentifiable. When we do this, the sentence will read: "All persons who put their eggs in one basket are persons who take great risks."

RULE B: **Supply the missing quantifier.**

When no quantifier is present, supply the missing quantifier. Unless it is clear from the context that "some" is intended, the rule is that "all" is meant. Thus, in a proposition such as "Psychotics are dangerous," one should add the word "all." This will put the proposition into standard logical form, e.g., "All psychotics are dangerous." In such a proposition as "Americans are great sprinters," however, "some" is intended, not "all." The revised proposition should read "Some Americans are great sprinters," unless, of course, we mean by it "All **American sprinters** are great sprinters."

Further examples of such revisions follow:

(*a*) "Dogs bark" should be rendered as "All dogs bark."

(*b*) "Cats are carnivorous" should be rendered as "All cats are carnivorous."

(*c*) "Germans suffer from Buerger's disease" should be translated as "Some Germans suffer from Buerger's disease."

RULE C: **Add the missing complement.**

Since the terms of logic designate classes, it is sometimes necessary to add what is called a **"complement"** to an adjective or to a describing phrase to show that they refer to classes. For example, if I say "Some lions are docile," since we cannot point to "a docile," strictly speaking we must say "docile creatures," or "docile animals." Consider the following examples:

(*a*) "Communists are losing ground" should be rendered as "Communists are persons who are losing ground."

(*b*) "The foolhardy are losers in the end" should be rendered as "All foolhardy persons are losers in the end."

RULE D: **Supply the missing copula.**

In propositions such as "Dogs bark" and "Some ancients believed in devils," the copula (i.e., the word "are" or "is") is missing. These propositions should be rendered as "All dogs *are* barking animals" and "Some ancient peoples *are* people who believed in devils."

RULE E: **Exclusive sentences.**

Some sentences begin with words such as "only" or "none but." For example, if I say "Only men are priests" or "None but nonsmokers need apply," these sentences are not in standard form. It is important in such cases that we reflect upon the meanings of these sentences before putting them into standard logical form. For example, "Only men are priests" surely does not mean that "All men are priests." Rather, it means that "All priests are men." The rule therefore with regard to such sentences is: Drop the word/words "only" or "none but," and add "all" as a quantifier; then reverse the order of subject and predicate. Thus, in order to transform such sentences into standard form, two steps are required: (*a*) **Drop the word/ words "only" or "none but," and replace them by "all."** (*b*) **Interchange subject and predicate terms.**

Example: "None but adults are admitted" is equivalent in meaning to "All those persons admitted are adults."

RULE F: **Negative sentences.**

To begin with, such words as "nothing," "none," and "no one" are to be treated by replacing them with the quantifier "no." Thus, such a sentence as "None of the damned is happy" is to be rendered as a standard proposition as follows: "No person who is damned is a happy person." Or again, such a sentence as "Nothing human frightens me" will require the following steps in order to transform it into a standard proposition:

1. The quantifier becomes "no."
2. Subject is "human being."
3. Add the copula.
4. Complement the predicate.

The result of these operations is a proposition in standard form: "No human beings are things that frighten me."

Secondly, it should be noted that propositions of the form "All . . . are not" are frequently ambiguous. It is not clear sometimes whether they should be interpreted as an O proposition or as an E proposition. **The rule is that we should interpret them in every case as an O proposition unless an E is clearly intended.** Thus if I say "All Germans are not Christian Democrats," I do not mean "No Germans are Christian Democrats" but, rather, "Some Germans are not Christian Democrats," which is, of course, an O proposition.

RULE G: **Exceptive sentences.**

Sentences that contain the word "except" cannot be exactly translated into any *one* of the A, E, I, O propositions. For instance, if I say "Everyone except women may at-tend," I mean something that is expressed by the following two propositions:

1. All who are not women may attend.
2. No women may attend.

The first proposition is an A proposition, and the second is an E proposition. Since a syllogism can contain only three propositions, if we were to allow *both* propositions as being the translation of the exceptive sentence, arguments in syllogistic form would no longer be syllogisms, since they would contain more than three propositions. Hence **the rule is that either the A proposition or the E proposition may be used, but not both. Any argument that contains an exceptive sentence and that is valid will remain valid if the exceptive sentence is interpreted either as an A proposition or as an E proposition.**

RULE H: **Sentences containing "anyone," "anything," "whoever," "the," "if . . . then," "whatever."**

Consider the following sentences:

1. Anyone who comes must participate.
2. Anything that comes must participate.
3. Whoever comes must participate.
4. Whatever comes must participate.
5. Everyone who comes must participate.
6. If anyone comes, he/she must participate.
7. The person who comes must participate.

Sentences containing the above terms can all be translated into A propositions, e.g., "All who come must participate" or "All persons who come must participate," and so on.

RULE I: **Sentences containing "someone," "something," "there is," or "there are."**

Consider the following:

1. Someone opened the door.
2. Something opened the door.
3. There are things that opened the door.
4. There is something that opened the door.

All such sentences are to be translated into I propositions, e.g., "Some persons are persons who opened the door."

The reader should study the above rules carefully, since by following them he/she will be able to translate sentences of ordinary discourse into propositions of standard logical form. Once this is accomplished, it is simple to determine whether arguments containing such propositions are valid or invalid. The above list of rules, it should be mentioned, is not complete; and thus the reader who examines a body of discourse taken from literature or the daily newspaper will frequently have to exercise his/her ingenuity in order to transform irregular sentences into the standard position of logic.

EXERCISE 8

Put the following into standard logical form:

1. Ships are beautiful.
2. Joan is a blonde.
3. The whale is a mammal.

4. Whoever is a child is silly.
5. Snakes coil.
6. None but golfers appreciate the game.
7. Only indicative sentences make assertions.
8. Nothing ventured, nothing gained.
9. All but the brave die many deaths.
10. All swans are not white.

Equivalent sentences

There is one further logical technique that we must consider before concluding the formal theory of the syllogism. This is a technique that, like the foregoing discussion, enables us to put reasoning that is not in syllogistic form into a form in which its validity can be assessed. The purpose of the technique is to transform certain propositions into other propositions, which are equivalent in meaning but which may have a different logical form—**with the advantage that an argument that may not be in strict syllogistic form can be transformed into a syllogism** by the use of these techniques. Perhaps this can be explained more clearly by an example. Consider the following:

No unwise people are trustworthy.
All wise people are unaggressive.
No trustworthy people are aggressive.

This argument clearly seems to be valid, but we cannot test it by the rules we have formulated above, since it contains more than three terms. In fact, it seems to contain five terms: "unwise people," "trustworthy people," "wise people," "unaggressive people," and "aggressive people." But the second premise means the same thing as "All aggressive people are unwise." Consequently, if we substitute this latter proposition for the original proposition, we get the following argument:

No unwise people are trustworthy.
All aggressive people are unwise.
No trustworthy people are aggressive.

The argument now contains three and only three terms, and hence is a syllogism. We can now test it with our five rules, and can thus ascertain that the argument is valid.

The techniques that allow us to transform a given proposition into an equivalent one are called **"obversion," "conversion,"** and **"contraposition."** Let us turn to an examination of these techniques now, beginning with obversion.

Obversion

In **obverting** a given proposition, we do two things:

(*a*) We change the **quality** (but not the quantity) of the proposition. That is, **if it is negative, we make it affirmative; and if affirmative, we make it negative.**

(*b*) We then **negate the predicate.**

Example: "No marines are unreliable."
First we change the quality. Thus the proposition becomes:
"All marines are unreliable."
Then we negate the predicate:
"All marines are not unreliable."

The proposition "All marines are not unreliable" is equivalent to "All marines are reliable" (two negatives make a positive), and thus our final proposition, "All marines are reliable," is equivalent to our original one, "No marines are unreliable."

It is possible to obvert every A, E, I, O proposition. There follows a diagram with the original proposition and its obverse:

Type of sentence	Original	Obverse
A	All men are mortal.	No men are nonmortal.
E	No men are mortal.	All men are immortal.
I	Some men are mortal.	Some men are not immortal.
O	Some men are not mortal.	Some men are immortal.

Care must be exercised in obverting propositions in ordinary speech, since one may use an English term that does not negate the predicate. Some of the English prefixes such as "im" or "un" or "in" do not always express simple negation. Furthermore, words such as "small" and "poor" are not the negations of "large" and "rich." In such cases, in order **to negate the predicate, the prefix "non" is ordinarily employed by logicians.** Thus, the negation of "wealthy" is not "poor" but "nonwealthy."

In obverting, there must be no change in the **quantity** of the sentence, but only in its **quality.** Thus, **a universal sentence remains universal, a particular remains particular.**

Conversion

When we **convert,** we merely **interchange subject and predicate.** Thus, the proposition "No cats are dogs" is equivalent to the proposition "No dogs are cats." Unlike obversion, **not every standard proposition of logic has an equivalent converse.** In fact, **only the E proposition and the I proposition can be converted.** Thus, "No horses are mice" is equivalent to "No mice are horses." Likewise, the I proposition "Some horses are animals" is equivalent to "Some animals are horses."

The O proposition cannot be converted. From "Some men are not priests," we cannot infer "Some priests are not men."

The A proposition cannot be converted simply. From such a proposition as "All horses are animals," we cannot infer "All animals are horses." However, it is possible **partially to convert** the A. Logicians call this **"conversion by limitation." When we convert a true A proposition, we can transform it into a true I proposition.** Thus, "All horses are animals," when partially converted, gives us "Some animals are horses." Partial conversion, however, does not result in a statement that is exactly equivalent in meaning to the original, since the quantity of the original statement is changed.

The following is a table of permissible conversions:

Type of sentence	Original	Converse
E	No men are mortal.	No mortals are men.
I	Some men are mortal.	Some mortals are men.
A	All men are mortal.	Some mortals are men. (Partial conversion)

The O, it must be remembered, cannot be converted.

Contraposition

Contraposition is the third method of altering propositions into their equivalents. To obtain the **contrapositive** of a proposition, three operations must be performed: **first we obvert, then convert, then obvert once again.** The contrapositive of a given proposition has, for this reason, sometimes been defined as the **"obverse of a converted obverse."** Let us illustrate this by an example:

Original sentence: All dogs are animals.
Step 1: Obvert: No dogs are nonanimals.
Step 2: Convert: No nonanimals are dogs.
Step 3: Obvert: All nonanimals are nondogs.

Contraposition, like conversion, cannot be applied to all four standard propositions of logic. The A and O propositions have contrapositives. The I has no contrapositive. The E has a partial contrapositive. Since contraposition is generally applied only to A propositions, we shall not discuss this form further here.

The above discussion completes our informal disquisition upon methods of translating irregular propositions into regular ones, and of translating certain propositions into equivalent ones. Given the above machinery, as well as the formal theory of the syllogism explained earlier, it should now be possible for the reader to transform large parts of English discourse into arguments of a syllogistic form, and then to test their validity.

A. Obvert the following:

1. Some humans are braggarts.
2. No trains are buses.
3. Some magazines are not articulate.
4. Only dwarfs are kind.
5. All fairies are immortal.
6. All except John will be admitted.
7. Whoever is intelligent is appreciated.

B. Convert the following:

1. Some cats are white.
2. No lions are tame.
3. Some Russians are not Communists.
4. All cars are expensive.
5. Some golfers are champions.
6. Some cars are not expensive.
7. Nothing ventured, nothing gained.

C. Contrapose the following:

1. All superstitions are ridiculous.
2. All prejudices are unwarranted.
3. Some horses are not unintelligent.
4. Some horses are not intelligent.
5. Only the considerate deserve the fair.

Fallacies

In the preceding pages, we discussed the rules for determining when reasoning of the kind called "syllogistic reasoning" is valid or invalid. The five rules we formulated are tests that determine whether an argument is valid; and they are likewise tests that determine whether an argument in syllogistic form is invalid. **When an argument that has the form of a syllogism seems valid, but is not, we say that it is "fallacious."** Such errors as "undistributed middle" and "illicit process" are examples of fallacies.

However, the word "fallacy" has a much broader signification than merely the violation of one or another of the five rules above. **A fallacy is any sort of mistake in reasoning or inference; it is a term used to denote anything that causes an argument to go wrong.** The number of types of fallacy, in this sense of the term, is so great that no complete list has ever been drawn up. For this reason, it is difficult to specify in general why an argument is fallacious. It may be fallacious for all sorts of different reasons. The usual way of treating fallacies, therefore, is to discuss specific fallacies in order to show how they employ incorrect reasoning. We shall follow this procedure here, but at the same time we shall attempt to classify some of the more common types of fallacies.

Fallacies of Ambiguity

Ambiguity is one of the major sources of fallacious reasoning. We say **a term is ambiguous if it has more than one meaning.** Thus, if I say "He has a good grip," it is not clear whether I mean "He has a strong handshake" or "He has a good suitcase." The word "grip" is thus ambiguous, since it may be interpreted in at least two different ways. Ambiguity, it should be mentioned, is not always a source of confusion or of invalid reasoning. Words may have more than one meaning, but it may be clear which meaning is intended from the context in which they are used. **It is only when we cannot tell which meaning is intended that confusion may result.** Consider a common noun such as "brother." It may be used in a number of different ways without leading to confusion. For instance, examine the following utterances:

John is the brother of Jane.
All men are brothers under the skin.
Bill and Max are fraternity brothers.
"Oh brother!"

Although the word "brother" is being employed differently in each of the above cases, no confusion results; but consider what happens when the sense of "brother" in the first sentence is confused with the sense of "brother" in the second. We may be led into a fallacious argument of the following sort:

All men are brothers in a common fraternity.
All brothers in a common fraternity are college students.
All men are college students.

The fallacy here is one of ambiguity. When we say that "all men are brothers in a common fraternity," we mean that there are no fundamental differences among men with regard to their being human beings and with regard to their having certain universal human rights (e.g., freedom of speech, religion, etc.). But when we say "all brothers in a common fraternity are college students," we mean that each and every member of a college fraternity is a college student. The resulting argument is invalid because the same word is used in two different senses. (The word "fraternity" is also ambiguous in

the argument.) The fallacy that occurs when an inference is invalid because a single word may be used in two different senses is called **"equivocation."**

A second type of fallacy involving ambiguity occurs when the whole sentence, as contrasted with single words, is ambiguous. Each and every word in the sentence may not be ambiguous, yet the whole sentence will be because of its grammatical structure. Such a fallacy is called an **"amphiboly."**

There is a legend that the oracle at Delphi, in ancient Greece, was never wrong. One reason for its infallibility was that it made its predictions in an amphibolous way—they could be taken in at least two different senses; hence, if either event happened, the oracle's prediction could be confirmed as correct. During the conflict between the Greeks and Persians, a Greek commander is supposed to have asked the oracle who would emerge as the eventual victor. The oracle replied, "Apollo says that the Greeks and Persians shall subdue." Here it is not clear whether the Greeks are to be the victors or the Persians. Again, when Cyrus the Great contemplated war against a certain king, the oracle answered his request about who would conquer by saying, "The king yet lives that Cyrus shall depose."

It should be noted that amphibolies occur because of the construction of a sentence. The ambiguity in such cases is not due to the fact that individual words are taken in two senses, but that **we do not understand the meaning of the whole sentence.**

Two common types of amphibolies are due to (*a*) **dangling participles,** and (*b*) the

inexact use of negation signs in ordinary speech.

In committing the grammatical error called "dangling participle," one fails to attach a noun to a participial phrase that precedes it. For example, I would have committed this error if I had written the previous sentence as follows: "In committing the grammatical error called "dangling participle," a phrase is left unattached." Here it looks as if it is a phrase that has committed the error, rather than a person using the phrase who has committed the error. Since a phrase is not the sort of thing that can commit errors, the ambiguity here is not seriously misleading; but it is grammatically incorrect, and in other contexts this kind of misleading sentence structure can make it impossible to be clear about the meaning of the sentence. Sometimes amphibolies that are due to a dangling participle can be very amusing. A certain newspaper once described a boat race as follows:

"The *Newport Beach* was far ahead of the others when she crossed the finish line. Her nose up in the air, salt water pouring across her bows, Mrs. Williams guided her skillfully past the cheering crowd."

The use of "not" in ordinary speech is another source of confusion. Sentences which begin "All . . . are not . . ." can be interpreted in two different ways, as an E proposition or as an O proposition. Since we have discussed this point earlier, we shall not comment upon it here again, except to mention that one must be on guard against an improper interpretation of negative sentences beginning with "all."

Contextual Fallacies

Some very common types of fallacies do not depend upon grammatical misuses of language or upon formal mistakes in reasoning. They depend upon the context in which an utterance is made. The context may tend to suggest that the utterance has a certain significance, but in fact it may not have such significance at all. Hence the utterance will be misleading to one who hears or reads it. Such fallacies we call "contextual fallacies." Let us consider some of these now.

THE FALLACY OF SIGNIFICANCE

One of the most common is the **fallacy of significance.** Suppose I say, "Twenty-eight per cent of the people in Birmingham have cavities in their teeth!" Before one can know whether this is a "significant" remark or not, one would have to compare Birmingham with cities of a similar size in order to see whether it has a high or low proportion of people suffering from dental defects. Advertising claims very often commit the fallacy of significance. It is not uncommon to see such a slogan as "62 percent of those doctors who smoke, smoke Raspies!" This is misleading, since it does not say how many doctors do *not* smoke, nor does it say that they smoke *only* Raspies. It may well be that most doctors who smoke, smoke some other brand more frequently than Raspies, although they may try them, too, when they wish to change brands.

THE FALLACY OF EMPHASIS

Another common contextual fallacy depends upon the **incorrect emphasis of the** words in a sentence. Thus an insurance firm may make such a claim:

PROTECTION GUARANTEED AGAINST EVERYTHING
except death, injury, disease

By printing the first sentence in large type, they suggest that they are giving full protection, but by printing the exceptions in very small type, they are taking back most of their claims. Again, advertising firms often employ this fallacy—the **fallacy of emphasis**—to full advantage in order to sell their product.

THE FALLACY OF QUOTING OUT OF CONTEXT

The **fallacy of quoting out of context** is another common fallacy that depends upon the context. A critic in reviewing a novel may write:

> I would enjoy this book if, and only if, it were the only book in the world, or if I were on a desert island and had nothing else to read.

But the publisher, in order to sell the book, might lift certain of the critic's remarks from the whole sentence, and the review would then look as follows:

> I would enjoy this book . . . if I were on a desert island . . .

By careful manipulation of the context, the publisher thus gives the reader the impression that the review was favorable, when the contrary was the case.

FALLACY OF *ARGUMENTUM AD HOMINEM*

One of the most difficult fallacies to expose, as well as being one of the most common, is what is called **"argumentum ad hominem."** These words refer to an argument that is directed **against a person, rather than against what a person says, in order to show what he/she says cannot be true.** Politics affords us many examples of *argumenta ad hominem*. Suppose a Democratic representative in Congress should argue: "It is extremely important that we abolish or limit nuclear bomb tests, since it is possible that their long-range effects will poison the atmosphere." A conservative Republican might retort by saying: "Oh well, you can't believe what he says, since he is a left-wing Democrat, and you know that they are always trying to control military expenditure." The Republican has directed his argument against the *man;* he has tried to refute what the Democrat has said by pointing out that the speaker is a member of the opposing party. But such a refutation is based on a fallacy, since the proper way to refute such an argument would consist in marshaling facts to show that what the speaker said is false—namely, that atomic tests are not likely to poison the atmosphere.

What makes the *argumentum ad hominem* so persuasive, and so difficult to refute, can be shown by the following example. Suppose a witness in a trial is testifying that he saw a crime committed by the defendant. Suppose, further, that in cross-examining the witness the defense proves that he has testified in other cases, and that in some of them his testimony was false (assume, for purposes of the example, that he has even been convicted of perjury). One's temptation, as a juror, would be to disregard what the witness has said *in this case* on the ground that he is an unreliable source of information. But to disregard his testimony entirely is to commit the fallacy of *argumentum ad hominem*. What he says on this occasion may be true; if possible, his testimony should be tested against other evidence that might be or might become available during the course of the trial. The important thing to recognize is that one should consider what is said apart from who says it. **A statement cannot be shown to be false merely because the individual who makes it can be shown to be a person of defective character.**

THE FALLACY OF ARGUING FROM AUTHORITY

Argument from authority is another common type of fallacy. It has the following form. Smith says that a certain statement is true. If questioned, he answers. "Because X, who is an authority, says so." **One cannot prove the truth or falsity of a given statement merely because someone, even an authority, says so. It is not the prestige of an authority that makes a statement true or false but, rather, the citing of evidence either to confirm or to confute the statement.** Thus, if I say "Jack Nicklaus was a greater golfer than Sam Snead," and someone challenges this remark, I would be committing a fallacy to say "Because Arnold Palmer, who played against both of them and therefore is an authority, has said so." One could prove the proposition only by citing tournaments won by Nicklaus and Snead, by comparing their records in other respects, and so forth. The fact that an authority has made a statement cannot be *itself* regarded as evidence; what constitutes evidence are the *facts* that the authority pro-

duces—and these are quite different from a mere verbal pronouncement. We might be prepared, however, sometimes to take on trust the pronouncement of an expert on some matter within his/her expertise, but there can never be any good reason for accepting his/her assertions in other fields. I may not go far wrong if I accept Arnold Palmer's word on a golfing matter; I am likely to go very wrong if I place as much credence in his views of politics.

ARGUMENTS THAT APPEAL TO SENTIMENTS

There are a number of arguments that commit the following fallacy. **These arguments attempt to establish that a given statement is true or false by reporting how people feel about it.** Thus, if I say "The world is flat," and you challenge my remark, I might attempt to beat down your challenge by saying "But everybody believes that." Such an answer would be to commit a fallacy, since one cannot prove whether the world is flat or not by citing the beliefs of the majority of people—but rather, by citing evidence from geography, astronomy, and so forth. There are numerous cases, the above example being a famous one, where the majority have held beliefs that are false.

The appeal to pity, or to emotion, which is a variant of the above argument, is sometimes called the *"argumentum ad misericordiam."* An attorney who implies that the defendant could not have committed the crime because he has a wife and six children is employing the *argumentum ad misericordiam*. His family responsibilities are irrelevant with regard to his guilt, although they may be relevant with regard to determining his punishment.

ARGUMENTUM AD IGNORANTIAM

A common type of argument that commits a fallacy is called the **"argument from ignorance." This argument contends that some statement must be true because there is no evidence to disprove it.** The argument from ignorance is plausible because it apes a legitimate type of argument. One might hold (legitimately) that a certain view is true because we have considerable evidence, all of which shows that the view is true, and none of which shows that it is false. Thus one might hold that, under specified conditions, the statement "Water boils at 100° Celsius" is true because every time we have tried to boil water it has boiled at 100°, under these specified conditions—and, moreover, there have been *no* contrary instances. But the argument from ignorance, which looks like this argument, holds that a certain statement is true *simply* because there is no evidence against it. But this is fallacious since **it is not enough to show that a view is true simply because there is no contrary evidence; we must also show that there is positive evidence in favor of it.** Otherwise, we could prove that dragons, elves, sea serpents, and unicorns exist, since there is no contrary evidence against them. Religious disputes often employ the argument from ignorance. People will assert that "God exists" is true, since there is no evidence that He does not. But if this is the matter of proof, it is inconclusive, for the reasons we have stated above.

PETITIO PRINCIPII

The fallacy of begging the question. This fallacy occurs when either the same statement is used both as a premise and a conclusion in an argument, or when one of the premises could not be known to be true unless the conclusion were first assumed to be true. This fallacy is sometimes described as **"assuming what you are trying to prove,"** or **"circular argumentation."** The closer the premises of a circular argument are to the conclusion, the easier the fallacy is to detect; but sometimes when premises and conclusions are widely separated by a long chain of argumentation, it may be difficult to discover that the whole argument is circular. An example of the fallacy of begging the question is the following:

A: "Moses is divinely inspired."
B: "How do you know?"
A: "Because the Bible says he is."
B: "But how do you know the Bible is reliable?
A: "Because it was written by Moses, who is divine."

THE FALLACY OF COMPOSITION

In the fallacy of composition, what is assumed to be true of a part is asserted to be true of the whole. This fallacy is made plausible because it looks like a sound inductive argument. Let us exhibit the difference between the fallacy of composition and a sound inductive inference by the following two examples:

(a) John O'Brien is an Irishman and belligerent; therefore, Ireland is belligerent.

(b) John O'Brien is an Irishman and belligerent; therefore, Irishmen are belligerent.

Example (a) commits the fallacy of composition because it says that what is true of a member of a country is true of the whole country. This is simply mistaken. From the fact that X is wealthy, we cannot conclude that the country in which he resides is wealthy (e.g., Pablo is wealthy; therefore, Spain is wealthy). On the other hand, Example (b) is a sound inductive inference. Whether the conclusion is true or false, of course, will depend upon how many Irishmen besides John O'Brien can be found to be belligerent; but the inference is itself sound.

THE FALLACY OF DIVISION

The fallacy of division commits the opposite mistake from that made by the fallacy of composition. **It holds that what is true of a whole must be true of all its parts.** Thus if I say "The United States is a wealthy country; therefore, Joe Smith is wealthy," I am committing the fallacy of division. It does not follow that because the whole country is wealthy, each and every citizen of it will be wealthy. Tourists who are frequently charged exorbitant rates in foreign countries may protest against such charges on the grounds that the fallacy of division is being committed (although this protest will probably be unsuccessful). From the fact that one comes from a wealthy nation, it does not follow that one is wealthy.

The fallacy of division is plausible and easy to commit because it looks like one type of valid argument, called **"argument by specification."** If we say "All Americans are wealthy; Joe Smith is an American," we can validly infer that Joe Smith is wealthy. This is because the statement "All Americans are wealthy" attributes wealth to each and every American. And if it is true and if Joe Smith is an American, then it will be true that he is wealthy. But what is true of the whole country (i.e., that the United States is wealthy) is not true of each and every one of its members.

THE FALLACY OF *IGNORATIO ELENCHI*

This fallacy, also called **"irrelevant conclusion"** is an argument in which one starts out to prove that something is the case, but instead proves something else. For instance, if I attempt to prove that the French League has better soccer players than the Italian League, but instead establish that the French League is wealthier than the Italian League, I have committed the fallacy of irrelevant conclusion. For even if it is true that the French League is wealthier than the Italian League, it still does not follow that wealthier leagues have better players than poorer ones. What happens in an *ignoratio elenchi* is that the disputant thinks he is proving *p* (the French League has better players) when in reality he is proving *r* (that the French League is wealthier). Thus he arrives at a conclusion that is irrelevant to the conclusion he was trying to prove.

THE FALLACY OF *NON SEQUITUR*

Almost every fallacy involves, in some respect, a *non sequitur*. The phrase *"non sequitur"* means the same as **"does not fol-**

low." Thus the fallacy of *ignoratio elenchi*, which we discussed above, involves a type of *non sequitur*. From the fact that the French League is wealthier than the Italian League, it does not follow that French League players are better than Italian League players. This would have to be shown by marshaling sets of statistics concerning the relative performances of the players in both leagues. Sometimes the phrase *"non sequitur"* has a formal meaning. In this case, we say that **the conclusion of an argument does not follow from the premises when it is possible for the premises to be true and the conclusion to be false.** But generally *"non sequitur"* is used in a broader sense; for example, **where a conclusion may be true, but irrelevant, we will say that a *non sequitur* has been committed.** This fallacy is also sometimes called "argumentative leap."

STATISTICAL FALLACIES

It is commonly asserted that "you can make statistics prove anything." This is so, to be sure, if one misuses the statistical method. There is a famous story that exhibits a misuse of statistics. Two philosophers decided to find out why they kept becoming intoxicated; and they decided to apply the statistical or scientific method to discover the cause. They proceeded to their favorite tavern, where they had dinner, and during the process they consumed several drinks composed of Scotch whiskey and water. They became intoxicated and had to be taken home. The next night they repeated the process. They had exactly the same food, but this time, for a beverage, they drank Irish whiskey and water. Again they became intoxicated and had to be carried from the prem-

ises. The third night they repeated the same steps, varying only the drink. This time they drank rye whiskey and water, again becoming drunk. They concluded, in accordance with the statistical method, that since water was the only constant factor in all their drinks, it must have been water that was making them intoxicated!

One must handle the findings of statistics with extreme caution unless one knows the methods that were applied, the controls over the data that were exercised, and so forth. These are highly intricate and technical matters, which demand careful supervision to maintain proper controls over all possible variables. Thus, such a statement as "Schnooko, the great washday detergent, washes 91 times cleaner than any other soap" must be disregarded unless one knows what sorts of tests were applied, how one defines "cleaner than," and so forth.

With the above remarks, we shall conclude our discussion of types of fallacy. We reiterate that the list is not complete—indeed, it may be impossible to provide such a list—but in any case, we have tried to select some of the commoner types of mistakes in reasoning. A reader who seriously studies the above mistakes in reasoning, and who applies what he has learned to everyday speech, is not apt frequently to be misled.

EXERCISE 10

Identify the fallacies committed in the following:

1. Water the plant when thoroughly potted.
2. He: "Dance?"
   She: "Love to!"

He: "Marvelous, that's better than dancing!"

3. Jones was not intoxicated today.

4. Your contention that alcohol is injurious is without merit since you drink.

5. It has been argued that the Crusades were a noble endeavor, since men of high purpose founded them and whole peoples supported them.

6. "Educated people do not believe in ghosts," he said. "Ah," I replied, "some college people do." "Oh, but they are not educated just because they went to college," he answered, "for if they were, they would not believe in ghosts."

7. There can be no doubt that atomic bombs can poison the atmosphere. Einstein himself said so.

8. But, Doctor, surely your advice to me to stop smoking cannot be serious, since I happen to know that you smoke.

9. Socrates is a man; man is a species; therefore, Socrates is a species.

10. Every attempt to prove that people are not immortal has failed. No evidence can be found that shows that people's souls do not exist after death; hence immortality must be true.

Logic, semiotics, and semantics

Our account of the nature of logic would be incomplete without a brief reference to the relationship between logic and semantics. We should preface such an account by pointing out that the word "semantics" is currently used in a number of different senses—by ordinary persons, teachers, and linguists. But philosophers, who invented the concept, use the term in a narrow and precise sense. As they employ it, the term is used to denote one of three branches of the general science or study of language. This general science is called "semiotics," and it has three subdivisions, of which semantics is one. The other branches are known as "pragmatics," which deals with the relationship of speakers and hearers to the words they utter or hear, and "syntax," which deals with the relationship holding between words and words. In contrast, semantics as a discipline concerns itself with the relationship between language and what language refers to or signifies. More generally, the relationships of reference and signification are taken to be identical to the notion of "meaning." Words may mean in a referential way—for instance, the word "John" may be used by me to denote a certain person; naming would thus be one kind of semantical meaning, or referential relationship. But I may be able to speak about things that do not exist—for instance, a mythological object like Medusa or a fictitious object like Hamlet. Here my words express a certain sense or concept. "Hamlet" (the word) expresses a certain concept I understand, e.g., "the Prince of Denmark in a play by Shakespeare." Semantic theory explains how, via concepts, we can significantly speak about things or persons or places that do not exist.

According to semantic theory, words thus "mean" in at least two different ways. This can be illustrated by considering a word like "brother." If someone were to ask us, "What do you mean by the word 'brother'?" we could answer in two different ways: either we could point to someone who was a brother, or we could define the term verbally. We could say in the latter case, "By the word 'brother' I mean anyone who is a male and a sibling." In the latter case, we employed words to do the job that pointing did in the former case. Logicians employ a technical vocabulary to distinguish between giving the meaning of an expression in the former case and giving the meaning in the latter. Where we point, we are giving the **extensional** meaning of the word; we are indicating the object or event that the word refers to. In the latter case, where we produce a verbal definition, we are giving the **intensional** meaning. The notions of extension and intension (also called **"denotation"** and **"connotation"** respectively) are among the basic concepts in semantical meaning analysis: for one explains the meaning of a term by giving either its denotation or its connotation.

Syntax

Syntax, as we have indicated, is the branch of the science of language that deals with the relations between words. Here we are no longer concerned about the relation of a word to its user or interpreter, or even about what the word or phrase or sentence refers to or means (as in semantics). Instead, **we deal in syntax with the grammatical structure of the arrangement of the elements of language.**

Logic, it should be clear by now, is a type of language. It is not a language, of course, of the same kind as English or French, which are languages that have developed *naturally*. **It is instead a well-formed or artificial language; but a language it is, since it employs signs or symbols.** These signs or symbols have certain properties. Depending upon the properties that we are interested in when we study logic, **logic falls either into syntax or into semantics.** Let us illustrate each of these points. We have in the foregoing discussed the syllogism. The syllogism is an argument containing terms that refer to classes of things. **The relation between a term and its referent (i.e., the relation of "referring," or "naming" or "designating") is a semantical relation.**

On the other hand, **the relation of "inclusion," which we have also studied in logic, is a syntactical relation rather than a semantical one.** We can abstract from any semantic considerations when we speak about such a relation as "inclusion." We can state that **an argument will be valid regardless of what the terms in the argument refer to, provided that the terms are arranged in a certain order.** Thus, an argument having the following form (regardless of what descriptive meaning we give to its constituent terms) will be valid:

All M is P
All S is M

All S is P

On the other hand, merely by analyzing the syntactical arrangement of the terms in the following argument, we can state that it is invalid:

All P is M
All S is M

All S is P

We may summarize our long discussion of the nature of logic by pointing out that logic falls both within semantics and within syntax, depending upon what sort of logical relations we are emphasizing at the time. If we are dealing with "referring," we are concerned with semantics; if we are dealing with "logical form," we are in the branch of the study of language called "syntax."

Summary

In this chapter, we have tried to present a brief account of the nature of logic. It should be understood that we have done little more than introduce the reader to the barest essentials of logic. **The system of inference that we have studied is called the "syllogism."** This is one common type of argument. Logic in its more advanced branches deals with many types of inference, as well as with syllogistic inference.

In the foregoing, we have tried to define "logic" and to show how logic differs from psychology. In doing this, we have called attention to the difference between reasoning and other types of thinking, such as supposing, remembering, guessing, doubting, believing, and so forth. We then distinguished between deductive logic and inductive logic. In deductive logic, we argue from general to particular statements so that the reasons adduced as evidence for the truth of the conclusion of an argument are conclusive, whereas in inductive logic, where we are attempting to argue from the particular to the general, they merely make the conclusion more probable. We then considered the syllogism as one type of deductive inference, and then discussed various types of fallacy.

The result of the above discussion has been to prepare readers for further study of logic and to give them a substantial amount of equipment for distinguishing good from bad reasoning. One who studies the above material carefully will find not only that it has numerous applications to discourse in everyday life, but moreover, that by continuing to apply logic to such discourse, he/she will become clearer and sounder in his/her own reasoning.

Answers to exercises

EXERCISE 1

Identify the subject term, predicate term, copula, and quantifiers (if any). The following letters will stand for the corresponding term: "S" for subject term; "P" for predicate; "C" for copula; "Q" for quantifier.

```
        Q        S       C        P
1. Some   mad dogs   are   happily married.
   Q    S          C                      P
2. All   bats   are members of the class of   rodents.
       S     C      P
3. James   is   wicked.
      S      C        P
4. Horses   are   man's best friend.
```

$$\begin{array}{llll} Q & S & C & P \end{array}$$
5. Some   tables   are not   mahogany.
$$\begin{array}{llll} Q & S & C & P \end{array}$$
6. Nothing   green   is   in the room.

EXERCISE 2

Determine whether the following propositions are affirmative or negative:

1. James is very unhappy. (affirmative)
2. Lions are not untrustworthy. (negative)
3. She was not disinclined to come. (negative)
4. None but the lonely heart is filled with sadness. (affirmative)
5. Nothing tried, nothing gained. (negative)
6. He has been unwell for months now. (affirmative)
7. Some philosophers are intuitive. (affirmative)
8. No nonaddicts can understand the problem. (negative)
9. All non-S are non-P. (affirmative)
10. All except women may attend. (affirmative)

EXERCISE 3

Determine whether the following propositions are universal or particular:

1. Fish are mammals. (universal)
2. Some dragons are fierce. (particular)
3. This table is brown. (universal)
4. That system is useless. (universal)
5. They are crazy. (universal)
6. Hardworking students are successful. (universal)

7. Albert Einstein was a genius. (universal)
8. Those tins seem heavy. (universal)
9. That bottle of aspirin is not full. (universal)
10. No human beings are infallible. (universal)
11. Some cats are not wise. (particular)
12. Men have climbed Mount Everest. (particular)
13. All policemen are not cruel. (particular)
14. All golfers are wealthy. (universal)
15. Some babies are small. (particular)

EXERCISE 4

Determine whether the following propositions are to be designated as "A," "E," "I," or "O," and also determine their quantity and quality, i.e., whether they are universal and affirmative, etc.:

1. No Americans are explorers. (E, universal-neg.)
2. All doctors are interested in medicine. (A, universal-affirm.)
3. Some lawyers are golfers. (I, particular-affirm.)
4. Muhammad Ali is no longer heavyweight champion. (E, universal-neg.)
5. Martin Luther King was a champion of freedom. (A, universal-affirm.)
6. Some conductors are nonluminous. (I, particular-affirm.)

7. All football players are excluded from the class of authors. (E, universal-neg.)

8. Some tennis players are not authors. (O, particular-neg.)

9. That paper was well read. (A, universal-affirm.)

10. Each and every lion is ferocious. (A, universal-affirm.)

Indicate which terms are distributed and which are undistributed in the following examples. "D" will stand for distributed, and "U" for undistributed.

	D		U
1.	All Americans are		good swimmers.
	D		D
2.	No conductors are		overpaid.
	U		D
3.	Some swans are not		black.
	U		U
4.	Some swans are		beautiful.
	D		U
5.	Jane is		a model.
	D		U
6.	All Iowans are		nonfarmers.
	U		D
7.	Some Nevadans are not		farmers.

Identify the major, middle, and minor terms of the following syllogisms; also, designate the premises as major and minor. "M" will stand for middle, "Ma" for major, and "Mi" for minor.

       M   Ma
1. All men are fallible. (major premise)
   Mi   M
I am a man. (minor premise)
          Mi   Ma
Therefore, I am fallible.
       Mi   M
2. Some politicians are ignoble. (minor premise)
     Mi   Ma
No one who is ignoble is wise. (major premise)
      Mi   Ma
Some politicians are not wise.
    Mi   M
3. All singers are temperamental. (minor premise)

Ma   M
No truck drivers are temperamental. (major premise)
   Mi   Ma
No singers are truck drivers.
   Mi   M
4. All S   is M. (minor premise)
   M   Ma
No M is P. (major premise)
_____
   Mi   Ma
No S   is P.

EXERCISE 7

Determine whether the syllogisms in this exercise are valid or invalid. If invalid, state the fallacy they commit.

1. Invalid. Undistributed middle.
2. Invalid. Undistributed middle.
3. Invalid. Illicit process (Rule 2 violated).
4. This example has more than three terms, hence is not a syllogism.
5. Invalid. Undistributed middle.
6. Invalid. Undistributed middle.
7. Invalid. Illicit process (Rule 2 violated).
8. Invalid. Affirmative conclusion derived from a negative premise.
9. Invalid. No conclusion can be drawn from two negative premises.
10. Invalid. Illicit process (Rule 2 violated).

EXERCISE 8

The following are the results of putting the corresponding sentences into standard logical form in Exercise 8:

1. All ships are beautiful things.
2. Joan is a blond woman.
3. All whales are mammals.
4. All children are silly creatures.
5. All snakes are coiling things.
6. All persons who appreciate the game are golfers.
7. All sentences that make assertions are indicative sentences.
8. No nonventured things are gained things.
9. Nothing that is brave is a thing that dies many deaths,

or

All things that are not brave are things that die many deaths.
10. Some swans are not white.

EXERCISE 9

A. The following are the results of obverting the corresponding sentences in Exercise 9:

1. Some humans are not nonbraggarts.
2. All trains are nonbuses.
3. Some magazines are nonarticulate.
4. No kind persons are nondwarfs.
5. No fairies are mortal.
6. No one who is not John is a nonadmitted person.
7. No one who is intelligent is a nonappreciated person.

B. The following are converted propositions:

1. Some white things are cats.
2. No tame creatures are lions.
3. The O cannot be converted.
4. Some expensive things are cars. (partial conversion)
5. Some champions are golfers.
6. The O cannot be converted.
7. Nothing gained, nothing ventured.

C. The following are contraposed propositions:

1. All nonridiculous things are nonsuperstitious.
2. All warranted things are nonprejudices.
3. Some intelligent things are not nonhorses (i.e., some intelligent things are horses).
4. Some nonintelligent things are not nonhorses (i.e., some unintelligent things are horses).
5. All nonconsiderate persons are non-deservers of the fair.

EXERCISE 10

The following are the fallacies identified in Exercise 10:

1. Amphiboly.
2. Emphasis.
3. Significance or amphiboly.
4. *Ad hominem.*
5. Appeal to sentiment.
6. Begging the question.
7. Appeal to authority.
8. *Ad hominem.*
9. Equivocation.
10. *Ad ignorantiam.*

Suggested further reading

Elementary Texts

Bergman, M., and Moon, J. *The Logic Book.* 1980. More advanced than the following two, but lucidly written and easy to follow.

Copi, I. *Introduction to Logic.* 6th ed. 1982. A solid, simple introduction to the elements of traditional and modern logic.

Hurley, P. *A Concise Introduction to Logic.* 1985. Excellent modern treatment of elementary logic, with accompanying handbook of exercises.

Martinich,, A. P. *Philosophical Writing.* 1989. The best simple introduction to elementary logic and critical thinking.

Thouless, R. H. *Straight and Crooked Thinking.* 1959. A discussion of the many ways in which argument can go wrong.

More Advanced Texts

Copi, I. *Symbolic Logic.* 1965.

Jeffrey, R. *Formal Logic.* 1981. Another very sound text.

Mates, B. *Elementary Logic.* One of the best treatments of formal logic at an intermediate level.

CHAPTER SEVEN

Contemporary philosophy

In this final section, we shall examine some of the major movements in modern philosophy. In selecting pragmatism, the various forms of philosophical analysis, and existentialism, we are not, of course, exhausting the possibilities. Many forms of traditional philosophy continue to hold the interest of twentieth-century philosophers and still command many adherents.

However, primary consideration is owing to those developments that have had a decisive effect upon modern philosophical activities. **Pragmatism**, a movement of American origin, has deeply influenced intellectual life in America. **Philosophical analysis,** which originated in England and Vienna, has had a great impact on thought, first in Britain and more recently in the United States. **Existentialism**, which has its roots in various nineteenth-century ideas, in the twentieth century became prominent in Continental European thought, especially in France and Germany, and has also received considerable attention in the English-speaking world.

Pragmatism

In the late nineteenth century, a method of philosophizing called "pragmatism" developed in America as a revolt against what some thinkers (e.g., William James, Charles Sanders Peirce, and John Dewey) felt to be a sterile philosophical tradition in the American colleges, and the useless metaphysical tradition then flourishing in Europe. The pragmatists felt that their method and theory could be of tremendous utility in solving intellectual problems and in forwarding man's progress.

Background of Pragmatism

The America in which this movement developed was just beginning to awaken in the post–Civil War period to its cultural potentialities. For a long time, American philosophical activity—such as it was—merely reflected European influences. Early in the nineteenth century, the very astute observer of the American scene, Alexis de Tocqueville remarked that in no country in the civilized world was philosophy taken less seriously than in the United States. Philosophy probably seemed too abstruse and too remote from the immediate concerns of a young, vigorous nation.

The views of the seventeenth-century New England Calvinists, for example, were a continuation of English philosophical discussion, and the objective was the application of these views to then current problems of their new society. Even the man who was perhaps the most original metaphysician in American history, the great New England preacher Jonathan Edwards, was greatly influenced by such European contemporaries as John Locke, the Cambridge Platonists, and possibly Nicolas Malebranche. In the eighteenth century, American philosophy felt the impact of the French Enlightenment philosophers; and in the early nineteenth century, it felt that of the German Romantics. By the end of the eighteenth century, "academic" philosophy had become a sterile and rigid version of the ideas of the **Scottish commonsense realists,** whose purpose was to refute the "dangerous" skepticism of David Hume.

In the mid-nineteenth century, there were gathering indications of a philosophic revival that would repudiate the exhausted academic and European traditions. German immigrants (refugees from the failure of their revolution of 1848), disciples of Hegel who were impressed with the implications of new scientific theories, especially with the theory of evolution, provided the essential impetus for the revival. Known as the **St. Louis Hegelians,** they founded the first philosophical journal in the United States, the *Journal of Speculative Philosophy*, which presented translations of contemporary European philosophers and provided an outlet and audience for American philosophers who were venturing on fresh approaches.

William James

Amid this intellectual ferment, the man who was to contribute fundamentally to the new philosophical movement, **pragmatism**, developed his system. William James (1842–1910), brother of the great novelist Henry James, was the son of Henry James, Sr., who was himself a philosopher and a man of immense learning. Trained as a doctor, William taught at the Harvard Medical School but later turned his attention to psychology, in which field he became one of the most important theorists of his day. From his studies of the psychology of man's intellectual and religious life, James turned to philosophy, becoming professor of philosophy at Harvard and the foremost advocate of pragmatism.

WHAT IS PRAGMATISM?

Pragmatism is, first of all, a method for solving or evaluating intellectual problems, and a theory about the kinds of knowledge we are capable of acquiring. William James shared in the American distrust of purely theoretical or intellectual activity, and asked bluntly, what is the point of theorizing? What difference does it make? Why is it important to deal with the intellectual problems that theorists bother about?

"CASH-VALUE"

Before determining if any given philosophical claim is true, James first thought it necessary to determine the **"cash-value"** of the claim—that is, what function it had and what difference it would make if it were true. According to the pragmatic theory, our intellectual activity, our philosophizing, has as its purpose the attempt to resolve difficulties that arise in the course of our attempts to deal with experience. The cash-value of our ideas is to be found in the use to which ideas can be put. With regard to any theory, we can ask what difference it would make if I believed it, and what consequences would follow from my activities if I acted on the theory. If a theory has no cash-value, this means that it would not make the slightest difference whether one believed it true or false and that it would not at all affect one's actions.

THEORIES AS "INSTRUMENTS"

According to James, we think only in order to solve our problems, so that our theories are **instruments** that we employ in order to solve problems in our experience, and the theories, therefore, ought to be judged in terms of their success at performing this function. If one is walking in the woods and loses one's way, then, according to the pragmatic view, one way of dealing with this situation is through theoretical activity. Taking into account such data as the sun's position, the direction in which one has been walking, and one's previous knowledge of the terrain, one can develop a theory about how to extricate oneself from this predicament. The cash-value of the theory can be evaluated in terms of the possible differences it would make if it were true or false. The theory will be judged according to whether it serves as a successful way of dealing with the problem.

In contrast to such instances in which theories have obviously foreseeable consequences for experience, many classical philosophical theories have little or no cash-value. What difference would it make if one believed that the universe was really only one vast mind, or if one believed such a theory false? The immediate problems that one is faced with would remain exactly the same, and one would get no clues as to how to resolve them. At best, a metaphysical belief, such as the one just mentioned, might make one happy or sad; but beyond that, it would have almost no cash-value. There would be no foreseeable consequnces to evaluating the merits of such a metaphysical theory about the ultimate nature of the universe.

From judging that the function of theory is to deal experience, **the pragmatists conclude that a theory is true if it works.** If we ask, what do we mean by saying that a given theory or belief is true, the pragmatists answer that it has been verified if it has been found to deal successfully with experience. Conversely, the falsity of certain ideas is determined by showing that attempts to verify them fail or that they do not "work" in our experience.

Pragmatism and Science

This criterion of evaluation of the truth of theories, the pragmatists claim, is essentially that of science. When a scientist tests a theory, he designs an experiment that tests whether the theory works under specified conditions. Thus, in the test of the Salk polio vaccine, the method employed was to see whether the vaccine worked as a preventative for the disease. The success of the experiments was the basis for the claim that the theory was true.

Pragmatism and Traditional Philosophy

Pragmatists such as William James have opposed the traditional philosophical view that the truth of ideas is a property independent of human experience. Philosophers such as Plato had held that a theory was true absolutely, whether anyone knew it or not. The pragmatists contend, in opposition to such a theory of truth, that the only reason people have for calling one view true and another false is that the one works in human experience and the other does not, not that it does or does not conform to some absolute standards independent of all human experiences. Our only basis for judging the alleged absolute truths of Plato, Descartes, or any other great philosophical rationalist is by evaluating them in relation to their effect on concrete aspects of life. **James maintained the only reason we have for asserting that anything is true is that it works.** Any claims about the independent, objective, absolute nature of truth are meaningless, as far as we can ever determine from our experience and judgments.

Pragmatic Truth

One consequence of the pragmatic theory of truth is, then, that truth is something that happens to an idea, rather than being a fixed property of an idea that we are trying to uncover. Before one discovers whether an idea, a theory, or belief, works, it is neither true nor false. Through the process of testing the view in terms of its consequences and its compatability with other beliefs, the idea becomes true or false, or more true or less true. Thus,

prior to the discovery of America, the view that "There is a large land mass located between Europe and Asia" was neither true nor false. However, as a consequence of the discoveries of Columbus and other early explorers, this theory became true. When this view became true, its denial became false.

In the course of time, various ideas have different developments. As they are employed in relation to the problems and difficulties that confront mankind, as means for dealing with these difficulties and problems, the ideas become true insofar as they work, and false insofar as they do not. Thus, an idea might work for a while, and hence become true. Later it might cease to yield satisfactory results, or no longer be verified by further experience, and so, then, become false. Various now-discarded scientific theories have had such a career. The phlogiston theory of chemistry worked fairly well for a while, but after certain experiments in the eighteenth century, it no longer yielded satisfactory results, and so it was discarded.

Truth, then, is not something static and unchangeable; instead, it grows and develops with time. At various times in human history, certain theories and ideas may be satisfactory for the problems then current. However, with further experience and difficulties, that which is true expands and grows to meet the new conditions. Presumably, at no time will we ever reach a completion or culmination of this process. There has been, and will be, a continuous process of developing new ideas to meet new situations. The attempts of human beings to cope with their universe will lead to unending inquiries, which in turn will lead to newer theories, which in turn will become either true or false, or truer or falser. At each stage in the development without end, what we will call "truth" will be that which enables us to deal satisfactorily with the problems that are then current.

Pragmatism and Ethics

There is also, according to James, an intimate connection between the pragmatic conception of truth and the notion of goodness. Since truth is that which works, or yields satisfactory results in terms of our experience, what is true, in these terms, turns out to be what is profitable for us to believe, or what is good. So put, a type of ethical theory can be developed from pragmatic theory. The pragmatist's method of determining what is good or bad, or right or wrong, is the same as that for determining if an idea is true or false. Thus, given a problem in human behavior, we can ask, "Would performing certain actions be right in order to solve a given problem?" The answer to the question is to be judged in terms of whether the actions yield satisfactory results in the resolution of difficulty. If one ponders whether the right way to solve one's financial problems is to rob a bank, the test is the pragmatic one. Here, presumably, a careful evaluation of the possible consequence of bank robbing would lead one to the conclusion that such a theory does not work, because of all the possible unsatisfactory consequences to oneself, like imprisonment, and the unsatisfactory consequences to others. Therefore, one would conclude, that the bank-robbing solution to one's difficulties is "wrong." On the other hand, one might just as readily con-

clude that this solution is "right." Clearly, then, pragmatism cannot offer any absolute moral principles. We must always act on the hypothesis that works, and this must involve a purely subjective evaluation.

The pluralistic universe

Corresponding to his theory of truth and goodness, James developed a conception of the universe. To begin with, experience is not an object that we examine; instead, there is just a "humming-buzzing confusion" out of which we differentiate various aspects that we call "ourselves," "physical objects," etc. These differentiations are made with reference to problems or difficulties that arise in experience and are carved out of experience as ways of dealing with the problems. The organization and selection of the items that make up our universe relate to our need to deal satisfactorily with various obstacles to successful action. **There is no fixed world to be uncovered through experience but, rather, a continuous quest for workable solutions to difficulties.** No single concept of the universe is to be regarded as the final and complete answer. Instead, the continuing development of our knowledge of the world represents the meaningful idea that we have of the natural world. As new ways of organizing and selecting aspects of our experience are tried, new features of the universe emerge. Both our knowledge and the world are regarded as having an **evolutionary quality of growth and development to meet new situations and new needs.**

This novel conception of the universe was in direct opposition to the more rigid and all-encompassing metaphysical schemes of earlier philosophers. The materialists, the idealists, and others offered a picture of the universe in which certain determinate features pervade it for all time. In contrast to this, the pragmatists envisaged a **pluralistic universe, one with many kinds of features and possibilities,** which cannot be examined and unraveled all at once. Instead, the universe has to be studied tentatively as it emerges and develops. As the process of nature unfolds, our understanding of it will also, in the same progressive and developing manner.

Instrumentalism

In the twentieth century, the form of the pragmatist view that has been most prevalent was constructed by John Dewey, a view sometimes called "instrumentalism." Dewey, who was perhaps the most influential American thinker in recent times, developed **a theory of knowledge essentially in terms of the biological and psychological role that the knowing process plays in human affairs, and then tried to employ this conception as a guide in directing the application of human intellectual activities to contemporary social problems.**

Dewey's Concept of Experience and Thinking

According to Dewey, what constitutes our brute experience is the **interaction between a biological organism and its environment.** Experience is not an object known but, rather, **an action performed.** In the course of the organism's activities, it encounters situations in which it can no longer act. **Thinking arises as a means of dealing with these disturbing situations by working out hypotheses, or guides to future actions.** The merits of these intellectual acts are determined by a practical criterion, by whether the organism can now function satisfactorily again. **Thought, especially scientific thought, is instrumental in problem solving.** The occurrence of problems sets off a chain reaction of mental activity directed toward discovering a functional solution to the difficulties that confront the organism.

Much of earlier philosophizing, Dewey claimed, is actually a hindrance to the task of problem solving. In separating theorizing from practical concerns, and searching for absolute solutions to philosophical questions, philosophers have got away almost completely from the human needs that give rise to thought, and have also tried rigidly to impose certain preconceived schemes upon human thought, and have refused to allow any new beliefs and new solutions in human affairs. What is needed nowadays, Dewey insisted, is a reconstruction of philosophy in terms of the problems that now confront us. In this role, philosophy will no longer be an abstruse subject, of little or no value in the immediate concerns of the day, but will, instead, be the overall directive force in developing new instrumental techniques for assisting the human organism in its struggles with its environment, and in building a better world in which some of the problems now confronting us will gradually be resolved.

Some Applications of Pragmatism

In terms of the more practical point of view of much of American culture, one can easily conceive of the appeal of pragmatism in America. Some of its success has been in the application of its philosophy to certain social problems. By and large, the earlier pragmatism of William James was directed toward resolving certain individual questions of belief, whereas the later instrumentalism of John Dewey was concerned more with broader social questions confronting America in its rapid development in this century.

Possibly owing to his personal heritage, James devoted much effort to examining religious beliefs in pragmatic terms. Unlike the theologicans with their insistence upon the truth of certain religious beliefs, and the scientifically inclined persons with their insistence upon judging religious views by the latest scientific findings, James was concerned to examine the "cash-value" of belief. Why do people accept certain beliefs and not others, and what difference does it make to them in their lives?

James on Religious Belief

In his studies *The Varieties of Religious Experience* and *The Will to Believe*, which were mentioned in Chapter 4, James claimed that there were some people, "tough-minded people," who were temperamentally inclined not to believe anything except on scientific evidence. They were more concerned not to risk holding possibly false beliefs than to hold beliefs that, if they turned out to be true, might be very pleasant, but for which not much evidence was available. On the other hand, there was another group, the "tender-minded," who wanted to believe, and who wanted to believe things about the world that made them happy. Which group was right? A pragmatic analysis, James suggested, revealed that it was actually a question of which attitude worked best. If one could regard the problem of belief undogmatically, that is, without worrying about whether a given belief was actually true or not, one could see that for some people, a certain set of beliefs worked, that is, a certain set of beliefs, when accepted, provided a more satisfactory life. Insofar as these beliefs worked as guides to life, or as satisfactory attitudes, then, pragmatically speaking, these were true beliefs for certain people. Thus, James felt, his pragmatic analysis could remove questions of moral and religious belief from the realms of theological controversy or scientific scrutiny.

Dewey and "Progressive" Education

John Dewey regarded his type of pragmatism as having far-reaching applications in our society. One such employment of his theory was in the realm of education. Previous educational techniques, Dewey felt, were aimed primarily at inculcating a mass of factual information into students without giving them any means of utilizing it. They were crammed with the experience of the past rather than prepared to meet the problems of the future. Instead, he proposed that the educational system should try to develop methods for **problem solving.** If the student learned how to solve problems, presumably he/

she would be better fit for living in our ever-changing world with its manifold perplexities and ever-new problems.

Out of this application of Dewey's theory grew the progressive education movement. Rather than being trained in various disciplines, the child would be trained by being confronted with various situations in which he/she would have to develop methods for overcoming the difficulties that beset him/her. The child would learn how to make satisfactory "adjustments" to his/her environment, and thus develop various means that would aid him/her in solving the larger problems of the social world in which he/she would have to live.

The type of education would train people for living in a democratic society, and it would strengthen the development of this type of social and political organization. A democratic society is one that is better able to confront new situations and try new solutions, since it does not have any rigid or preconceived ideology. It is essentially a system of social organization that is open to exploration of new means for meeting difficulties. It is designed to evolve, to meet change, and to adapt to new developments. The student trained in problem solving would be able to be an active citizen of such a society, utilizing his/her techniques for dealing with unresolved problems in cooperation with the larger social group in their common search for satisfactory ways of dealing with the practical difficulties that hinder the best functioning of society.

Some criticisms of pragmatism

In spite of the evident appeal of the pragmatic point of view for Americans, and its apparent success in becoming for a while the dominant philosophy in America, some philosophers have objected to this theory. They have attacked the basic pragmatic conception of what constitutes true knowledge, and asked if we can really evaluate ideas in terms of whether they work. At what point, they demanded, can one tell if an idea has worked? In considering the example offered earlier, of the man who believed that the way to solve his financial difficulties was by bank robbing, we saw that it would be easy to conclude that this solution was "right," and one cannot deny that there have been occasions on which it has worked. In attempting to deal with this anomaly, the pragmatists insist that one should take into account not only immediate consequences but also the long-run effects. In response, the critics point out that one can never be sure whether an idea has worked, since its long-run consequences can go on forever. At certain times the idea might work successfully, then fail, and then again be successful. One would have to wait indefinitely in order to be able to evaluate the consequences of any belief, and to determine whether it worked. Furthermore, it is not possible to make an evaluation, to say whether something works or not, unless one has some sort of criteria to appeal to. Such criteria the pragmatist expressly denies us. What is meant by "what works"? Are we to be concerned with what works for us as individuals, for our society, for humanity, or what? We need some moral framework, some idea of what is good and bad, desirable and undesirable, some notion of aims and objectives, in order to know what it might mean to say that something works or does not. But the pragmatist wants us to settle our moral disputes also in the same way, by an appeal to "cash-value"; he/she sees "good" itself as synonymous with "what works"; and thus he/she denies the validity of all other criteria and makes it impossible for us to decide what works.

In addition, some of the critics hold, in assessing the working of ideas in terms of the satisfaction certain beliefs afford people, all sorts of personal idiosyncrasies and preferences will become the standards for judging truth and falsehood. Some people may enjoy believing that the moon in made of green cheese, but does that make it true? The critics contend that the pragmatists are confusing the human problems and feelings that are often involved in our attitudes toward various ideas with the merits of the ideas themselves, and are making human "adjustment" the ultimate goal of all investigations, instead of seeking objectively true knowledge.

The pragmatists, in response to these objections, insist that there is no way of investigating the truth or falsehood of theories and beliefs except in terms of how they affect human beings, and that their critics are introducing abstruse and artificial standards that have nothing to do with the real problems of human experience.

Philosophical analysis

What Is Philosophy?

Although people in the Western world have philosophized for more than 2,500 years, the exact nature of philosophy is still a matter of dispute. Philosophy began originally as a curious mixture of scientific, theological, magical, and ethical "explanation" of the common and uncommon features of the world. The early Greek thinkers, such as Thales, Heraclitus, Anaxagoras, Pythagoras, and others, thought of philosophy as we now think of contemporary science. **They assumed that through philosophical reflection the nature of the world would be revealed to them.** Thales, for example, invented an ingenious hypothesis about the fundamental composition of the universe. He believed that all objects are variations of one basic ingredient—water. For water, he argued, if heated becomes steam, and thus all entities that are gaseous, such as the atmosphere, can be described as rarefied water; water in its natural state is a liquid, and all things that flow must be made up of it; and finally, if water is cooled sufficiently, it becomes a solid, ice. It seemed plausible, therefore, that all solids must be condensed forms of water. Thales, with a minimum amount of factual information, was able by reflection to devise an ingenious hypothesis to account for such diverse things as the gaseous, liquid, and solid characteristics of the earth.

Subsequent philosophers, pursuing substantially the same method (i.e., reflection), devised even more striking theories. Democritus, for example, worked out a crude version of the atomic theory some 2,000 years before careful investigation could produce any empirical confirmation of it. As man's curiosity about nature grew and as knowledge of it increased, explanations became both more sophisticated and more satisfactory. In time, the study of nature became an activity that broke away from philosophy, and a new discipline was developed called "science." But this, it should be pointed out, has been a comparatively recent development. Even as late as the nineteenth century, university courses in physics, for instance, were described as "natural philosophy." Now science itself has been fragmented into a host of subdisciplines; each science, so to speak, has selected some aspect of nature for intensive study—physics, for example, deals with the nature of inanimate objects; botany, with plants; astronomy, with celestial phenomena; and so on. Nevertheless, all these scientific activities, as different as they are from one another, each utilize a common method: a method that is too complex accurately to be described here, but **one that not only employs reflection about the world but, more important, also involves the patient observation of, and experimentation with, it.** The main presupposition of scientific activity is that it is only through such observation of, and experimentation with, the objects in the world (as well as reflection about them, of course) that we can acquire accurate information about the characteristics of these objects. Put briefly, **knowledge of the world can be acquired only through the use of scientific method.**

The Problem of Knowledge

Now this method differs importantly from philosophical activity. The philosopher does not perform experiments; he/she does not patiently observe the behavior of natural objects, either animate or inanimate (except his students). And yet philosophy purports to give us knowledge about the world. What kind of knowledge does philosophical activity result in? Is philosophy like science except that it deals with a different subject matter— that is, is it like physics or botany or astronomy, but treating of different kinds of things (e.g., universals, concepts, theories)? Or is philosophy different from science? Does it give us a kind of knowledge, but one that is different from scientific knowledge of the world? Or is it possible that philosophical activity does not result in knowledge at all? But if not, then how can philosophy be justified? Put simply— what, then, is philosophy and what does it tell us about the world?

Recent Developments

In the twentieth century, several influential philosophical movements have developed, each with a different answer to the above questions. Some contemporary theorists, Saul Kripke (1940–) for instance, think that philosophy is and ought to be concerned with an analysis and investigation into the most general features of the world—the concepts of identity, personhood, natural kinds. Willard van Orman Quine (1908–) sees philosophical activity as a theoretical extension of science; that the difference between what a philosopher does or ought to do and what a scientist does are merely differences in emphasis and interest. Ludwig Wittgenstein (1889–1951), whom many regard as the greatest philosophical genius of the twentieth century, thought of philosophy as an autonomous discipline, as dealing with its own peculiar sorts of problems. He did not think that science could solve philosophical problems, and indeed felt, in his last works, that philosophy could not give us any factual information about the world at all.

In the early 1990s, a group working in the philosophy of mind, and calling themselves "empirical philosophers," have taken the view that recent scientific findings in cognitive science and neurobiology will bear importantly on classical philosophical problems about perception, knowledge, and consciousness, and indeed may even solve some or all of these issues. This is still a minority position, but it is growing in importance. Thus, as we approach the end of the twentieth century, a lively debate has been generated about the nature of philosophy: whether it is a substantive discipline with results that give us information about the world, or whether its problems are unique and are basically different from those of science. Let us trace the history of the subject, briefly of course, during the twentieth century.

In the first part of the century, three important movements laid the groundwork for what followed in the second part: **logical atomism, logical positivism** (or **logical empiricism**), and **ordinary language philosophy.** In various forms they are still with us today, having resonances in the work of Quine, Donald Davidson, Hilary Putnam, Richard Rorty, Daniel Dennett, Paul Churchland, and others. Unquestionably, the single most influential philosopher in the second half of the century has been Ludwig Wittgenstein. Wittgenstein died in 1951, and with one exception (*Tractatus Logico-Philosophicus*), his most important writings have been published posthumously. Many of these have re-

cently been edited and published, and more are scheduled to appear in the near future. The impact of his work, especially that deriving from his *Philosophical Investigations* (1953), has been phenomenal. In 1989 the centenary of his birth was celebrated with innumerable worldwide national and international conferences, and more than thirty books dealing with his life and thought were published in that year alone. In speaking about recent developments, we shall focus our attention on the "later philosophy" of Wittgenstein. This discussion will be followed with a description of the state of the field as we approach the year 2000.

Logical atomism: The philosophy of Bertrand Russell and the early Ludwig Wittgenstein

It is difficult to explain the philosophy of logical atomism in a simple and brief way for the average (nonspecialist) person. This is because in order to understand it such a person must know the essentials of a highly technical new discipline called **"mathematical (or symbolic) logic."** In a sense that does not too greatly distort the facts, logical atomism may briefly be described as the philosophy of mathematical logic, or perhaps more accurately, of *Principia Mathematica*, the great work on mathematical logic by Alfred North Whitehead and Bertrand Russell, published in three volumes between 1910 and 1913. Let us try here to give an account in a simple way of the main ideas of *Principia Mathematica*.

The New Logic

It had been assumed, even as late as the nineteenth century, that Aristotle had said the last word on logic. Kant, for instance, had asserted that logic as developed by Aristotle was, of all philosophical disciplines, a finished and complete subject, even down to its details. This view was shown to be wholly mistaken by Russell and Whitehead. Around the turn of the twentieth century, and after more than ten years of work, **they developed a new type of logic that was much broader in scope than Aristotelian logic; indeed, it contained classical logic as a very minor part.** This new logic resembled a mathematical calculus, such as Euclid's elements, except, again, that it was of much greater generality: it did not mention lines, points, and planes, but talked merely about the relations of symbols to each other. (This is why it has been named "symbolic logic.") The main difference between Aristotelian logic and the new logic can be put as follows: **Aristotelian logic was essentially a logic of classes, whereas Russell's logic was a logic of propositions.** By a class we mean an entity denoted by a term such as "man," or "brother," or "mortal," etc. The basic propositions of Aristotelian logic, such as "All men are mortal," and "Some men are mortal," state the relations of classes of things to each other. For example, the proposition "All men are mortal" states that the class of men is included in the class of mortal things, while the proposition "Some men are mortal" states that some of the class of men are included in the class of mortal things. Russell's logic, on the other hand, talked about the relation of propositions to each other (e.g., "If it is raining, then the streets are wet"). The sentences "It

is raining" and "the streets are wet" both express propositions, which stand in a certain relation to each other—a relation that Russell called **"implication."** Russell was able to show that in terms of this logic, the relation between classes of things could also be explicated; hence his logical system not only included Aristotle's treatment of logic, but at the same time went beyond it.

Principia Mathematica was of great importance for philosophy for at least two reasons: (*a*) **It argued that mathematics, which had been thought to be a distinct discipline, is in fact a part of logic.** Russell showed this by deducing from purely logical notions a set of postulates laid down by the great Italian mathematician Giuseppe Peano; and from these postulates it was known that arithmetic could be derived. (*b*) **Russell claimed, further, that everyday, or "natural," languages, such as English, have a basic structure similar to that of *Principia Mathematica*.** Although natural languages resemble *Principia* in this respect, they are defective for purposes of philosophical analysis, since they are less precise. **It was accordingly believed that mathematical logic would provide philosophy with a tool of razor sharpness for clarifying the meaning of the sentences of any natural language, for instance English and French.** This in turn gave rise to the hope that philosophical disputes at last could be treated definitively with the use of a new logical machinery. Since we are interested in the influence of *Principia* upon philosophy, rather than in its treatment of the foundations of mathematics, we shall restrict our discussion to that aspect of it.

The Nature of Sentences

What, then, is meant by the "basic structure" of the sentences of any natural language, such as English? This can be explained as follows: Russell distinguished between what he called **"atomic propositions"** and **"molecular propositions." An atomic proposition is a proposition that has no parts that are themselves propositions.** Thus, "John is human" is an atomic proposition, since its parts are individual words, not propositions. On the other hand, a proposition like "John and Mary are going to the cinema" is a molecular proposition. Upon analysis, it can be seen to be a **complex proposition containing two parts, each of which is itself a proposition,** i.e., (a) "John is going to the cinema," and (b) "Mary is going to the cinema." A molecular proposition is built up out of atomic propositions by the use of what Russell called **"connecting words,"** such as "and," "or," and "if . . . then." In part, symbolic logic can be regarded as the study of such words, since the rules for the employment of these words allow us to build up complex propositions out of more simple ones. Through the logical machinery of *Principia*, Russell laid down a set of rules that, if followed, would allow one to build molecular propositions out of atomic ones. **He was thus able to analyze any molecular proposition into a set of atomic propositions, plus the logical connectives.** Thus the meaning of a molecular proposition could, so to speak, be unraveled by breaking it down into its constituent atomic propositions. The question now remained—how do we analyze the meaning of an atomic proposition?

Russell's answer was that **an atomic proposition is always of the subject-predicate form.** For example, "John is mortal" can be analyzed into a subject term, which is a proper noun or proper name, "John," and into a predicate term, such as "is mortal." The subject term in such a case always refers to an individual thing—in this case the person, John—and the predicate term to a characteristic, or "property," which the subject term possesses, in this case the characteristic of being mortal.

At this point, the philosophical implications of Russell's system become apparent. When an atomic proposition is true, the subject term denotes an individual thing or object, and the predicate term refers to some characteristics of this thing or object. And in showing that atomic propositions refer to such objects and characteristics, *Principia* gives us information about the real world. **It informs us that the world is made up of "facts," and that all such facts are atomic in nature, i.e., every fact can be described by an atomic proposition.** There are no molecular facts in nature, since every molecular proposition can be translated into, or reduced to, a set of atomic propositions, plus the logical connectives, such as "and," "or," "if . . . then," and so forth. These connectives, of course, themselves refer to nothing in the world; they are linguistic devices that enable us to combine atomic propositions in various ways; their use is thus, as Russell put it, "syntactic" only. It should also be stressed that there are no "general" facts in the world either. There is no fact corresponding to the general proposition "All men are mortal," since this proposition again reduces to a set of atomic propositions such as "John is mortal," "James is mortal," and so forth, for every individual human who is mortal. **The ultimate constituents of the world are thus "facts," and a fact is made** up of an individual thing with its individual characteristics.

Through the study of mathematical logic, then, we are able to discover the essential structure of the world, i.e., we are able to discover that the world is made up of atomic facts. The answer of logical atomism to the set of questions we posed about philosophy can now be stated: **The function of philosophy is to inform us about the world.** In particular, it is to inform us that the structure of the world is mirrored by the structure of the basic propositions of *Principia*.

The Theory of Descriptions

But this was not the sole use to which *Principia Mathematica* could be put for philosophical purposes. Further, and perhaps as important, its machinery could be used to solve problems that had puzzled thinkers for centuries—problems that had important **ontological** consequences. We can illustrate this by a discussion of what Russell called the **"theory of descriptions."**

The point of the theory of descriptions is to show that philosophers, through the faulty analysis of language, have been misled by specious arguments into believing that the sorts of things that ordinary people regard as fictitious or nonexistent actually do, in some sense, exist. The problem that these philosophers found perplexing is an ancient one; it occurs even in Plato. It can be stated as follows: We seem to be able to make significant, and indeed sometimes even true, statements about "objects" such as Medusa, Hamlet, the mythical country of Atlantis, and so forth. When we say, for example,

"Hamlet murdered Polonius," this proposition seems to be true; and yet, upon reflection, we realize that there never was any such thing as Hamlet. But how can the proposition be true unless it is about something existent? Or again, when we say "Medusa does not exist," are we not saying "There exists something, Medusa, which does not exist"? But this is an obvious contradiction. Is it then impossible for one to deny the existence of anything without contradicting oneself? There is something obviously wrong here, and through the machinery of *Principia Mathematica*, Russell set out to eliminate the difficulty.

Russell put the puzzle in this way. He asked: How is it possible for a sentence such as "The present King of France is wise" to be significant even though there is no King of France? Now the answer given to this question by a group of philosophers who preceded Russell, notably Alexis Meinong, was that such entities as "The present King of France," "Medusa," and "Hamlet" are real things. True, they do not exist in the actual world, but at least they do exist; they exist in some shadowy realm. Meinong described them as "subsisting" instead of "existing"—but his point is that in some sense they *are*. "Medusa," "Hamlet," "the present King of France," etc., are genuine constituents of the world, but they do not exist in the same sense as you and your friends do. Meinong and those influenced by him were led into this curious way of thinking (something called **"philosophical idealism"**) by an argument that might be stated as follows:

(*a*) The phrase "The present King of

France" is the subject of the sentence "The present King of France is wise."

(*b*) Since the sentence "The present King of France is wise" is *significant*, it must be about something, i.e., it must be about the present King of France.

(*c*) But unless the present King of France existed, the sentence would not be about anything and hence could not be meaningful at all.

(*d*) Since "The present King of France is wise" is meaningful or significant, it therefore must be about some entity—the present King of France—hence such an entity must exist (or "subsist").

Symbolic Logic

Russell now showed, through the techniques developed in his symbolic logic, that this argument rests upon a fallacy. In order to understand his criticism, and accordingly to understand the theory of descriptions which is part of the criticism, it is necessary to make a distinction between what Russell called the **"grammatical form"** of a sentence and its **logical form.** A sentence may be of the subject-predicate form from a standpoint of English grammar, and yet when translated into the language of *Principia Mathematica*, it may be of a different form, logically speaking. Thus, consider the sentence "God exists." In such a sentence, the word "God" is grammatically the subject of the sentence, and "exists" is the predicate. If we were to rephrase this sentence and put it into its proper logical form, i.e., if we were to make clear the proposition it asserts, the word "God" would no longer be the logical subject but, instead, would be the logical predicate; and the word "exists" would no longer be the logical predicate but would have a different function. It would be what Russell called a **"logical quantifier,"** that is, it would have the same function as an indefinite pronoun such as "someone" or "something." Such words are used to refer ambiguously to an indeterminate class of things, and because they refer *indefinitely*, they are words expressing generality. Thus, when put into its proper logical form, the sentence "God exists" says: "Something, and only one thing, is omnipotent, omniscient, and benevolent." In short, when we analyze the meaning of the sentence "God exists," we see that it means that a certain indefinite something has a certain set of properties (being omnipotent, omniscient, and benevolent). **The sentence is thus, logically speaking, not of the subject-predicate form but is a general proposition, a proposition of an entirely different structure from that of an atomic proposition.**

Now the same thing is true of the sentence "The present King of France is wise." Its grammatical structure leads us to believe that the phrase "the present King of France" is logically the subject term, and "is wise" is logically the predicate term, and that such a sentence therefore is an atomic proposition, denoting a fact of the world. But such a sentence is not *logically* of the subject-predicate form. When it is analyzed according to the techniques developed in *Principia Mathematica* it analyzes into the following propositions:

1. Something is current monarch of France.
2. Not more than one thing is current monarch of France.

3. Whatever is current monarch of France is wise.

It should be noticed that each of these three propositions, which together comprise the meaning of "The present King of France is wise," is a *general* proposition, not an atomic proposition. This can be seen since **no proper names** occur in them, but, instead, such *general* words as "something," "whatever," etc. The phrase "the present King of France," which occurs in the sentence "The present King of France is wise," is thus, from a logical point of view, not the subject of the proposition at all, for upon analysis it is eliminated from the analyzing propositions. Instead, we have propositions containing **no proper names at all, but only indefinite pronouns and predicates.** Thus the phrase "the present King of France" is not logically a proper name, although from a grammatical standpoint it has the same function as a proper name. Meinong would have been right, Russell argued, in inferring that if such a phrase *were* a proper name, it would refer to something, and thus right in inferring that the present King of France "subsists." But analysis into logical terminology shows us that the grammatical form of the sentence is misleading with respect to giving us the *actual form* of the proposition; for when so analyzed, it turns into a set of general propositions. Now general propositions do not refer to anything *directly in the actual world*, since only atomic propositions can designate facts. Meinong's fallacy was to conclude that the phrase "the present King of France" was a proper name because it functioned as the grammatical subject of a sentence. In showing that

"The present King of France is wise" is logically a *general* proposition, not an atomic proposition Russell was in effect showing that such a phrase does not directly denote any object in the world. **Only the subjects of atomic propositions are capable of direct denotation or reference.**

Russell called such expressions as "the present King of France" **"definite descriptive phrases." They are "definite" because they connote that one and only one individual satisfies the description—this is the function of the word "the."** Russell's point about descriptions not being logically proper names can be put in yet a different way. He elsewhere described them as **"incomplete symbols"** rather than as "proper names." Such phrases are "incomplete" because they have no meaning by themselves. They function much as brackets do in a sentence, which also have no meaning by themselves. However, definite descriptive phrases can take on meaning in the context of a whole sentence that contains them. Thus, if one were to ask "What does the phrase 'the present King of France' mean?" then, according to Russell, a proper reply would be "It means nothing at all—by *itself*." This is because only proper names *mean* independently of a whole sentence; they *mean* the object they are used to refer to (for instance the name "Julius Caesar" means the object Julius Caesar). Now since the phrase "the present King of France" can be shown by analyzing it (as above) into the language of *Principia* not to be a proper name, it has no meaning of its own, i.e., it does not by itself directly refer to anything in the world. However, sentences containing such a phrase may have meaning. Thus the sentence "The present King of France is wise" means the same as "One and only one thing is the current monarch of France, and this thing is wise." In this way, through the notion of an "incomplete symbol," Russell was able to solve Meinong's perplexity about how it is possible for a sentence like "The present King of France is wise," to be significant even though the phrase "the present King of France" does not directly denote anything.

Logical Atomism

The assumptions upon which the theory of descriptions rests are those of logical atomism. **It is assumed by Russell that *Principia Mathematica* gives us the sketch of a perfect language; it is perfect because it mirrors the structure of the actual world.** When we translate a sentence of ordinary English into this perfect logical language, its meaning becomes clear. **If it turns out, upon such translation, not to be of the subject-predicate form, then there is nothing that its grammatical subject will directly refer to, since in the perfect language every subject term will denote an actual object in the world, and every predicate term will denote an actual characteristic of that object.**

Logical atomism received its most careful and complete statement in a cryptic work written by a philosophical genius named Ludwig Wittgenstein, who was a pupil of Russell's. Wittgenstein, in a book called the *Tractatus Logico-Philosophicus*, published in 1922, developed a version of logical atomism that is now called the "picture theory." According to Wittgenstein, the ideal language (*Principia*) pic-tured or mirrored the world, just as a map mirrors it. If we wish to discover whether town A is north of town B in Scotland, we can do so by referring to a map, since a map in a sense pictures the terrain. It pictures it because there is identity of structure between the points on the map and the points on the ground. A perfect language is like a map. It pictures the structure of reality. For every proper name in the language, there is a corresponding entity; and for every predicate, a corresponding property. The ideal language thus gives us the structure of facts, since facts are composed of objects and their properties.

We may summarize the main tenets of logical atomism as follows:

Philosophy is a genuine activity, just as science is. Unlike science, though, philosophy does not discover new facts for us. The knowledge we acquire through the study of philosophy is not knowledge of new facts. Instead, philosophy tells us about the structure of the world, how its basic ingredients are constructed. Roughly speaking, it tells us that the world is composed of a set of atomic facts, i.e., objects and their properties.

The Proper Function of Philosophy Is Analysis

Analysis consists in rewriting sentences of natural languages in such a way that these sentences will exhibit their proper logical form. When put into their logical form, their meaning will become clear, and philosophical perplexity will be eliminated.

As can be seen from the above remarks, **the philosophy of logical atomism is a metaphysical system in the traditional** sense. It contends that philosophy is an activity that gives us knowledge of the world; not the same kind of knowledge that science gives us, to be sure, but knowledge nonetheless.

The philosophy of logical atomism flourished, especially in England, in the 1920s and 1930s; but it has declined steadily in popularity since then. One of the main reasons for its eclipse was the rise of **logical positivism, another philosophy influenced by the development of mathematical logic. But this doctrine utilized mathematical logic to show that metaphysics was nonsense, and since logical atomism was clearly a form of traditional metaphysics, it was rejected by thinkers who accepted the newer view.**

Logical positivism: Schlick, Carnap, Ayer

Logical positivism is often thought to have been initiated by a remark of Wittgenstein in the *Tractatus* to the effect that **philosophy is not a theory but an activity.** Logical positivism was the philosophical movement initiated by a group of thinkers who lived in Vienna in the 1920s. (This group later became famous under the name of the Vienna Circle.) Among its members were Moritz Schlick, professor at the University of Vienna, Hans Hahn, Friedrich Waismann, Herbert Feigl, Otto Neurath, and Rudolf Carnap. These men held informal seminars and, in particular, closely studied the writings of Wittgenstein. They elaborated upon the view that philosophy is not a theory but an activity. **They held that philosophy does not produce propositions that are true or false; it merely clarifies the meaning of**

statements, showing some to be scientific, some to be mathematical, and some (including most so-called "philosophical statements") to be nonsensical. Their views, put in brief, were that every significant statement either is a **statement of formal logic** (in the broad sense of *Principia Mathematica*, and thus including mathematical statements) or is a **statement of science** (again the phrase "scientific statement" was broadly interpreted to include singular sentences such as "This is white," as well as statements of physical laws). All other types of statement were, strictly speaking, nonsensical. If they had any meaning whatsoever, it was described as **"poetical,"** or **"emotive,"** or **"pictorial,"** or **"motivational,"** but it was **not cognitive.** The statements of theology such as "God exists in a heavenly place" fell into this category, as did such traditional philosophical statements as "We can never directly observe physical objects," "I can never know that you have a mind," "No men are free, but everyone is determined by his past," and so forth. It was not held, it must be made clear, that such statements were *false*; they were literally without sense, just as the statement " 'Twas brillig, and the slithy toves" is without sense. Philosophy pursued in the traditional manner was thus deprecated; philosophy had a legitimate function, to be sure, but it was not a function that resulted in propositions. Rather, it was an activity that led to the clarification of the meaning of questions in order to show how these could be answered by the appropriate disciplines. Herbert Feigl's witty remark about the nature of philosophy, practiced in the traditional way, beautifully epitomizes the outlook of this school of philosophers. "Philosophy," he remarked, "is the disease of which it should be the cure." Let us trace the steps that led to this position.

The Verification Principle

In order to understand the powerful attack that logical positivism made upon traditional philosophical systems, including logical atomism, it is necessary to analyze two of their basic tenets: first, a distinction that they adhered to between what are called **"analytic"** and **"synthetic"** propositions, and secondly, **their criterion for determining when a proposition is cognitively meaningful,** sometimes called the **"verification principle."** Let us explain first the distinction they drew between analytic and synthetic propositions.

Consider, by way of introducing the distinction, the following two propositions: (*a*) All husbands have heads, and (*b*) All husbands are married.

Now both of these propositions are similar in being true; yet they differ in the way they are true. Proposition (*a*) happens to be true of every husband. We never see a husband without a head. But, and this is the important point, it would be possible to imagine a husband who had no head. Imagine a man born without a head, who lived, who was fed through tubes, who married. This man would be exactly like other men except that he would lack a head. But because he would have married someone, he would be a husband. On the other hand, proposition (*b*) is not merely true as a matter of fact; but it is *impossible* to imagine or conceive of any circumstances whatever in which somebody could be a husband and yet not be married. It does not merely happen to

be the case that all husbands are married; it follows from the very meaning of the word "husband" that anyone who is a husband *necessarily* is married. We can thus see that if anyone were in doubt about the truth of these propositions, he would establish them in quite different ways. In order to prove the first proposition true, he would actually have to observe every single husband. This would require, as we say, empirical investigation: some sort of actual survey of existing husbands. But one does not have to conduct any investigation to prove that the proposition "All husbands are married" is true. He merely has to understand the meaning of the words that make up the proposition. Once he understands these words, he can see that it is part of the *meaning* of the word "husband" that all husbands are married—for "husband" means the same as "married male." Thus the proposition can be seen to be true without any sort of empirical investigation at all.

Propositions that require some sort of empirical investigation for their confirmation are termed "synthetic" while those whose truth follows from their meaning are called "analytic." It is the contention of logical positivism that every significant proposition must be either analytic or synthetic, but none can be both. Broadly speaking, all analytic propositions belong to formal logic—they are true by virtue of their formal structure; while all synthetic propositions are like the propositions of science—they require empirical investigation before their truth can be established. To put it differently, analytic propositions are so called because, since their predicate is contained in the definition of the subject term, all that the proposition is doing is **to assert something of the subject that is obtained by analysis of the subject term** (e.g., "All husbands [i.e., married males] are married"). Hence we verify such propositions by examining the words they contain. Synthetic propositions, on the other hand, are so called because they are the result of **joining together, i.e., making a *synthesis* of, two logically unrelated things** (e.g., "This desk is brown"). Hence they can be verified only by observation and empirical investigation of whether in fact this relation is true.

One further consequence of this distinction must be mentioned. Analytic propositions, it was held, do not refer to the world in the way in which synthetic propositions do. From the truth of an analytic proposition, we cannot infer that the items mentioned by the terms in the proposition exist. Thus, from the analytic truth that "All giants are giants," we cannot infer that there are any giants. On the other hand, if such a proposition as "This desk is brown" is true, we can infer that the world contains at least one desk. The logical positivists described the difference between the two types of proposition by saying that analytical propositions are **"trivial,"** whereas synthetic propositions are **"informative."** The former are trivial in the sense that although they appear to be talking about items in the world, upon analysis it can be seen that they make no claim about the world; this was put by saying that **they are true merely in virtue of their logical form, or by definition** (i.e., the definition of a "husband" is that husbands are married males), or by saying that they are **assertions about words.** On

the other hand, a synthetic proposition is **"informative" in the sense that it purports to make some claim about reality, and when true, in fact does make such a claim.**

Now it is easy, through the mathematical and logical techniques developed by Russell and Whitehead, to tell whether a proposition is analytic or not. But how can we tell when a synthetic proposition, or one which purports to be about the world, is significant?

Is such a proposition as "God exists in a heavenly place" significant? It purports to be about the world—but is it?

In order to answer this question, the positivists developed a test for the significance of synthetic propositions: the famous verifiability criterion of meaning. Any proposition that passed this test was held to be significant in a factual sense. If it failed to pass the test, it must either be analytic (and hence not about the world) or nonsignificant, i.e., nonsensical. All propositions that therefore aim to express genuine knowledge about the world must pass the test of being empirically verifiable before they can be admitted to be significant. What, then, is the verifiability criterion?

This criterion has been formulated in various ways by different philosophers. Schlick, in a famous paper called "Realism and Positivism," formulates the principle in at least five different ways. One of its most famous statements is to be found in a book by A. J. Ayer, published in 1936, called *Language, Truth, and Logic.* According to Ayer, **a sentence will be factually (i.e., not analytically) significant to a given person if, and only if, he knows how to verify the proposition that it purports** to express; that is, if he knows what observations would lead him under certain conditions to accept the proposition as being true, or reject it as being false.

The important word in the above formulation is the word **"observation."** The point of the principle is that it must be possible to describe what sorts of observations would have to be made in order to determine whether a proposition is true or false. **If some observation can be described that would be relevant in determining the truth or falsity of a proposition, then the proposition will be significant; if not, it will be meaningless.** Schlick produced a striking example to illustrate the use of this principle. Suppose somebody asserted, "The universe is shrinking uniformly." Suppose further that by "uniformly" he meant that everything would remain exactly proportional to everything else; all our measuring sticks would shrink at the same rate; all people would grow smaller proportionately; and thus there would be no discernible or measurable difference between things after the universe had shrunk and things before it had. Would it then make sense to say that the universe had shrunk? Obviously not, since no possible observation could prove that it had shrunk. Since the word "universe" denotes everything that exists, no one—even in principle—could get outside of it; thus no one could measure any such shrinkage; and thus to assert such a set of words is to assert something nonsensical.

Philosophical theories, according to Schlick, make just such assertions. To say "We never directly perceive physical objects" is either to utter a triviality or to make a remark that is, if significant, false.

But if a philosopher holds that it is neither trivially analytic or false, then, according to Schlick, since it cannot be verified, it will be nonsensical, since no possible observation can be described that will determine it to be either true or false.

In explaining the verifiability criterion, a further distinction must be made. It is necessary to distinguish between propositions that are veri*fied* and those that are verifi*able*, or to put it in other words, between *practical* verifiability and verifiability *in principle*. Consider the following proposition: "There is extraterrestrial life." Now this proposition has never been verified by anyone; yet it is a proposition that is verifiable. We can describe the steps we must take in order to verify it. We must first find some means of getting to other parts of the universe and then looking to see if there is life there. If there is determined to be such life, then the proposition will be true; if not, it will be false. The proposition in any case is significant, since we have described the conditions under which it would be known to be either true or false. Even though we cannot at the present time actually verify the proposition, since we do not have the available means for traveling to outer space, nonetheless it is in principle verifiable, and hence is significant.

Now consider by way of contrast such a proposition as "God exists in a heavenly place." What conditions would reveal this proposition to be true? What steps could we possibly take in order to show it to be verifiable, even in principle? There is no relevant observation we could make that would show the proposition either to be true or false (to argue that if we died, we could then determine which it was, is simply another way of stating that no observation, in the present sense of that word, would be relevant). Since no conceivable way of verifying the proposition, even in principle, exists, this sentence expresses no propositions—it is not a **cognitively significant** utterance.

Implications

What are the consequences for traditional philosophy if we accept the tenets of logical positivism? The main effect of accepting such a doctrine will be that insofar as philosophy purports to tell us something about reality, and insofar as it claims that the propositions purporting to tell us something about reality are neither empirically verifiable nor analytic, we can reject such claims as being without sense. Thus, consider the following example of philosophical prose from a book by a contemporary existentialist, Martin Heidegger, *What Is Metaphysics?* Heidegger writes:

> Why are we concerned about this nothing? The nothing is rejected by science and sacrificed as the unreal. Science wants to have nothing to do with the nothing. What is the nothing? Does the nothing exist only because the not, i.e., negation exists? Or do negation and the not exist only because the nothing exists? We maintain: the nothing is the simple negation of the totality of being. Anxiety reveals the nothing. The nothing itself nots.

Rudolf Carnap in an examination of the above discourse shows that its propositions are not capable of confirmation, since it is not possible to formulate an observation statement by which the proposition can be tested. He thus rejects them as nonsensical, and the above piece of writing, he believes, is typical of traditional philosophy. **Traditional philosophy purports to tell us something about the world, but because its utterances are in general empirically unverifiable, they are either trivially analytic or meaningless.**

Does this then mean that philosophy has no legitimate function whatever? The positivist thinks that philosophy does have a legitimate function—what we have called "**analysis.**" But by "analysis" he does not mean analysis in Russell's sense, i.e., **the translation of statements in ordinary language into statements that accurately exhibit their logical form.** Rather, **the function of analysis is to take any problem, to show which questions in it are capable of being answered by mathematical or logical reasoning, and which questions are capable of being answered by some sort of empirical investigation.** It is not the function of philosophers, as such, to *answer* these questions: it is merely their function to **clarify the meaning of the questions so that one will know what sort of questions they are and how to proceed to answer them.** Philosophical problems of the traditional sort, as we have tried to show elsewhere in this book, are extraordinarily complex. They are a composite of a whole host of queries, puzzles, questions—some of which are answerable only by empirical investigation, some of which require mathematical or logical techniques for their solution. Some questions are the products of emotion and bias; some are simply senseless, for one reason or another. Philosophical analysis is thus conceived as a process that is *preliminary* to any sort of answer to a question. One must first **analyze the question in order to discover what it means**—indeed, as David Rynin in his excellent statement of the verifiability criterion puts it—**to discover what a question means is identical with discovering how one would go about answering it.** The analyst himself suggests no answers—and hence when he philosophizes properly, no propositions are forthcoming. Philosophy thus makes no claims about the world—it merely attempts to unravel those perplexities of everyday life and science that bother people, and that people cannot sensibly answer without first discovering what sort of an answer would be relevant. Insofar, then, as philosophy solves puzzles and clears heads, its function is therapeutic. Those who advocate the use of philosophy for such purposes have often been described as **"therapeutic positivists."**

Ordinary language philosophy: Moore and the later Wittgenstein

A third important contemporary movement in analytical philosophy has sometimes been styled the **"ordinary language school"** of philosophy. Although many of the philosophers described as "ordinary language philosophers" would deny that they form a school, or that there is one method they follow, they have enough in common to justify grouping them together in some rough fashion. Basically, what they have in common is a rejection of the notion that philosophical problems can be understood or solved by the use of techniques deriving from formal logic. So they share a negative outlook, but though differing widely in their positive views,

they also share the positive commitment that one must begin from an analysis of ordinary speech in order to see what light it casts on philosophical issues.

One of the founders of this movement, if it can be called a movement, was G. E. Moore (1873–1958). Moore defended a commonsense view of the world, holding that ordinary persons who claimed that they knew—and knew with certainty—that tables, chairs, etc., existed, were correct. They were correct because they were using the word "know" in its common, ordinary way in making such a claim. Therefore, those philosophers—skeptics or idealists—who denied that we can have knowledge of the external world were either mistaken in such claims or were using the word "know" in some peculiar, technical sense that did not undermine the claims of those, speaking ordinary English, who claimed that they did know that tables, persons, planets existed.

Moore's approach was greatly extended by John L. Austin (1911–60), whose meticulous and subtle investigation of how words are used by ordinary speakers had an enormous influence upon philosophy in the post–Second World War period. Austin's philosophical writings rest upon two assumptions:

1. That everyday speech is built up over a long period of time and, accordingly, that the different words and other types of expressions it contains are not merely accidental occurrences in the language but are there to serve specific purposes. It is thus part of his approach to assume that different words tend to be subject to different uses and that these in turn

mark out different logical distinctions. One of the main purposes of philosophy is to explore such distinctions and then to see how they bear upon traditional philosophical issues. A good example of his technique is to be found in *"Three Ways of Spilling Ink,"* where he describes a scene in which a young boy in school pours ink on the hair of the girl sitting in front of him. Did he spill the ink **deliberately** or **purposively** or **intentionally?** One might think that these words are synonymous, but Austin shows they are not. A person who spills ink **deliberately** does so after weighing various options (he/she doesn't act hastily); one who spills ink **intentionally** is operating from a plan (he/she has thought out the scheme in advance); and one who does it **purposively** has an end or goal in mind. Via these distinctions, Austin brilliantly brings out different ways that persons can be held **responsible** for what they do; his work thus amounts to a new and inventive approach to such old problems as the free will problem, which raises questions about whether one can be held responsible for one's actions.

2. Austin's second assumption is that philosophers tend to approach a philosophical problem before they are clear about the facts of a case, especially the linguistic facts. In his *Sense and Sensibilia* (1960), Austin points out that the so-called "argument from illusion," which is designed to show that some of our perceptions of the world are **delusive,** assumes that cases of illusions and cases of delusions are the same thing. A wheel that appears to be rotating in the opposite direction that a cart is moving is an illusion all right, but not a delusion. There is nothing wrong psychologically with the person who sees the wheel rotating "backward." But people who have delusions are suffering from an illness and may need treatment. A person seeing his/her face in a mirror is not seeing an illusion at all and, if normal, is not suffering from a delusion. Unless one gets these linguistic facts straight, Austin argues, one cannot come to grips with serious issues about our knowledge of the external world.

The Later Wittgenstein

In the 1930s Wittgenstein came to realize that the search for a perfect language that accurately mirrored the world could not be realized. We cannot here reliably state in detail his reasons for abandoning logical atomism—the view he propounded in his *Tractatus Logico-Philosophicus*, published in 1922—but his later works were primarily directed toward attacking his own earlier views. He was to claim that his "older" theory was the only possible alternative to his newer outlook, was indeed an attractive view, but that it was deeply and fundamentally mistaken. The new approach is to be found in his masterpiece, *Philosophical Investigations* (1952), published after his death. This has had enormous influence on contemporary philosophy. Literally hundreds of books and articles have been devoted to Wittgenstein's later philosophy in the four plus decades since his death, in 1951.

Wittgenstein's later philosophy is difficult to summarize because it is not presented in a didactic or argumentative form. It is presented as a series of numbered remarks or comments. Sometimes it is not clear whether it is the author who is speaking or whether he is alluding to an opponent (perhaps his earlier self) whom he is attacking. It is therefore often difficult to tell whether a line of reasoning represents a main theme, and if it does where it begins and ends, and what its point is supposed to be. Wittgenstein himself recognized that the reader would find it difficult to follow his thought, but he believed that it was necessary to present his views in this fashion—that a philosophical investigation is a series of "sketches of landscapes," as he says in the introduction to the *Investigations*. Wittgenstein begins the *Investigations* by quoting from St. Augustine's *Confessions* (Book I, Chapter 8). According to Wittgenstein, Augustine presents the following view about the nature of language. Wittgenstein writes as follows:

> These words, it seems to me, give us a particular picture of the essence of human language. It is this: the individual words in language name objects—sentences are combinations of such names. In this picture of language we find the roots of the following idea: every word has a meaning. This meaning is correlated with the word. It is the object for which the word stands.
>
> Augustine does not speak of there being any difference between kinds of words. If you describe the learning of language in this way you are, I believe, thinking primarily of nouns like "table," "chair," "bread," and of people's names, and only secondarily of the names of certain actions and proper-

ties; and of the remaining kinds of words as something that will take care of itself.

But though explicitly speaking about St. Augustine, Wittgenstein is really describing the view he advanced in the *Tractatus*—the so-called "picture theory"—which in turn was connected with the doctrine of logical atomism. According to the picture theory, significant discourse is possible about the world because the elementary sentences of such discourse mirror the world; and this is due to the fact that their elements—conceived of as logical atoms—stand in a one-to-one correspondence with the individual elements of the world. As we remarked earlier, the resulting picture of language is that it has a simple essence: namely, its basic propositions can be significant because they stand in an isomorphic mapping relation to the world.

It is the whole conception of what language is, and how it works, that Wittgenstein now rejects. The new view shows that language has no simple essence, that it is an enormously complicated activity, learned in a variety of ways and used in ways too numerous to count. It is the search for an essence, the search for the "real" meaning behind the everyday flow of experience, that characterizes the activity of the philosopher. He is driven by the impulse to find a simple picture, a simple model that will fit all phenomena and in terms of which he can understand them. The theory of meaning thus ultimately gives way to a theory about the nature of philosophical activity, and this becomes the central theme of the later philosophy.

For Wittgenstein, typical philosophical

"problems" have the peculiarity that they cannot be solved either by mathematical or empirical procedures (in part, this is why any attempt to solve them by means of an ideal language will prove abortive). The reason for this is that they involve "perplexities" that arise from the attempt of a reflective person to give a theoretically satisfactory picture of facts that are known to him/her. In giving such a picture, the person in question is not attempting to discover new facts (to make a scientific contribution). Instead, he/she is trying to order these facts in a way that makes them seem significant to him/her. He/she is, in short, trying to give a general explanation of the world. But the results of this activity often issue in statements that are unverifiable and run counter to common sense. As Wittgenstein says in a remarkable passage: **"Language is a labyrinth of paths. You approach from one side and know your way about; you approach the same place from another side and no longer know your way about."** Thus, the person who says **"Everybody is basically selfish"** is aware of the fact that some people are motivated to act only in their own interest, and that some people are motivated to act so as to further the interests of others—yet he is inclined to describe both sets of people as "selfish." In doing this, something has gone wrong with his way of characterizing or describing these facts. The result is perplexity, because he is inclined to say both that such people are selfish and yet, in view of the obviously contrary facts, that they are not selfish. In the end, he does not know what to say.

How, then, is such perplexity to be resolved? Not by an appeal to the facts, since the person suffering from such perplexity knows the facts as well as anyone. His problem is that he does not know how to describe them. The solution to this problem, accordingly, does not consist in giving him new information, but (as Wittgenstein puts it) "by arranging what we have always known." We must convince him that the ordinary way of describing these facts is the correct way. "What we do," Wittgenstein says, "is to bring words back from their metaphysical to their everyday use."

What have caused our reflective person to fall into this kind of intellectual confusion are certain subtle misuses of ordinary language. In one way or another, he/she has gradually extended the ordinary uses of words in ways that importantly change their meaning. He/she may, as a consequence, begin to doubt that his/her normal, unhesitating application of these words is in fact correct. When this occurs, he/she is in the state of perplexity described above. The way to resolve such perplexity, therefore, is to exhibit the ordinary, correct use of the key terms in his/her discourse in order to show how, in subtly misusing them, his/her activities give rise to such conceptual bewilderment.

The aim that lies behind Wittgenstein's writings is thus mainly therapeutic. It is to rid philosophy of conceptual confusion by diagnosing its causes. In the *Investigations*, all sorts of procedures for achieving this result are adopted. The main one is the technique that Wittgenstein calls the use of "language games." This technique assumes that everyday language is learned analogously to the way in which certain games are learned. The rules that we learn for the proper employment of certain terms have much the same function as the rules we learn in order, say, to play chess. To illustrate, then, how the philosopher misuses ordinary expressions, Wittgenstein shows, through developing various language games, what the actual rules for the use of these expressions are: what they will and will not allow us to do with these expressions. In the light of this sort of description (which replaces explanation), he is able to pinpoint those deviations from actual use that lead to conceptual confusion—those confusions that arise, as he puts it, "when language goes on a holiday."

The therapeutic impulse in the *Investigations* is thus not dissimilar to that we have found in the *Tractatus*. In the *Tractatus*, the claim was that philosophical pronouncements are literally senseless; and some such notion pervades the *Investigations* as well. Wittgenstein say (paragraph 109):

> And we may not advance any kind of theory. There must not be anything hypothetical in our considerations. We must do away with all explanation and description alone must take its place. And this description gets its light, that is to say its purpose, from the philosophical problems. These are, of course, not empirical problems; they are solved, rather, by looking into the workings of our language, and that in such a way as to make us recognize those workings: in despite of an urge to misunderstand them. The problems are solved, not by giving new information, but by arranging what we have always known. Philosophy is battle against the bewitchment of our intelligence by means of language.

And in paragraph 124 he adds:

> Philosophy may in no way interfere with the actual use of language; it can in the end only describe it. For it cannot give it any foundation either. It leaves everything as it is.

Philosophy After Wittgenstein

As was indicated earlier, Wittgenstein held that philosophical problems are different from scientific problems, and that no "factual" solution to a philosophical problem is possible. Wittgenstein, of course, did not deprecate science per se. He thought science to be an important activity for an investigation of the world, but one that philosophers should not take as a model of how to proceed in pursuing their characteristic activities. There has been a long tradition of twentieth-century philosophy that disagrees with this Wittgensteinian attitude. Among its earlier, main proponents, were Bertrand Russell, Rudolf Carnap, and A. J. Ayer. Though differing from one another in certain ways, they held that science is indeed the model that should inspire philosophical activity. Carnap and Ayer, in fact, held that the only significant statements that can be made about the world belong to one or another of the physical sciences.

With the death of Wittgenstein, this tradition that sees philosophy as modeled upon science has had its most influential proponent in Willard van Orman Quine (1908–), who until his retirement in 1978 was Edgar Pierce Professor of Philosophy at Harvard University. The main influences on Quine have been three: the logical work of Russell, the positivism of Carnap, and the pragmatism of Dewey and James. These unite in his philosophy in complex ways, but the main thread through these somewhat differing points of view is the notion that when done correctly, philosophy is just an extension or subdiscipline of science. The distinction is one of abstractness with respect to subject matter, not one of method. Given that there are physical objects, it is the scientist who discovers whether there are quarks and other subatomic particles, and what their properties are. On the supposition that there are sets and classes, it is the mathematician who decides whether there are negative numbers and what their properties are. But whether there really are sets or classes is a matter to be dealt with by the philosopher. In a famous paper, "On What There Is" (1948), Quine addresses the question of whether it is possible to decide whether there are abstract entities such as classes and universals, and he lays down an important criterion—too technical to be discussed here in detail—to decide this question. Roughly speaking, the criterion says that certain idioms we use in ordinary language, words such as "some," "there is," which Quine calls "quantifiers," allow one to decide what a given "ontology" is committed to. So if we quantify over physical objects, saying *there are such things,* our ontology must contain physical objects. Quine thus disagrees with Wittgenstein, who says that the sentence "There are physical objects" is nonsense (see Wittgenstein's *On Certainty*, entry 35). He thinks this sentence is both meaningful and true, and can be proved to be such by his criterion of "quantifying over."

Quine's ideas that science and science alone is the key to reality, and that philosophy when done correctly is an extension of science, is sometimes called "Quine's naturalism," i.e., the idea that the exploration of nature (including human nature) is properly done only by science. In a series of famous articles and books, such as "Two Dogmas of Empiricism" (1950), *Word and Object* (1960), and *The Roots of Reference* (1973), this idea has been applied to a wide range of traditional philosophical topics. In "Two Dogmas of Empiricism," for instance, Quine challenged the received view that there is a distinction of *kind* between analytic and synthetic propositions, contending in a series of brilliant arguments that all arguments to this effect are either question-begging or incoherent. His own view is that propositions do not differ in kind but only in degree, and that in principle, depending on how future experience judges these matters, any proposition can be given up or revised. The point of view here is a sophisticated form of pragmatism.

Quine's influence in contemporary analytical philosophy has been enormous. One of its most prominent developments is in the philosophy of mind, where a wide variety of views, ultimately tracing back to Quine's thought, can be found today. Hilary Putnam (1925–), for instance, says in *Representation and Reality* (1989), "The way to solve philosophical problems is to construct a better scientific picture of the world" (p. 107). Putnam, who is the inventor of a theory of the human mind called "functionalism," assumes on scientific grounds that the human mind works like a computer. This is a form of materialism that rests on the notion that computer science, or more generally cognitive science, will give us a true picture of the mind—an idea that has its origins in Quine's philosophy. Another major contemporary philosopher, Donald Davidson (1917–), follows Quine in rejecting any form of Kantian transcendental idealism. In a famous paper, "On the Very Idea of a Conceptual Scheme" (1974), Davidson argues that the Kantian conceptual scheme, which assumes that the physical world is somehow to be contrasted with the mental, and that mental activity somehow conditions the human apprehension of the world, rests upon a fallacious distinction. The world is as science describes it, and any idealist or philosophical gloss that holds that the mental is not subject to scientific investigation, such as Kant's, is to be rejected. Even stronger neo-Quinean views about the nature of the mind are to be found in later writers, called "eliminative materialists." They hold that a scientific approach to the so-called "mind" will reveal that the mind is nothing but the brain. We have no need for thoughts, ideas, intentions, and other types of "metaphysical" notions in developing a correct explanation of human behavior and cognition. All that is needed is a scientific investigation of the brain and its activities. This view has been criticized by those who claim that such eliminativists *believe* that there are no such things as beliefs, a view that is either self-contradictory or self-defeating. Eliminativists have rejected this analysis, and in the decade of the 1990s a vigorous debate on the question is taking place in advanced philosophical circles.

Conclusion

The twentieth century has seen a remarkable surge of philosophical activity, much of it of great power and originality. We are still too close to the most recent developments to assess their ultimate significance, but there can be no doubt that the greatest philosophers of the analytical tradition will continue to be read and studied for many years to come.

Existentialism and phenomenology

The last types of contemporary philosophy we shall consider are the views called "existentialism" and "phenomenology." These are the names given to a number of very different philosophies and should not be seen as implying that these philosophies have more than a very tenuous connection with each other. They have little more in common than that they are all "philosophies of life"; they all try to answer in different ways the questions that men are inclined to ask about human existence; they are all, therefore, opposed to "rational" philosophy, and they see philosophy as having a more positive role to play than any of the modern analytical movements are willing to ascribe to it. This kind of view has been extremely popular in France, Germany, and Latin America since the Second World War, and is becoming influential in the English-speaking world as well. In order to understand these philosophical theories, it is best to go back to their origins in the nineteenth century and then examine certain of the most general features of contemporary existentialist and phenomenological thought.

Søren Kierkegaard

The underlying theory of this movement goes back to a brilliant Danish philosopher and theologian, Søren Kierkegaard, and his war against rational philosophy and theology. Kierkegaard was born in 1813, lived most of his life in Copenhagen, and wrote a series of strange books until his death, in 1855. By and large, these writings and the career of their author made a very slight impression on his times. In Copenhagen, Kierkegaard was regarded as a peculiar crank, as a nuisance to the Danish church. Outside of his homeland he was hardly known at all. However, near the beginning of this century, his works were translated into German, French, English, and other languages, until now, a century after his death, his influence is deep and widespread. The histories of philosophy written eighty years ago hardly mention him, but current philosophical journals and publications contain more and more studies of his work each year. So, although Kierkegaard has been dead over a century, he is really a contemporary thinker.

The Works

One of the puzzling features of his works is that they are attributed to a series of authors with names like Johannes Climacus, Johannes de Silentio, and Anti-Climacus, and occasionally to himself. The works vary from almost fictional writings such as *Either/Or*, to philosophical studies such as *Philosophical Fragments* and *Fear and Trembling*, to religious rhapsodies such as *Edifying Discourses*, to bitter satirical diatribes such as *Attack upon Christendom*. However, as Kierkegaard argued in one of his works, there is a method in all this apparent madness, a problem and a message that the author felt could only

be conveyed in this peculiar fashion through the points of view presented by the various pseudonyms.

The Central Question

Fundamentally, in its most simplified form, the problem that Kierkegaard raised in his works was "What is the point of man's life?" "What sense can people make out of human existence?" "What is the purpose of human events?" Kierkegaard attempted in his literary works to reveal an image of human life as anguished and absurd, harrowing and meaningless. In his philosophical writings, he developed arguments on the basis of this view of human existence. His religious writings and his satires attempted in other ways to make the reader acutely conscious of these questions.

"Johannes Climacus"

For our purposes, the clearest presentation of Kierkegaard's view is set forth in *Philosophical Fragments*; his proposed solution also appears there. This work is alleged to have been written by one Johannes Climacus. This name was probably chosen because there had been such an author at least a thousand years earlier who wrote a work entitled *The Ladder to Paradise*. On the title page of Kierkegaard's book, the supposed author, Climacus, posed the problems of the book in three questions: Is an historical point of departure possible for an eternal consciousness? How can such a point of departure have any other than a mere historical interest? Is it possible to base an eternal happiness upon historical knowledge? What Climacus wished to point out is that the solution to a person's problem lies in somehow being able to find a link between historical or temporal life and some sort of eternal knowledge. As the argument of the book is intended to make out, the answer to each of the questions must be both completely negative and also completely affirmative.

The Socratic Paradox

In order to develop his paradoxical theory, Kierkegaard begins *Philosophical Fragments* with a classic philosophical puzzle posed by Plato. In the dialogue entitled *Meno*, Socrates asked, can we learn that which we do not know? He argued that if we really do not know it, then we will not be able to recognize this knowledge when we learn it. If I do not now know what 7,689 times 4,547 is, how can I distinguish the right answer from the wrong answer when I see it? If I can tell the right answer from the wrong one, then, Socrates insisted, in some sense I must already have known the right answer (see pages 190–91). On the basis of such an argument, Socrates came to the conclusion that learning is impossible—that is, it is not possible to acquire true knowledge that one does not already have. Either one learns what one already knows, in which case one does not *learn*, or one has no way of learning anything, since one has no way of recognizing the truth of what one is trying to learn. The significance of all this, for Socrates and Plato, was that one does not actually learn anything new, but must have all possible knowledge within oneself, and that what we call learning is really nothing but recollecting true knowledge that we already have within us. The stimulus of certain occasions, such as conversations with Socrates, only have the effect of jarring our memories, so that we become aware of something we already know.

Kierkegaard's Solution

Kierkegaard accepted the problem raised by Plato as genuine, but suggested that a different solution could be offered in place of the Platonic theory of recollection. Let us suppose that the learner does not have all knowledge within him/her. Then prior to acquiring knowledge, the learner has no means of recognizing truth when he/she encounters it. But if one does learn anything, then, according to Kierkegaard's hypothesis, something extremely strange must occur. Something must happen at the moment of learning that makes the learner different from what he/she was before, that makes him/her capable of recognizing a truth that he/she previously could not do. Prior to this change in the nature of the learner, he/she must have been in complete ignorance, incapable of telling truths from falsehoods, knowing no truths. Then, suddenly, a moment of enlightenment must have taken place, which has removed the previous ignorance and made it possible for him/her to distinguish truth from falsehood. In other words, instead of explaining knowledge as recollection, Kierkegaard's hypothesis explains knowledge as miraculous, as due to some inexplicable transformation that takes place in the learner at some decisive moment in his/her existence.

Once the moment of enlightenment has

taken place, what one knows is absolutely certain for the learner; it is eternal knowledge for him/her. In view of the learner's inability to bring about his/her own enlightenment, since he/she was completely ignorant before it occurred, and in view of his/her own inability to comprehend what has happened to him/her, or how it has taken place, Kierkegaard suggests calling whatever is the cause of one's enlightenment—"God." Such a God, whatever He or it may be, must enter into the series of historical events that constitute man's life in order to produce this radical and complete transformation in the learner.

The Decisive Moment

One further element of the Kierkegaardian hypothesis must be introduced. Kierkegaard claims that his explanation differs from that of Socrates in one crucial detail. For Socrates, the moment of recollection is not really important, since the learner had all the knowledge within himself all the time. But in Kierkegaard's theory, the moment of enlightenment is decisive for the learner in two respects: he is completely changed from total ignorance to possessing eternal knowledge; and the moment is decisive as part of *his* life. What this latter claim means is that although the transformation is miraculous from the human point of view, it must still be significant for the individual as the dramatic culmination of something that occurs in his/her own life.

To make the moment of enlightenment decisive from a person's point of view, he/she must desire this transformation, but because of his/her ignorance must desire it without knowing what it would involve

and what it would be like. In order to illustrate this, Kierkegaard offers a possible interpretation of this theory in terms of a story. Suppose a mighty king (God) wants to marry a humble maiden (the human learner), but can marry her only if she loves him for himself and not because of his wealth and power. If he shows her his power and his wealth, she may marry him for the wrong reasons—she will merely be overpowered by his grandeur. If he forces her to marry him, again she will not do it because of love of the king. The only way the king can achieve his end—gaining her because she wants him for himself—is to conceal all those elements that might lead her to make her choice for the wrong reasons. Similarly, if the learner can see the *benefits* of enlightenment, he will be enticed. If God causes the enlightenment without any desire for it on the part of the learner, it will have no significance for him. So, Kierkegaard claims, if the moment is to be significant for a human being, it must involve his prior desire for enlightenment without his either being forced to desire it or being enticed into desiring it because of its possible advantages.

Skepticism and Faith

Put in less picturesque terms, the theory Kierkegaard set forth is that human beings of and by themselves are incapable of knowing anything that is certain, and that only through some sort of miraculous event in their lives can they ever acquire such knowledge. But this miracle of knowing can be significant or decisive for a human being only if he/she desires its occurrence without being able to form any judgment about the advantages or disadvantages of the transformation. A good deal of Kierkegaard's philosophical writing is devoted to developing a type of complete skepticism, to showing that human beings by themselves can know nothing. After developing that skepticism, he maintained that the solution to man's total ignorance lies first in recognizing our tragic plight and then, blindly, irrationally, seeking a way out of that wretched predicament through faith alone, faith that there can be a form of contact between man and God in man's historical existence.

The only information we have in our benighted state of ignorance is either factual, historical information about our experience, or logically derived information about concepts. But whether any of this is necessarily true about anything in this world, we can never tell. In our unenlightened state we are completely unable to tell if God exists. In fact, our ignorance is such that His nonexistence is more compatible with our information than His existence.

Uncertainty

Our sense experience and historical information are always changing. We cannot tell whether any of our sense information is necessarily true. We lack means for establishing the necessary truth of any knowledge we acquire by experience. In order to be absolutely certain, we would have to be able to show that it is impossible that it could be false. But the very fact that our sense experience deals with changing things, with things that come into being, change, and disappear, shows that anything we believe that we know could be false. There is nothing about the changing world that has to be the way it is, since it keeps altering its qualities. Hence, as regards anything historical, anything that takes place in time, we can notice only the temporary arrangements of qualities, but we can never be sure that experienced objects *must* have certain properties, and cannot be otherwise. (The point Kierkegaard is making is much like Hume's claim that we can never have necessary knowledge about matters of fact [see pages 222–32]).

With regard to the apparently certain knowledge that we have in mathematics and other such disciplines, here all that we know according to Kierkegaard's analysis is that *if* we define certain concepts in certain ways, *then* certain consequences follow. This tells us about the logical relationships of concepts but tells nothing at all about whether any items in our experience have these properties. Geometry may allow us to formulate certain theorems about "points," "lines," and "planes," but it does not allow us to tell whether there are objects in our experience to which these theorems apply. Even if there are no "points," "lines," or "planes" in our world, Euclidean geometry is still valid. But the geometry of objects in our experience is a matter of sense investigations, which can never yield any completely certain or necessary conclusion.

Kierkegaard's skepticism is summed up in his claim that a logical system of knowledge is possible, that is, a body of knowledge is possible in which the conclusions can be justified as necessarily true, since they are logical consequences of the initial concepts and definitions. **On the other hand, an existential system, a body of necessary knowledge dealing with experience, is not possible, because we are incapable of discovering**

any necessary truths about historical or changing events. As the logical positivists have contended, all our information consists either of logically true propositions that have no factual content, or of factual propositions that cannot be shown to be true by logical procedures.

The Problem of God

In view of these extreme limitations on the possibility of human knowledge, we have no way of proving the existence of God as an object that operates in our historical world. If we define God as many theologians do, as an eternal, unchanging being, it may be possible, if the definition is carefully contrived, to show that a proposition of the form "God necessarily exists" follows from the definition. But this procedure has no bearing on whether there is such a being in the world of our experience (see page 169). It merely shows the logical relationship that exists between concept and conclusion. If we try to discover from our experience whether God exists, we are confronted with a different kind of difficulty. Everything we experience is temporal and changing, and hence not God, since God is eternal and unchanging. Some of the items that we experience may be the effects of God's activities, but this we can tell only if we already know that there is a God.

With respect to the theologian's concept of God as an eternal and unchanging being, we can see that it would be logically impossible for God to be part of the historical world. By definition, no historical or temporal properties apply to God. If one believed that God existed in time, that God was able to act in human historical situations, one would be believing something that is logically absurd.

The Human Predicament

It is now possible to present the full flavor of Kierkegaard's theory, and then its more general formulation in contemporary existentialism. As human beings in our state of total ignorance, all that we can do is realize the necessity of complete skepticism, our inability to know anything about the world that is true or necessary. However, if we reflect on our plight, we realize also that we are trapped in an awful condition. We have no real knowledge, and yet we have a need for such knowledge to be certain of what we ought to do, what we ought to believe, and so on. The quest for knowledge, in the strongest possible sense, is unavoidable if we are concerned to find **the meaning of human existence.** But, in view of our ignorance, we have no means for discovering a solution. This can occur only if the miracle of enlightenment occurs, and we cannot even tell if there is an enlightener in the universe.

The "Risk" of Faith

Since there are no guides for us, no way of determining what we ought to do or how we can become enlightened, all that we can do is either to remain in our darkness as skeptics forever or to take **"the leap into absurdity," accept a belief, blindly and irrationally, that there is some agent called "God" who can and does act in time and who will, if we desire it, effect our enlightenment.** How does one know what to believe in? One cannot. All one can do is believe. Man's solution lies solely in **the decision to believe, to have faith.** One can never be sure before the event that it is the right decision, or if as a result of the decision, one's life may become meaningful, and the quest for knowledge be at the end. One may also have made the wrong decision, opted for the wrong belief. The risk is enormous, and there is no way of establishing a basis for belief.

Christian Belief

The faith that Kierkegaard advocated was **an interpretation of Christianity in terms of his theory.** Assuming his hypothesis about how knowledge occurs, he believed that the miracle of enlightenment took place through the incarnation of Jesus, through God's appearing in human history and saving those who believe. The crucial stumbling block for Kierkegaard's version of Christianity is involved in finding out what to believe, what form the incarnation took. God, like the king in Kierkegaard's story, has created a situation in which He is unrecognizable, so that human beings will believe in Him through faith alone. Those who were alive in Palestine in the first century A.D. were no better off than we in determining what to believe. The contemporary of Jesus saw only a human being and was aware that God cannot be a human being. At any time, the problem of being a believer is the same. There is *no* evidence. All that one can do is believe by faith alone. The evidence of Scripture is not convincing unless one already believes that the New Testament reveals the life of God. This one can never find out from the book. If one points out

that it is a contradiction in terms for God to have had a history, Kierkegaard answers with Tertullian's assertion "I believe that which is absurd." If one points out how implausible and ridiculous it is to believe that Jesus of Nazareth was God, Kierkegaard replies, quoting an earlier German irrationalist, "Lies, fables and romances must needs be probable, but not the foundation of our faith."

"Absurdity"

This idea of pure belief as the solution to man's problems is developed in Kierkegaard's brilliant portrayal of his hero, the Biblical Abraham, in *Fear and Trembling*. The knight of faith is somebody who believes and acts "in virtue of the absurd." The test of faith is whether one's beliefs can be held in the face of overwhelming evidence to the contrary, in the face of complete irrationality. Abraham—in consenting to sacrifice Isaac on God's command and God's promise that if Abraham sacrificed his only child he would then become the Father of the Faithful—was performing an action that was brutal and meaningless according to human standards. Its sole justification was that it was an act of faith.

In view of the irrationalism of Kierkegaard's solution, he saw that it would be a violation of his theory to claim that he could teach the truth. People could only find this in blind faith. For this reason, he claimed that his writings represented *indirect discourse.* All that he could do was raise certain questions, pose certain problems, but each person would have to find the solution in his own way. The point, apparently, in the use of various pseudonyms for his works was that each, in his own way, could raise certain questions, suggest certain answers. But the reader, himself, would have to find his own solution. Truth exists solely in the subjective, personal certainty of the believer.

Contemporary existentialism

If Kierkegaard's leap into religious faith was not acceptable, one might instead turn to Friedrich Nietzsche's atheism. Nietzsche insisted that the God of traditional religion was dead, no longer had any role in the lives of serious people. Instead, human beings had to create a meaningful world through their own will, and they had to be brave enough to live with and revel in the results. Nietzsche's somewhat nihilistic view shared with Kierkegaard's the subjectivity of the basic human decision about what to believe. Nietzsche rejected all supernaturalism and saw all theories as man-made. His view led to a form of humanistic existentialism, when joined with certain aspects of the philosophical theory called **"phenomenology."**

This movement was developed by Edmund Husserl in Germany early in the twentieth century. Husserl himself believed philosophy could be an exact science, based on certainty that rested on no presuppositions. Descartes had found such certainty in the *cogito* (I think, therefore I am). If we examine what we are aware of when we know the *cogito*, we see that such knowledge is completely certain. This needs no proof, but is evident just from examining it. If there are such intuitively certain truths in human con-

sciousness, we should study them as objects of consciousness, just as they appear to us and not as aspects of some hidden metaphysical world.

When we find out what is true in immediate experience and why it is true, we need no suppositions to justify or explain this. We perform a "phenomenological reduction" of consciousness and uncover what is intuitively certain, and what are the essences, or invariant features, of experience. These features give experience the genuine meaning it has. Husserl envisaged his phenomenological method as a descriptive procedure for examining conscious experience. It was not a psychological method but, rather, one that brought out certain and necessary aspects of experience. It did not deduce these from presuppositions, but revealed them by phenomenological reductions, a most arduous process as carried on by Husserl and his disciples. This would not lead to some kind of traditional metaphysics about the knower and what is known. Instead, it would delineate what is certain in conscious and intelligible experience. Husserl in his later writings seemed to be moving toward a kind of idealism in which the ego, the pure self, was the ultimate certainty. His last writings, only published after the Second World War, stressed the community of ego, and the world as the intersubjective community of individual egos. This could be studied without traditional metaphysical assumptions by describing what was indubitable in individual and group consciousness. And this would be a scientific study of knowledge.

Husserl died in 1938. As a Jew he had been persecuted by the Nazis. An enormous amount of his writing was smuggled out of Nazi Germany, and is still in the process of being published. His one-time assistant, Martin Heidegger, built on Husserl's efforts, as well as on the insights of Kierkegaard and Nietzsche to set forth modern existentialism. The French philosopher Jean-Paul Sartre studied Husserl's and Heidegger's views and developed his own version of existentialism.

Heidegger, a Catholic originally trained to be a Jesuit, studied with Husserl. He became Husserl's successor at the University of Freiburg. In 1927, after intensive studies in medieval philosophy as well as in phenomenology, Heidegger published his major work, *Sein und Zeit* (*Being and Time*), one of the most complicated philosophical treatises ever written. During the Nazi period, Heidegger supported Hitler at the beginning and was made rector of the University of Freiburg (and banned his teacher, Husserl, from using the library). Heidegger withdrew from active political life, but he remained a member of the Nazi party to the very end of the Second World War and was a staunch German nationalist. The extent of his participation in Nazism is currently being examined and debated, with various explanations being offered by his philosophical followers and his detractors. Some see his political activities as tainting his philosophy, while others insist on the value of his philosophical achievement independent of whatever links he may have had with Nazism.

Heidegger published no philosophical works during the Nazi period, but he made several public statements. After the Second World War, he indicated that his views had significantly changed from their original presentation in *Sein und Zeit*. That work starts from the methodology of Husserl's phenomenology, but then radically moves away from it. The work is presented in terms of a baffling vocabulary, building on German concepts and words, and Greek motifs, that are extremely difficult to translate into English (or any other language) without seeming to be meaningless or too opaque to understand. (This helps explain Rudolf Carnap's reaction cited above in the section on logical positivism.) We will not try to present Heidegger's entire theory but will explain only some selected key portions of his views.

Heidegger claimed that the basic problem of philosophy is to discover the nature of being. Philosophers from Plato onward had not succeeded because they abstracted and categorized being, but they did not see it where it really is. Using the phenomenological method, it becomes possible to seek for being without any presuppositions. It can be found in consciousness apart from conceptualizing. The key aspect of being for Heidegger is *Dasein*, human being. This does not refer to individual human beings but, rather, to the type of existence humans have. It is noticeable that only human beings try to find being. So, if we examine *Dasein*, we can start on the search for being itself.

Dasein in German has the meaning "being there." Human beings are always in a world that is already structured in various ways. People do not create their world, and to the extent *Dasein* is authentic. It is *there* and has to function in a situation whether it wants to or not. It adapts and participates by anticipating what is to occur. In this way, one understands one's world but does not comprehend the general relation of *Dasein* and *Sein*.

Man is to some extent determined by the character of the world. Yet man is also free insofar as a being can constitute its world. But people are enslaved by their relations to human being, *Dasein*, in general, and by the world they exist in. This is ordinary, in authentic existence.

Human being would become authentic if it turned away from the distractions of ordinary life and examined itself honestly, as a totality. Then it would recognize the human condition in terms of the kind of existence humans have. They have a life leading to death, and a dread of that situation. But in examining this, one realizes that one's potential death gives one authenticity. Each of us has a forthcoming death that is uniquely our own. We are each a being-unto-death. But realizing this makes us aware of our finitude, our responsibility, and our freedom and authenticity. We can each establish for ourselves what is meaningful for us without an ultimate framework. Heidegger adapted Nietzsche's view that man creates his/her own values. *Dasein* has no purpose beyond being in the world in a temporal sense. There is no transhuman God or structure to be discovered.

When one sees that human being is being-unto-death, then temporality and destiny become the fundamental features of one's world. Time as lived, existential time, is the measure of human being. In terms of existential time, each of us has a history that can be meaningful and yet can cease. Living in it, I may not be able to control it, yet insofar as it is *my* history, I am responsible for it. I and everyone, *Dasein*, are free to act in time and to make life meaningful in the face of death. With this freedom comes guilt, the realization of what could and should have been created freely. There is no objective role for humanity, only what humankind creates freely itself in time as history.

Heidegger's picture of the human condition is pretty bleak. Ahead of all of us is a pointless death. As we approach it through life, if we are aware of the situation, we freely, guiltily create what we can without any ultimate guideposts. We are responsible for the choices we make, but there are no ultimate or guaranteed right choices, only human choices.

Heidegger in later works became still more difficult to follow as he tried to carry on the quest for being, beyond just human being. He talked of humankind having fallen out of being, having lost the nearness and shelter of being. Philosophers and scientists probe into particular aspects of being rather than being itself. Poetry, Heidegger suggested, provides more possibility of providing a glimpse of being. Humankind through realizing its imminent nonbeing can become aware of nothingness, the opposite of being. If we examine nothingness, we can make room for being and maybe be in contact with it.

Heidegger's later works are very complicated, with mystical and nationalist motifs. They have been and are being variously interpreted. He himself kept revising his writings up to his death in 1976, but did not really make the message of his later years sufficiently clear, except for dissociating himself from the best-known off-shoot of his philosophy, French existentialism, which we turn to next.

French Existentialism

This movement, if a disparate group of thinkers can be called such, developed, generalized, and applied some of the views of Kierkegaard, Nietzsche, Husserl, and Heidegger, and used them to search for solutions to people's problems. Some, like Jean-Paul Sartre and Albert Camus, rejected Kierkegaard's irrational religious beliefs and insisted that any solution to the human situation must come from human beings themselves.

Many contemporary existentialists have grave doubts that there is any God to help us. Having taken seriously Nietzsche's message that God is dead, thinkers like Sartre have insisted that Kierkegaard's portrayal of man's plight properly describes our situation, but reject the claim that the solution lies solely and completely in the act of belief, in the decision to accept faith.

Sartre, perhaps the best-known French existentialist, was born in 1905 and studied philosophy, receiving his degree in 1929. He heard of the new approaches being developed in Germany, and from 1932 to 1934 studied Husserl's and Heidegger's formulations. He was active in the French Resistance to Hitler during the Second World War, and after the war emerged as one of Europe's leading thinkers. He played an active role in European politics for three decades after the war, usually advocating left-wing and humanitarian causes. His treatise *Being and Nothingness* and his novels present Sartre's own version of existentialism.

THE EXISTENTIALIST VIEW

We are "trapped in existence," living in a completely meaningless world. No prin- ciples that we use for ordering or comprehending events have any basis. But we cannot escape having to deal with "existence," having to make sense out of it. All that we can tell is that this world that we are confronted with is utterly arbitrary. When we realize the unintelligibility of the world, our inability to withdraw from contact with it, and our need for finding some principle of order or intelligibility, we are then ready for the existentialist message. One first has to be overpowered by the "nausea of existence," has to acknowledge that the pattern of our lives is due to totally arbitrary ways of living, and that any others would do as well.

At this point, we are confronted with our **"dreadful freedom," recognizing that we are completely free to choose our world view, our way of living in the world. However, there is no way in which we can find guides for our choice, no way we can avoid making a choice, and no way of escaping from the consequences of the choices**—our basic decisions.

NAUSEA

Sartre's famous novel *Nausea* portrays most forcefully this condition of man's plight. The hero has been moving through life on the basis of an unquestioned acceptance of a certain outlook. But his dissatisfaction with events forces him to ask whether this is the proper outlook. The quest for some justification for his way of life brings about its disintegration into pure nausea, as the arbitrary framework into which he has previously organized his world disappears. All that he is left with is the complete confusion of his inescapable existence, and the realization that it has no meaningful order. When he becomes aware that only by his decision can he find a means of organizing experience and a way of life, he is overwhelmed with the magnitude of the predicament that confronts him. He cannot avoid being a free agent. He cannot act unless he exercises his freedom and chooses some arbitrary outlook in order to make sense out of his world. Possibly most frightening of all, he is permanently burdened with all the consequences of his decision for which he, and he alone, is responsible. Even the saving grace of Kierkegaard's irrationalism is impossible, that there might be a right faith to choose, and once having chosen it, the responsibility for what follows is God's, not man's.

A Humanist Philosophy

The existentialist concern is not so much to understand the philosophical questions that interest the analytical philosophers (although in part this, too, is involved in their theory) as it is to answer the question **"How is man to live in this irrational, meaningless world?"** Some of the existentialists feel that the answer lies in religious faith, in the manner of Kierkegaard. Others, like Heidegger, Camus, and Sartre, being atheists or agnostics, **search for more humanistic beliefs,** ways of dealing with one's experience so as to make life meaningful. In general, the existentialists regard other philosophers either as wasting their time in defending intellectual systems that are indefensible, or as refusing to face the real problems that confront humankind and, instead, occupying themselves with unimportant concerns about language and logic, which cannot supply a solution to man's predicament.

On the other hand, many philosophers regard the existentialists as having abdicated the philosopher's quest, as having turned their backs on a rational examination of man's world. According to some, the existentialists are more poets of a harrowing variety than serious thinkers.

Deconstructionism

A further development from the ideas of Heidegger and the existentialists appears in **deconstructionism,** a theory presented by the Algerian-French thinker Jacques Derrida (1930–). The search for ultimate meaning that has been the central feature of Western philosophy since its beginnings is no longer viable. From Descartes to Husserl and Heidegger, the search has become more and more centered in subjectivity, without reaching ultimate meaning or ultimate certitude. What one can now do is "deconstruct" philosophy (and literature, language, and psychology as well).

Rather than arguing within a constructed philosophical world, and arguing about its components, its methods of proceeding, and its assumptions, the "deconstruction" seeks to make explicit the metaphysical suppositions and *a priori* assumptions that are involved in all philosophizing, whether it be the dogmatic presentation of a theory or the skeptical rejection of a philosophical claim. All philosophizing goes on verbally, in either written or oral form. There is an arbitrariness in all philosophical language, plus, as the late Michel Foucault has pointed out, a historical conditioning of all concepts, as well as nonphilosophical functions of them (such as using them as political signs).

Deconstruction not only elicits the tacit assumptions involved in so-called "rational thinking" but also is supposed to make one aware of the logocentrism involved in philosophizing, namely, the assumptions involved in using words and supposing that meaning and rationality somehow inhere in the text and in the world independently of human attempts to represent them in words. Derrida and the late Paul de Man of Yale deconstructed various philosophical and literary texts, exposing the many kinds and layers of assumptions and contradictions involved. What emerges from this process is a superradical skepticism about human communication. In its most extreme form, the contention is that a text, verbal or oral, is just marks on paper or sounds in the ear. Whether the text has an author is no longer relevant. The text only gets any significance in the mind of the reader or hearer, who is a member of an interpretative community that creates rather than discovers meaning. It makes no sense to talk of, or look for, some "objective meaning" that some "objective" author has set forth. What one can do is deconstruct texts in order to reveal what assumptions or presuppositions readers or hearers have put into them.

In this process, does one find a right or true meaning? Right or true for whom? A radical relativism seems to emerge from this process. Various interpretative groups, with various assumptions and presuppositions, make different meaning claims. Further, these groups have vari-

ous values that appear in their creative process of establishing texts. These value assumptions and presuppositions can be made apparent but are not thereby justified or rejected.

Deconstructionism has so far had little impact on the philosophical profession in America and England, but it has had a strong effect on literary criticism and literary studies. It has seriously challenged previous claims that there are fixed texts with fixed meanings and messages. It has challenged previous "objective" ways of interpreting texts, including logical analysis, linguistic analysis, etc. If carried over from literary examples to philosophical ones, the problematics of how to understand a passage in Plato, Hume, or Wittgenstein would no longer be just one of understanding the terms, the relations of the terms, or the purported conclusion. It would no longer involve historical research to find out what the historical author might have meant. Rather, it would consist of eliciting the assumptions, conflicting thoughts, etc., that the present reader or auditor finds there. The passage would not be considered for its objective worth, or truth value, but more for what it represents in present human contexts.

Some have contended that deconstructionism is a kind of nihilistic way of treating cultural artifacts. The assumptions underlying the Western philosophical enterprise are no longer taken for granted, even that of seeking rational (in the Western sense) understanding. Opponents have argued that since the theory of deconstruction derives from Heidegger, who was a Nazi, and was expounded in the United States by de Man, who was an anti-Semitic propagandist in Belgium at the beginning of the Second World War, the view may represent a way of justifying a dismissal of all accepted values. Others have suggested that deconstructionism is a new cultural outlook in the postcolonial world, where the values and standards of Western thought are no longer universally accepted or are applicable.

Nonetheless, at least in the field of literary criticism, deconstructionism has sometimes had a purgative effect in making one question oneself and become aware of what is involved in our expressing any position. It can lead to unending deconstruction of all attempts to find any objective basis for interpreting or understanding anything. Then this might lead to complete subjectivism, in which each deconstructer could express his/her point of view or understanding of texts, with no way of assessing which might be better or worse, or more true or false.

Rorty

The American philosopher Richard Rorty has attempted to reconcile the antimetaphysical antiabsolutist trends in twentieth-century English, American, and Continental philosophy, principally as expressed by John Dewey, Martin Heidegger, and Ludwig Wittgenstein. Rorty sees them all agreeing that the goal of Western philosophy—to reach an accurate and assured picture of reality—has had to be abandoned. In his book *Philosophy and the Mirror of Nature* (1979), he portrayed traditional philosophy as holding that knowledge is an accurate representation of reality made possible by special mental processes. The mind in traditional philosophy is a great mirror containing various representations, some of which provide accurate pictures of reality. From Descartes onward, philosophers have looked inward into the subjective mirror for any kind of certitude. Locke made this subjective study, according to Rorty, a study of ideas as representations of reality. The attempt to gain knowledge of ideas by this way has failed.

Starting with Dewey, twentieth-century thinkers tried first to find new ways of achieving the traditional goal, then ended up showing that the quest for certainty was illusory and could not reach its purported end. Dewey turned to the social uses of philosophy, offering the view that knowledge is what we are justified in believing in varying social circumstances. Justification is then a social phenomenon instead of a relationship between a fixed knowing subject, a mind, and reality.

Wittgenstein, in his later work, presented the view that language is a tool, not a mirror. Therefore, we should not expect that there are necessary conditions about the possibility of linguistic representation. And in Heidegger's view, according to Rorty, the effort to make the knowing subject, the mind, a source of necessary truths is just another self-deceptive attempt to avoid dealing with strangeness, which in the beginning led people to begin thinking.

When, following the insights of these three leading twentieth-century thinkers, one gives up the traditional philosophical task, and stops studying the mind as the mirror that can or might somehow give us a glimpse of reality, and drops the epistemological path that was trod from Descartes to Russell, one will realize that philosophers do not have special knowledge, or special access to knowledge, or a special method, or a special point of view. In a sense, as Rorty has argued more recently, a philosophy in its traditional guise is dead. The privileged position of philosophers as special guardians of the secrets of how we know and what we know has eroded.

What is left then? For Rorty it is an edifying role of philosophy and philosophers: to help people and society as a whole "break free from outworn vocabularies and attitudes, rather than to provide 'grounding' for the intuitions and customs of the present." This edifying role keeps inquiry and the pursuit of wisdom open to new and newer possibilities, rather than trying to enclose them within definitive systems, and makes it possible to see each system as part of some historical present that will be superseded.

Conclusion

Regardless of which kinds of contemporary philosophers are right in portraying their mission and their methods, one can appreciate why the existentialists and postexistentialists have so deeply influenced the intellectual life of Western Europe in the last few decades, and are gradually making inroads into the philosophical scene in England and America. The horrible experience of the Nazi dictatorship during the Second World War, the present economic and social turmoil throughout much of the civilized world, the frightening apocalyptic aspects that emerged during the Cold War, the fear of atomic annihilation, the fear of planetary environmental disasters, and the chaotic developments in various parts of the world after the Cold War, have left many people with a sense that their views and values are meaningless. The world in which they, and we ourselves, have to live no longer seems to many to be susceptible to rational examination. So, instead, they have concluded that only arbitrary beliefs seem able to give us a key to how to live in the face of an unintelligible universe.

In this section, we have attempted briefly to survey some contemporary philosophical trends. These indicate some of the means by which philosophers in our time have conducted the quest for comprehension, for some general statement of the significance of our experience, and for ways of dealing with some basic questions. All of these current views are of great significance for all branches of philosophy, since they concern themselves with the nature of philosophical activity and the kinds of questions it is appropriate for the philosopher to ask. From our brief discussion of them, readers will be able to see the kinds of views they lead their exponents to in the spheres of ethics, religion, politics, metaphysics, and epistemology. They should now be able, therefore, to round off for themselves our earlier discussions of these branches of philosophy by applying some of the techniques of contemporary philosophy to the questions that have concerned philosophers in these fields. They will thus discover for themselves what is meant by the "revolution in philosophy" that many claim has taken place in this century. They will also be starting out on their own philosophical inquiries, and the purpose of this book will have been fulfilled.

Suggested further reading

Pragmatism

Dewey, John. *Reconstruction in Philosophy.* London: Muller, 1956. One of Dewey's important statements of his philosophy.

James, William. *Essays in Pragmatism.* A collection of some of James's most famous papers.

———. *Pragmatism. A New Name for Some Old Ways of Thinking.* London: Longmans, 1943. One of James's best statements of his views.

Nagel, Ernest. *Sovereign Reason.* London: Collier-Macmillan, 1954. A statement of the pragmatic theory by one if its leading spokesmen.

Quine, Willard van Orman. *The Roots of Reference.* 1971.

Russell, Bertrand, *A History of Western Philosophy.* 2nd ed. London: Allen & Unwin, 1968. The chapter on Dewey is a rather severe criticism of pragmatism by one of the best-known twentieth-century philosophers.

Schneider, Herbert W. *A History of American Philosophy.* Oxford University Press, 1946. An excellent picture of the development of American thought, especially the pragmatic movement.

Wiener, Philip. *Evolution and the Founders of Pragmatism.* Oxford University Press, 1949. An important study of the origins of American pragmatism.

Analytic Philosophy

Austin, J. L. *Philosophical Papers.* It is important to get the 2nd edition of this work (1970). Major statement of ordinary language philosophy.

———. *Sense and Sensibilia.* 1962. A witty attack on sense-data theory from an ordinary language perspective.

Ayer, A. J. *Language, Truth, and Logic.* 2nd ed. 1948. A classical statement of logical positivism.

Churchland, P. *Matter and Consciousness.* 1988.

Hannay, A. *Human Consciousness.* 1990.

Kripke, S. A. *Naming and Necessity.* 1980.

Martinich, A. P. *Communication and Reference.* 1984.

———. ed. *Philosophy of Language.* 1985.

Monk, R. *Ludwig Wittgenstein: The Duty of Genius.* 1990.

Putnam, Hilary. *Representation and Reality.* 1989.

Quine, Willard van Orman. *Quiddities.* 1987.

Schwartz, S. P. *Naming, Necessity, and Natural Kinds.* 1977.

Stroll, Avrum. *Surfaces.* 1988.

Wittgenstein, L. *Tractatus Logico-Philosophicus.* 1921. Difficult, cryptic statement of logical atomism.

———. *Philosophical Investigations.* 1953. The classic statement of the "later" Wittgenstein.

Existentialism

Barrett, William. *Irrational Man. A Study in Existentialist Philosophy.* Garden City, N.Y.: Doubleday, 1962.

Blackham, H. J. *Six Existentialist Thinkers.* London: Routledge & Kegan Paul, 1952.

Collins, James. *The Mind of Kierkegaard.* Chicago: Regnery, 1955.

Grene, Marjorie. *Introduction to Existentialism.* Chicago: Midway, 1984.

———. *Sartre.* Washington, D.C.: University Presses of America, 1983.

Heidegger, Martin. *Being and Time.* New York: Harper and Row, 1962.

Kierkegaard, Søren. *Philosophical Fragments.* Princeton, New Jersey: Princeton University Press, 1962.

Lehman, David. *Signs of the Times. Deconstructionism and the Fall of Paul de Man.* New York: Poseidon, 1991.

Murdoch, Iris. *Sartre.* London: Fontana Books, 1967.

Natanson, Maurice. *Edmund Husserl. Philosophy of Infinite Tasks.* Evanston, Ill.: Northwestern University Press, 1973.

Rorty, Richard. *Philosophy and the Mirror of Nature.* Princeton, N.J.: Princeton University Press, 1979.

Sartre, Jean-Paul. *Being and Nothingness.* London: Methuen, 1957.

———. *Existentialism and Humanism.* London: Methuen, 1948.

———. *Nausea.* London: Penguin Books, 1965.

Schmitt, Richard. *Martin Heidegger on Being Human. An Introduction to Sein und Zeit.* Magnolia, Mass.: Peter Smith, Peter, Pub., Inc.

INDEX